CHAPTER 65 ... FROM THAT DAY FORWARD, HE AND THE GIRLS...

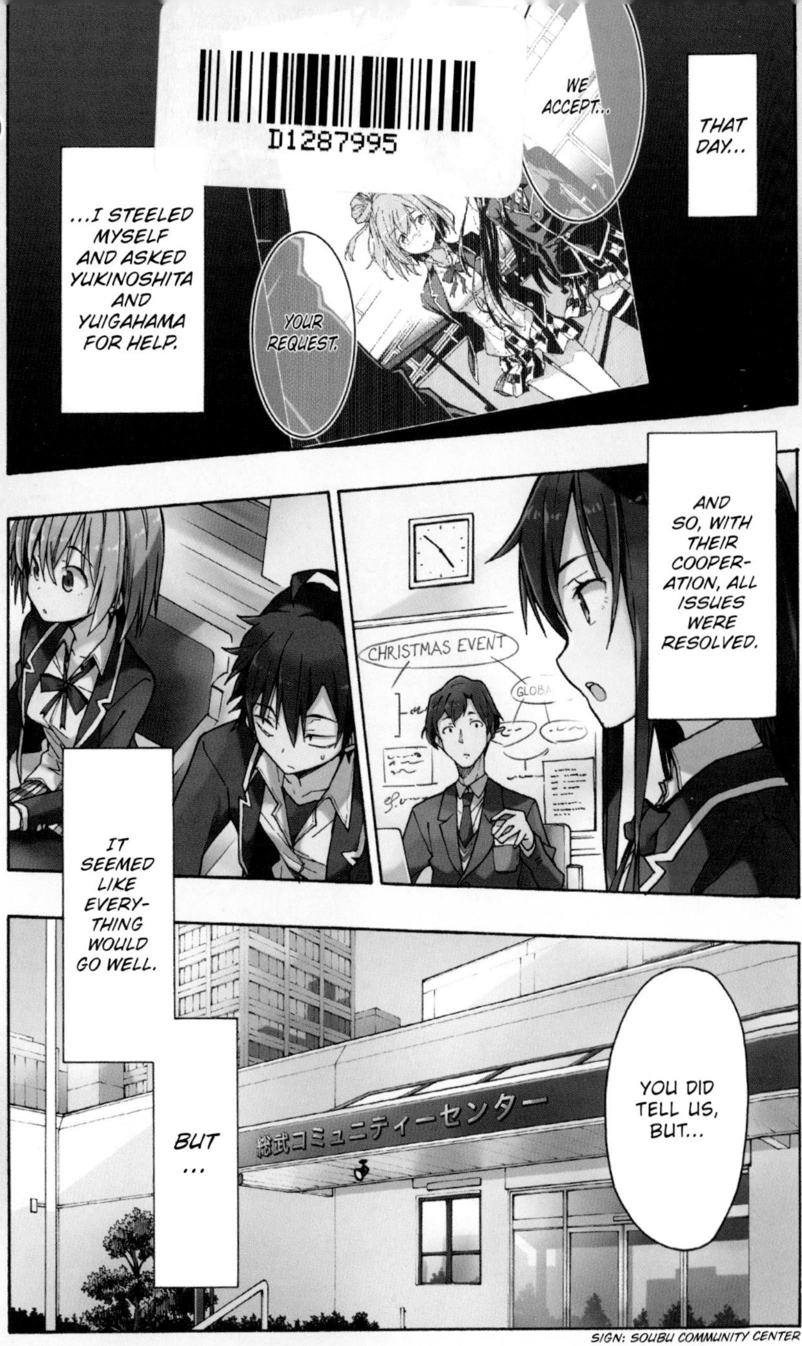
THAT DAY...
WE ACCEPT...
...I STEELED MYSELF AND ASKED YUKINOSHITA AND YUIGAHAMA FOR HELP.
YOUR REQUEST.
AND SO, WITH THEIR COOPERATION, ALL ISSUES WERE RESOLVED.
CHRISTMAS EVENT
IT SEEMED LIKE EVERYTHING WOULD GO WELL.
YOU DID TELL US, BUT...
総武コミュニティーセンター
BUT ...

SIGN: SOUBU COMMUNITY CENTER

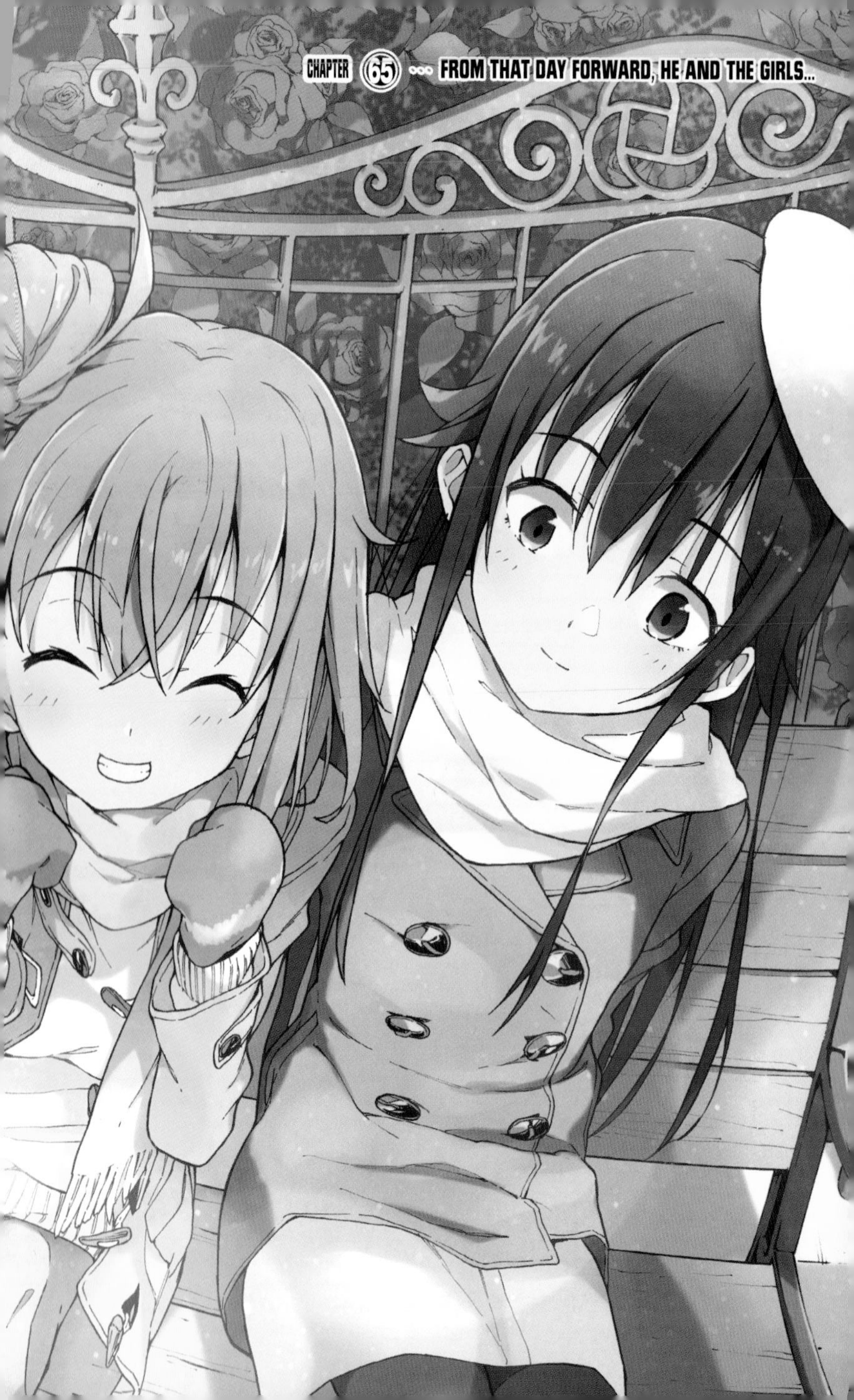
CHAPTER 65 ... FROM THAT DAY FORWARD, HE AND THE GIRLS...

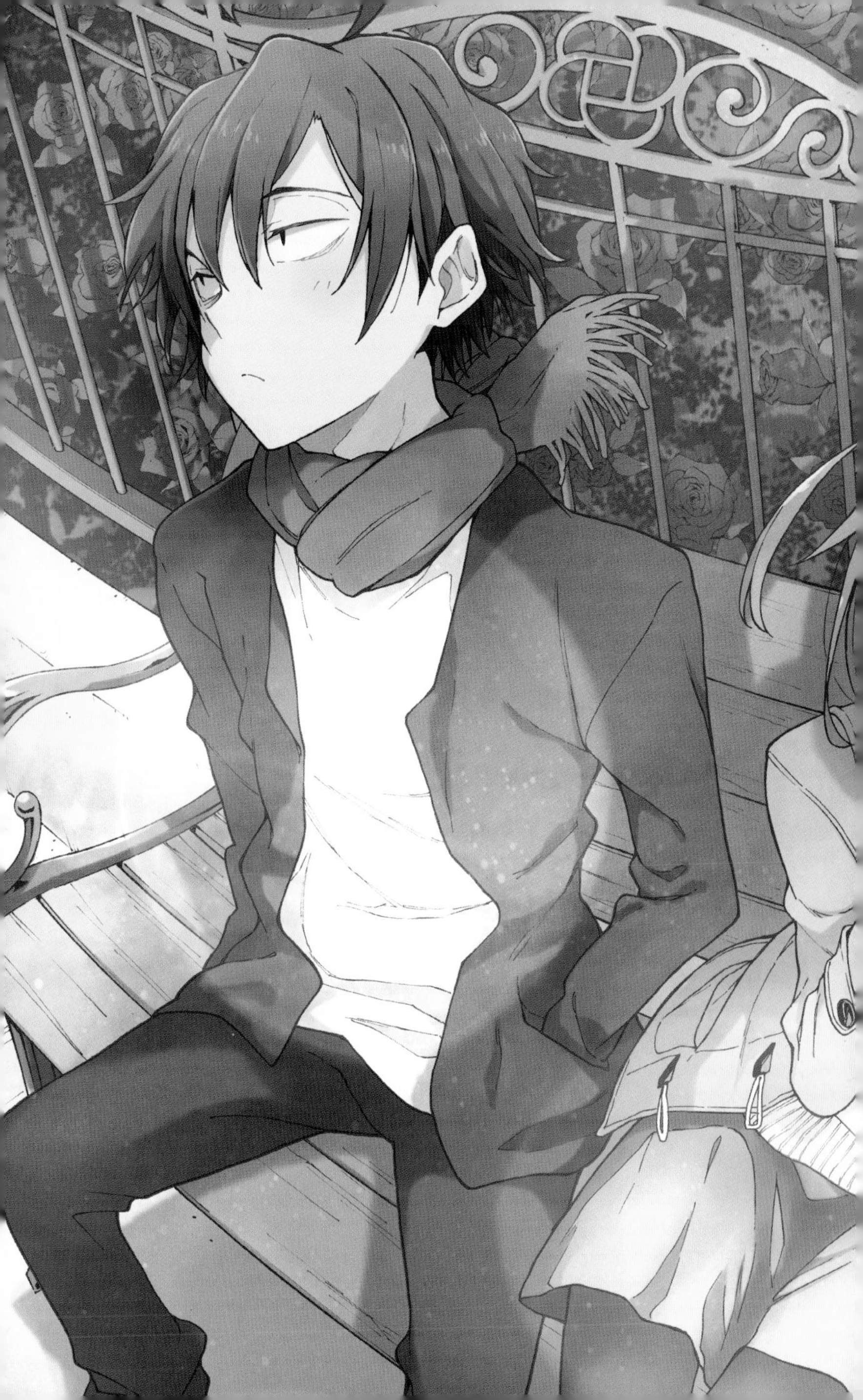

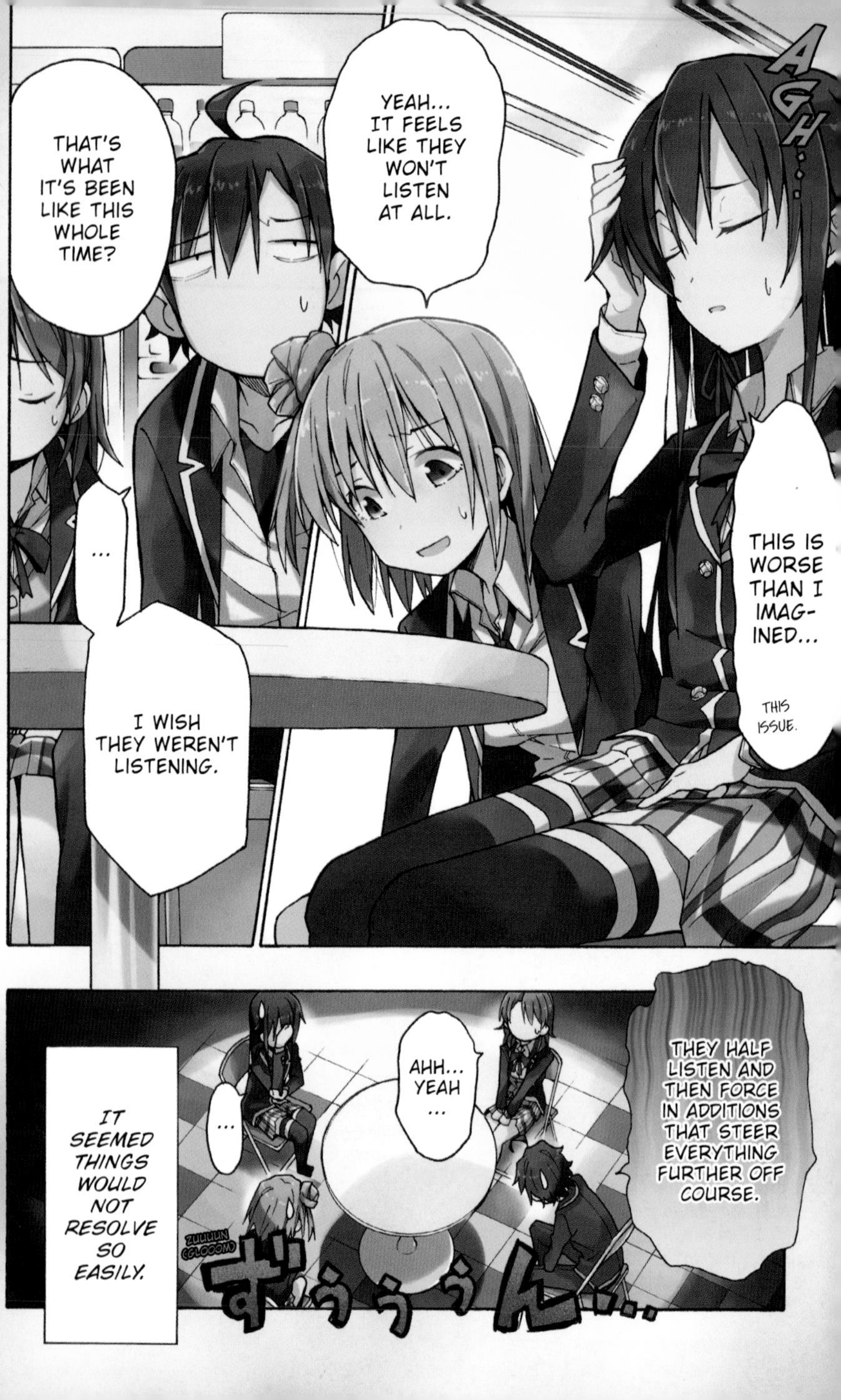
AGH...
YEAH... IT FEELS LIKE THEY WON'T LISTEN AT ALL.
THAT'S WHAT IT'S BEEN LIKE THIS WHOLE TIME?
THIS IS WORSE THAN I IMAG-INED...
THIS ISSUE.
...
I WISH THEY WEREN'T LISTENING.
THEY HALF LISTEN AND THEN FORCE IN ADDITIONS THAT STEER EVERYTHING FURTHER OFF COURSE.
AHH... YEAH...
...
ZUUUUN (GLOOOM)
ずううううん...
IT SEEMED THINGS WOULD NOT RESOLVE SO EASILY.

MY YOUTH ROMANTIC COMEDY is WRØNG, AS I EXPECTED @comic 12

■Original Story
Wataru Watari
■Art
Naomichi Io
■Character Design
Ponkan⑧

MY YOUTH ROMANTIC COMEDY IS WRONG, AS I EXPECTED @COMIC

CHARACTERS + STORY SO FAR

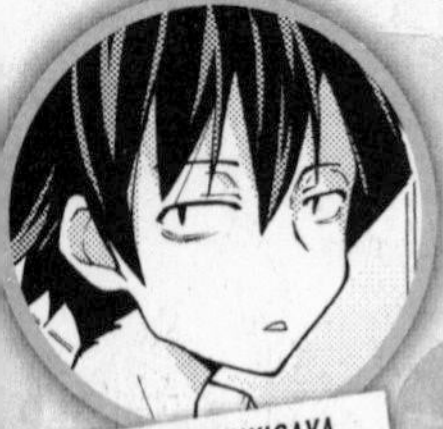

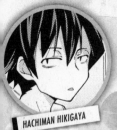

HACHIMAN HIKIGAYA

LONER AND A TWISTED HUMAN BEING. FORCED TO JOIN THE SERVICE CLUB. ASPIRES TO BE A HOUSEHUSBAND.

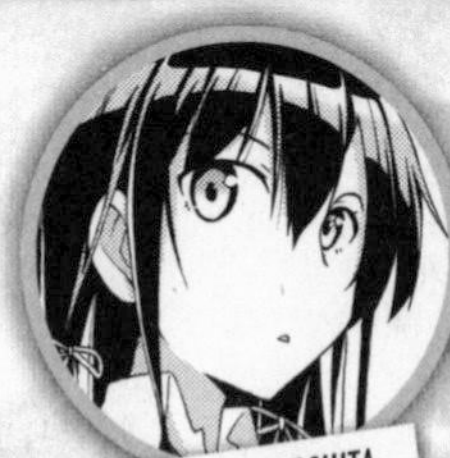

YUKINO YUKINOSHITA

PERFECT SUPERWOMAN WITH TOP GRADES AND FLAWLESS LOOKS, BUT HER PERSONALITY AND BOOBS ARE A LETDOWN. PRESIDENT OF THE SERVICE CLUB.

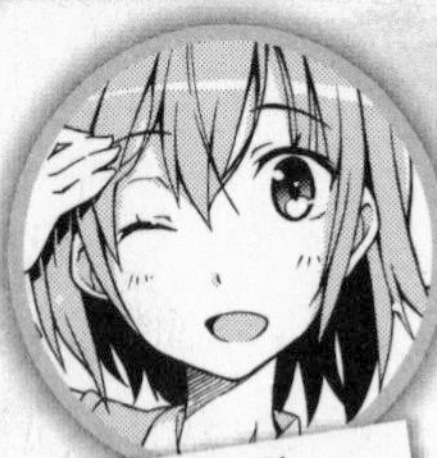

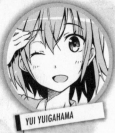

YUI YUIGAHAMA

LIGHT-BROWN HAIR, MINISKIRT, LARGE-BOOBED SLUTTY TYPE. BUT SHE'S ACTUALLY A VIRGIN!? MEMBER OF THE SERVICE CLUB.

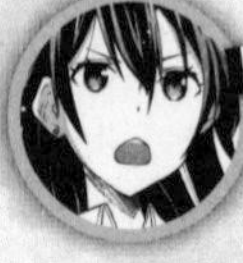

SHIZUKA HIRATSUKA

GUIDANCE COUNSELOR. ATTEMPTING TO FIX HACHIMAN BY FORCING HIM INTO THE SERVICE CLUB.

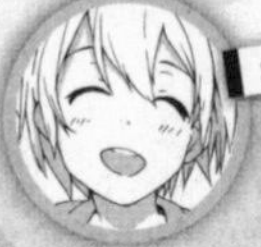

SAIKA TOTSUKA

THE SINGLE FLOWER BLOOMING IN THIS STORY. BUT...HAS A "PACKAGE."

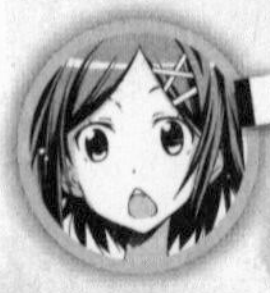

KOMACHI HIKIGAYA

HACHIMAN'S LITTLE SISTER. IN MIDDLE SCHOOL. EVERYTHING SHE DOES IS CALCULATED!?

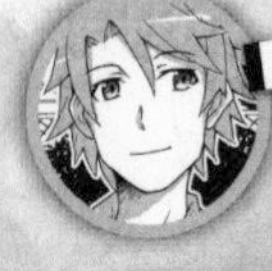

HAYATO HAYAMA

TOP RANKED IN THE SCHOOL CASTE. HANDSOME MEMBER OF THE SOCCER TEAM.

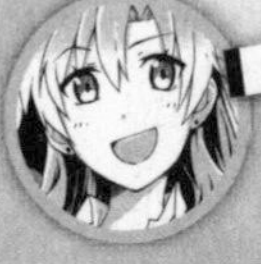

YUMIKO MIURA

THE HIGH EMPRESS NONE CAN OPPOSE.

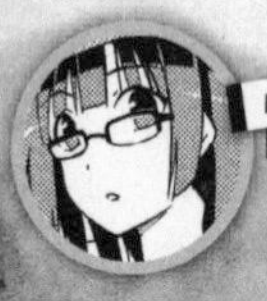

HINA EBINA

A MEMBER OF MIURA'S CLIQUE, BUT A RAGING FUJOSHI ON THE INSIDE.

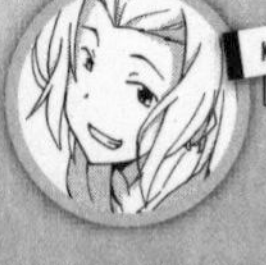

KAKERU TOBE

ALWAYS OVEREXCITED. MEMBER OF HAYAMA'S CLIQUE.

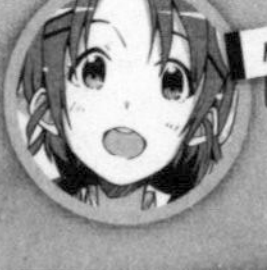

MEGURI SHIROMEGURI

THIRD-YEAR. THE PLEASANT AND GENTLE PRESIDENT OF THE STUDENT COUNCIL.

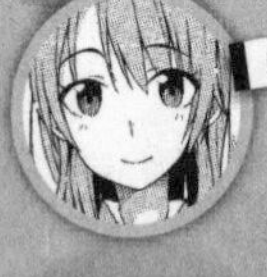

IROHA ISSHIKI

SOCCER CLUB ASSISTANT. FIRST-YEAR.

IN THE MIDDLE OF TRYING TO DEAL WITH A REQUEST IROHA ISSHIKI BROUGHT TO HIM REGARDING THE JOINT CHRISTMAS EVENT, HACHIMAN TAKES A BIG STEP WITH HIS RELATIONSHIP WITH YUKINO AND YUI. THIS ACTION LEADS THEM TO SET OUT TO TRY TO RESOLVE THE REQUEST AS A CLUB ONCE MORE, BUT THEY STILL CAN'T QUITE FIND A WAY TO FIX THE SITUATION. BUT THE DAY OF THE CHRISTMAS PARTY IS COMING CLOSER AND CLOSER...

CONTENTS

MADE IN COOPERATION WITH THE CHIBA CITY LOCATION SERVICE

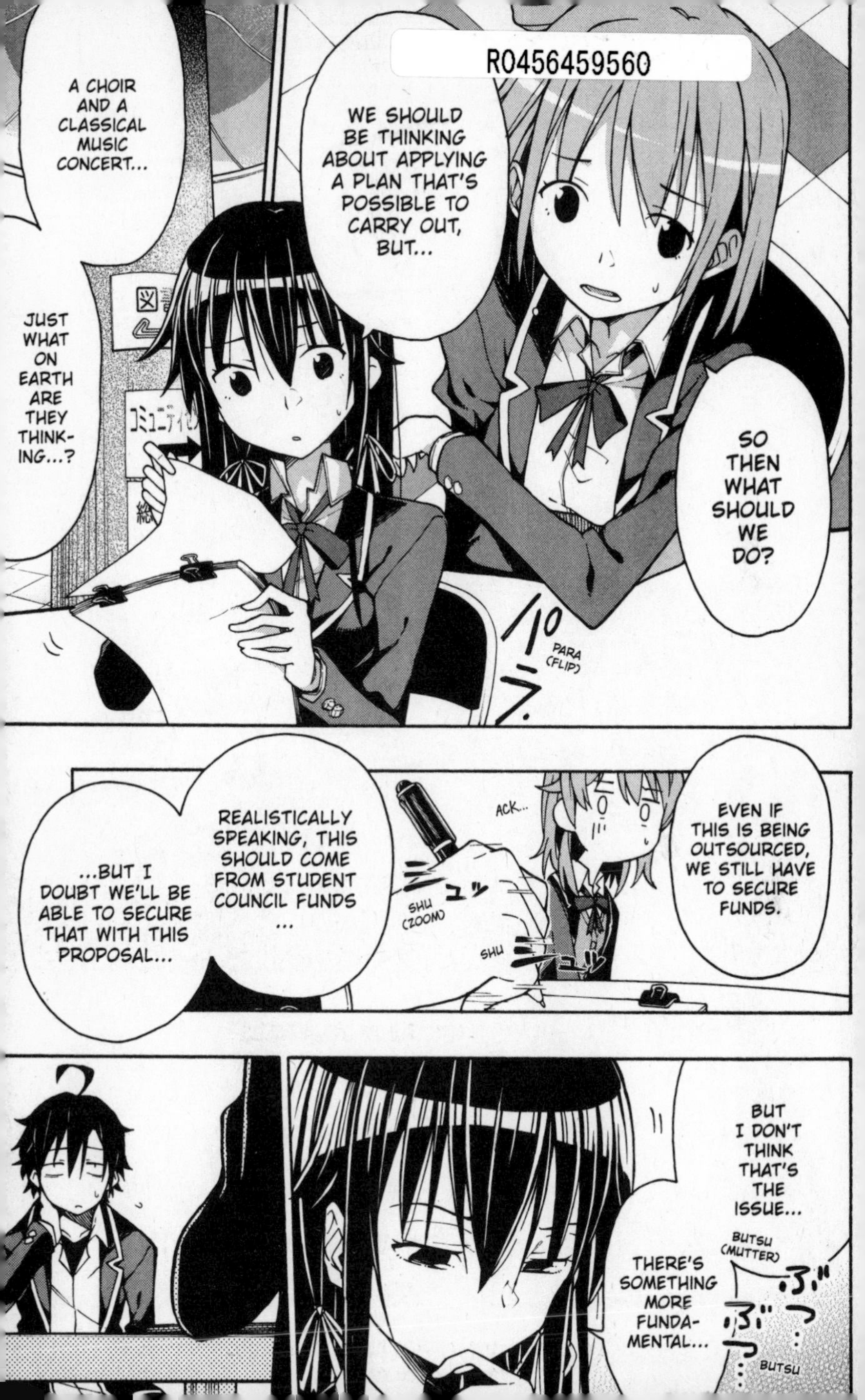
WE SHOULD BE THINKING ABOUT APPLYING A PLAN THAT'S POSSIBLE TO CARRY OUT, BUT...
A CHOIR AND A CLASSICAL MUSIC CONCERT...
SO THEN WHAT SHOULD WE DO?
JUST WHAT ON EARTH ARE THEY THINK-ING...?
PARA (FLIP)
EVEN IF THIS IS BEING OUTSOURCED, WE STILL HAVE TO SECURE FUNDS.
ACK...
SHU (ZOOM)
SHU
REALISTICALLY SPEAKING, THIS SHOULD COME FROM STUDENT COUNCIL FUNDS ...
...BUT I DOUBT WE'LL BE ABLE TO SECURE THAT WITH THIS PROPOSAL...
BUT I DON'T THINK THAT'S THE ISSUE...
BUTSU (MUTTER)
THERE'S SOMETHING MORE FUNDA-MENTAL...
BUTSU

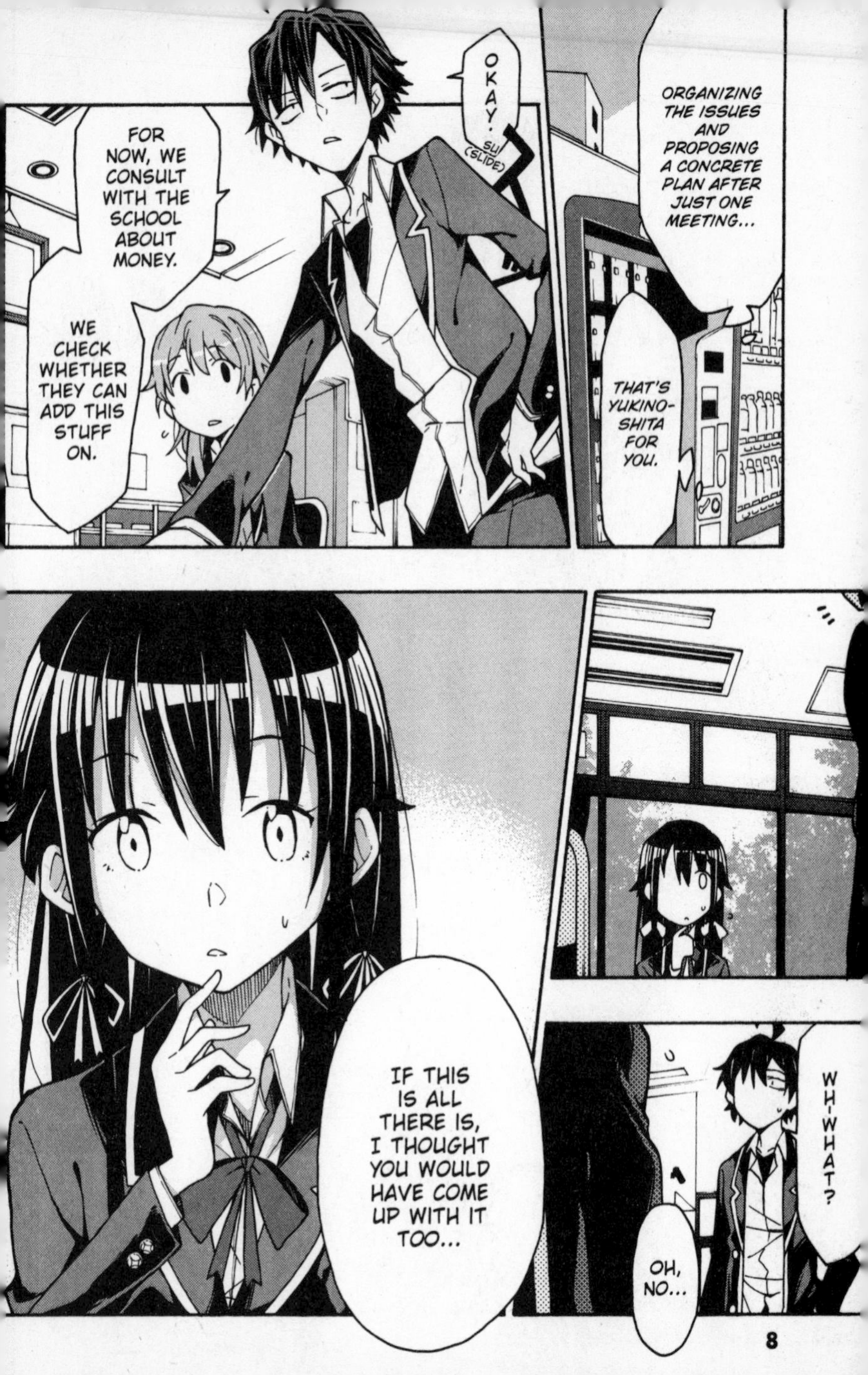
ORGANIZING THE ISSUES AND PROPOSING A CONCRETE PLAN AFTER JUST ONE MEETING...
THAT'S YUKINO-SHITA FOR YOU.
OKAY.
SLI (SLIDE)
FOR NOW, WE CONSULT WITH THE SCHOOL ABOUT MONEY.
WE CHECK WHETHER THEY CAN ADD THIS STUFF ON.
WHI-WHAT?
OH, NO...
IF THIS IS ALL THERE IS, I THOUGHT YOU WOULD HAVE COME UP WITH IT TOO...

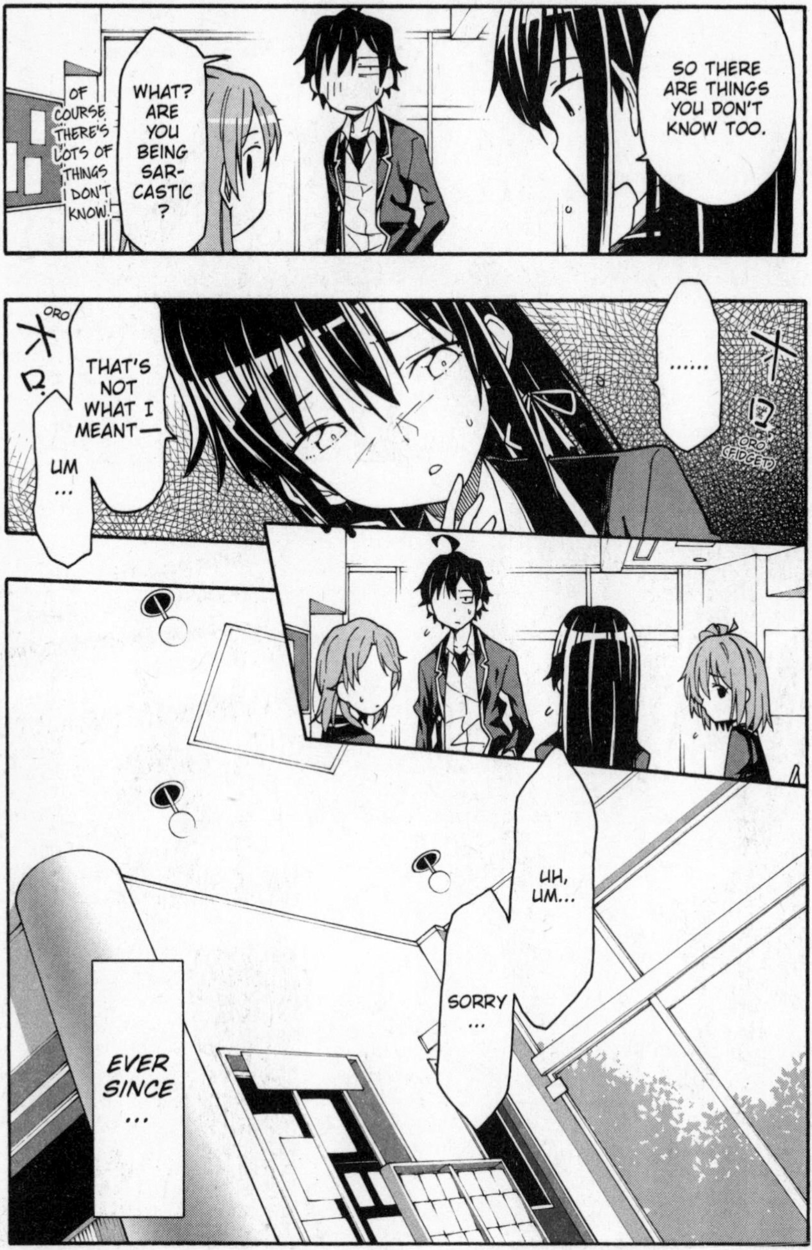
SO THERE ARE THINGS YOU DON'T KNOW TOO.
WHAT? ARE YOU BEING SARCASTIC?
OF COURSE THERE'S LOTS OF THINGS I DON'T KNOW.
......
ORO (FIDGET)
THAT'S NOT WHAT I MEANT— UM ...
ORO
UH, UM... SORRY ...
EVER SINCE ...

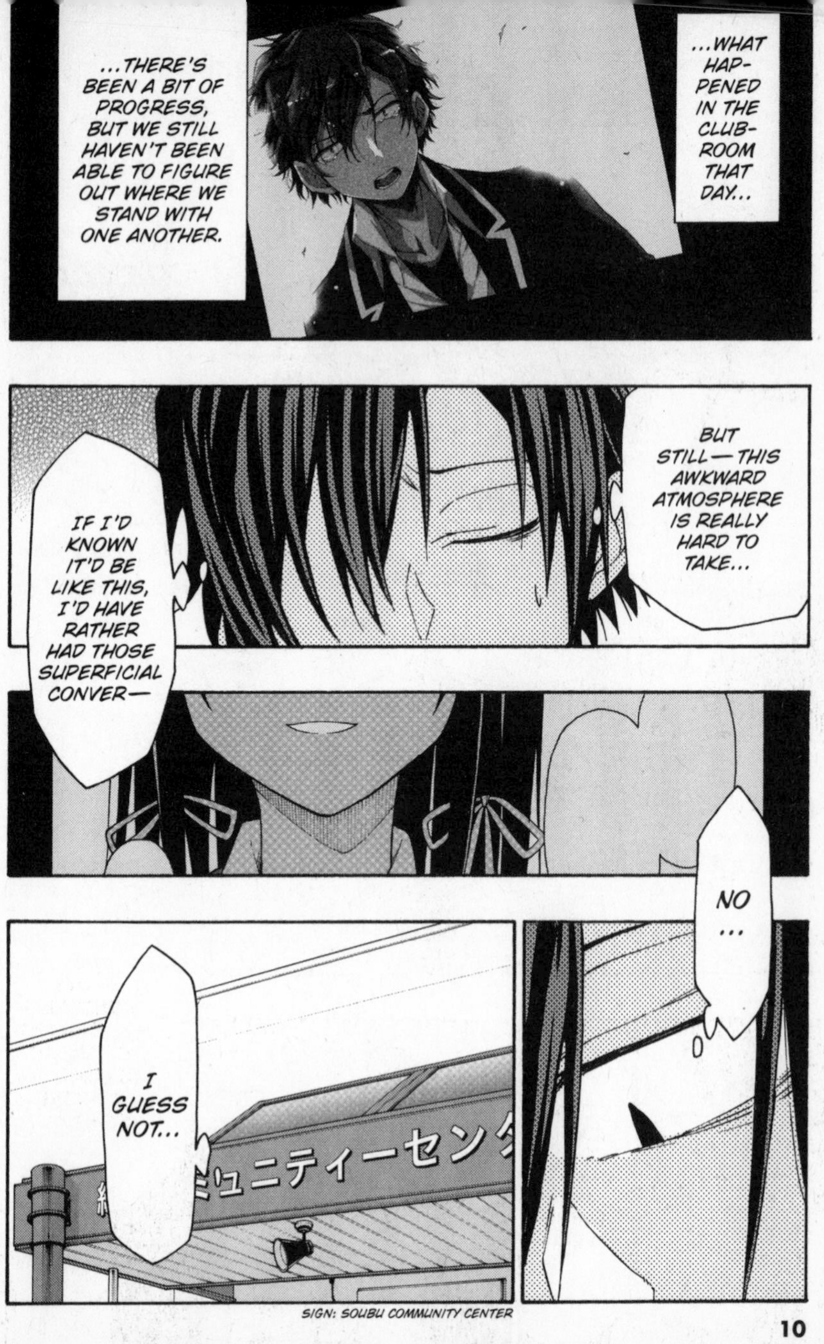
...WHAT HAPPENED IN THE CLUBROOM THAT DAY...
...THERE'S BEEN A BIT OF PROGRESS, BUT WE STILL HAVEN'T BEEN ABLE TO FIGURE OUT WHERE WE STAND WITH ONE ANOTHER.
BUT STILL—THIS AWKWARD ATMOSPHERE IS REALLY HARD TO TAKE...
IF I'D KNOWN IT'D BE LIKE THIS, I'D HAVE RATHER HAD THOSE SUPERFICIAL CONVER—
NO ...
I GUESS NOT...
SIGN: SOUBU COMMUNITY CENTER

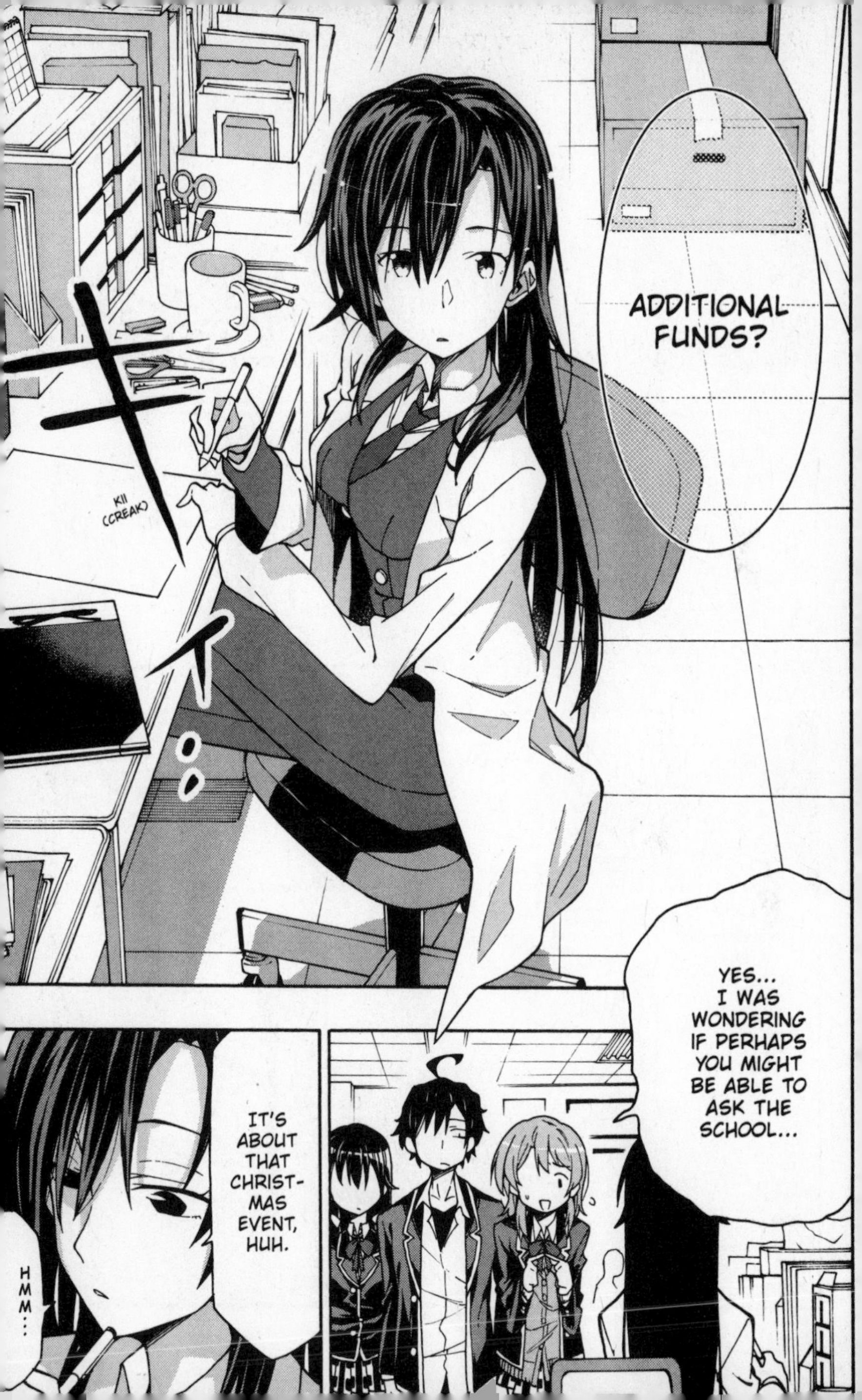
ADDITIONAL FUNDS?
KII (CREAK)
YES... I WAS WONDERING IF PERHAPS YOU MIGHT BE ABLE TO ASK THE SCHOOL...
IT'S ABOUT THAT CHRIST-MAS EVENT, HUH.
HMM...

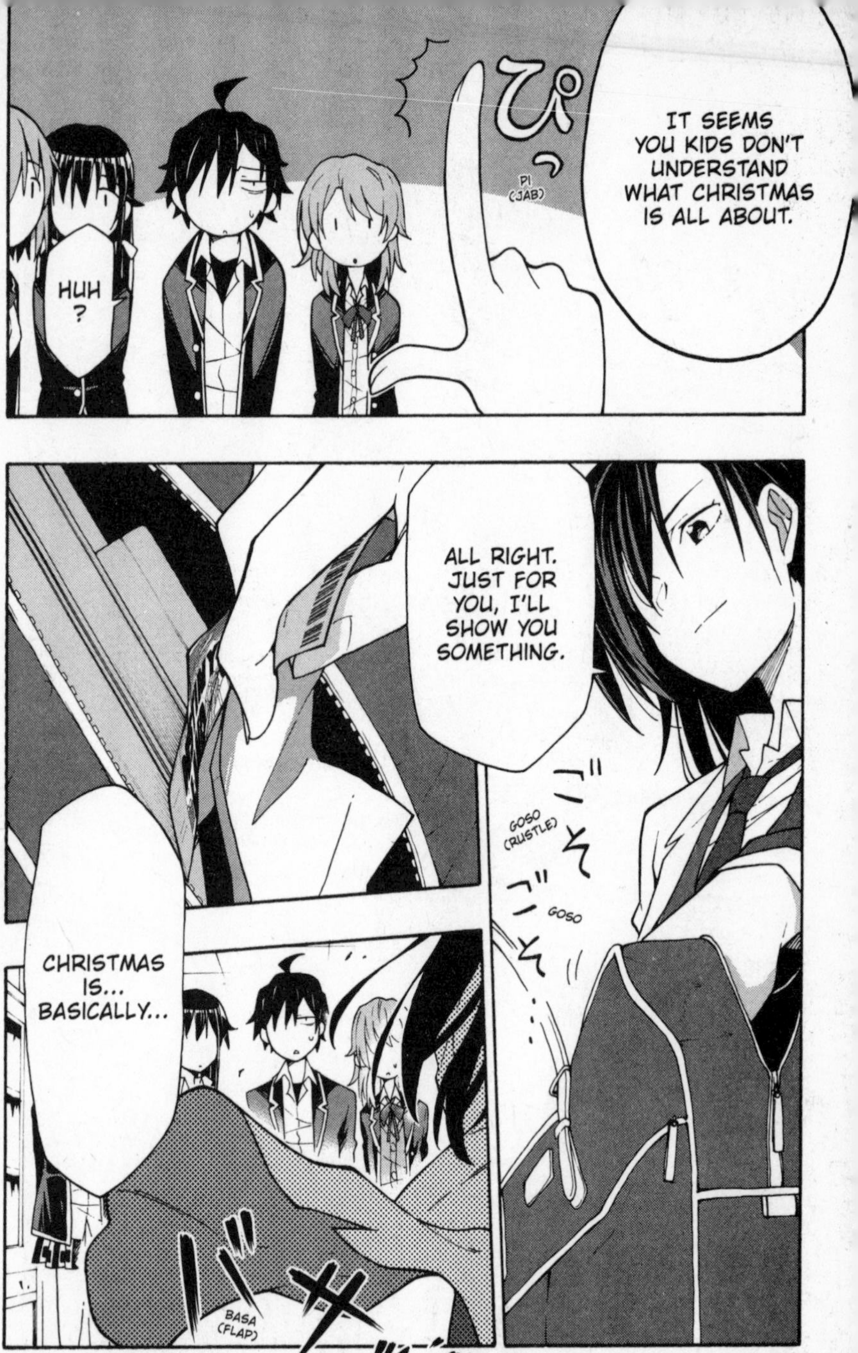
IT SEEMS YOU KIDS DON'T UNDERSTAND WHAT CHRISTMAS IS ALL ABOUT.
ぴっ
PI (JAB)
HUH?
ごそ
GOSO (RUSTLE)
ごそ
GOSO
ALL RIGHT. JUST FOR YOU, I'LL SHOW YOU SOMETHING.
CHRISTMAS IS... BASICALLY...
バサッ
BASA (FLAP)

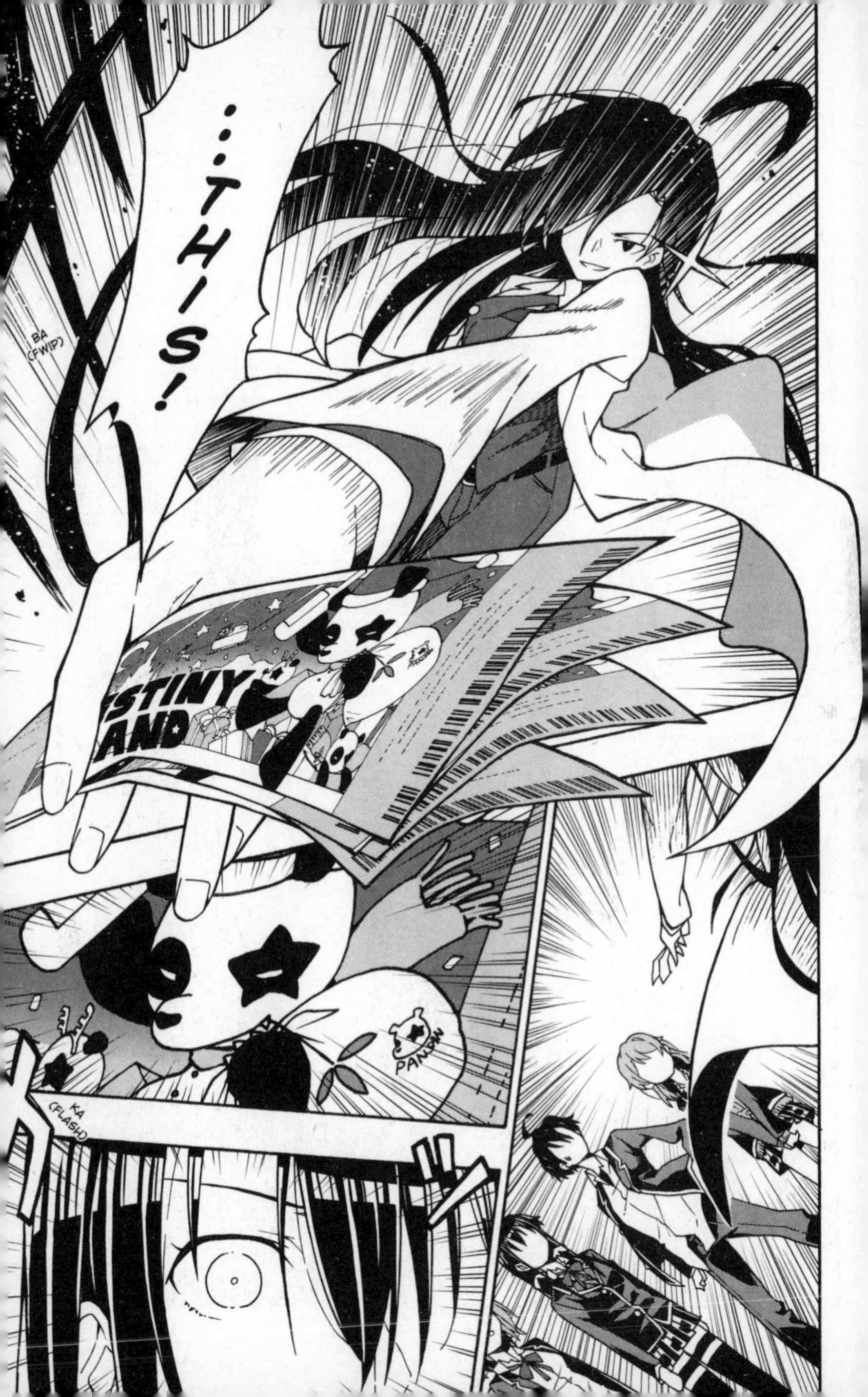

...THIS!
BA (FWIP)
STINY
AND
PANJAN
PANJAN
KA (FLASH)

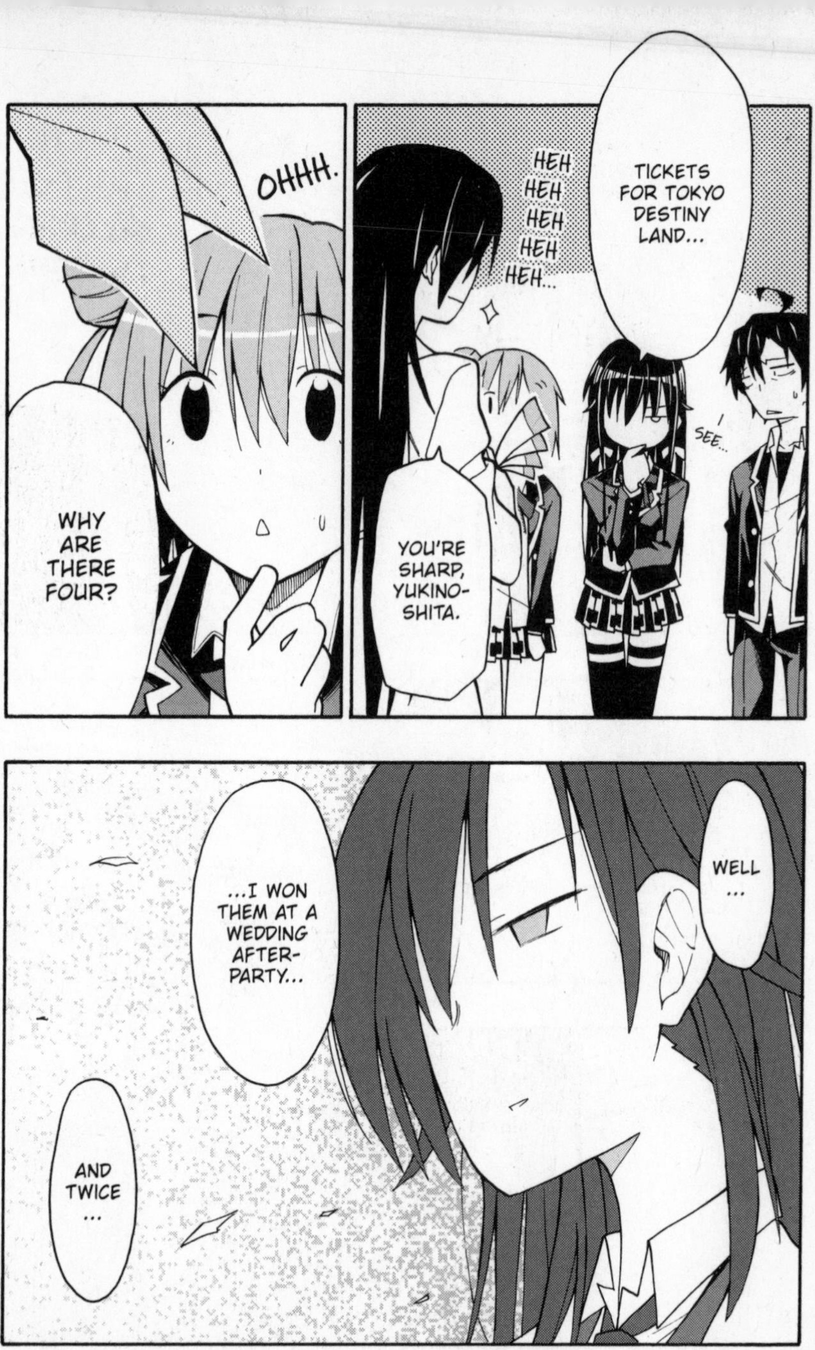
TICKETS FOR TOKYO DESTINY LAND...
I SEE...
HEH HEH HEH HEH HEH...
YOU'RE SHARP, YUKINO-SHITA.
OHHH.
WHY ARE THERE FOUR?
WELL ...
...I WON THEM AT A WEDDING AFTER-PARTY...
AND TWICE ...

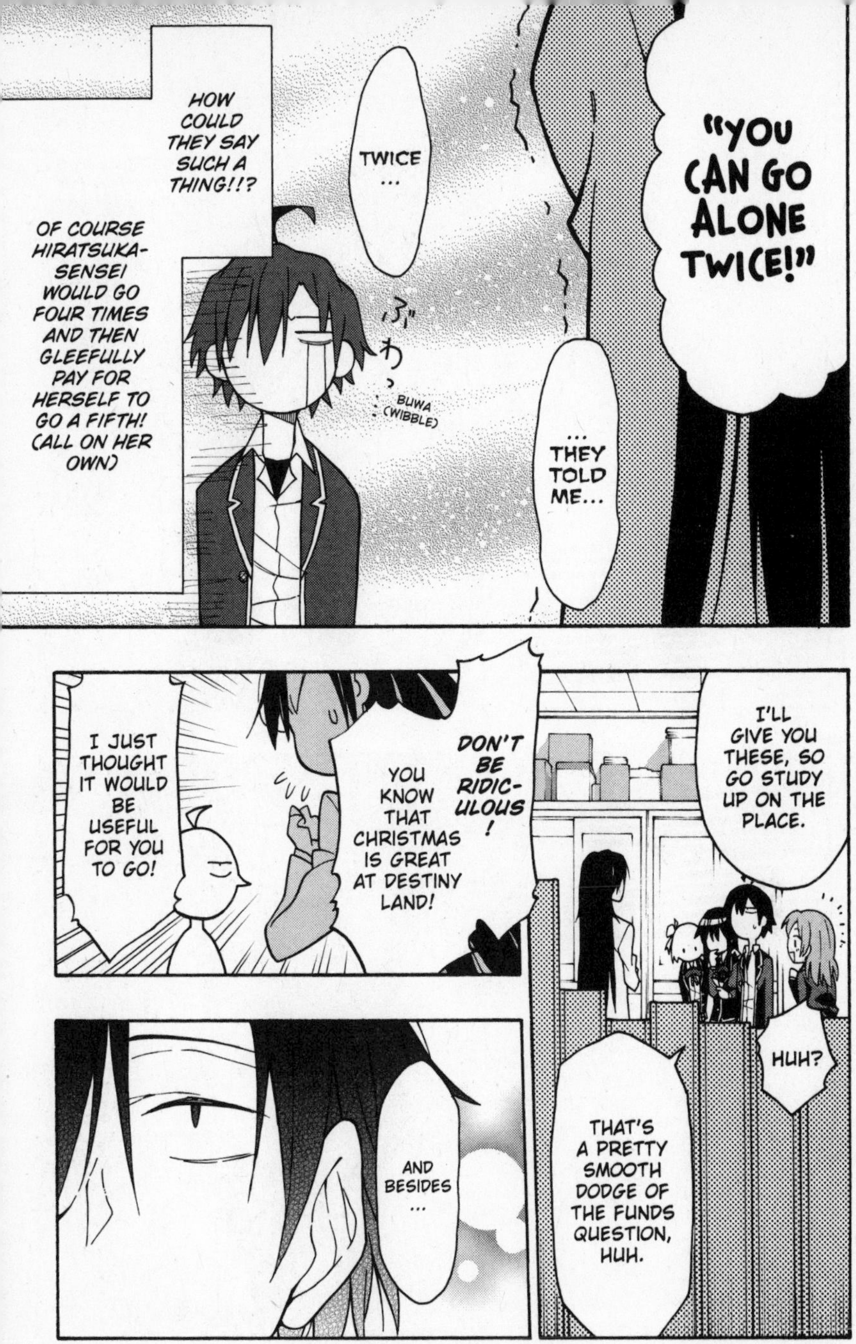
"YOU CAN GO ALONE TWICE!"
... THEY TOLD ME...
TWICE ...
ぶわっ
BUWA (WIBBLE)
HOW COULD THEY SAY SUCH A THING!!?
OF COURSE HIRATSUKA-SENSEI WOULD GO FOUR TIMES AND THEN GLEEFULLY PAY FOR HERSELF TO GO A FIFTH! (ALL ON HER OWN)
I'LL GIVE YOU THESE, SO GO STUDY UP ON THE PLACE.
HUH?
THAT'S A PRETTY SMOOTH DODGE OF THE FUNDS QUESTION, HUH.
DON'T BE RIDICULOUS!
YOU KNOW THAT CHRISTMAS IS GREAT AT DESTINY LAND!
I JUST THOUGHT IT WOULD BE USEFUL FOR YOU TO GO!
AND BESIDES ...

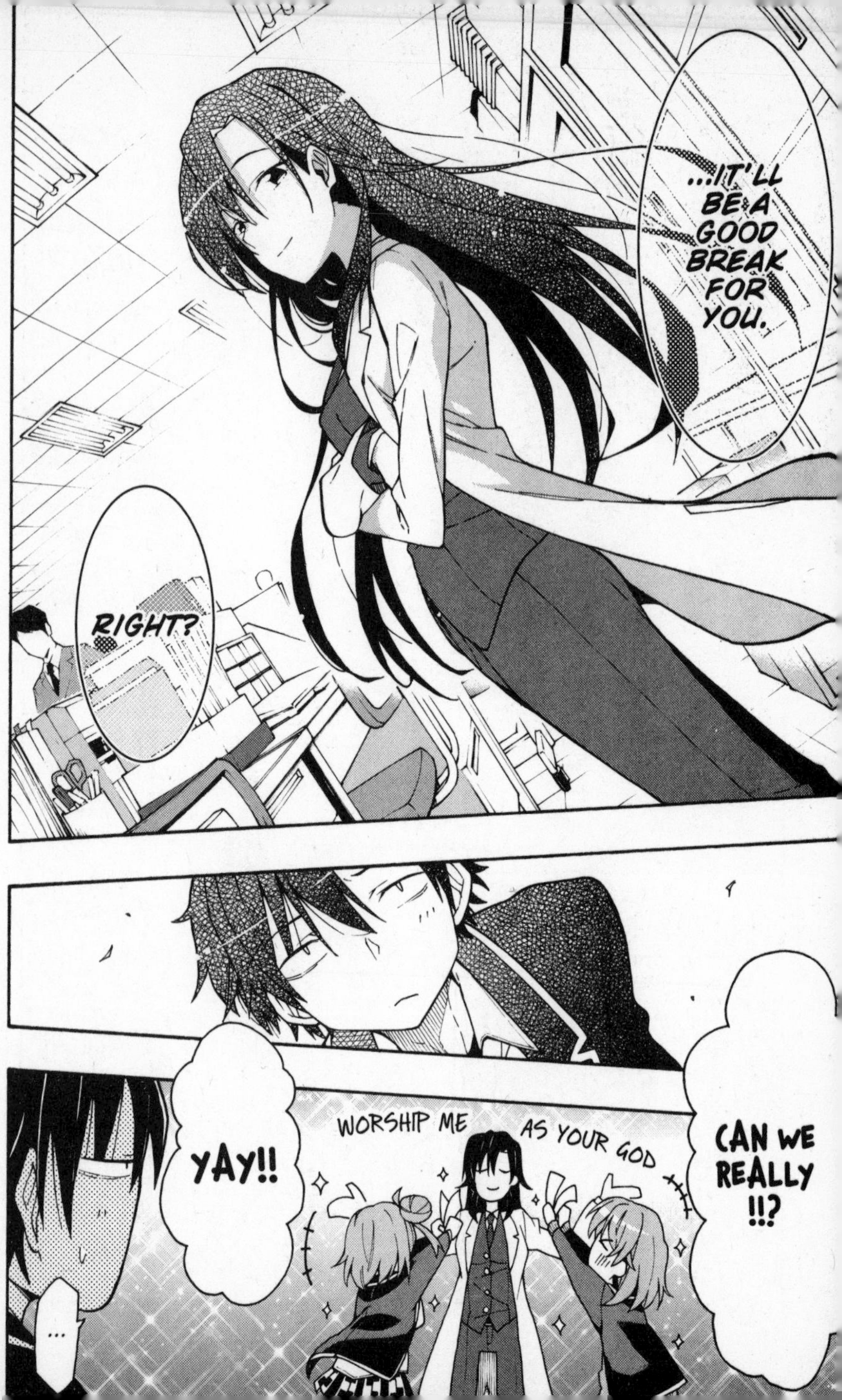
...IT'LL BE A GOOD BREAK FOR YOU.
RIGHT?
CAN WE REALLY !!?
WORSHIP ME
AS YOUR GOD
YAY!!
...

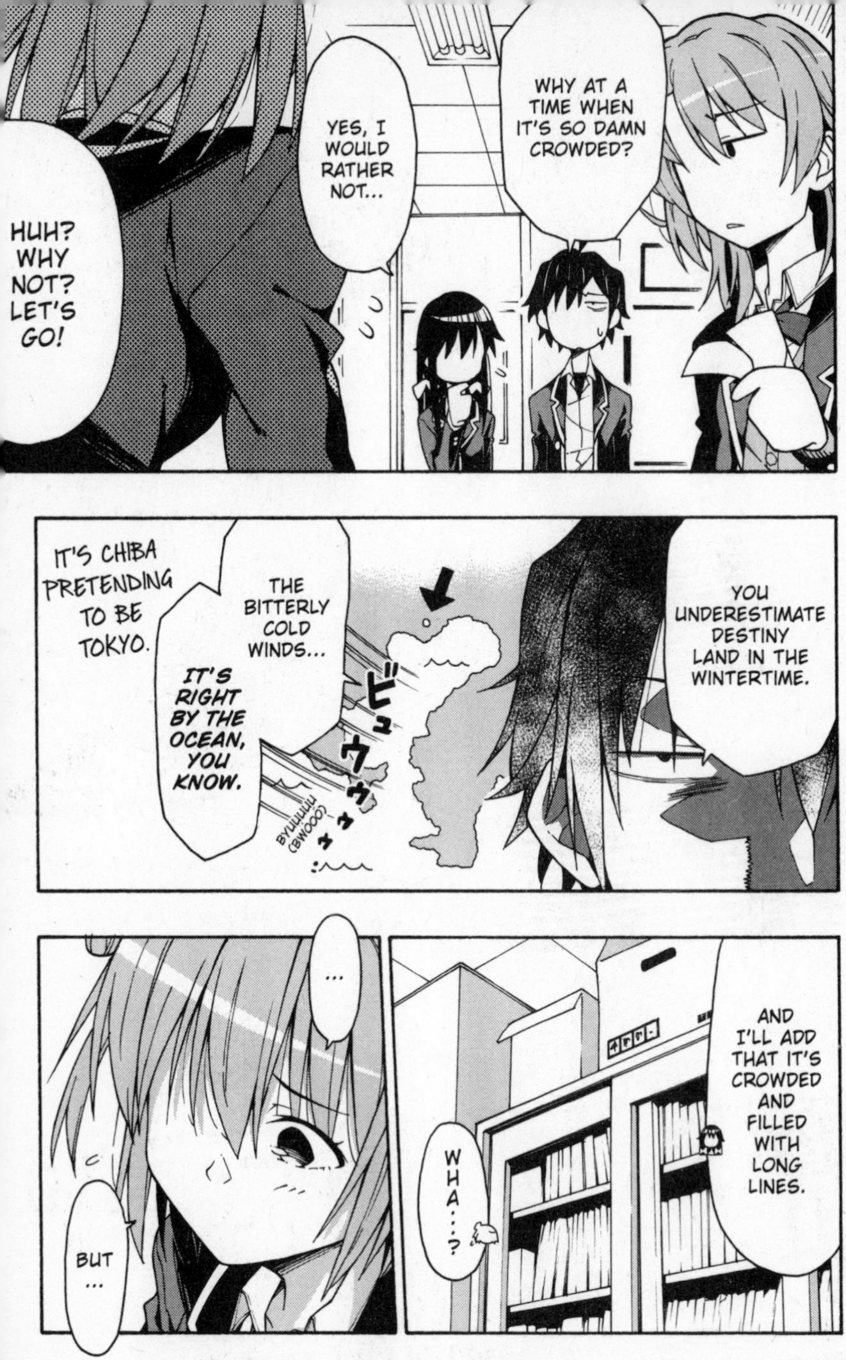
WHY AT A TIME WHEN IT'S SO DAMN CROWDED?
YES, I WOULD RATHER NOT...
HUH? WHY NOT? LET'S GO!
YOU UNDERESTIMATE DESTINY LAND IN THE WINTERTIME.
THE BITTERLY COLD WINDS...
IT'S RIGHT BY THE OCEAN, YOU KNOW.
ビュウゥゥ
BYUUUUU (BWOOO)
IT'S CHIBA PRETENDING TO BE TOKYO.
AND I'LL ADD THAT IT'S CROWDED AND FILLED WITH LONG LINES.
WHA...?
...
BUT...

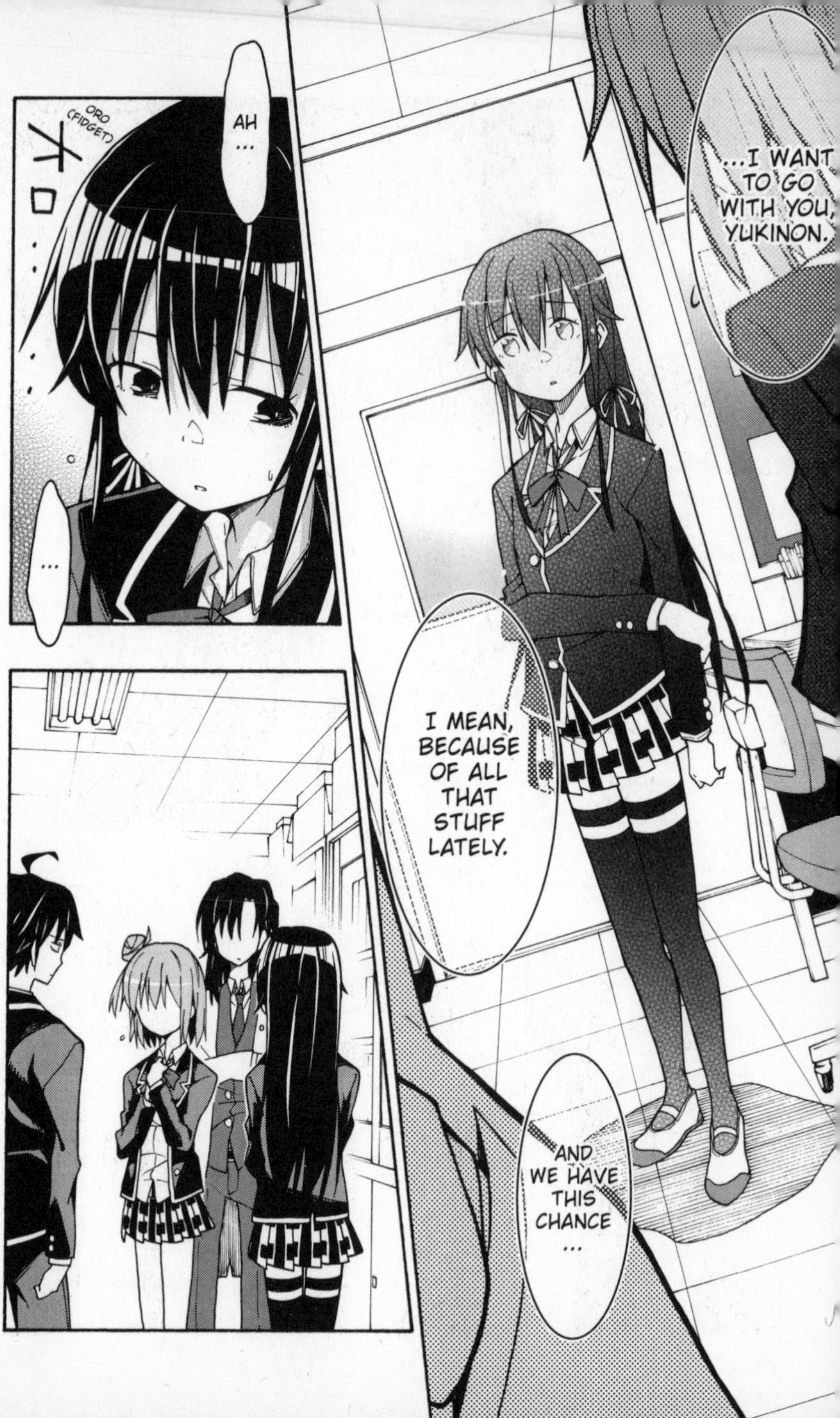
...I WANT TO GO WITH YOU, YUKINON.
I MEAN, BECAUSE OF ALL THAT STUFF LATELY.
AND WE HAVE THIS CHANCE ...
AH ...
ORO (FIDGET)
...

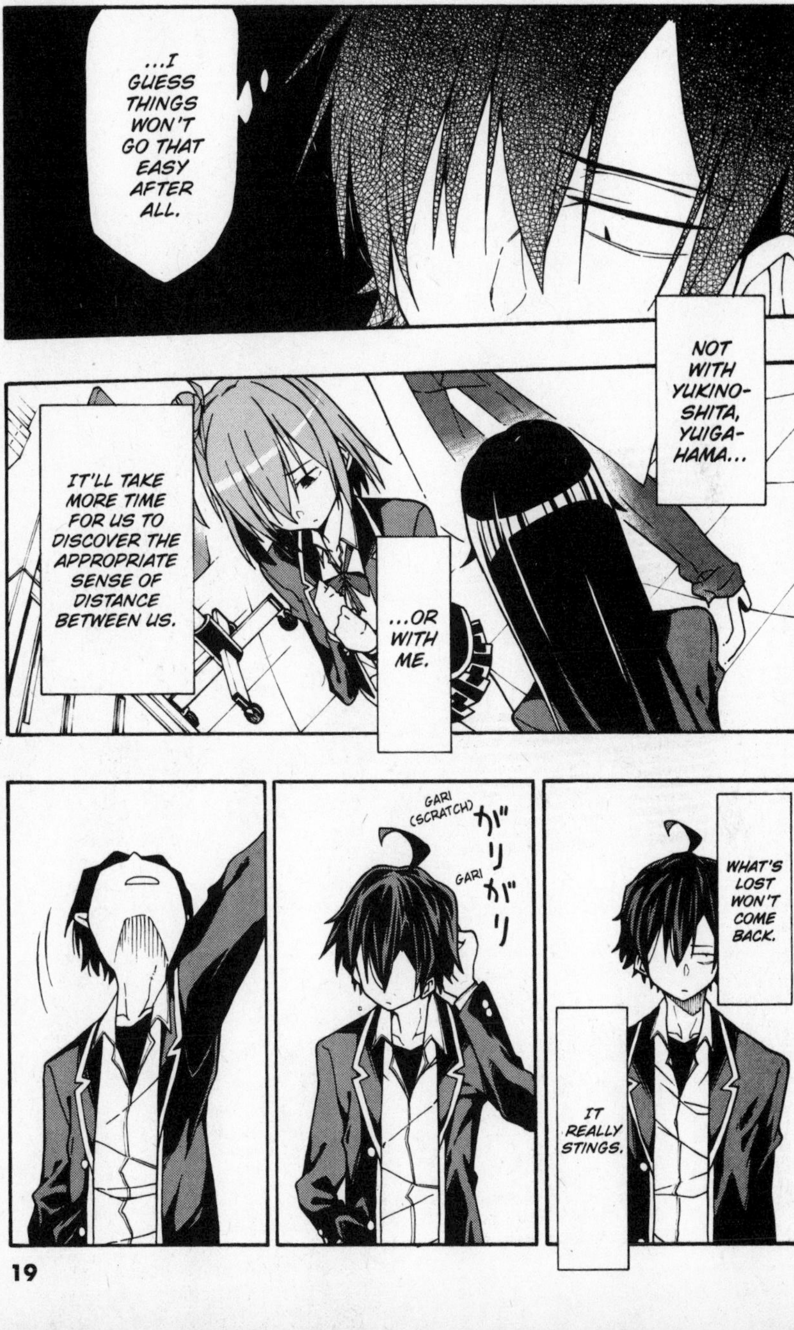
...I GUESS THINGS WON'T GO THAT EASY AFTER ALL.
NOT WITH YUKINO-SHITA, YUIGA-HAMA...
...OR WITH ME.
IT'LL TAKE MORE TIME FOR US TO DISCOVER THE APPROPRIATE SENSE OF DISTANCE BETWEEN US.
WHAT'S LOST WON'T COME BACK.
IT REALLY STINGS.
GARI (SCRATCH) ガリ
GARI ガリ

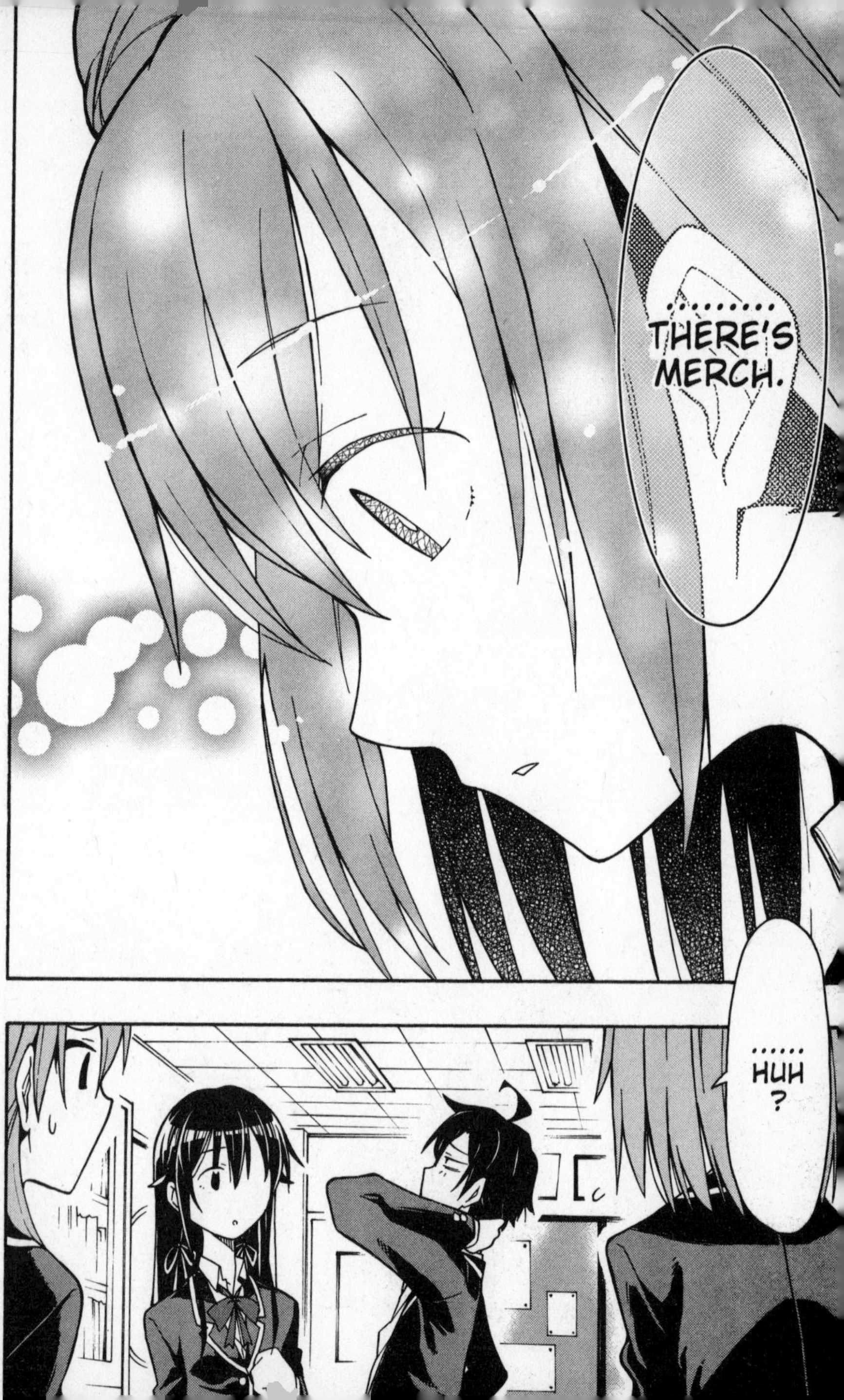
....
THERE'S MERCH.
......
HUH?

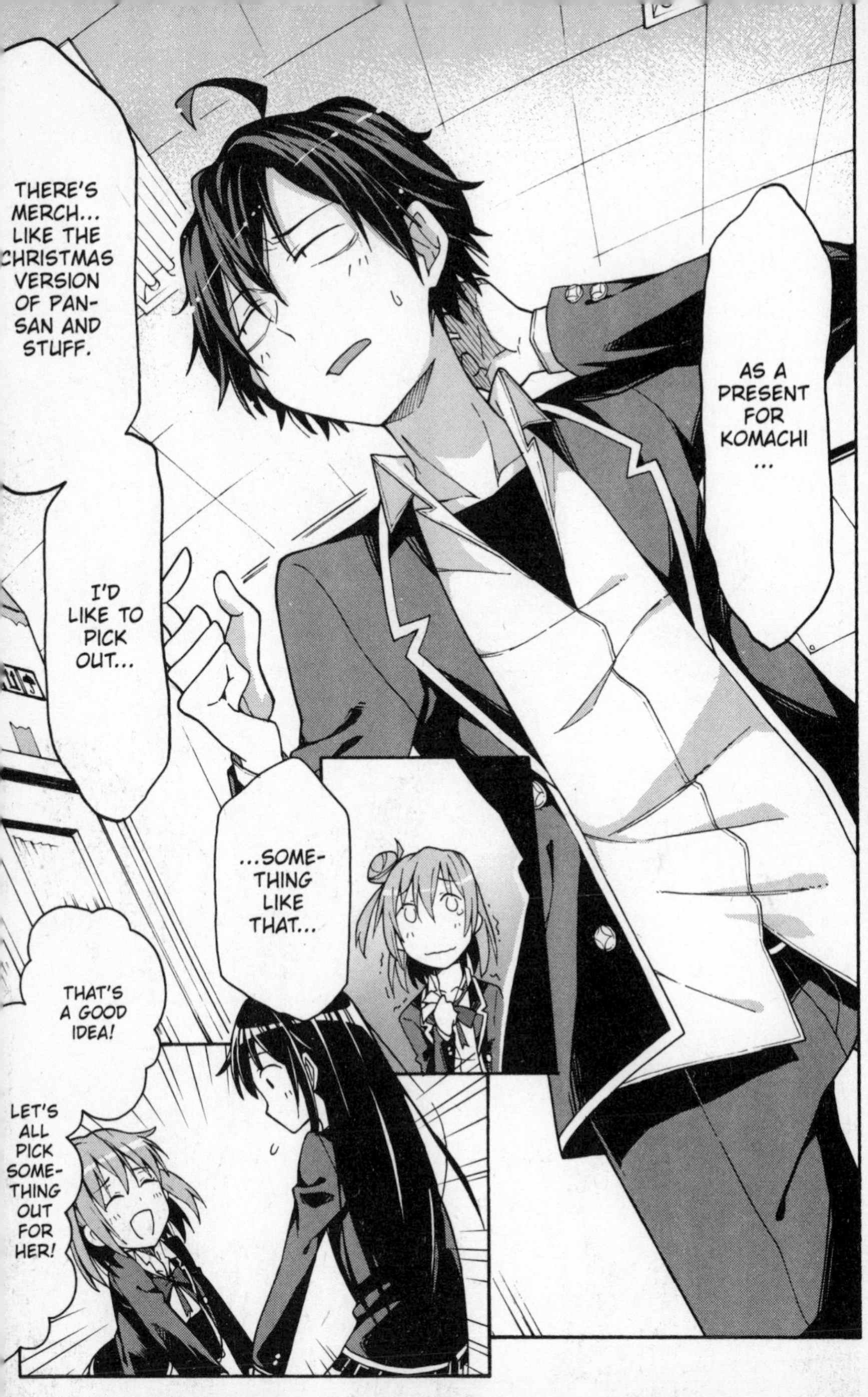
AS A PRESENT FOR KOMACHI ...
THERE'S MERCH... LIKE THE CHRISTMAS VERSION OF PAN-SAN AND STUFF.
I'D LIKE TO PICK OUT...
...SOME-THING LIKE THAT...
THAT'S A GOOD IDEA!
LET'S ALL PICK SOME-THING OUT FOR HER!

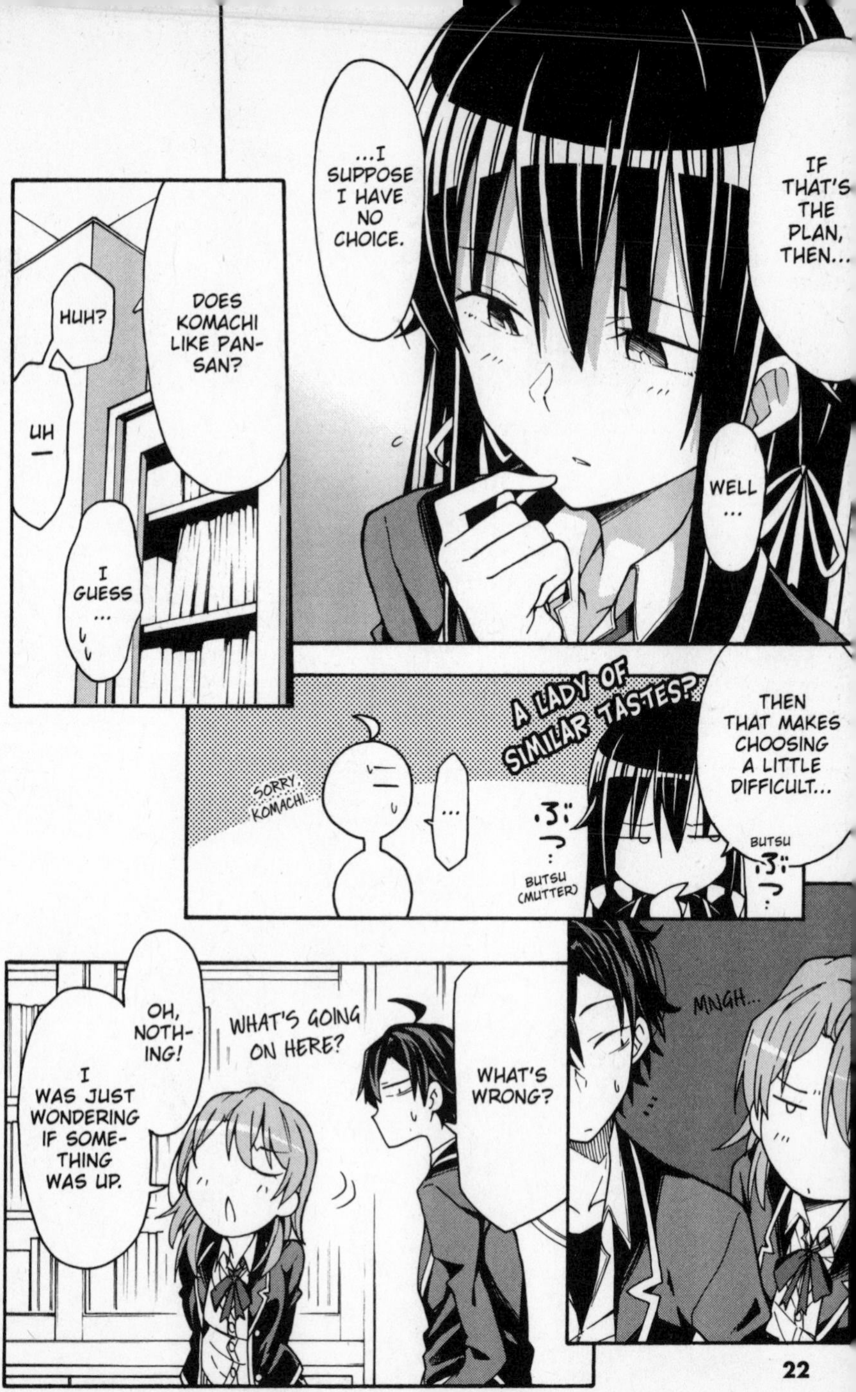
IF THAT'S THE PLAN, THEN...
...I SUPPOSE I HAVE NO CHOICE.
WELL...
DOES KOMACHI LIKE PAN-SAN?
HUH?
UH—
I GUESS...
THEN THAT MAKES CHOOSING A LITTLE DIFFICULT...
BUTSU
A LADY OF SIMILAR TASTES?
BUTSU (MUTTER)
...
SORRY, KOMACHI...
MNGH...
WHAT'S WRONG?
WHAT'S GOING ON HERE?
OH, NOTHING!
I WAS JUST WONDERING IF SOMETHING WAS UP.

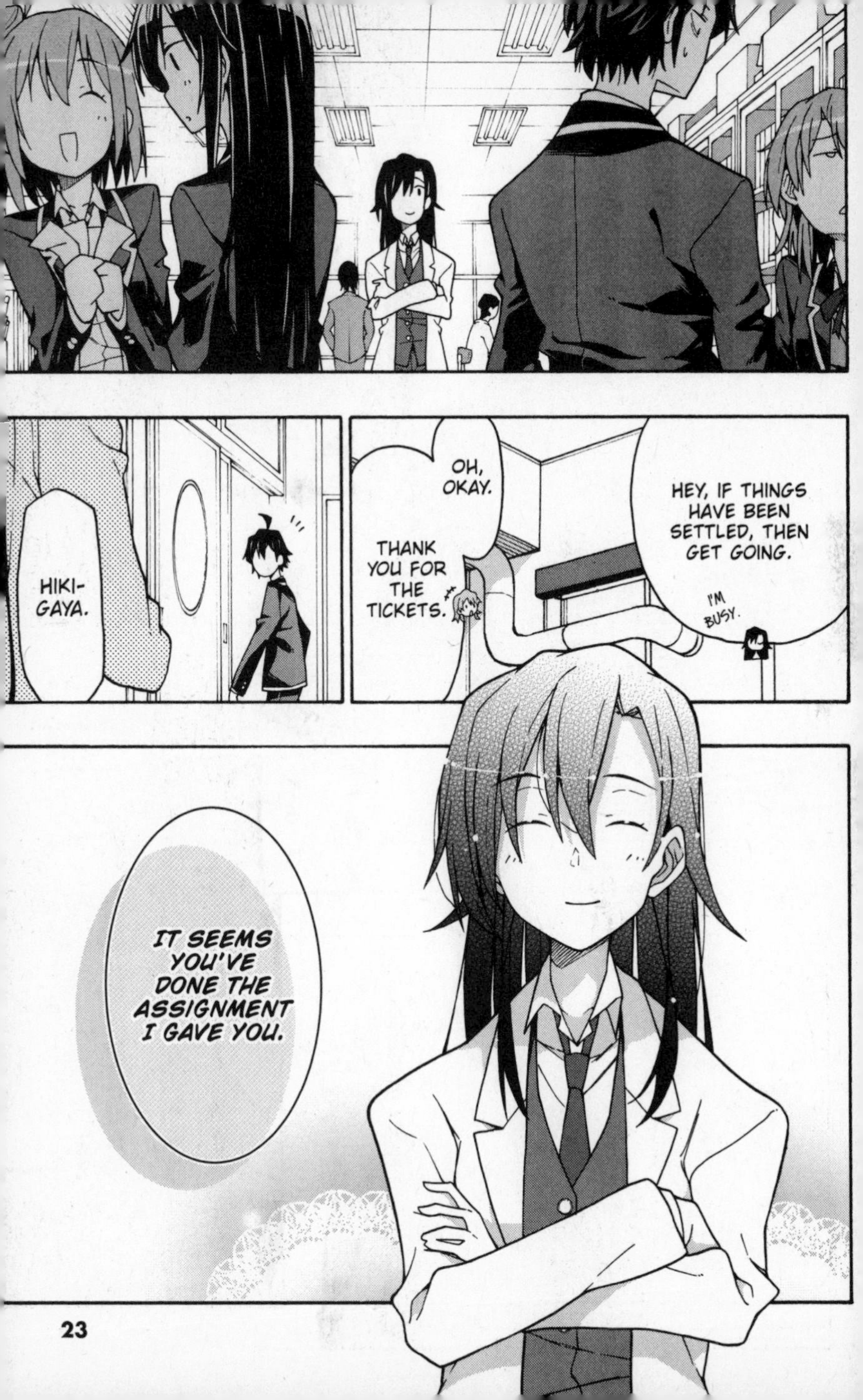
HEY, IF THINGS HAVE BEEN SETTLED, THEN GET GOING.
I'M BUSY.
OH, OKAY.
THANK YOU FOR THE TICKETS.
HIKI-GAYA.
IT SEEMS YOU'VE DONE THE ASSIGNMENT I GAVE YOU.

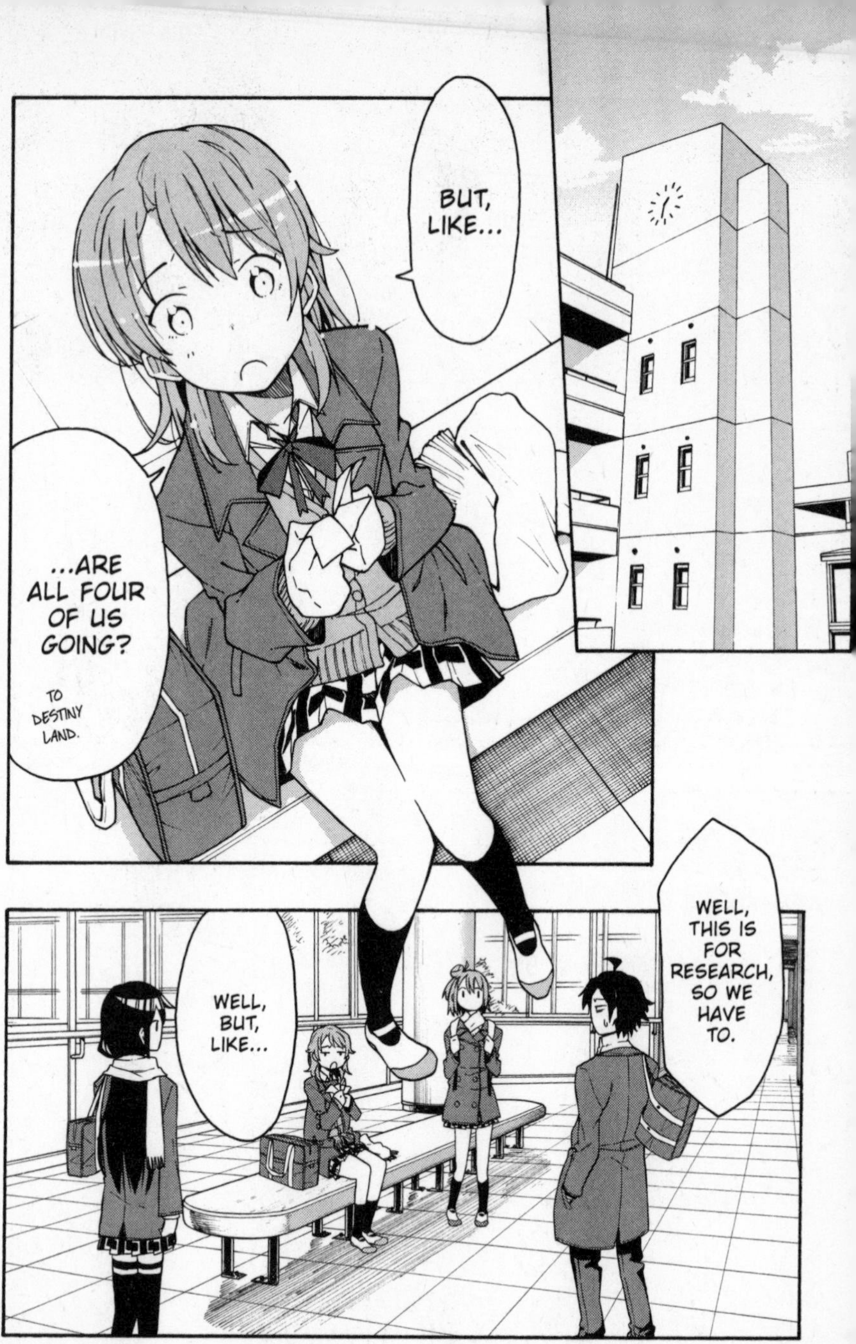
BUT, LIKE...
...ARE ALL FOUR OF US GOING?
TO DESTINY LAND.
WELL, THIS IS FOR RESEARCH, SO WE HAVE TO.
WELL, BUT, LIKE...

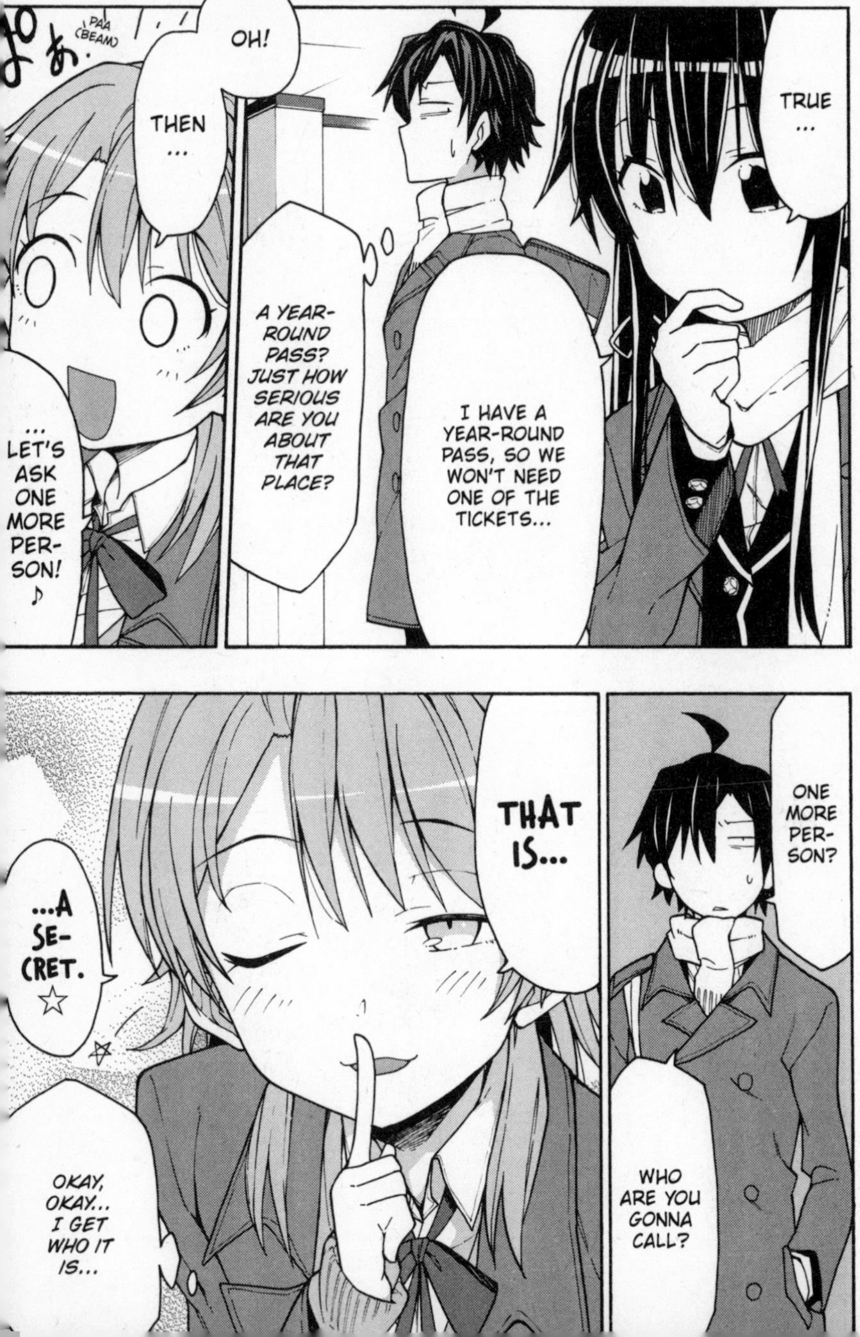

TRUE ...
I HAVE A YEAR-ROUND PASS, SO WE WON'T NEED ONE OF THE TICKETS...
A YEAR-ROUND PASS? JUST HOW SERIOUS ARE YOU ABOUT THAT PLACE?
PAA (BEAM)
OH!
THEN ...
... LET'S ASK ONE MORE PERSON! ♪
ONE MORE PERSON?
WHO ARE YOU GONNA CALL?
THAT IS...
...A SECRET. ☆
OKAY, OKAY... I GET WHO IT IS...

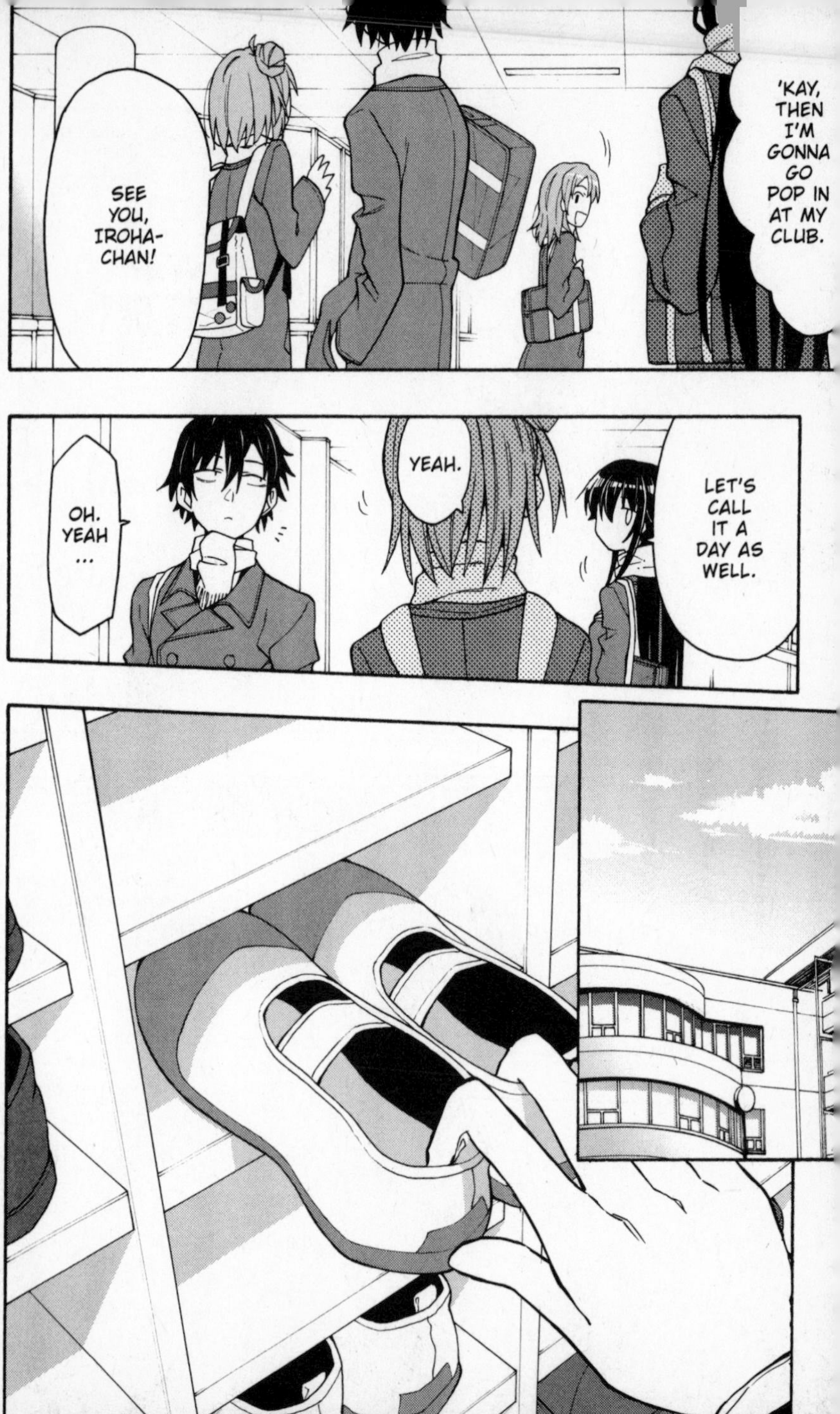
'KAY, THEN I'M GONNA GO POP IN AT MY CLUB.
SEE YOU, IROHA-CHAN!
LET'S CALL IT A DAY AS WELL.
YEAH.
OH. YEAH ...

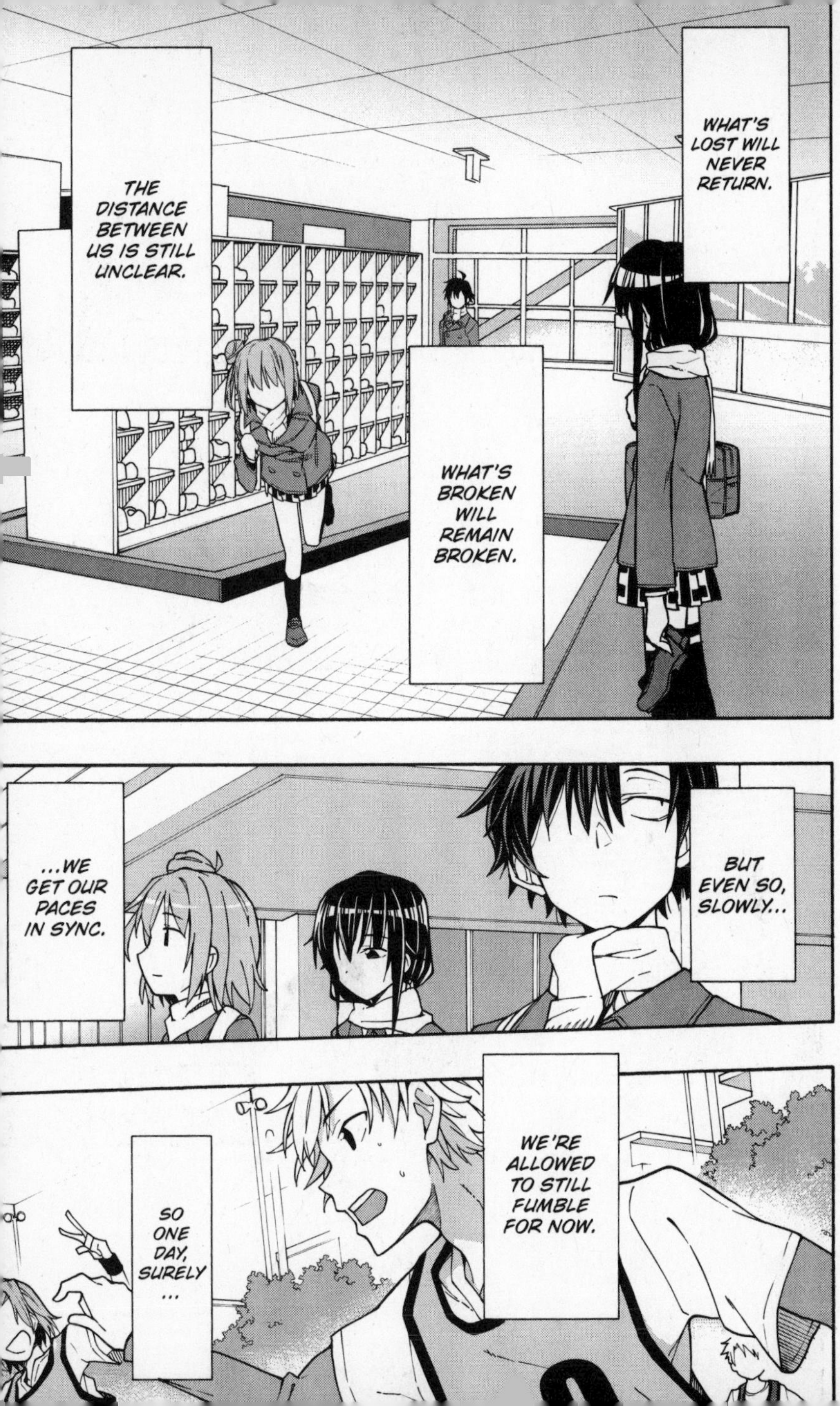
WHAT'S LOST WILL NEVER RETURN.
WHAT'S BROKEN WILL REMAIN BROKEN.
THE DISTANCE BETWEEN US IS STILL UNCLEAR.
BUT EVEN SO, SLOWLY...
...WE GET OUR PACES IN SYNC.
WE'RE ALLOWED TO STILL FUMBLE FOR NOW.
SO ONE DAY, SURELY...

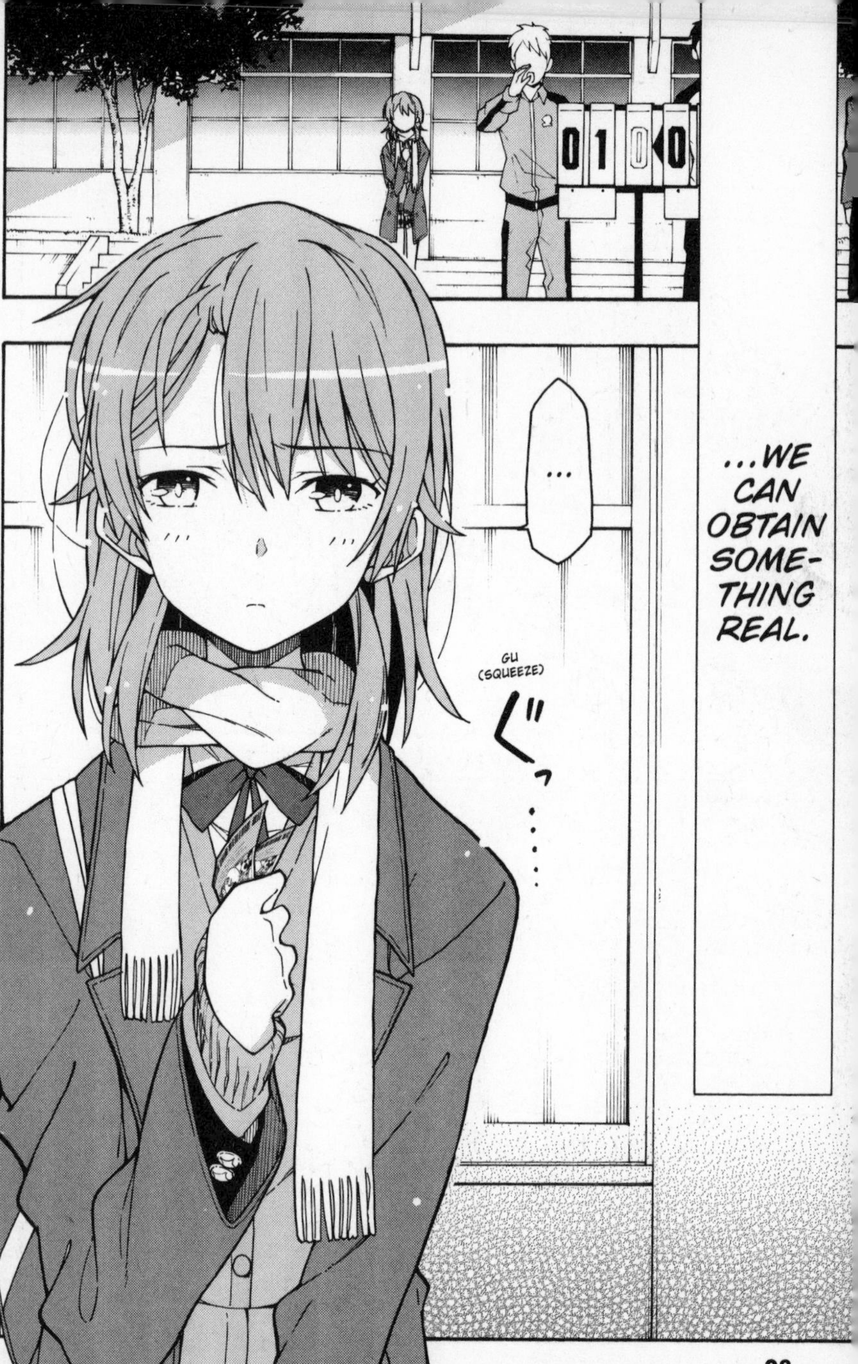
...WE CAN OBTAIN SOME-THING REAL.
...
GU (SQUEEZE)
ぐっ

CHAPTER 66 ... SOMEDAY, YUI YUIGAHAMA WILL...

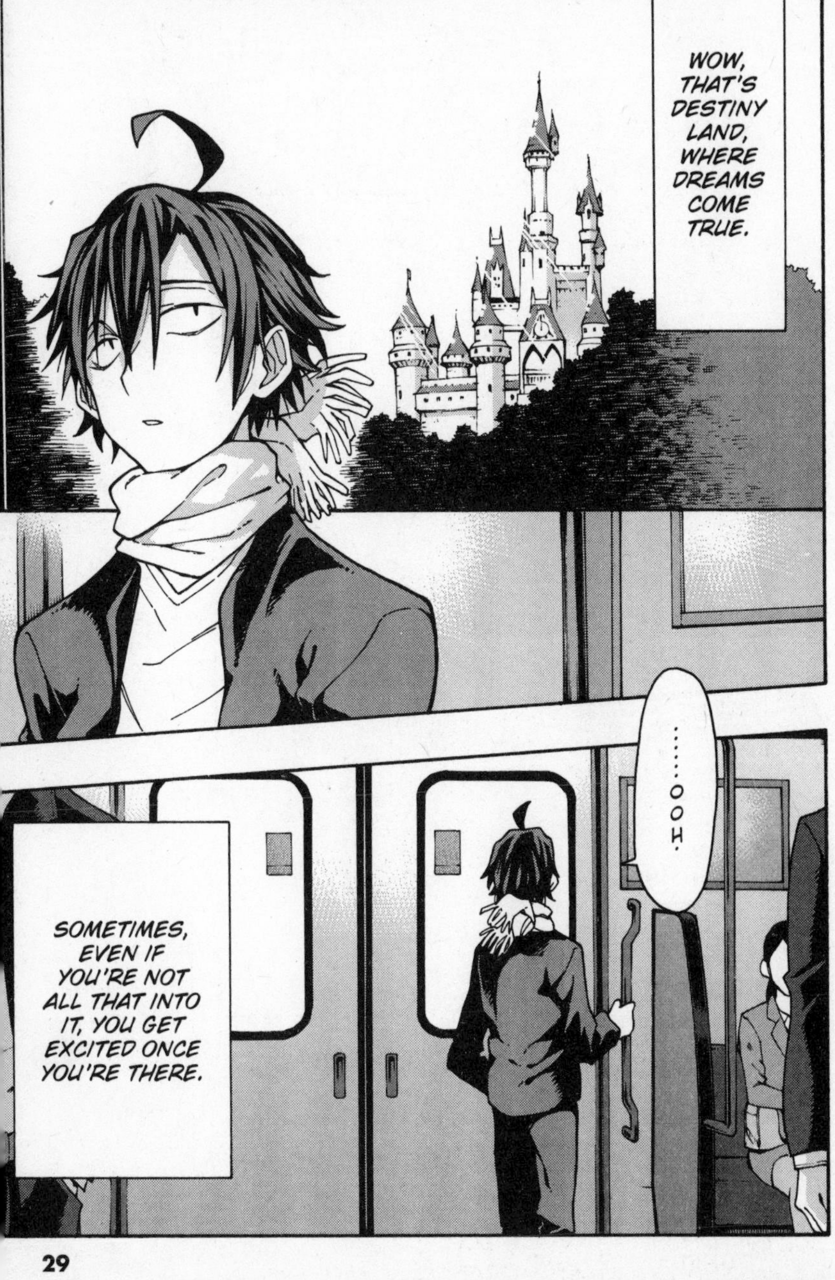
WOW, THAT'S DESTINY LAND, WHERE DREAMS COME TRUE.
.....OOH.
SOMETIMES, EVEN IF YOU'RE NOT ALL THAT INTO IT, YOU GET EXCITED ONCE YOU'RE THERE.

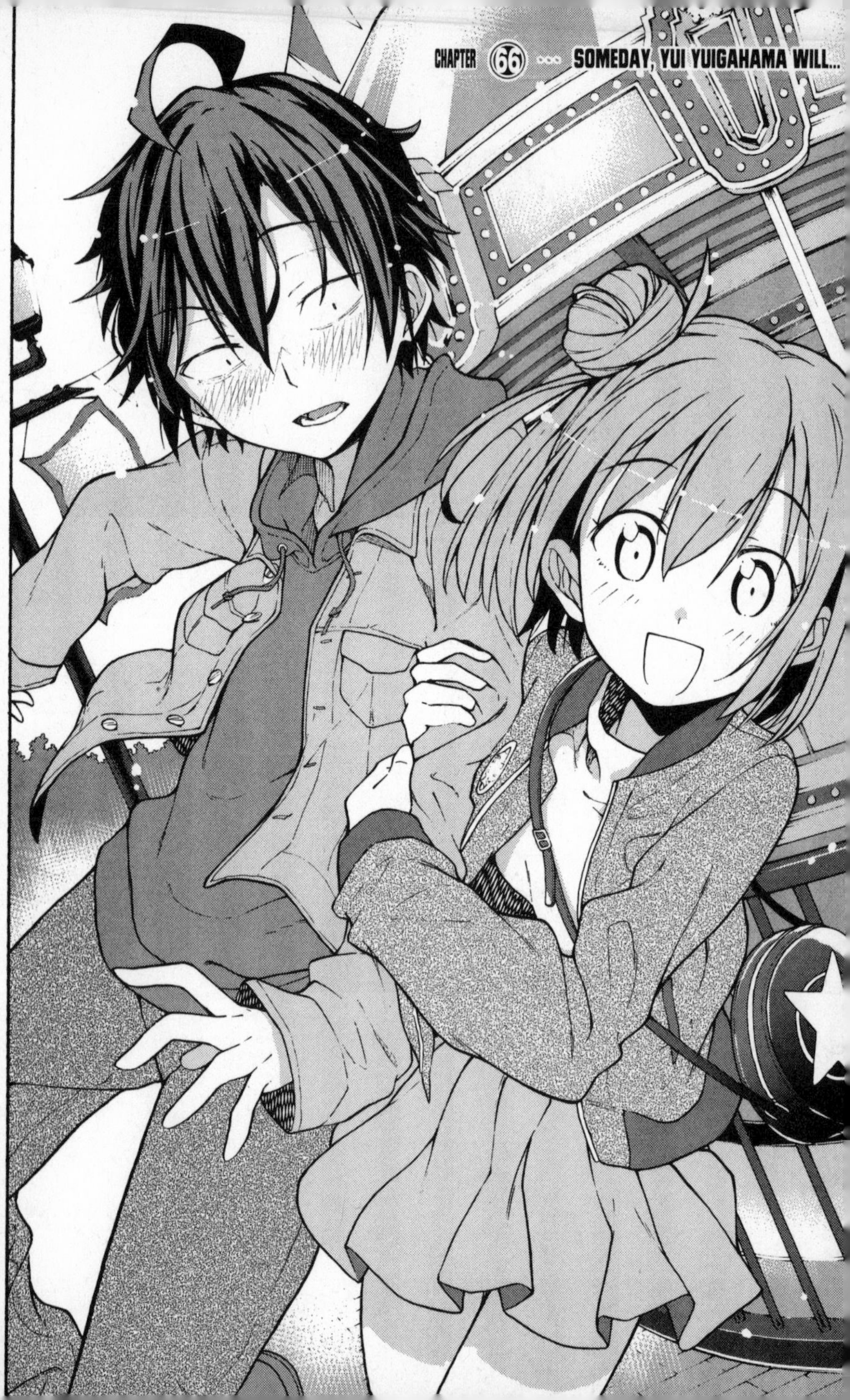
CHAPTER 66 ... SOMEDAY, YUI YUIGAHAMA WILL...

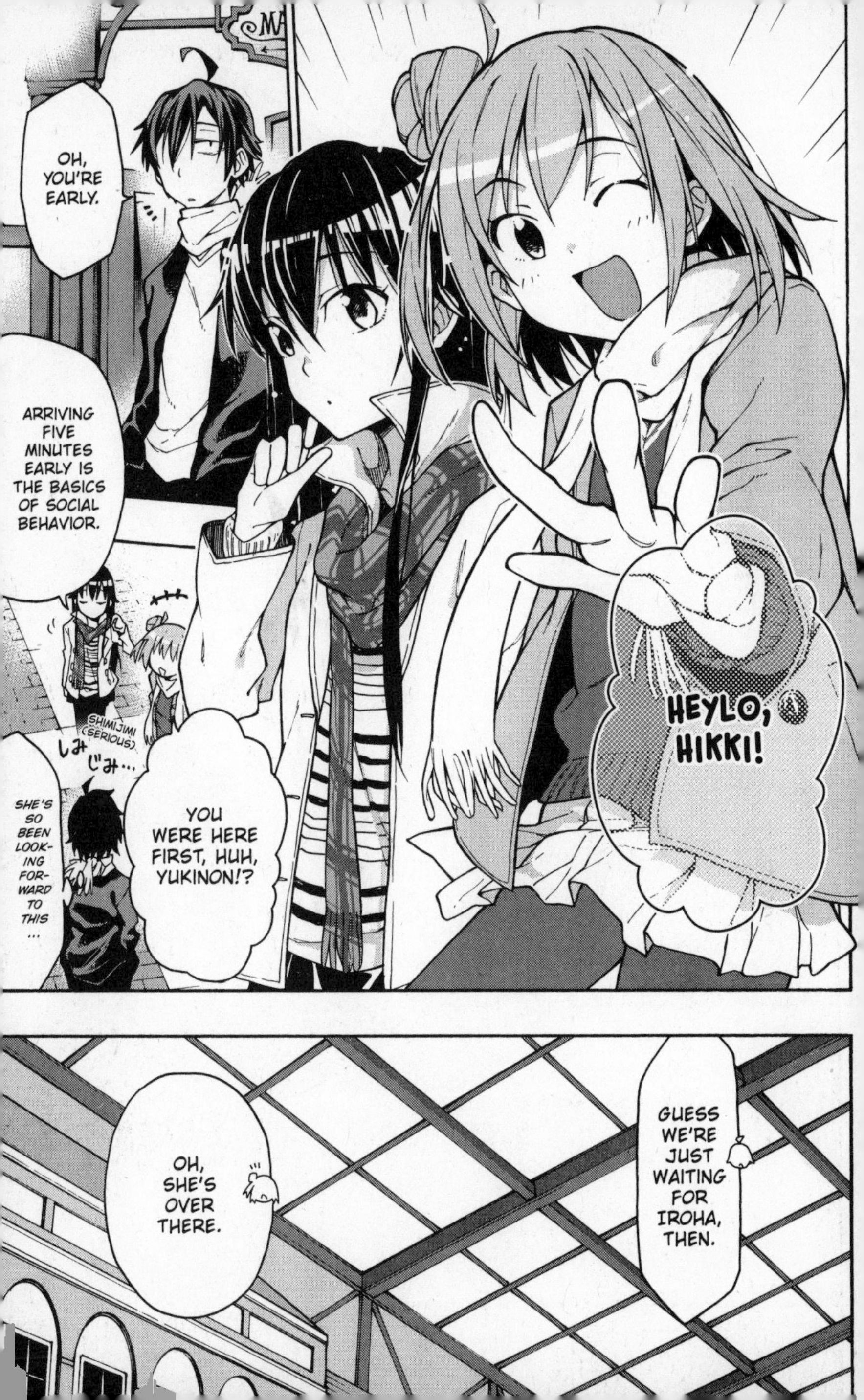
HEYLO, HIKKI!
YOU WERE HERE FIRST, HUH, YUKINON!?
OH, YOU'RE EARLY.
ARRIVING FIVE MINUTES EARLY IS THE BASICS OF SOCIAL BEHAVIOR.
しみじみ…
SHIMIJIMI (SERIOUS)
SHE'S SO BEEN LOOKING FORWARD TO THIS...
GUESS WE'RE JUST WAITING FOR IROHA, THEN.
OH, SHE'S OVER THERE.

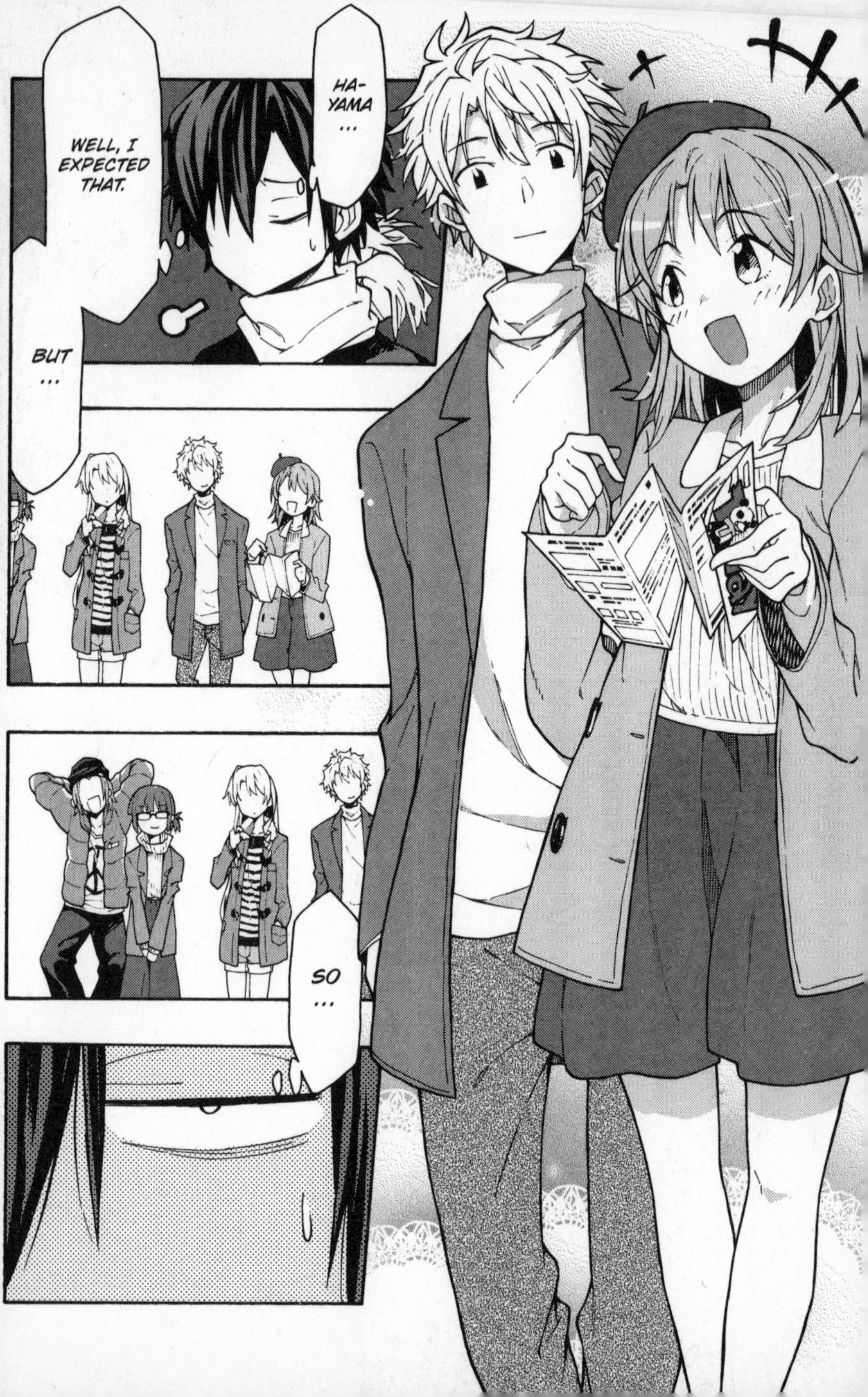
HA-YAMA ...
WELL, I EXPECTED THAT.
BUT ...
SO ...

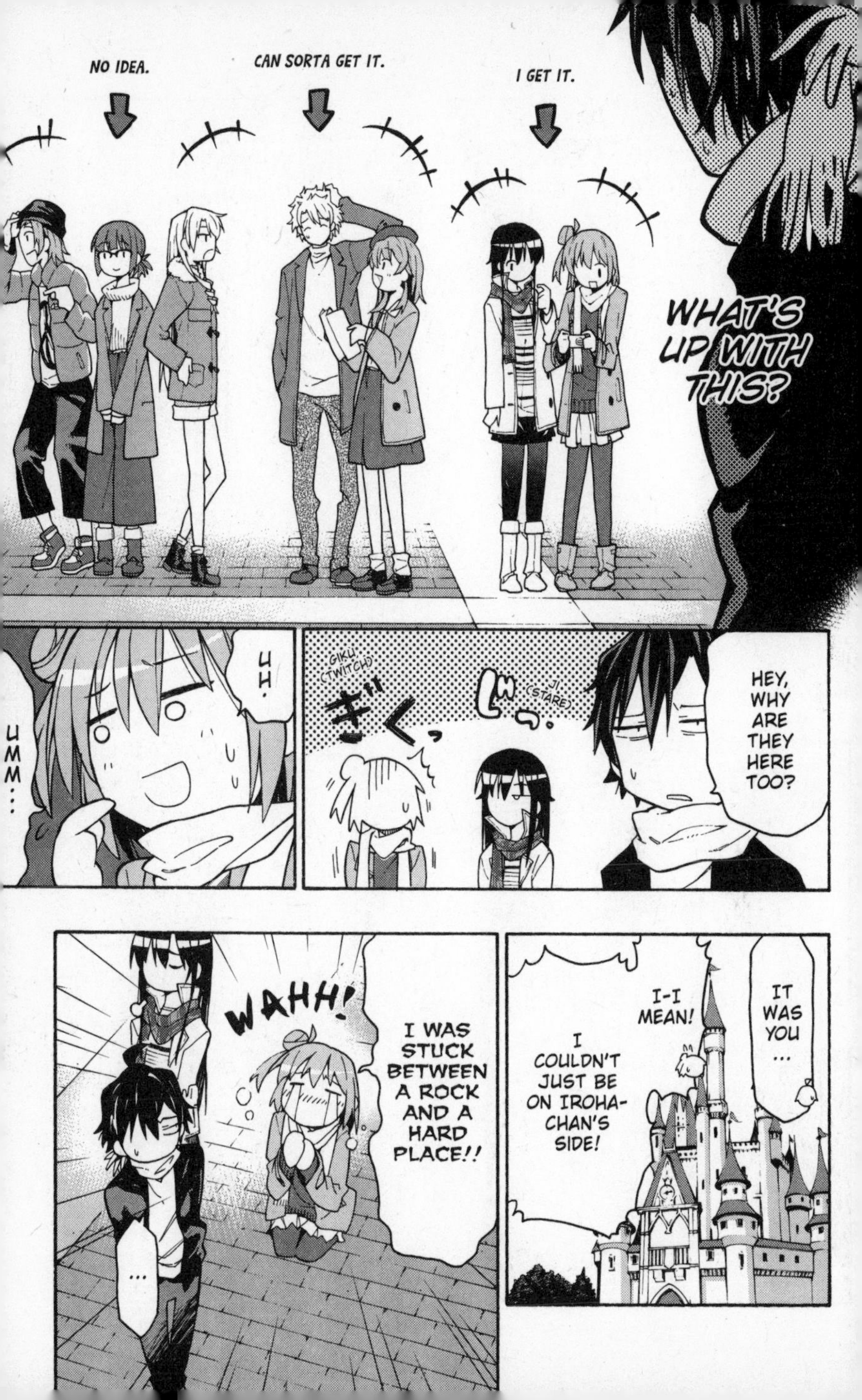
WHAT'S UP WITH THIS?
I GET IT.
CAN SORTA GET IT.
NO IDEA.
HEY, WHY ARE THEY HERE TOO?
JI (STARE)
GIKU (TWITCH)
UH.
UMM...
IT WAS YOU...
I-I MEAN!
I COULDN'T JUST BE ON IROHA-CHAN'S SIDE!
I WAS STUCK BETWEEN A ROCK AND A HARD PLACE!!
WAHH!
...

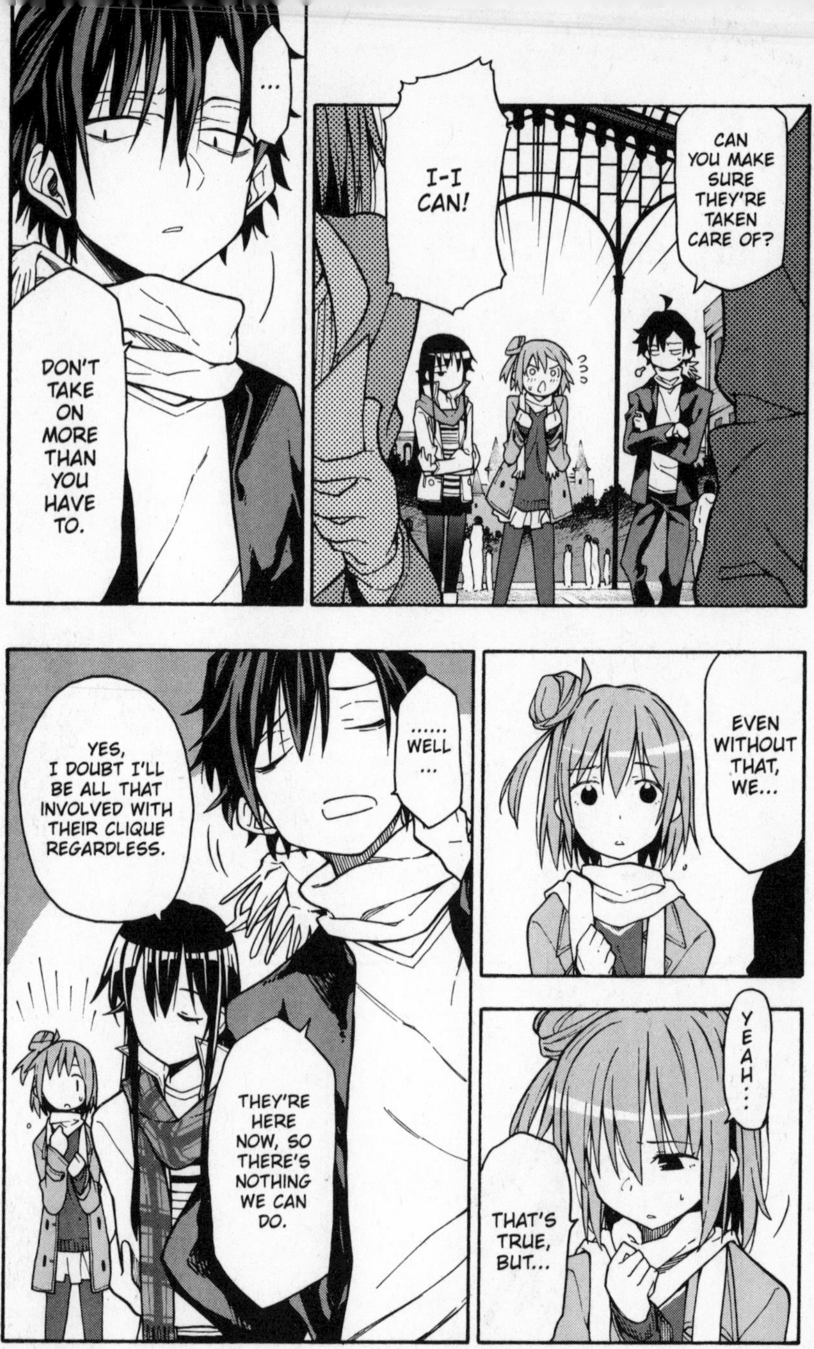
CAN YOU MAKE SURE THEY'RE TAKEN CARE OF?
I-I CAN!
...
DON'T TAKE ON MORE THAN YOU HAVE TO.
EVEN WITHOUT THAT, WE...
YEAH...
THAT'S TRUE, BUT...
......WELL...
YES, I DOUBT I'LL BE ALL THAT INVOLVED WITH THEIR CLIQUE REGARDLESS.
THEY'RE HERE NOW, SO THERE'S NOTHING WE CAN DO.

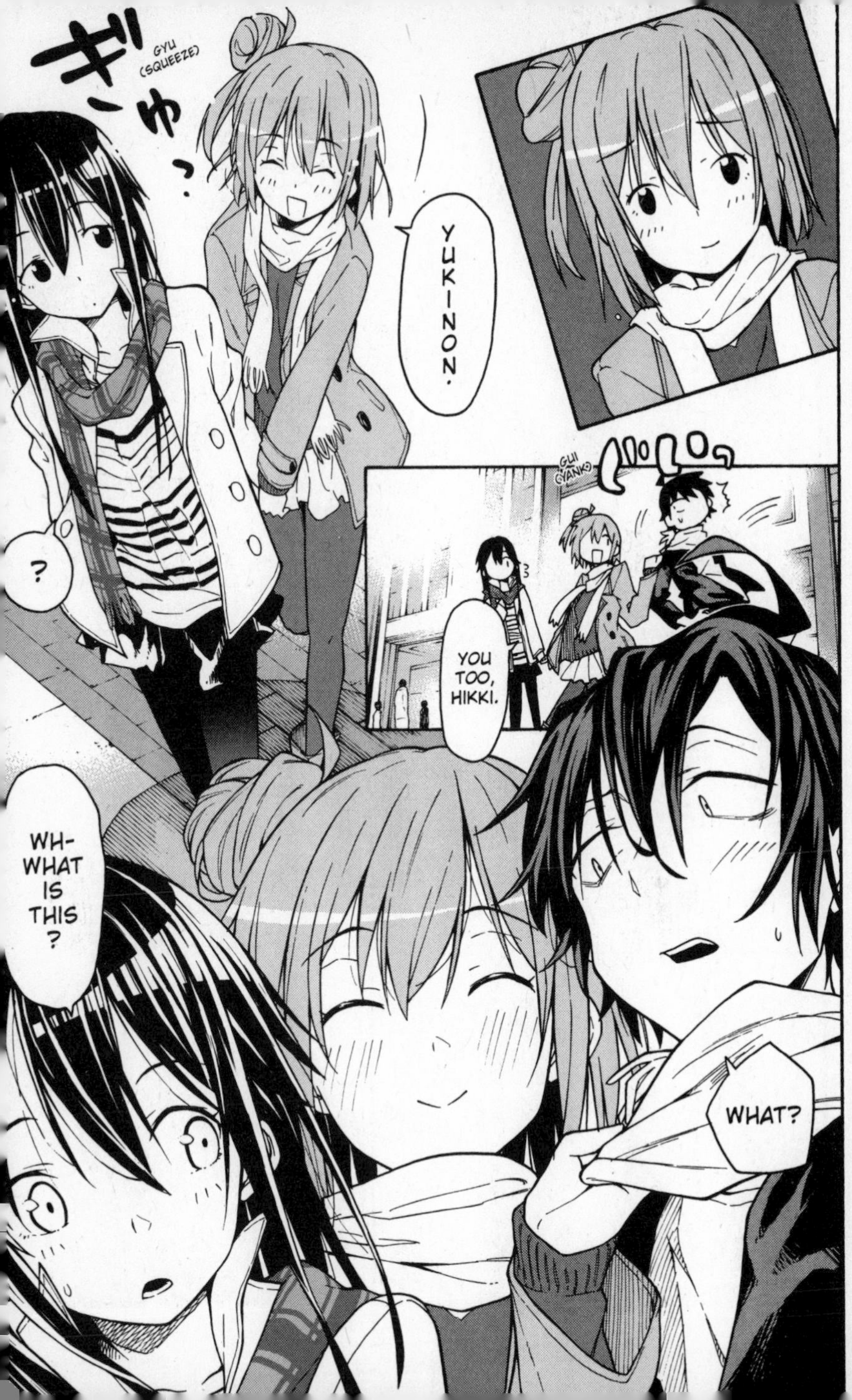
ぎゅっ
GYU (SQUEEZE)
YUKINON.
?
GUI (YANK)
ぐいっ
YOU TOO, HIKKI.
WH- WHAT IS THIS?
WHAT?

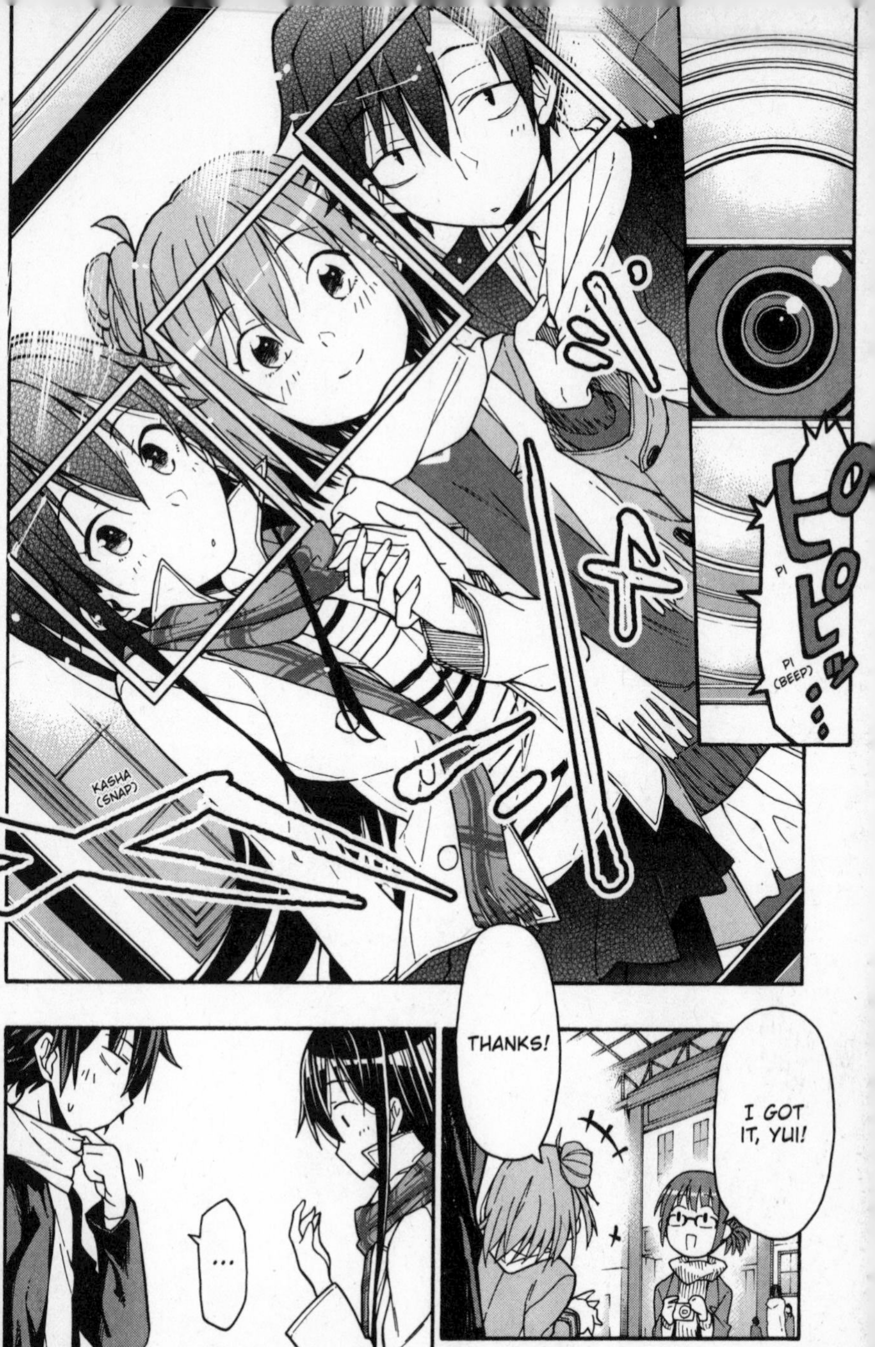
PI
PI (BEEP)
KASHA (SNAP)
I GOT IT, YUI!
THANKS!
...

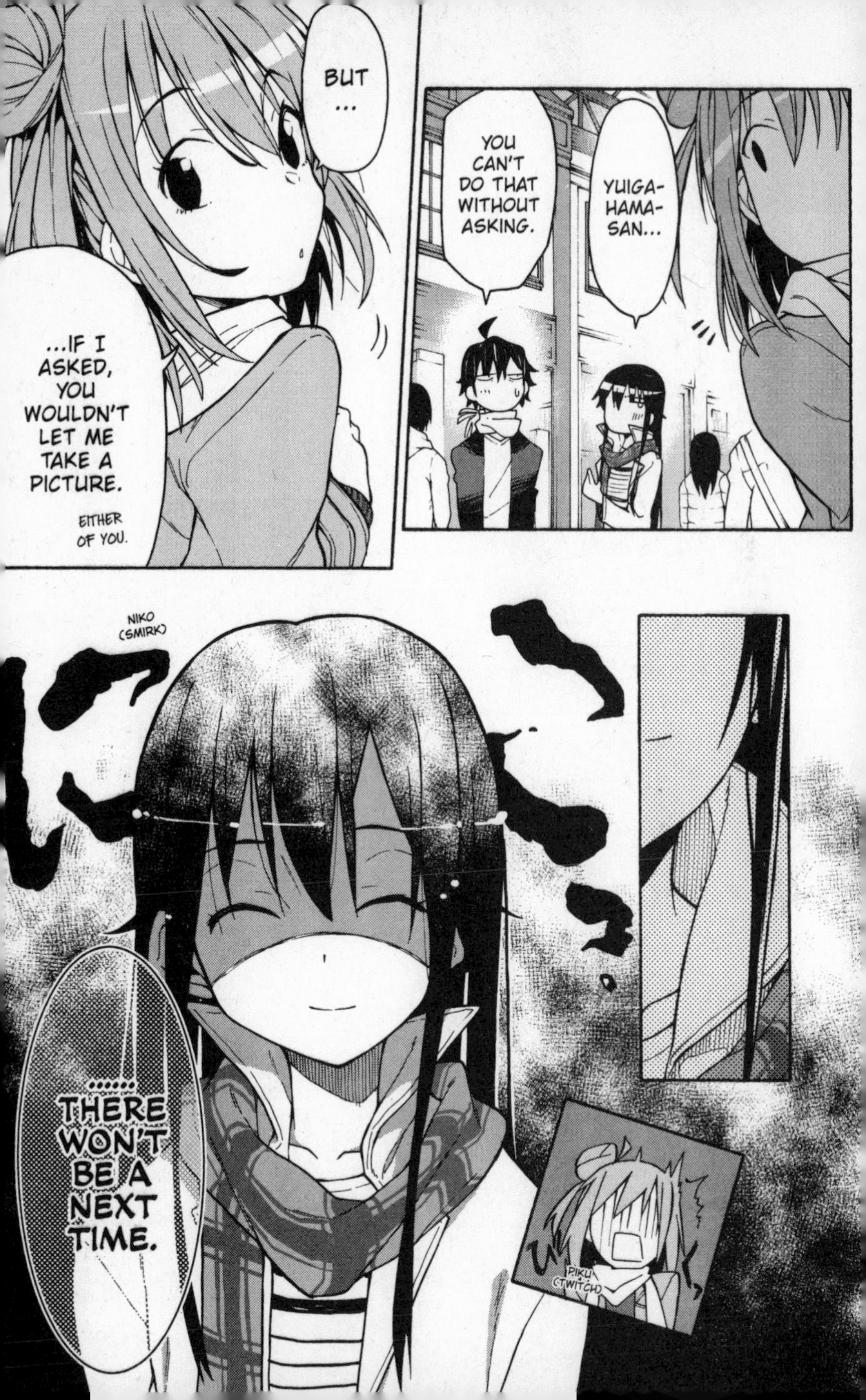

YUIGA-HAMA-SAN...
YOU CAN'T DO THAT WITHOUT ASKING.
BUT ...
...IF I ASKED, YOU WOULDN'T LET ME TAKE A PICTURE.
EITHER OF YOU.
NIKO (SMIRK)
......THERE WON'T BE A NEXT TIME.
PIKU (TWITCH)

I-I'M SORRY, YUKINON!

SUTASUTASUTA (TROT)

HOLD UUUP!

...IS PROBABLY BACK TO NORMAL NOW, AT LEAST.

THE DISTANCE BETWEEN THE TWO OF THEM...

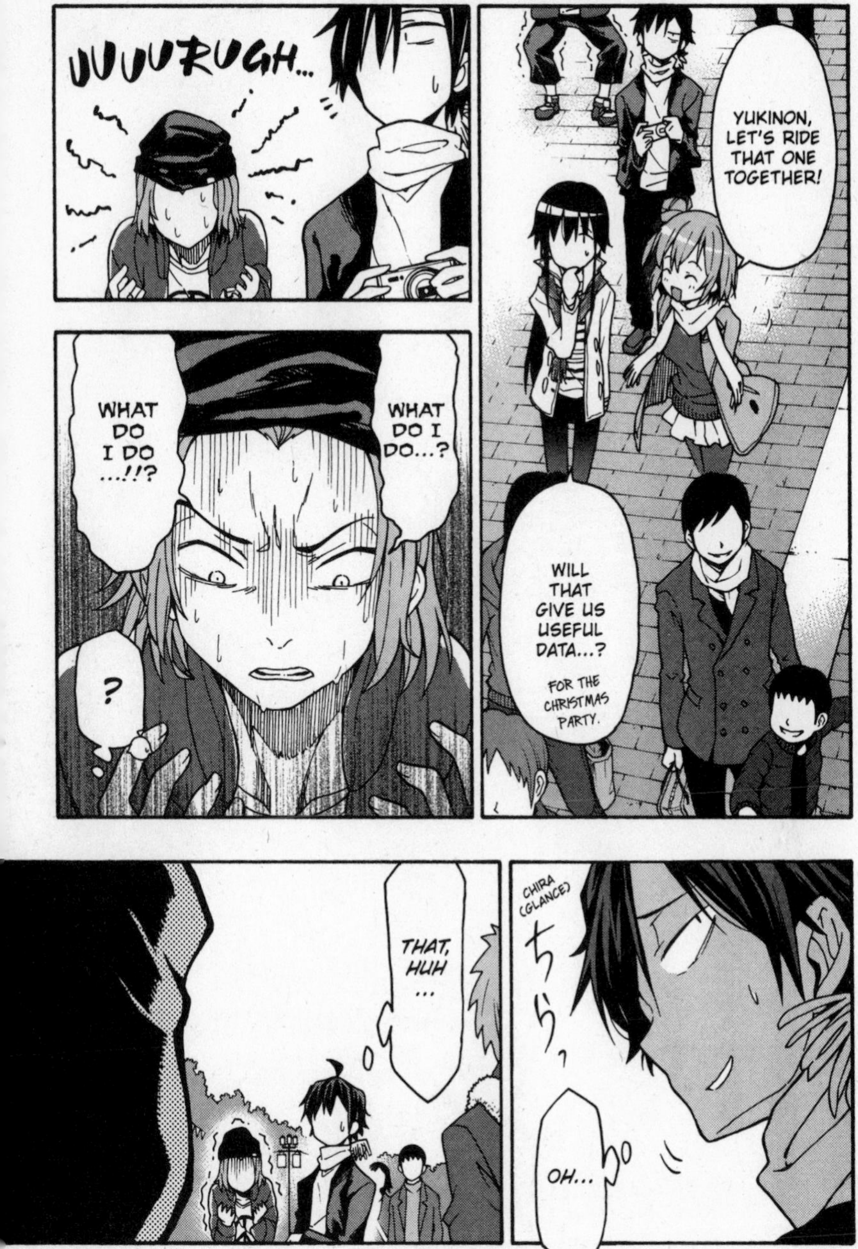
YUKINON, LET'S RIDE THAT ONE TOGETHER!
WILL THAT GIVE US USEFUL DATA...?
FOR THE CHRISTMAS PARTY.
UUUURUGH...
WHAT DO I DO...?
WHAT DO I DO...!!?
?
CHIRA (GLANCE)
OH...
THAT, HUH...

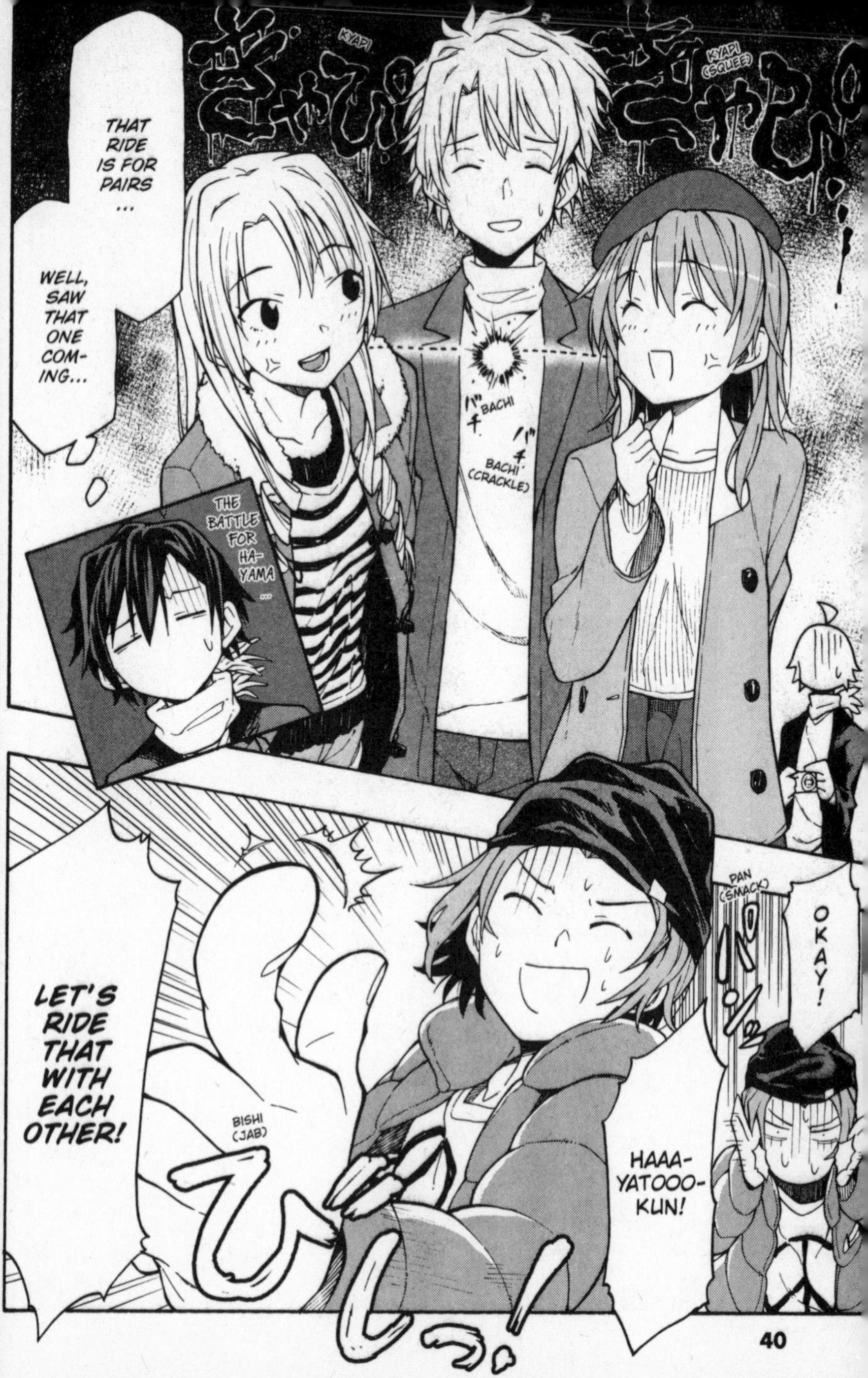
KYAPI (SQUEE)
KYAPI
THAT RIDE IS FOR PAIRS...
WELL, SAW THAT ONE COMING...
BACHI
BACHI (CRACKLE)
THE BATTLE FOR HAYAMA...
PAN (SMACK)
OKAY!
HAAA-YATOOO-KUN!
BISHI (JAB)
LET'S RIDE THAT WITH EACH OTHER!

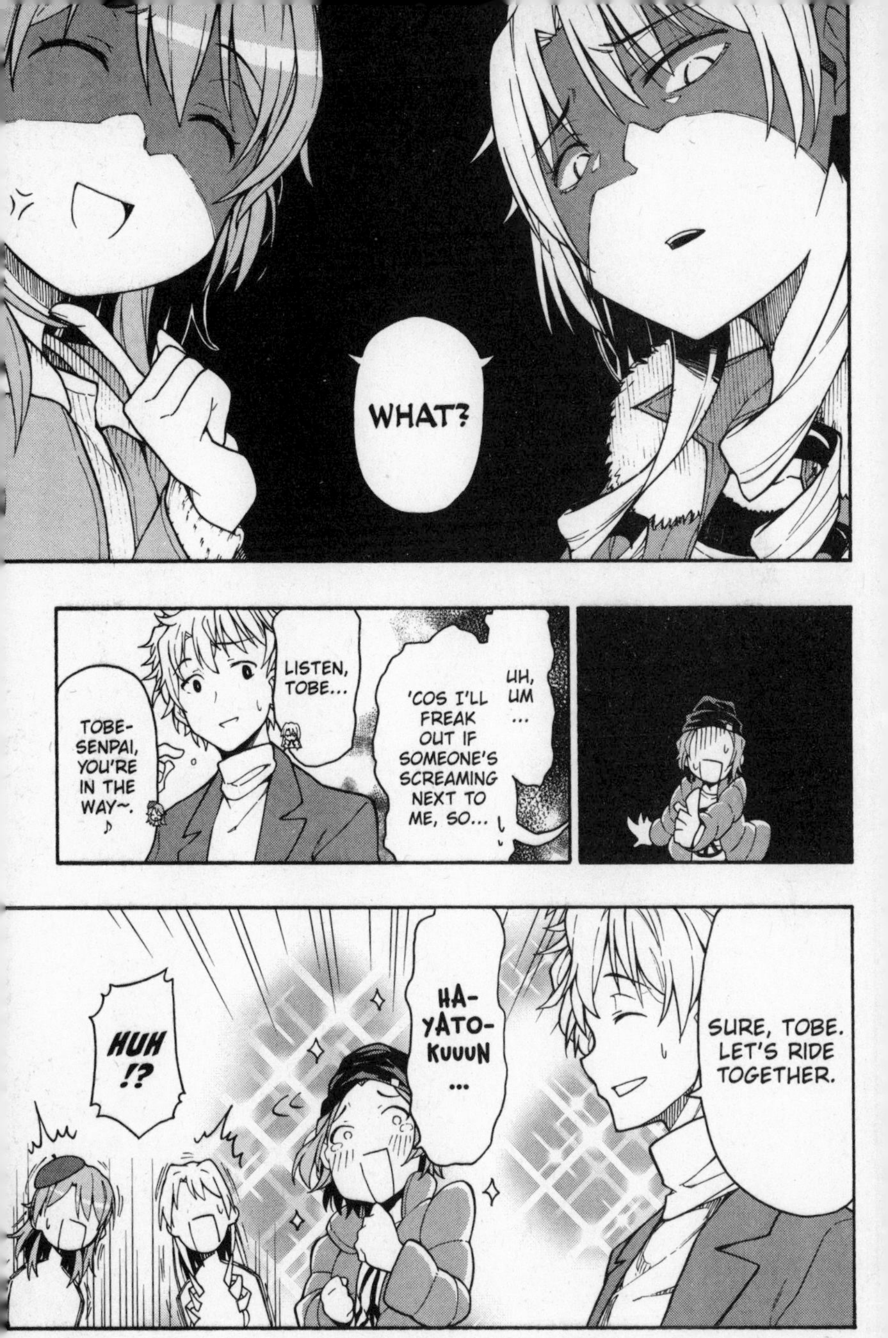
WHAT?
UH, UM ...
'COS I'LL FREAK OUT IF SOMEONE'S SCREAMING NEXT TO ME, SO...
LISTEN, TOBE...
TOBE-SENPAI, YOU'RE IN THE WAY~. ♪
SURE, TOBE. LET'S RIDE TOGETHER.
HA-YATO-KUUUN ...
HUH!?

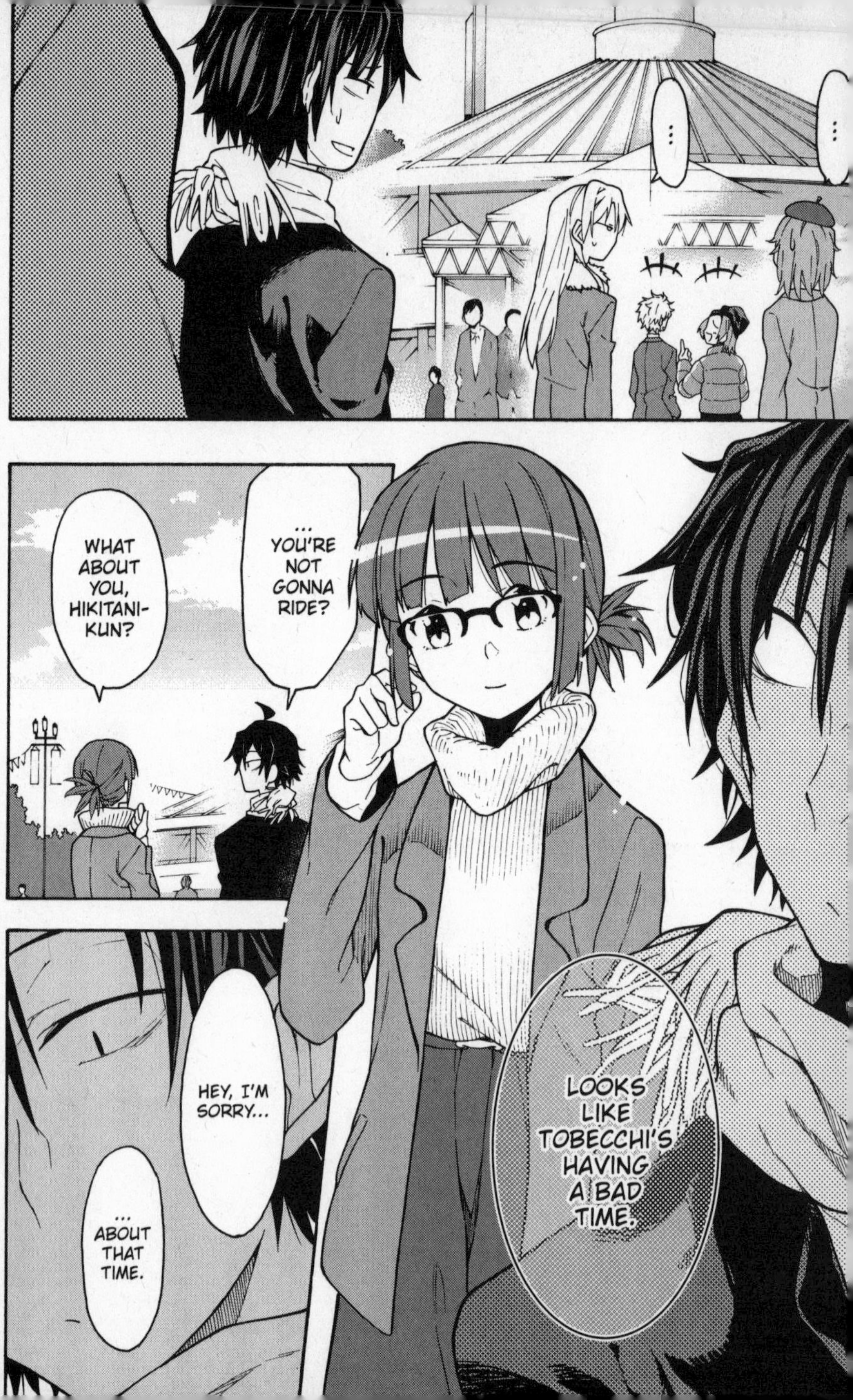
......
......
LOOKS LIKE TOBECCHI'S HAVING A BAD TIME.
... YOU'RE NOT GONNA RIDE?
WHAT ABOUT YOU, HIKITANI-KUN?
HEY, I'M SORRY...
... ABOUT THAT TIME.

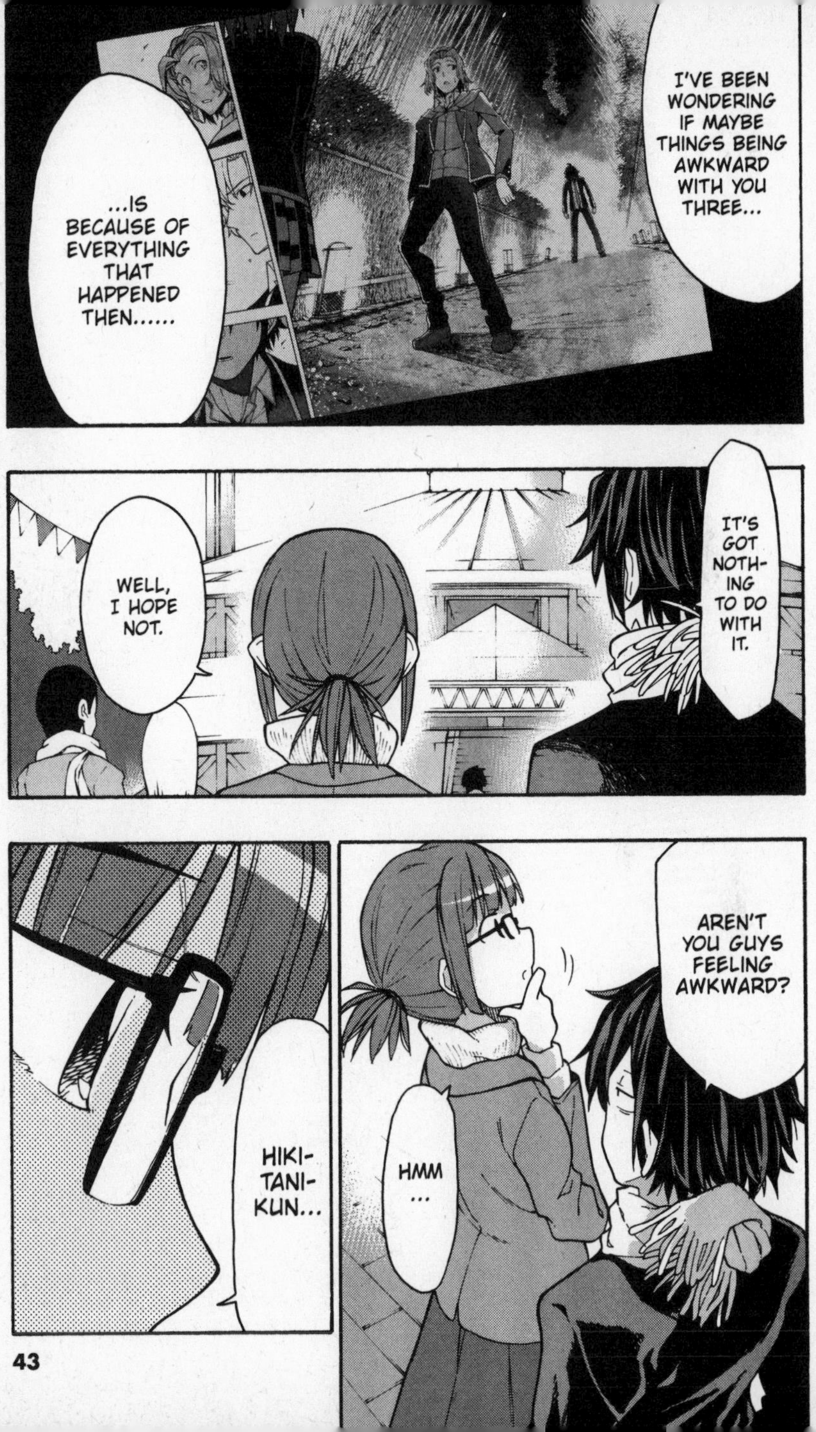
I'VE BEEN WONDERING IF MAYBE THINGS BEING AWKWARD WITH YOU THREE...
...IS BECAUSE OF EVERYTHING THAT HAPPENED THEN......
IT'S GOT NOTHING TO DO WITH IT.
WELL, I HOPE NOT.
AREN'T YOU GUYS FEELING AWKWARD?
HMM...
HIKITANI-KUN...

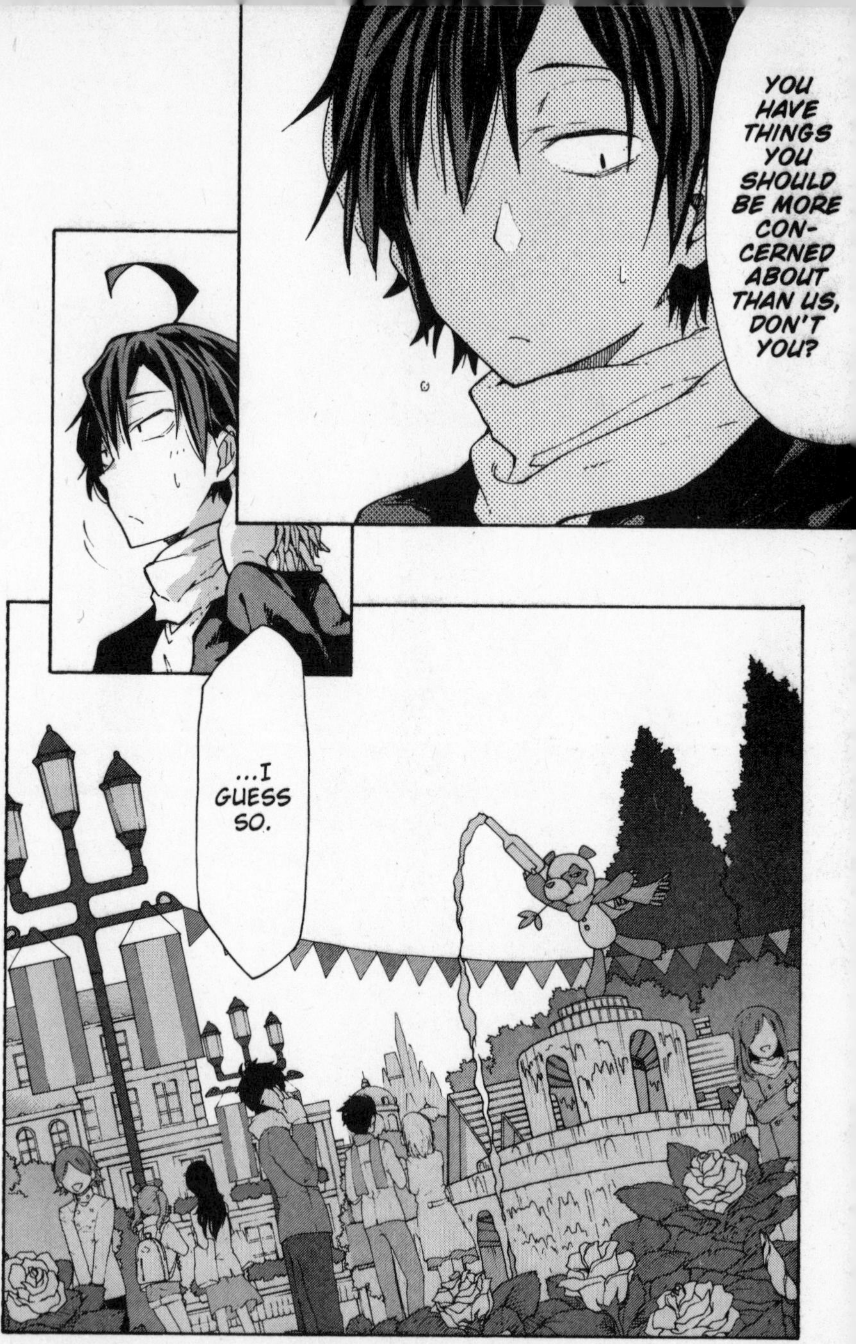
YOU HAVE THINGS YOU SHOULD BE MORE CON-CERNED ABOUT THAN US, DON'T YOU?
...I GUESS SO.

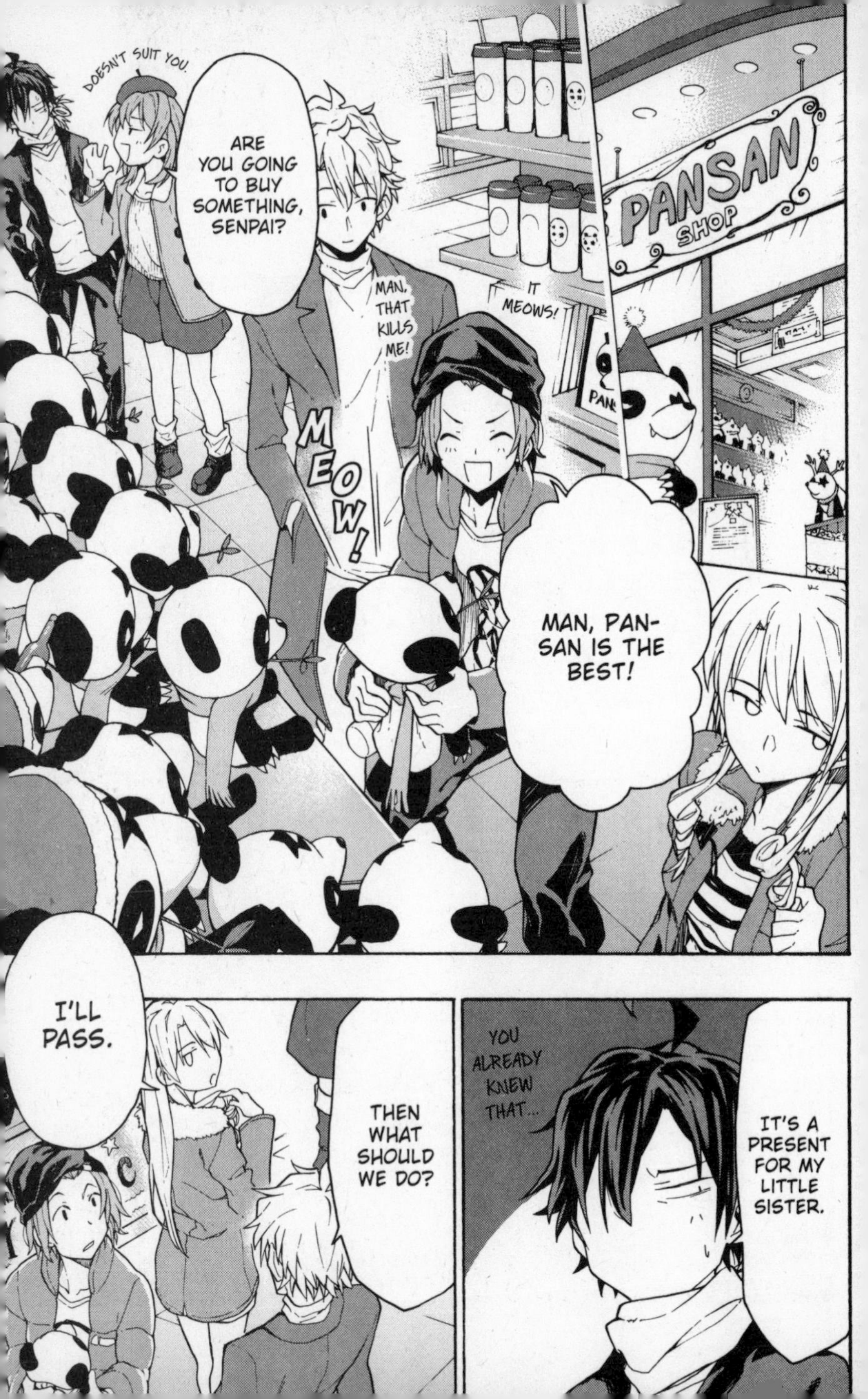
PANSAN SHOP
IT MEOWS!
MAN, THAT KILLS ME!
ARE YOU GOING TO BUY SOMETHING, SENPAI?
DOESN'T SUIT YOU.
MEOW!
MAN, PAN-SAN IS THE BEST!
IT'S A PRESENT FOR MY LITTLE SISTER.
YOU ALREADY KNEW THAT...
THEN WHAT SHOULD WE DO?
I'LL PASS.

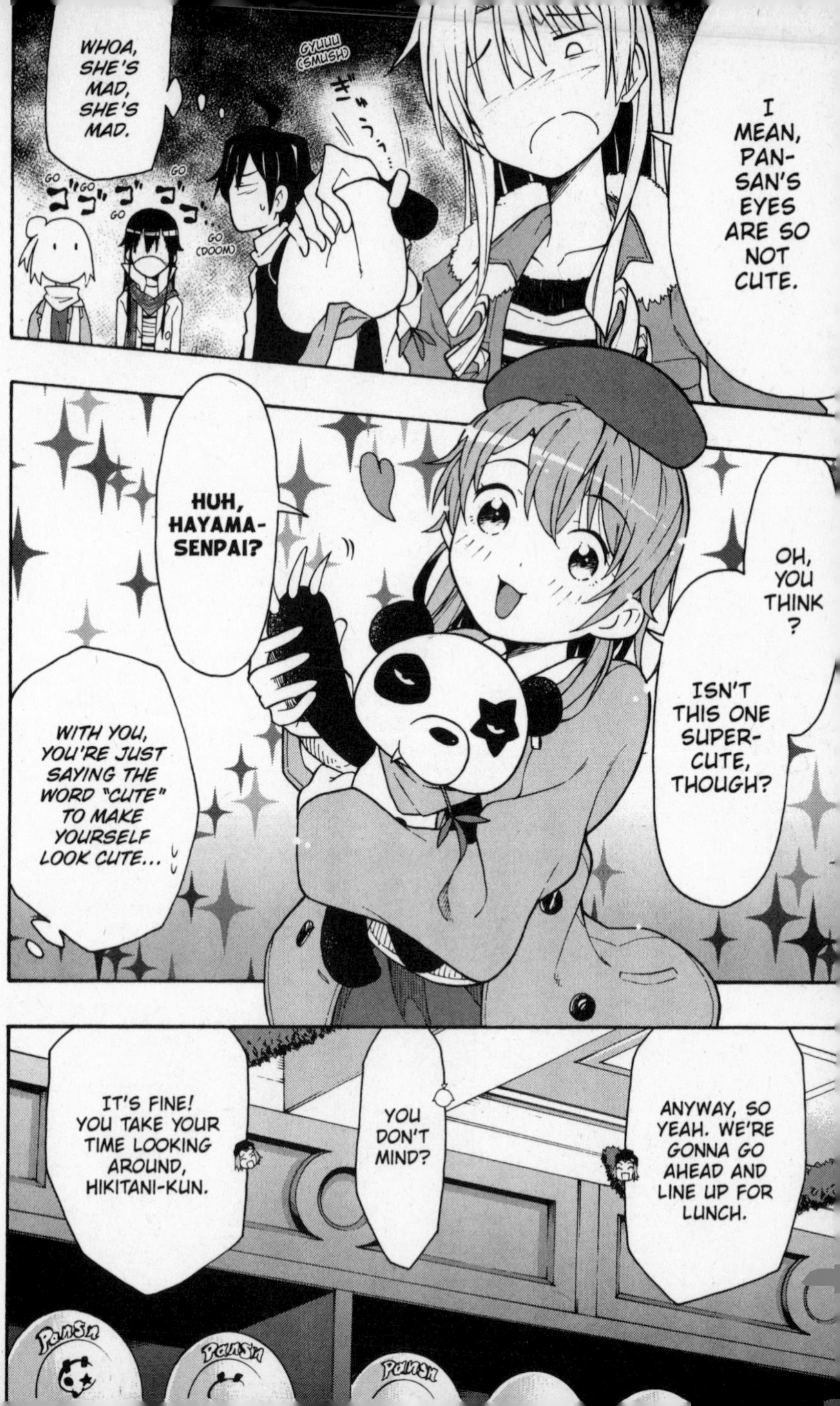
I MEAN, PAN-SAN'S EYES ARE SO NOT CUTE.
GYUUU (SMUSH)
GO GO GO GO GO (DOOM)
WHOA, SHE'S MAD, SHE'S MAD.
OH, YOU THINK? ISN'T THIS ONE SUPER-CUTE, THOUGH?
HUH, HAYAMA-SENPAI?
WITH YOU, YOU'RE JUST SAYING THE WORD "CUTE" TO MAKE YOURSELF LOOK CUTE...
ANYWAY, SO YEAH. WE'RE GONNA GO AHEAD AND LINE UP FOR LUNCH.
YOU DON'T MIND?
IT'S FINE! YOU TAKE YOUR TIME LOOKING AROUND, HIKITANI-KUN.

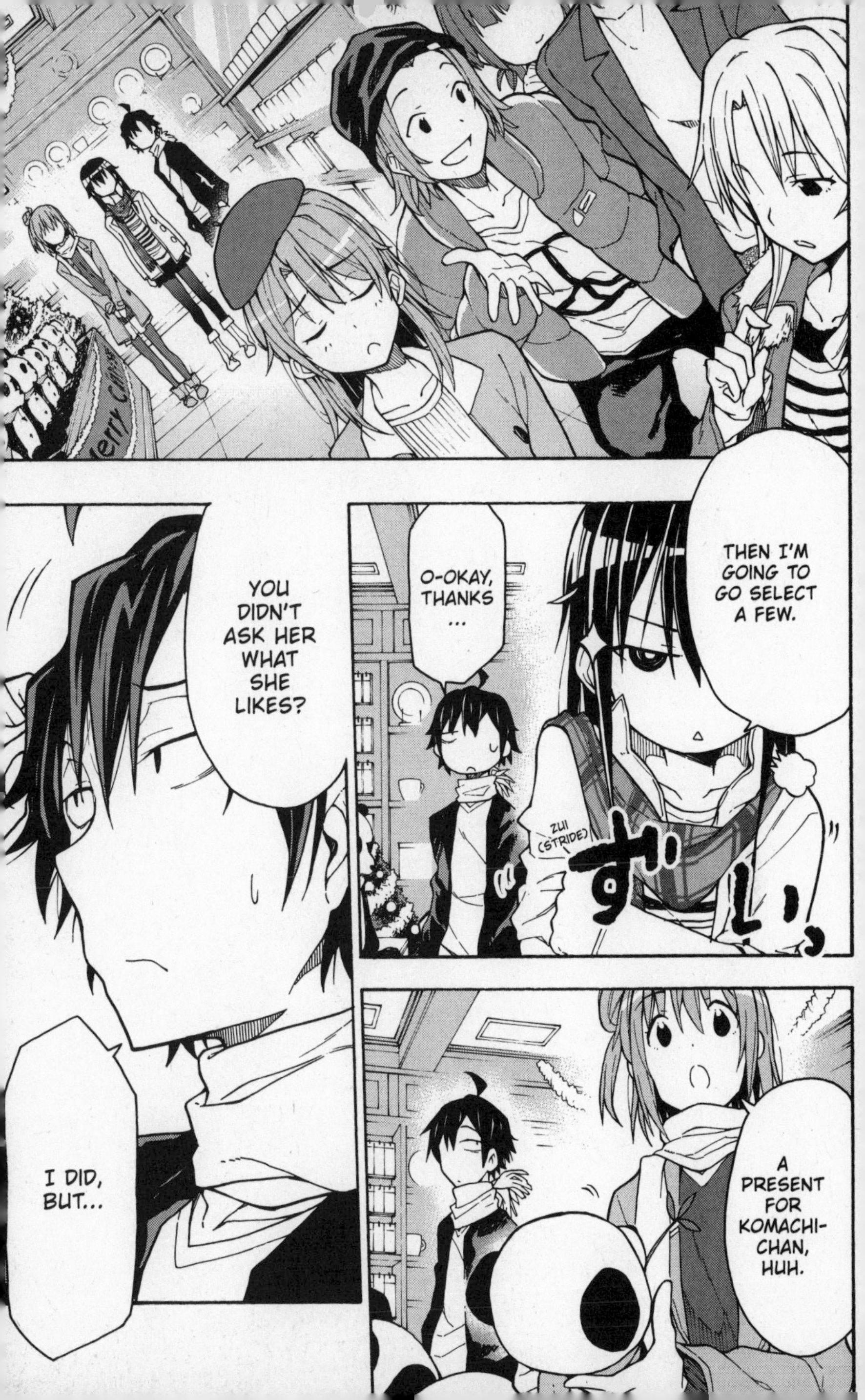
THEN I'M GOING TO GO SELECT A FEW.
O-OKAY, THANKS ...
ZUI (STRIDE)
A PRESENT FOR KOMACHI-CHAN, HUH.
YOU DIDN'T ASK HER WHAT SHE LIKES?
I DID, BUT...

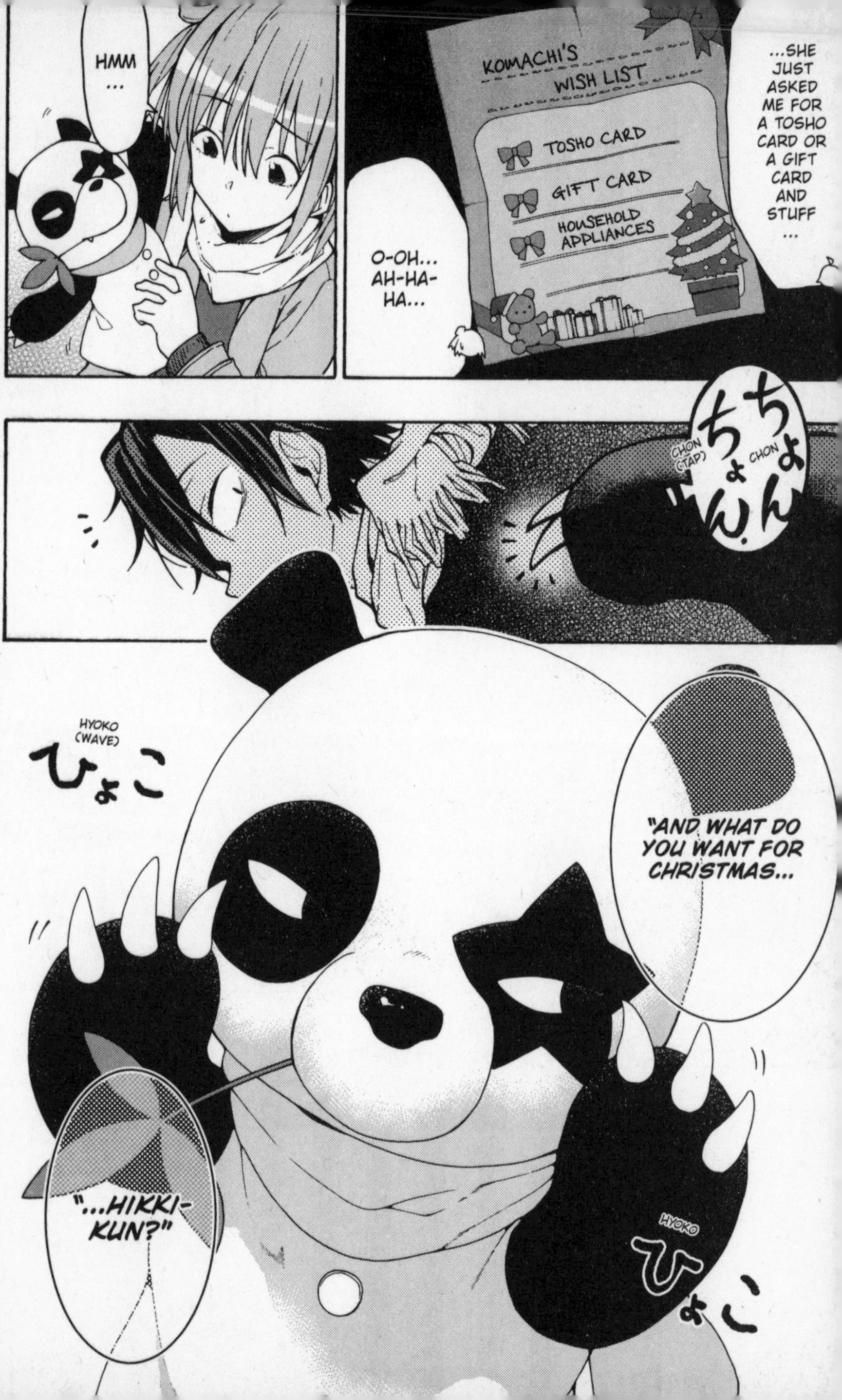

...SHE JUST ASKED ME FOR A TOSHO CARD OR A GIFT CARD AND STUFF...
KOMACHI'S WISH LIST
TOSHO CARD
GIFT CARD
HOUSEHOLD APPLIANCES
O-OH... AH-HA-HA...
HMM...
ちょんちょん
CHON (TAP) CHON
"AND WHAT DO YOU WANT FOR CHRISTMAS...
HYOKO (WAVE)
ひょこ
"...HIKKI-KUN?"
HYOKO
ひょこ

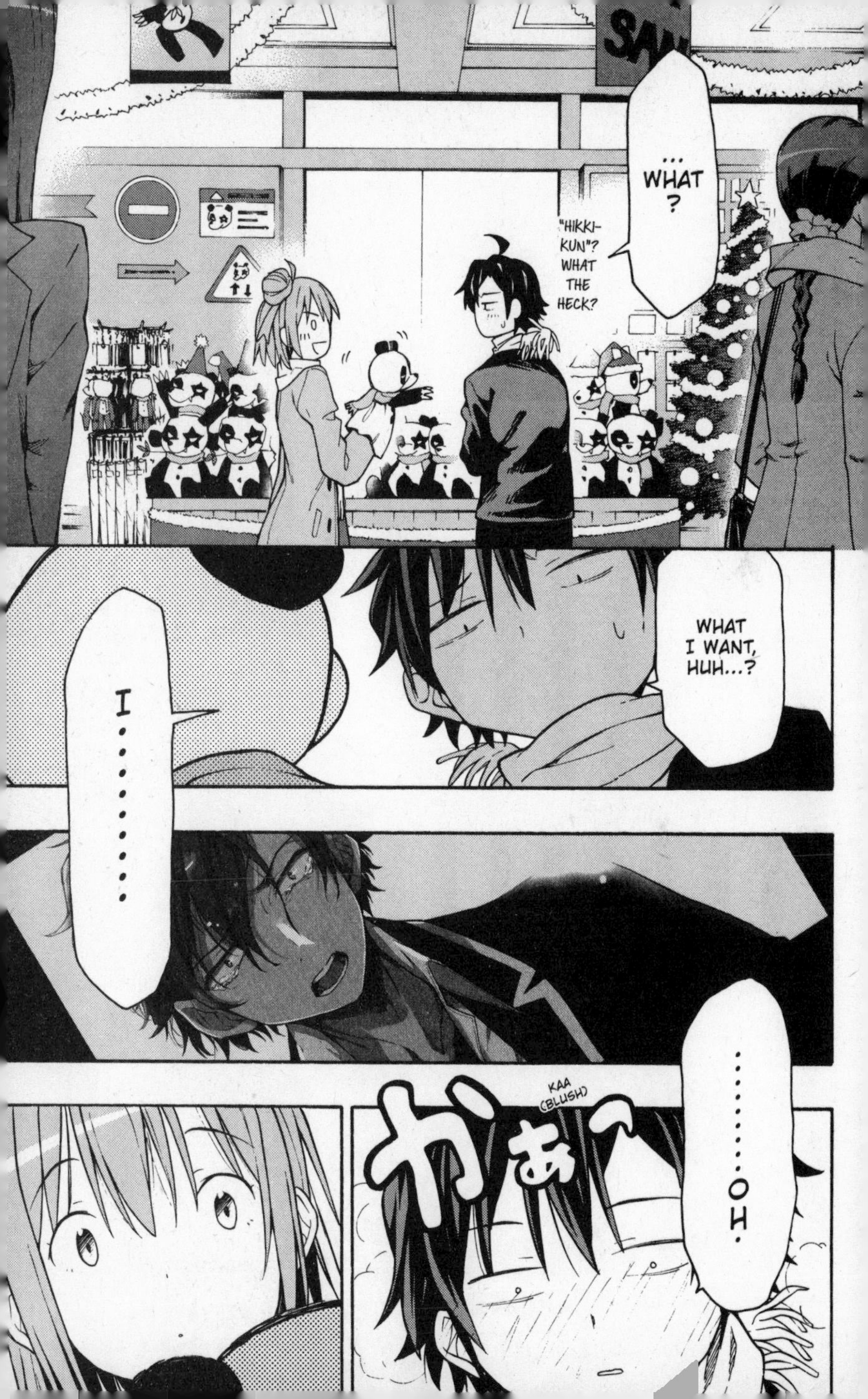
... WHAT ?
"HIKKI-KUN"? WHAT THE HECK?
WHAT I WANT, HUH...?
I.......
......OH.
かぁ
KAA (BLUSH)

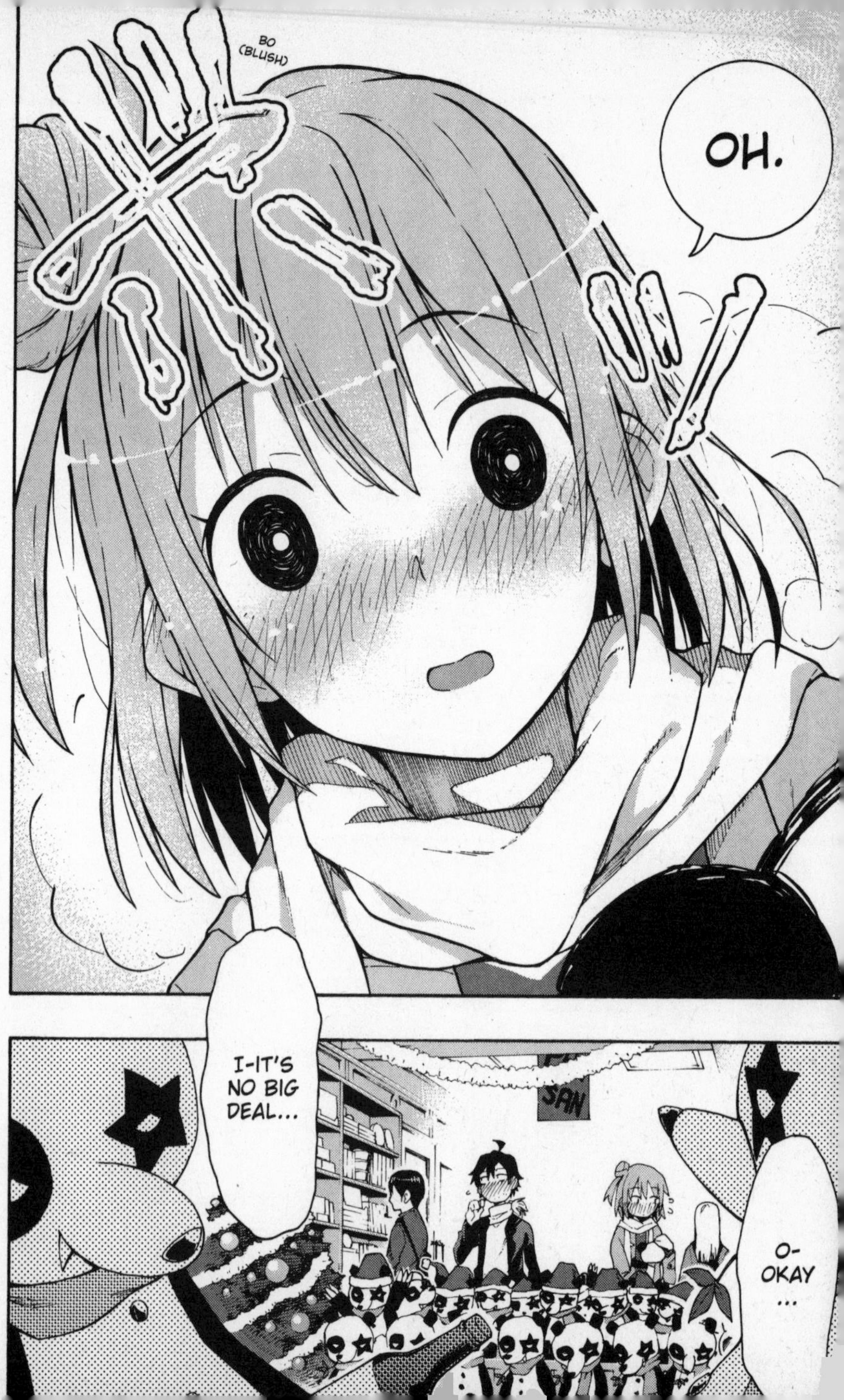
BO (BLUSH)
OH.
I-IT'S NO BIG DEAL...
O-OKAY...

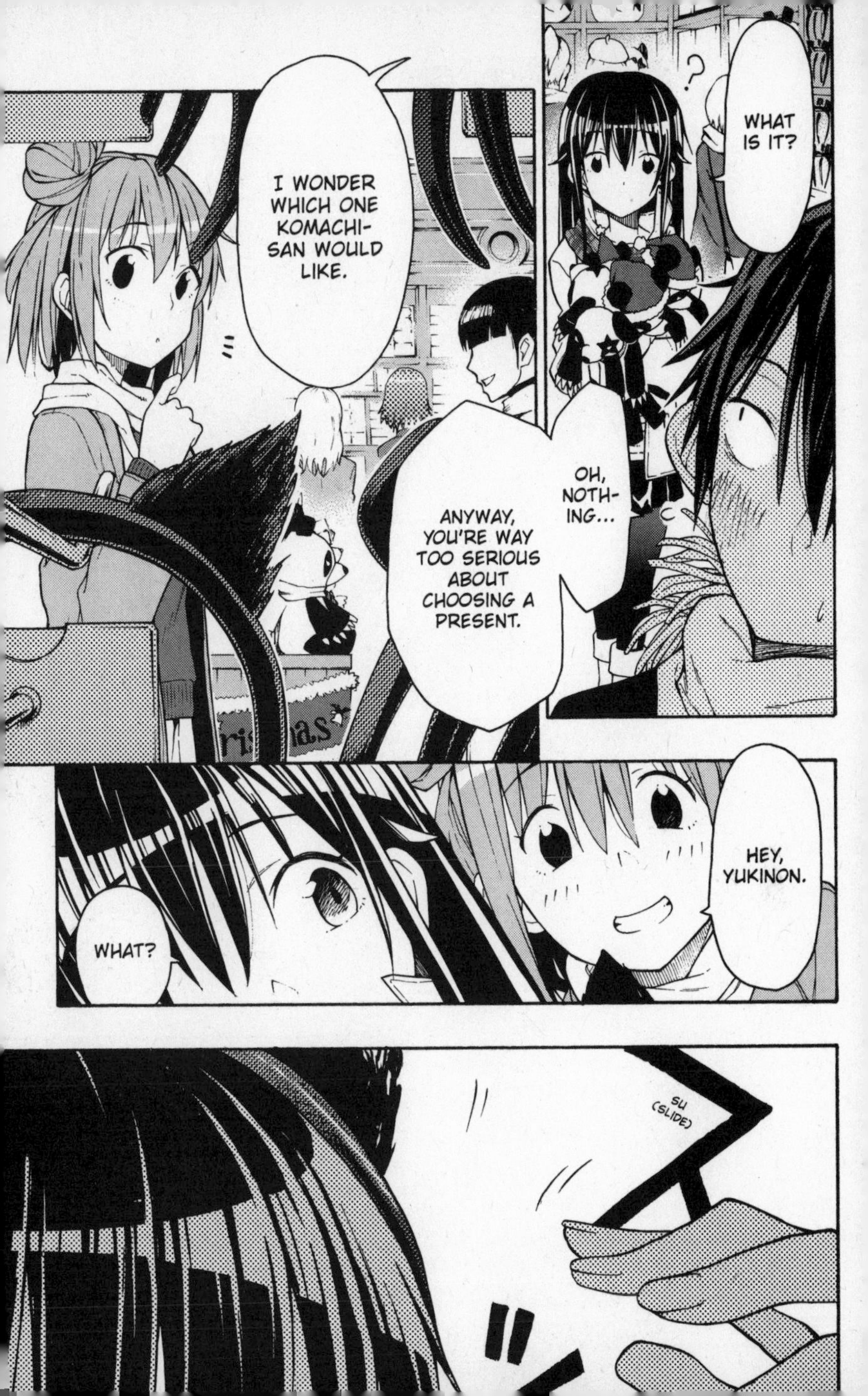
WHAT IS IT?
OH, NOTHING...
I WONDER WHICH ONE KOMACHI-SAN WOULD LIKE.
ANYWAY, YOU'RE WAY TOO SERIOUS ABOUT CHOOSING A PRESENT.
HEY, YUKINON.
WHAT?
SU (SLIDE)

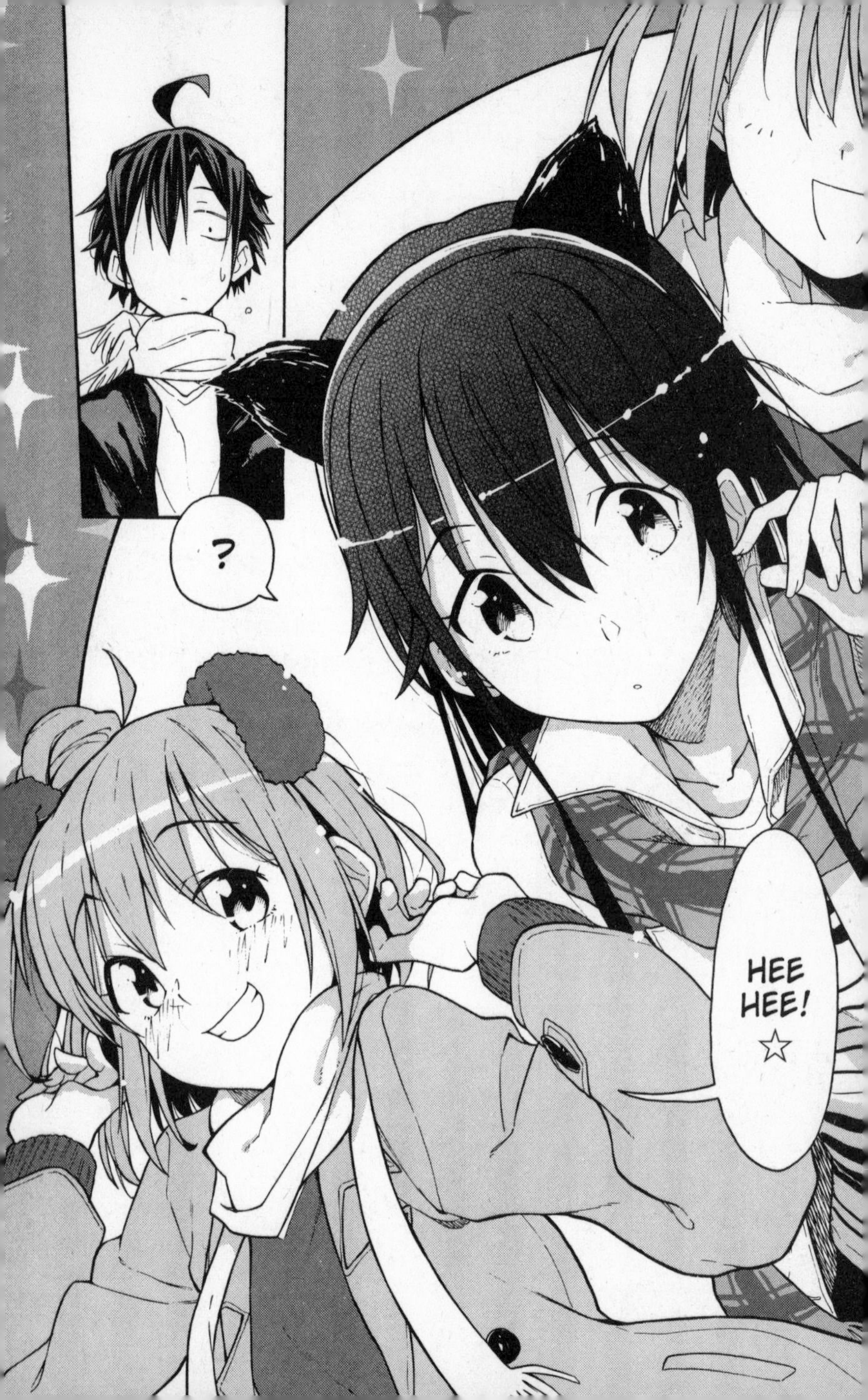
?
HEE HEE! ☆

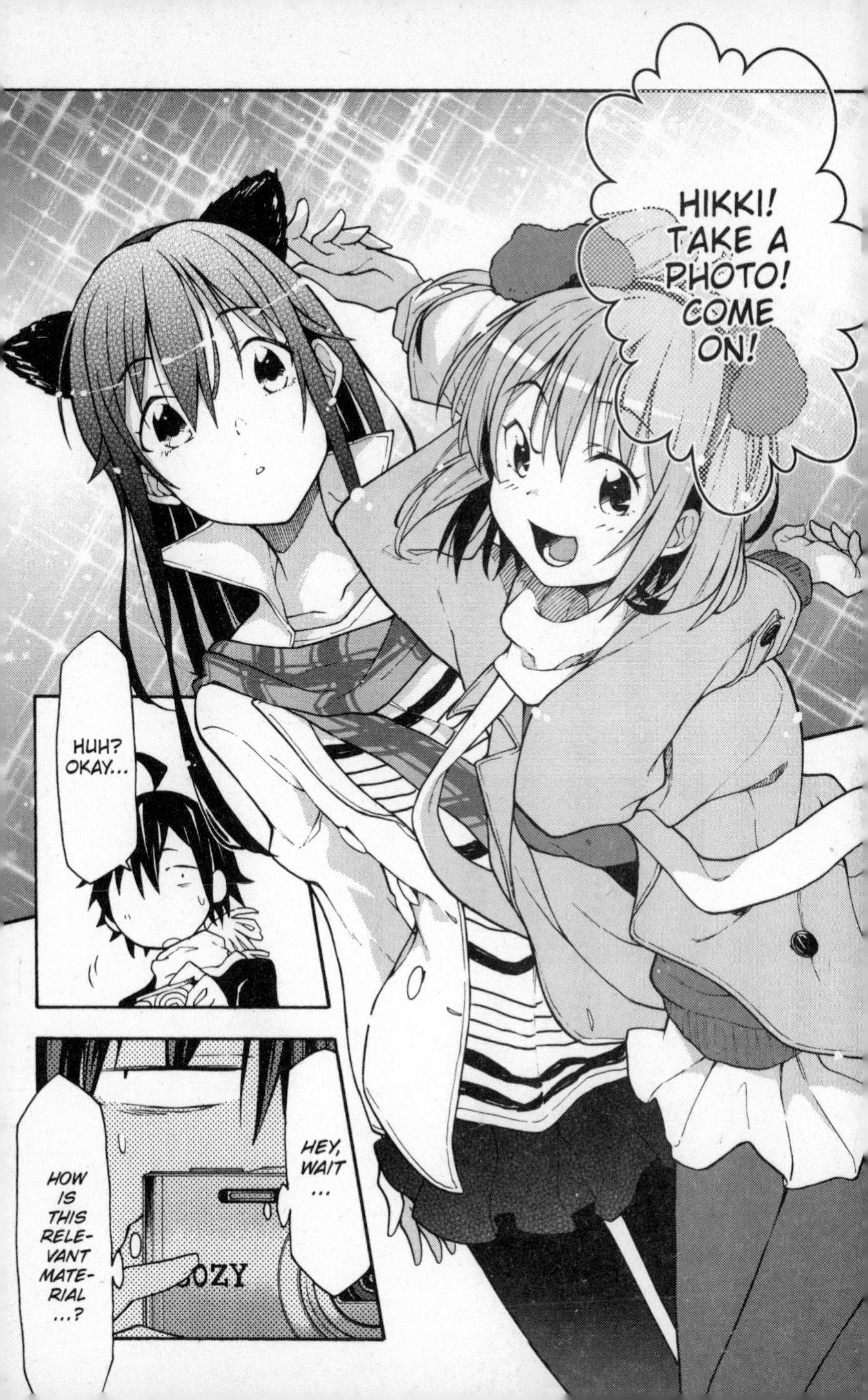
HIKKI! TAKE A PHOTO! COME ON!
HUH? OKAY...
HEY, WAIT ...
HOW IS THIS RELEVANT MATERIAL ...?

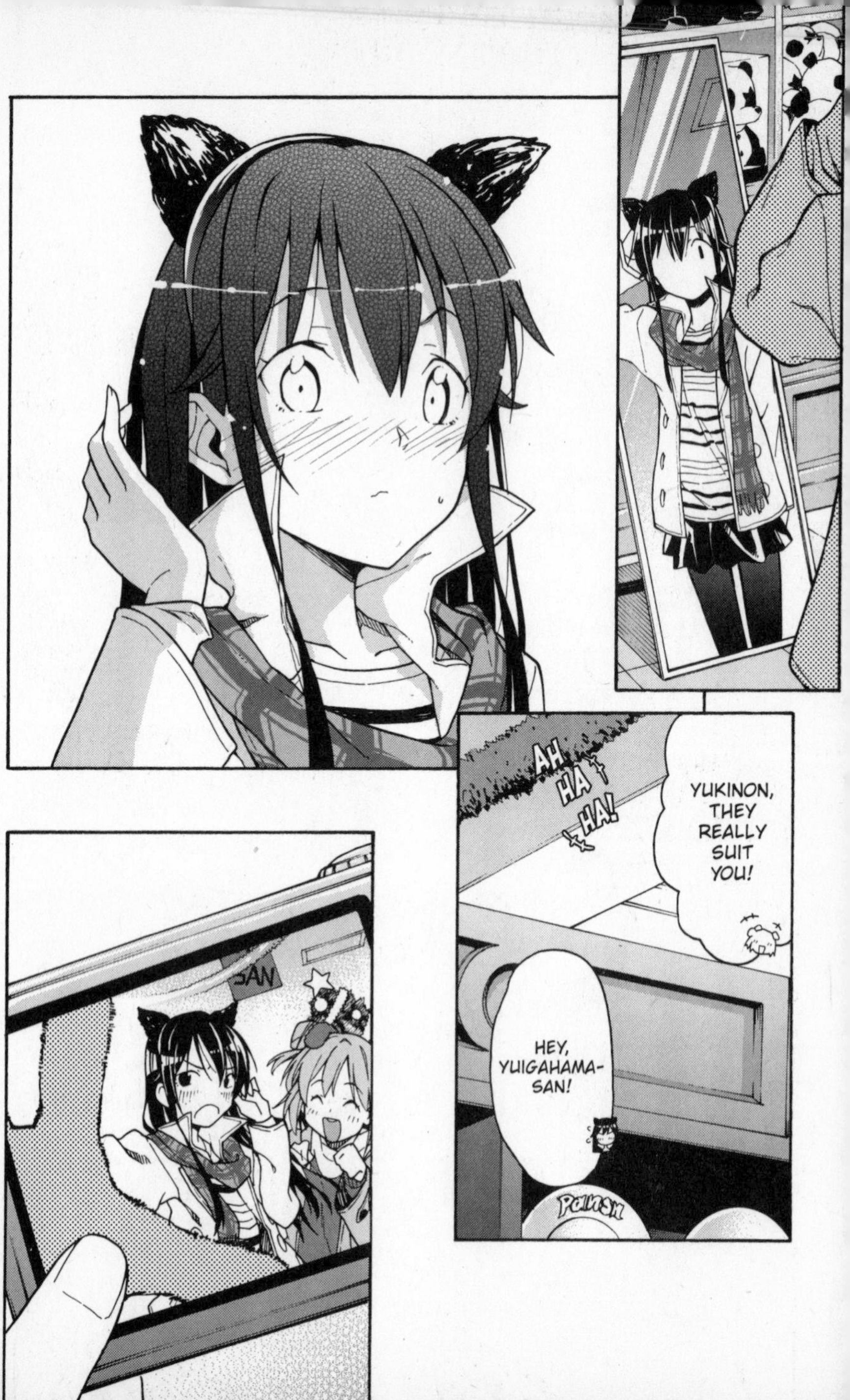
YUKINON, THEY REALLY SUIT YOU!
AH HA HA!
HEY, YUIGAHAMA-SAN!
SAN

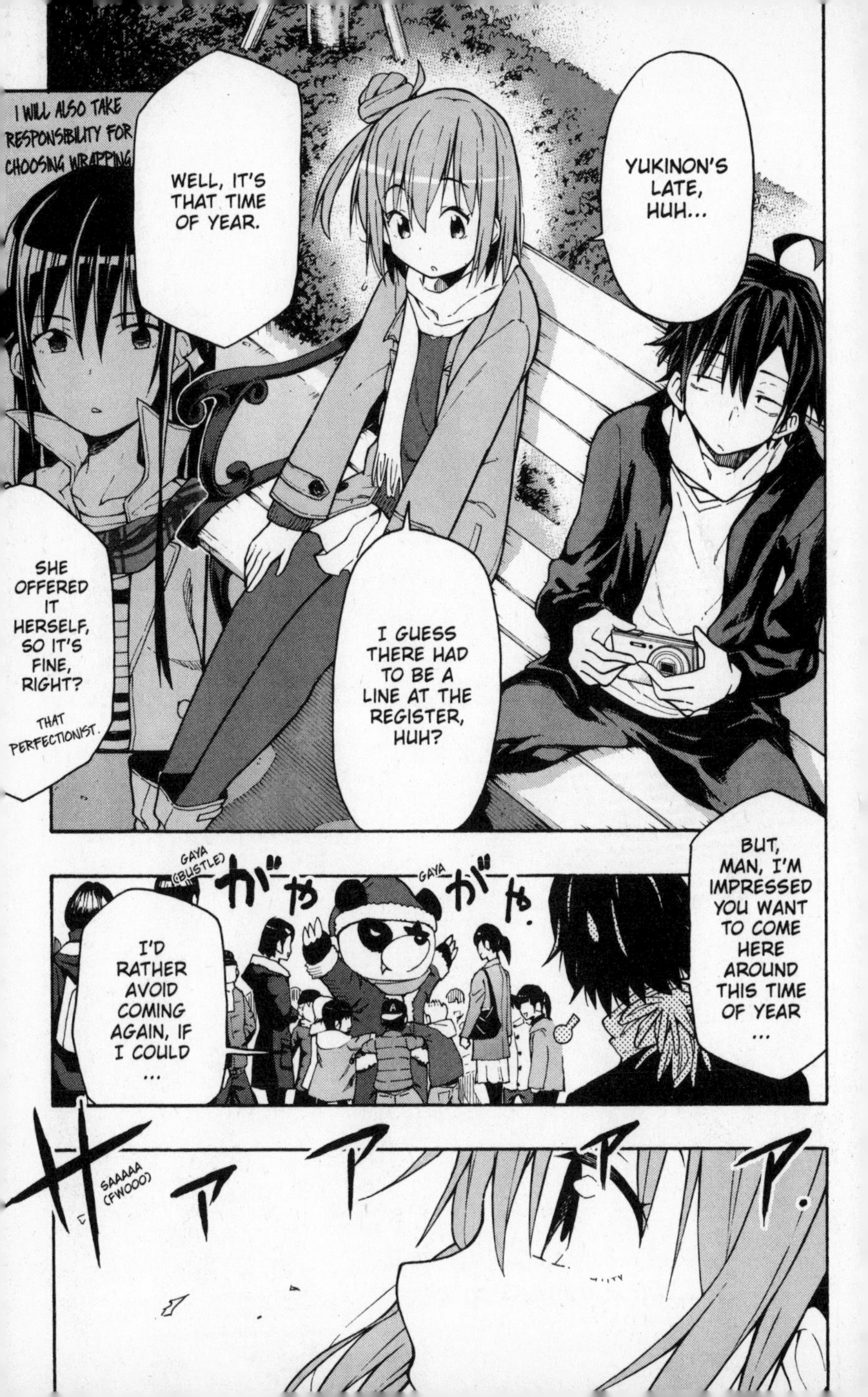
YUKINON'S LATE, HUH...
WELL, IT'S THAT TIME OF YEAR.
I WILL ALSO TAKE RESPONSIBILITY FOR CHOOSING WRAPPING
I GUESS THERE HAD TO BE A LINE AT THE REGISTER, HUH?
SHE OFFERED IT HERSELF, SO IT'S FINE, RIGHT?
THAT PERFECTIONIST.
BUT, MAN, I'M IMPRESSED YOU WANT TO COME HERE AROUND THIS TIME OF YEAR ...
がやがや
GAYA
GAYA (BUSTLE)
I'D RATHER AVOID COMING AGAIN, IF I COULD ...
サァァァァァ
SAAAAA (FWOOO)

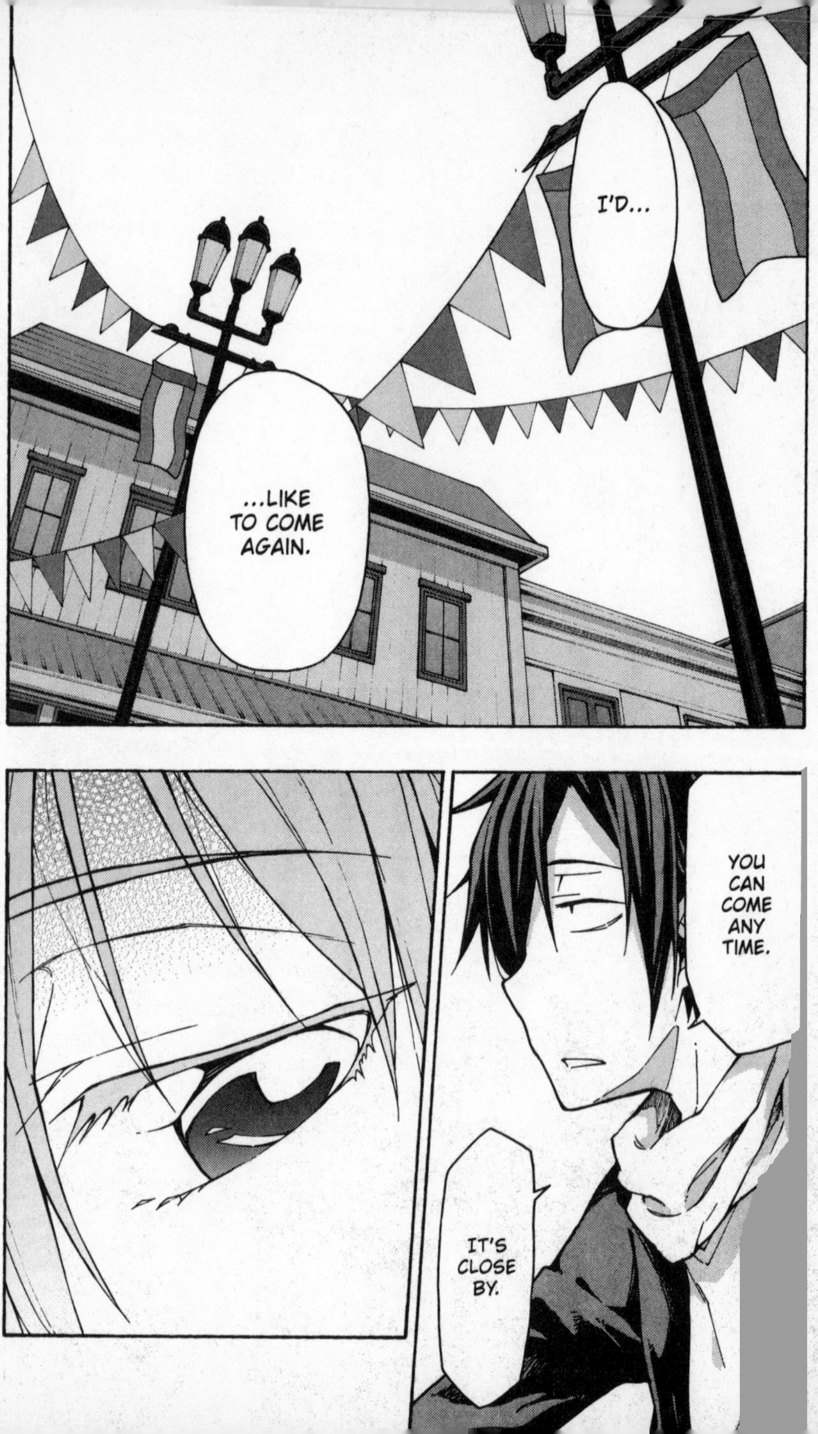
I'D...
...LIKE TO COME AGAIN.
YOU CAN COME ANY TIME.
IT'S CLOSE BY.

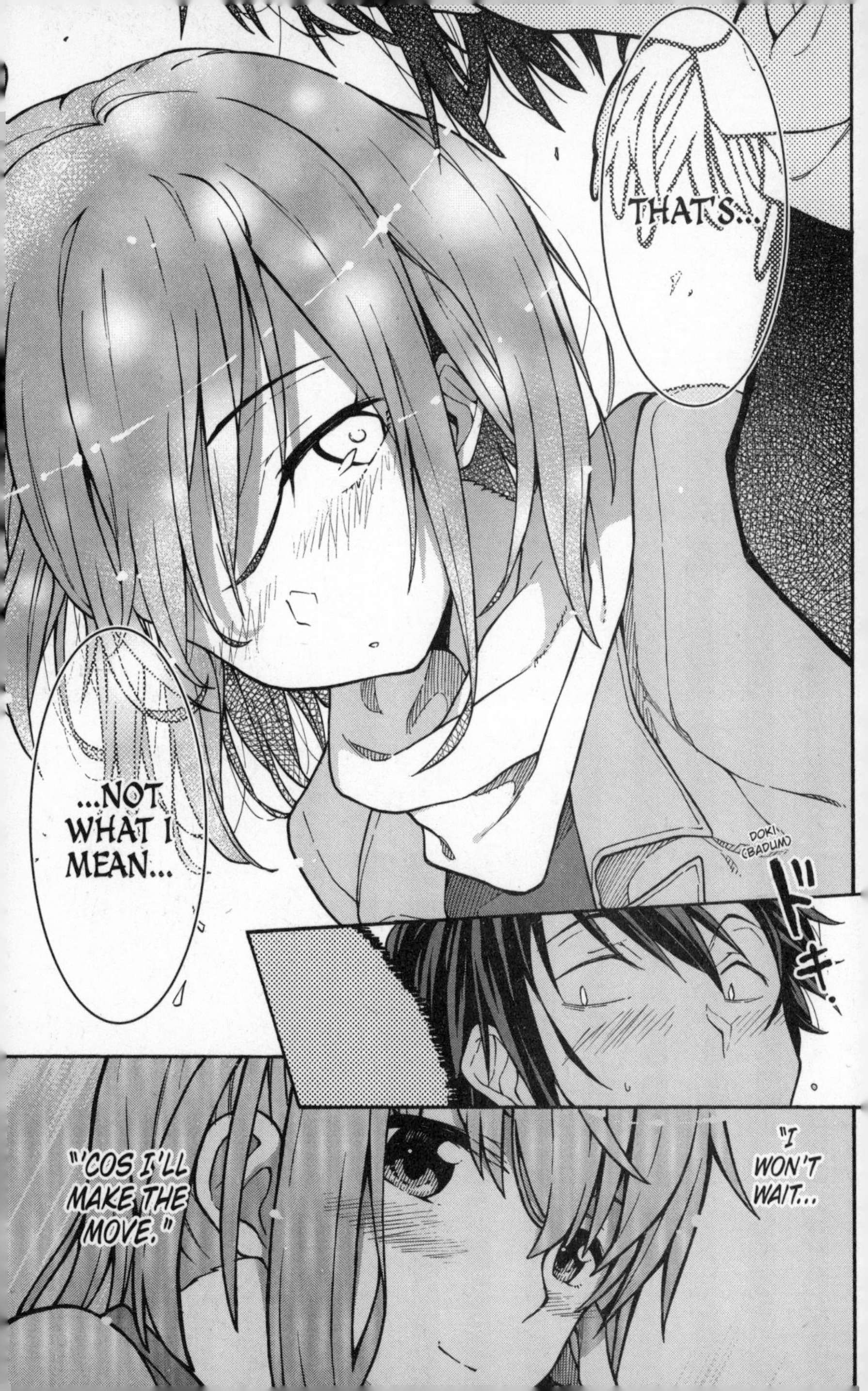
THAT'S...
...NOT WHAT I MEAN...
DOKI (BADUM)
ドキッ
"I WON'T WAIT...
'COS I'LL MAKE THE MOVE."

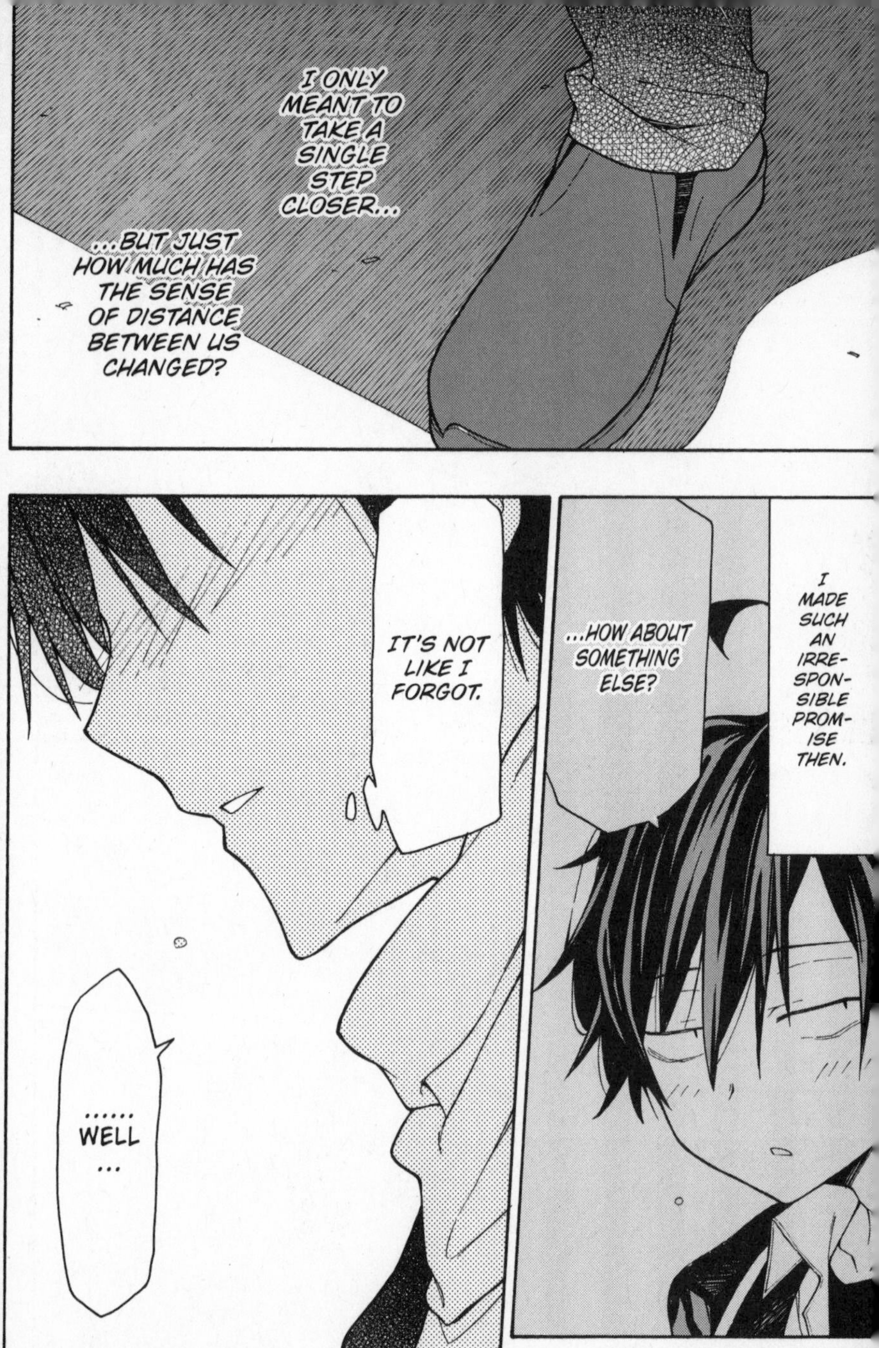
I ONLY MEANT TO TAKE A SINGLE STEP CLOSER...
...BUT JUST HOW MUCH HAS THE SENSE OF DISTANCE BETWEEN US CHANGED?
I MADE SUCH AN IRRE-SPON-SIBLE PROM-ISE THEN.
...HOW ABOUT SOMETHING ELSE?
IT'S NOT LIKE I FORGOT.
...... WELL ...

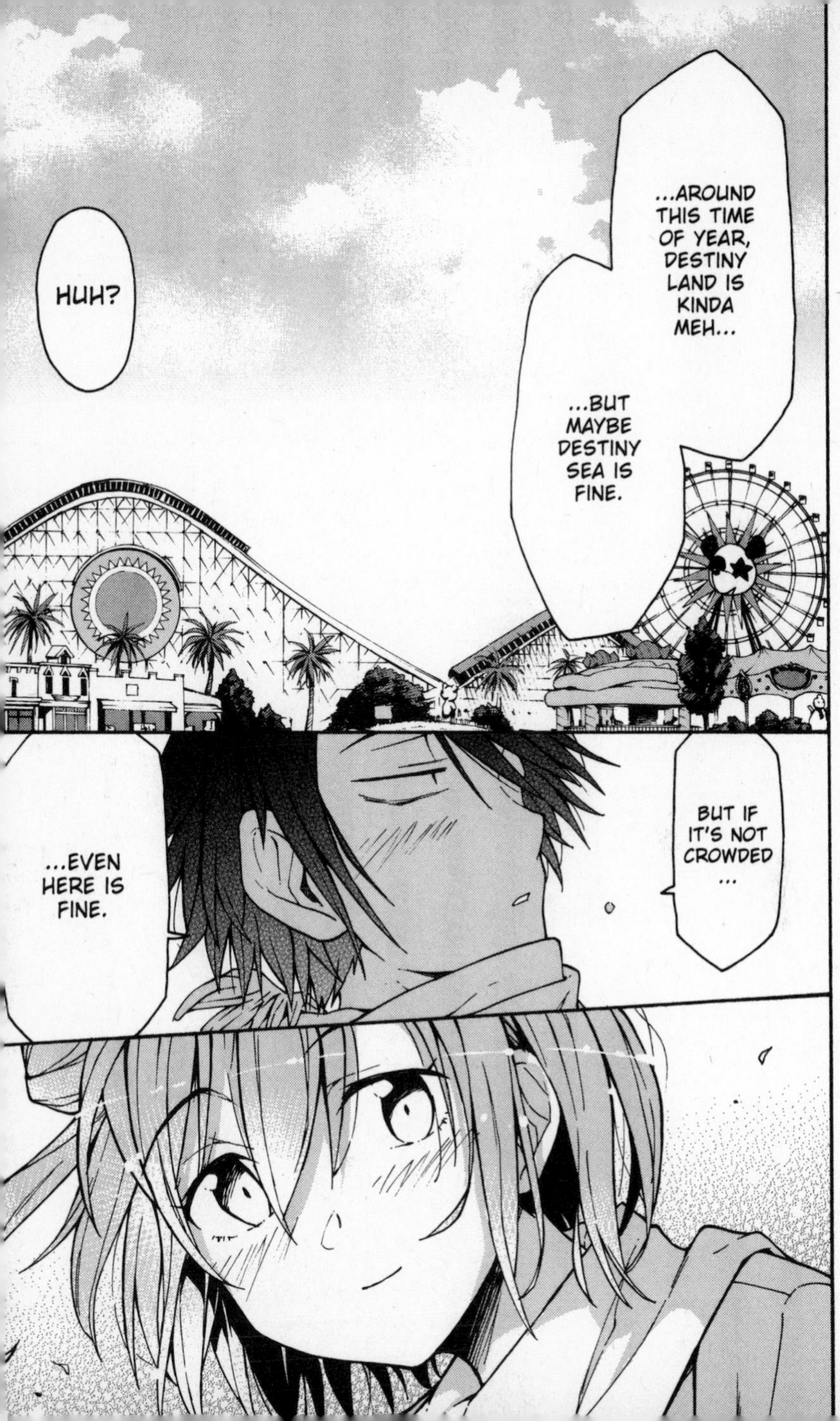
...AROUND THIS TIME OF YEAR, DESTINY LAND IS KINDA MEH...
...BUT MAYBE DESTINY SEA IS FINE.
HUH?
BUT IF IT'S NOT CROWDED ...
...EVEN HERE IS FINE.

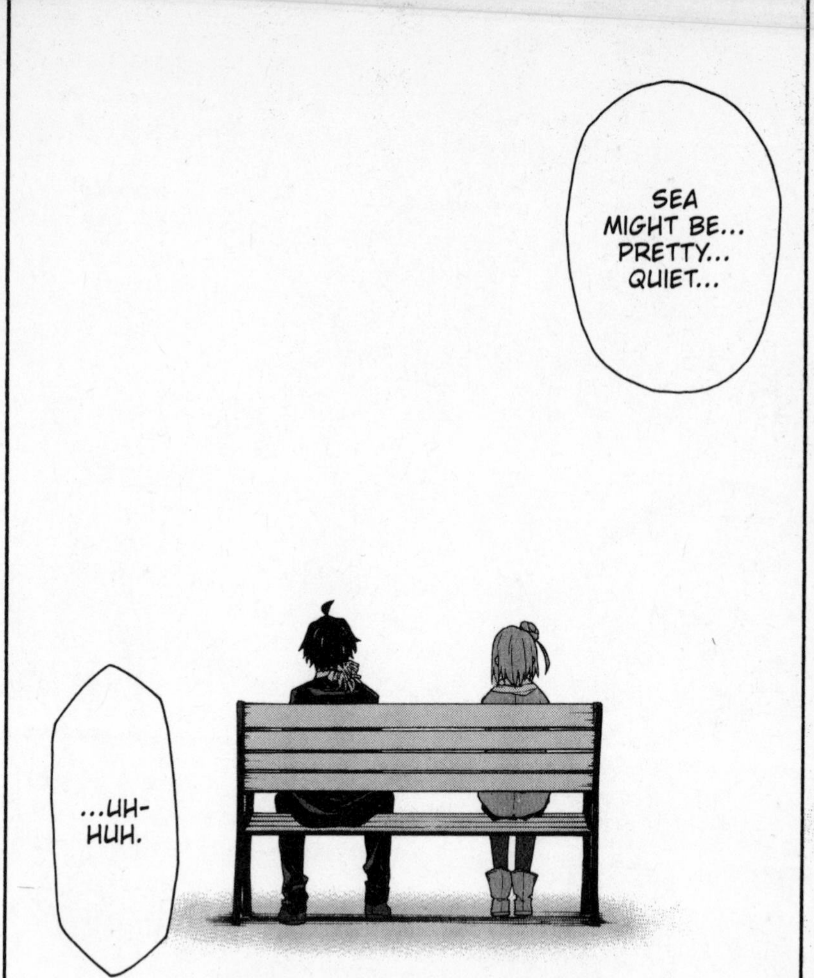
SEA MIGHT BE... PRETTY... QUIET...
...UH-HUH.
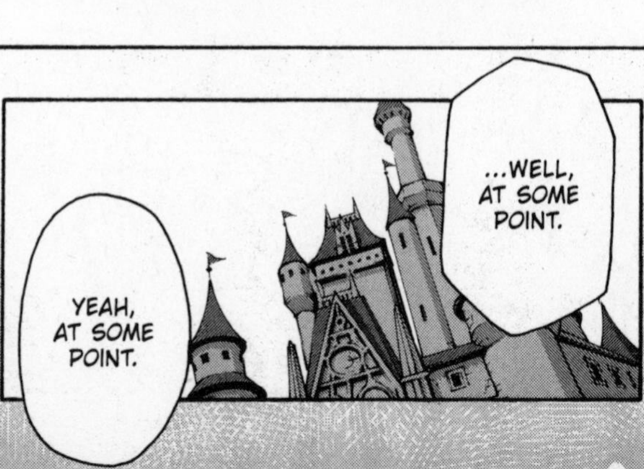
...WELL, AT SOME POINT.
YEAH, AT SOME POINT.

CHAPTER 67 ··· AND THEN YUKINO YUKINOSHITA...

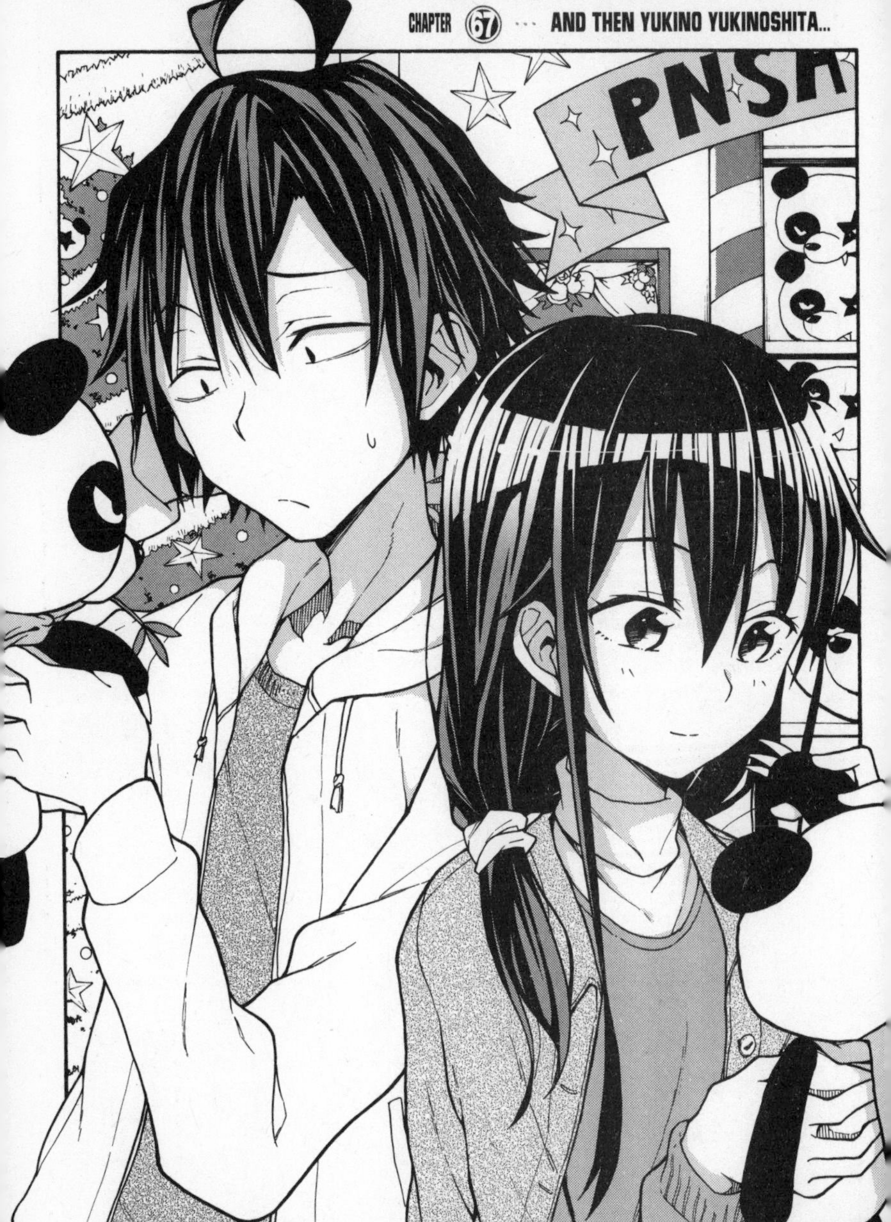
PNSA

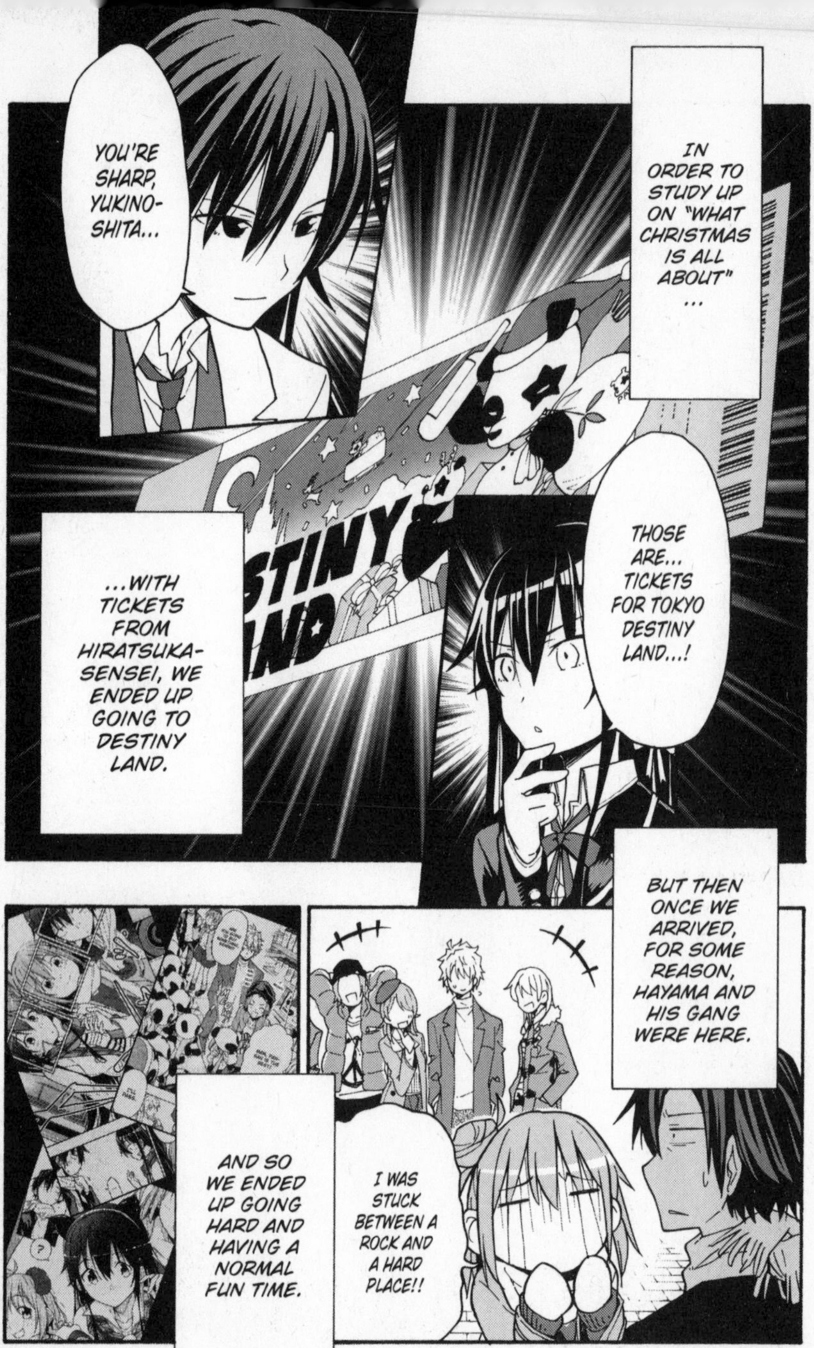
YOU'RE SHARP, YUKINO-SHITA...
IN ORDER TO STUDY UP ON "WHAT CHRISTMAS IS ALL ABOUT" ...
DESTINY LAND
THOSE ARE... TICKETS FOR TOKYO DESTINY LAND...!
...WITH TICKETS FROM HIRATSUKA-SENSEI, WE ENDED UP GOING TO DESTINY LAND.
BUT THEN ONCE WE ARRIVED, FOR SOME REASON, HAYAMA AND HIS GANG WERE HERE.
I WAS STUCK BETWEEN A ROCK AND A HARD PLACE!!
AND SO WE ENDED UP GOING HARD AND HAVING A NORMAL FUN TIME.

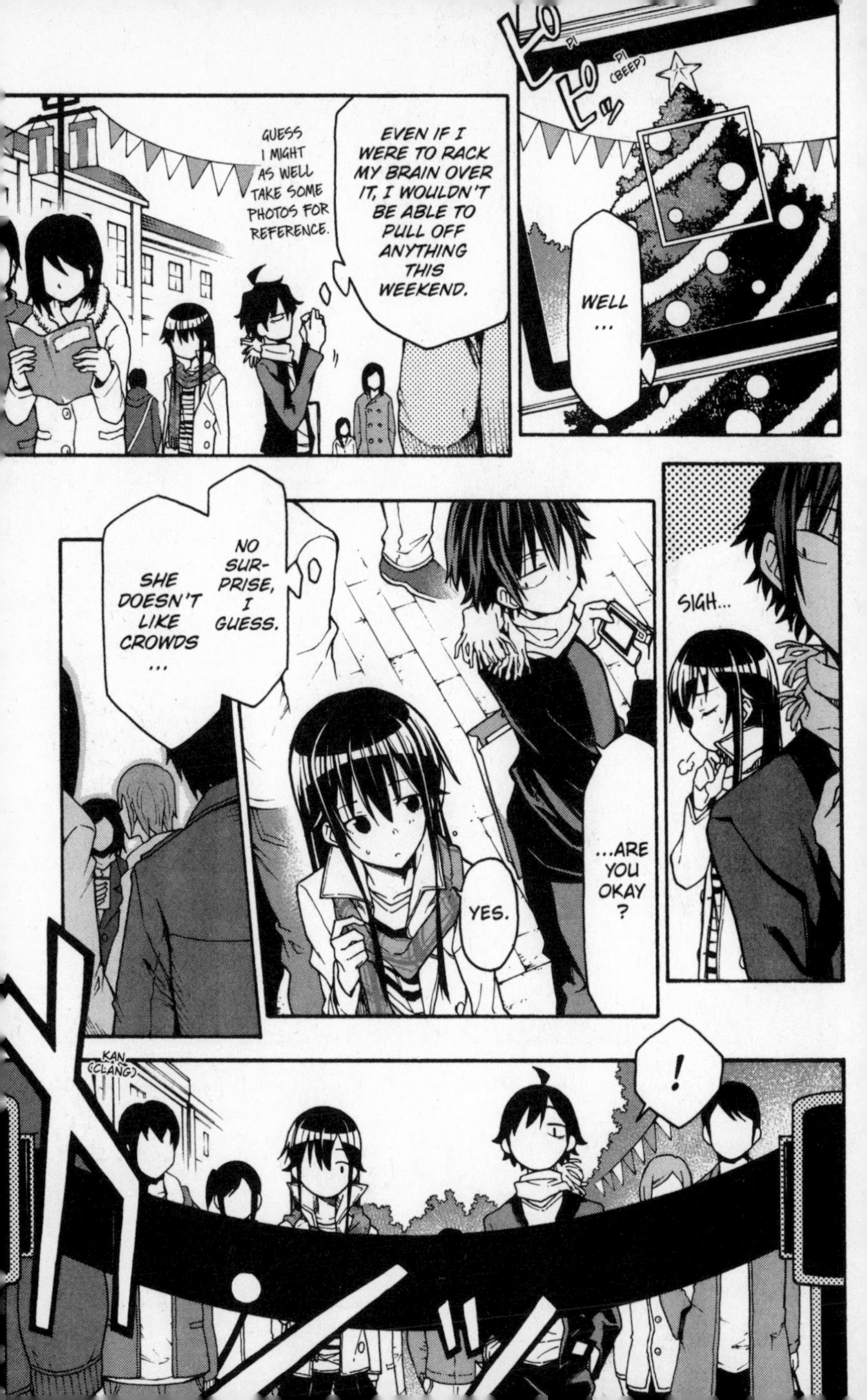
PI
PI (BEEP)
WELL...
EVEN IF I WERE TO RACK MY BRAIN OVER IT, I WOULDN'T BE ABLE TO PULL OFF ANYTHING THIS WEEKEND.
GUESS I MIGHT AS WELL TAKE SOME PHOTOS FOR REFERENCE.
SIGH...
...ARE YOU OKAY?
YES.
SHE DOESN'T LIKE CROWDS... NO SURPRISE, I GUESS.
!
KAN (CLANG)

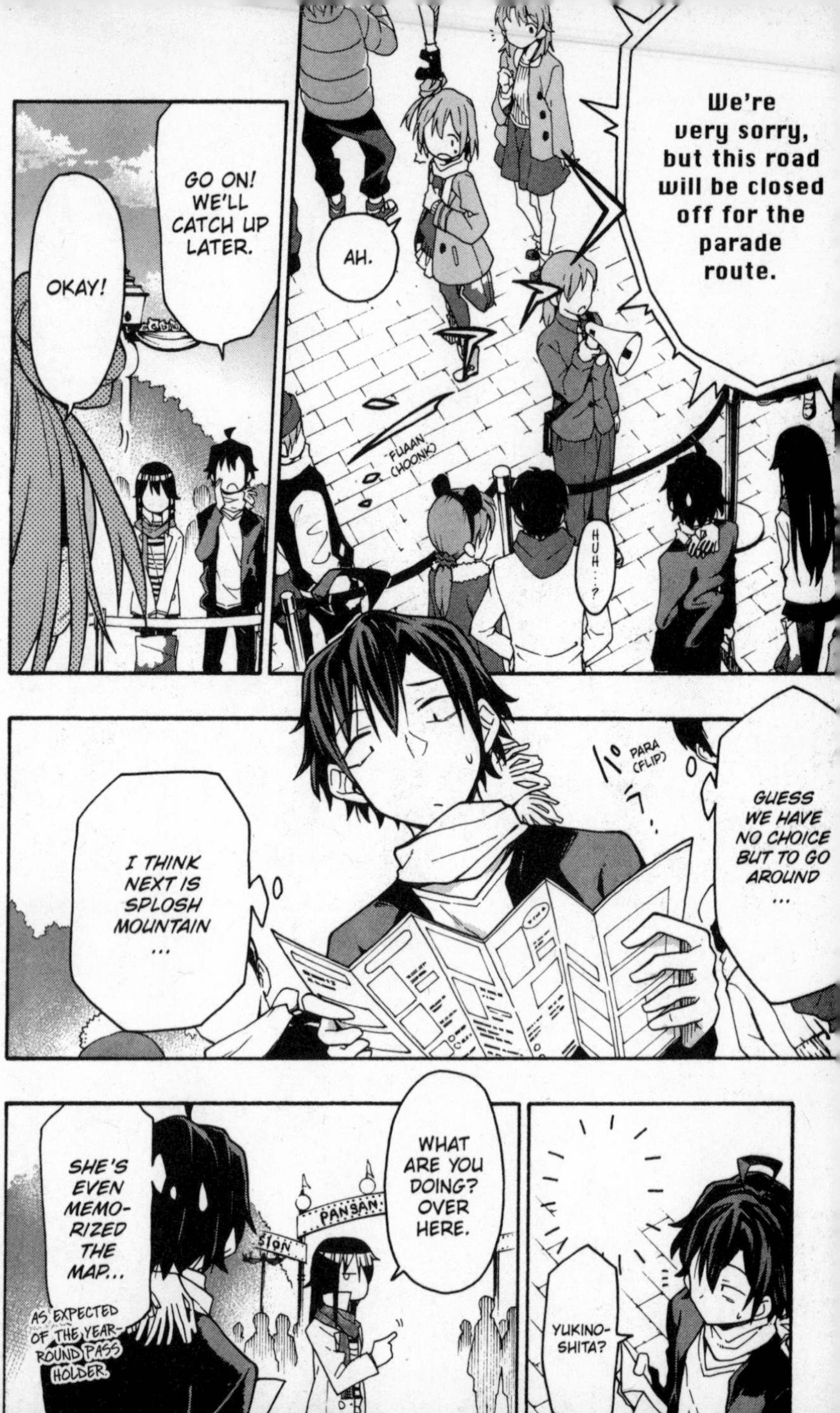
We're very sorry, but this road will be closed off for the parade route.
AH.
FUAAN (HOONK)
HUH...?
GO ON! WE'LL CATCH UP LATER.
OKAY!
GUESS WE HAVE NO CHOICE BUT TO GO AROUND ...
PARA (FLIP)
I THINK NEXT IS SPLOSH MOUNTAIN ...
YUKINO-SHITA?
WHAT ARE YOU DOING? OVER HERE.
PANSAN
SIGN
SHE'S EVEN MEMO-RIZED THE MAP...
AS EXPECTED OF THE YEAR-ROUND PASS HOLDER.

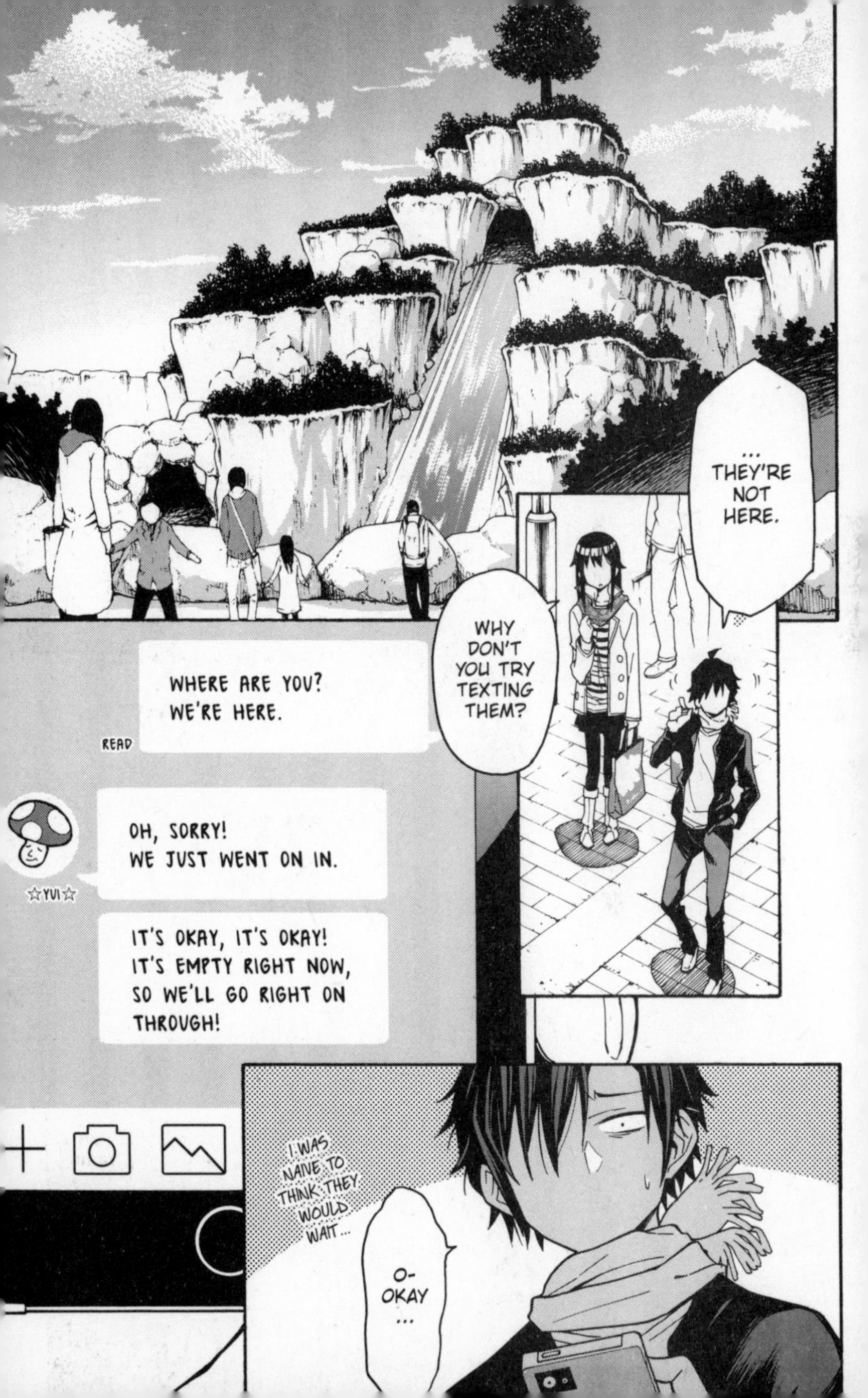
...THEY'RE NOT HERE.
WHY DON'T YOU TRY TEXTING THEM?
WHERE ARE YOU? WE'RE HERE.
READ
OH, SORRY! WE JUST WENT ON IN.
☆YUI☆
IT'S OKAY, IT'S OKAY! IT'S EMPTY RIGHT NOW, SO WE'LL GO RIGHT ON THROUGH!
O-OKAY...
I WAS NAIVE TO THINK THEY WOULD WAIT...

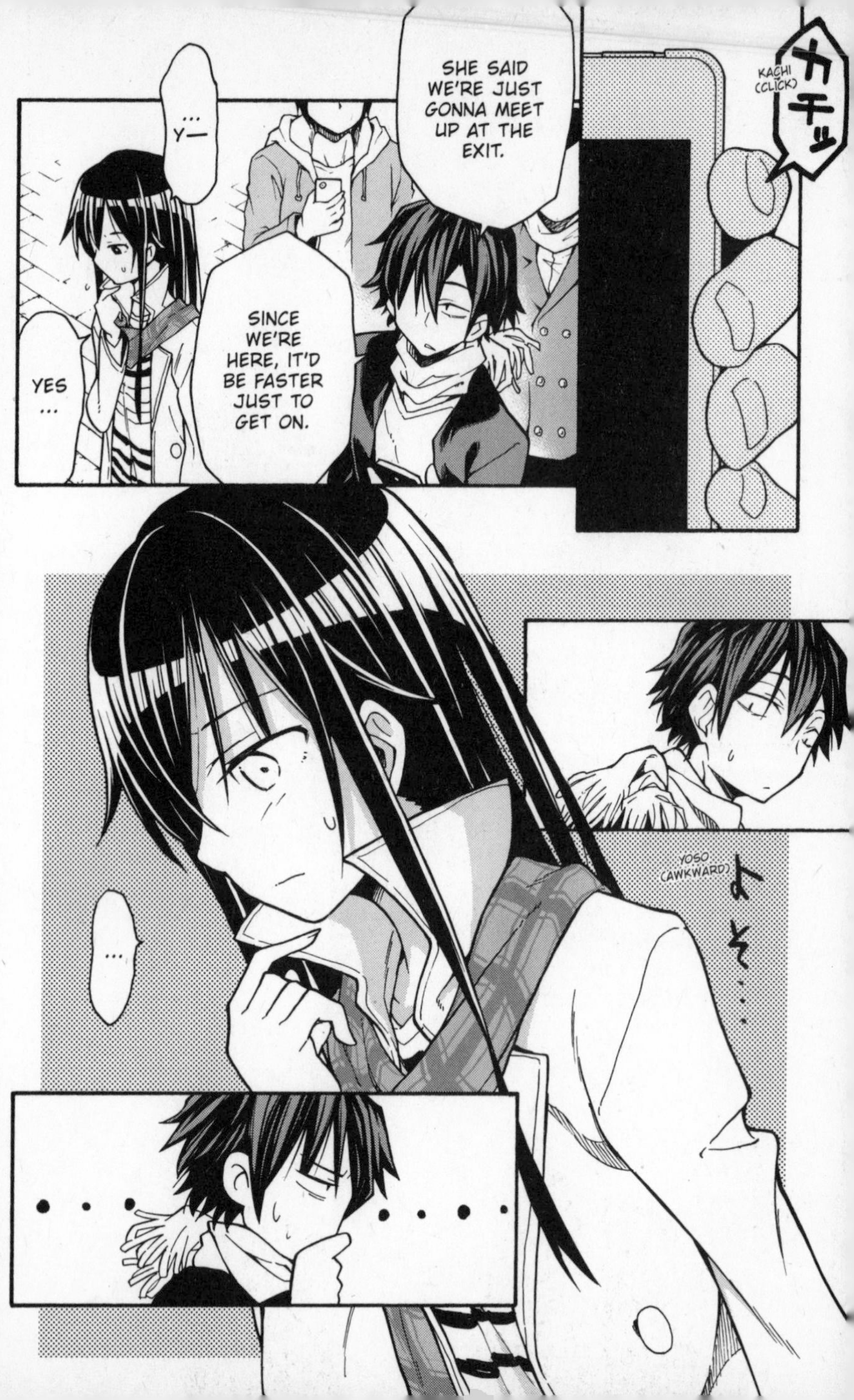
カチッ
KACHI (CLICK)
SHE SAID WE'RE JUST GONNA MEET UP AT THE EXIT.
SINCE WE'RE HERE, IT'D BE FASTER JUST TO GET ON.
... Y—
YES ...
YOSO (AWKWARD)
よそ…
...
• • • • • • • •

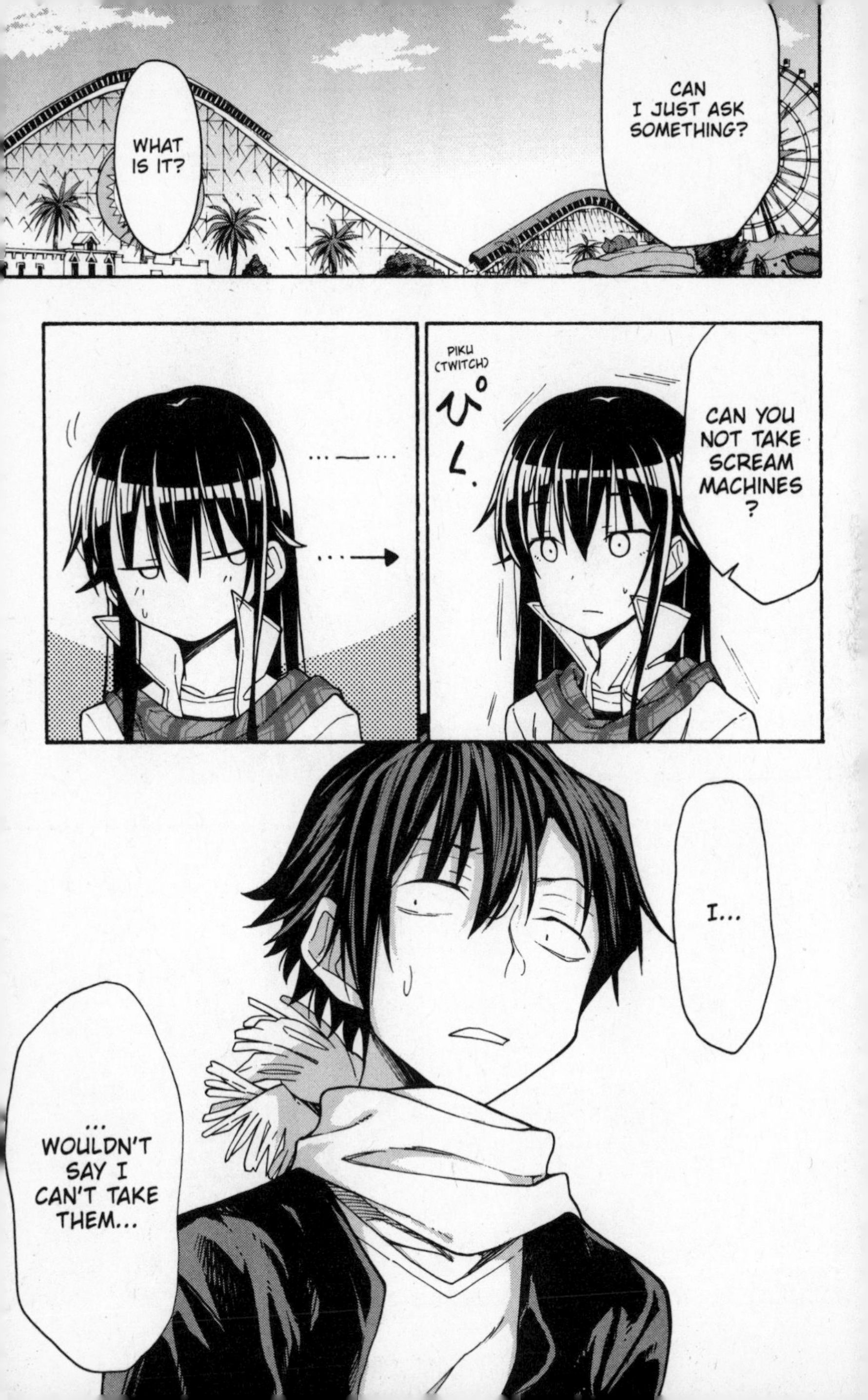
CAN I JUST ASK SOMETHING?
WHAT IS IT?
PIKU (TWITCH)
ぴく
CAN YOU NOT TAKE SCREAM MACHINES?
I...
...WOULDN'T SAY I CAN'T TAKE THEM...

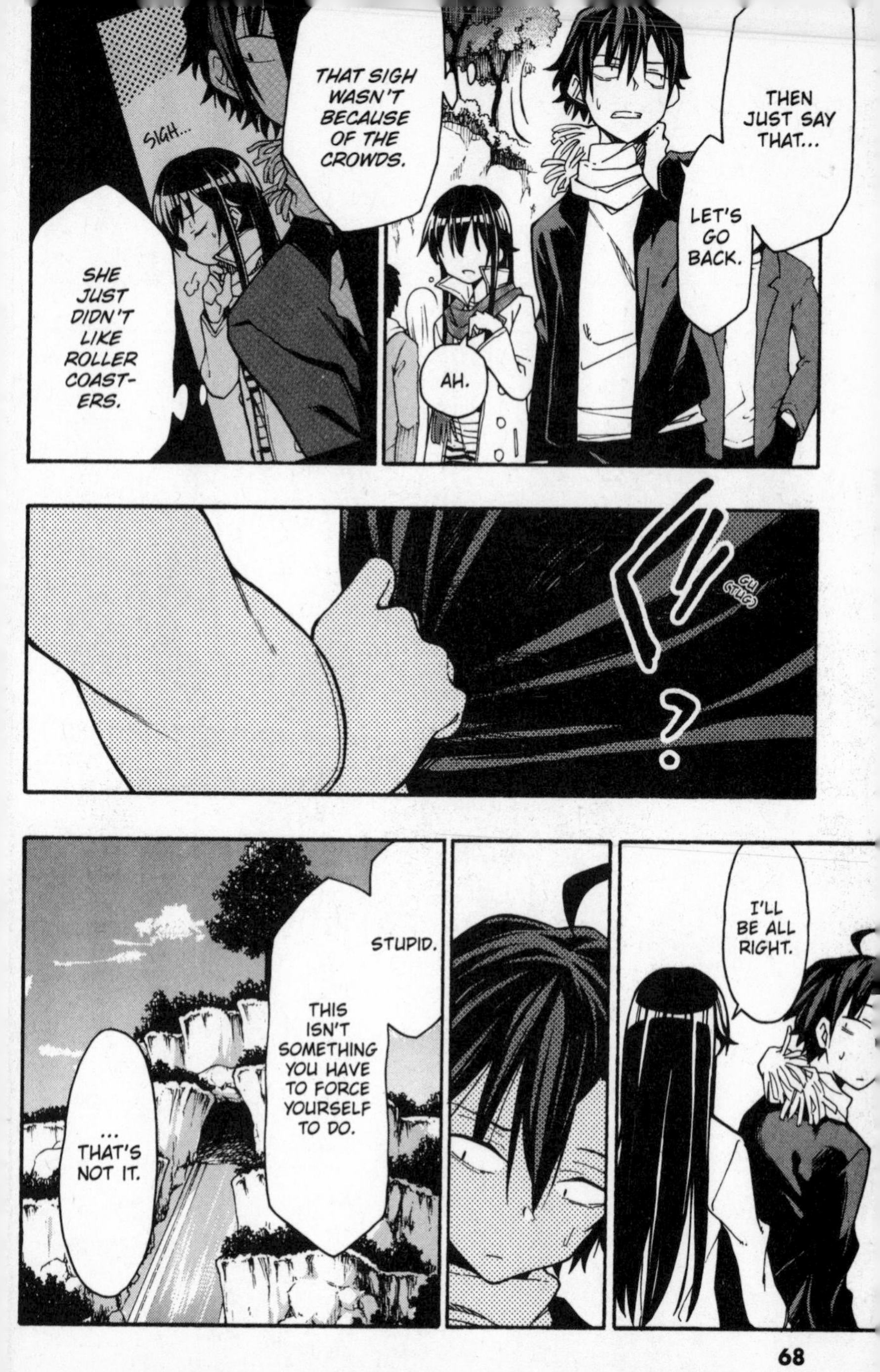
THEN JUST SAY THAT...
LET'S GO BACK.
AH.
THAT SIGH WASN'T BECAUSE OF THE CROWDS.
SIGH...
SHE JUST DIDN'T LIKE ROLLER COASTERS.
GU (TUG)
I'LL BE ALL RIGHT.
STUPID.
THIS ISN'T SOMETHING YOU HAVE TO FORCE YOURSELF TO DO.
... THAT'S NOT IT.

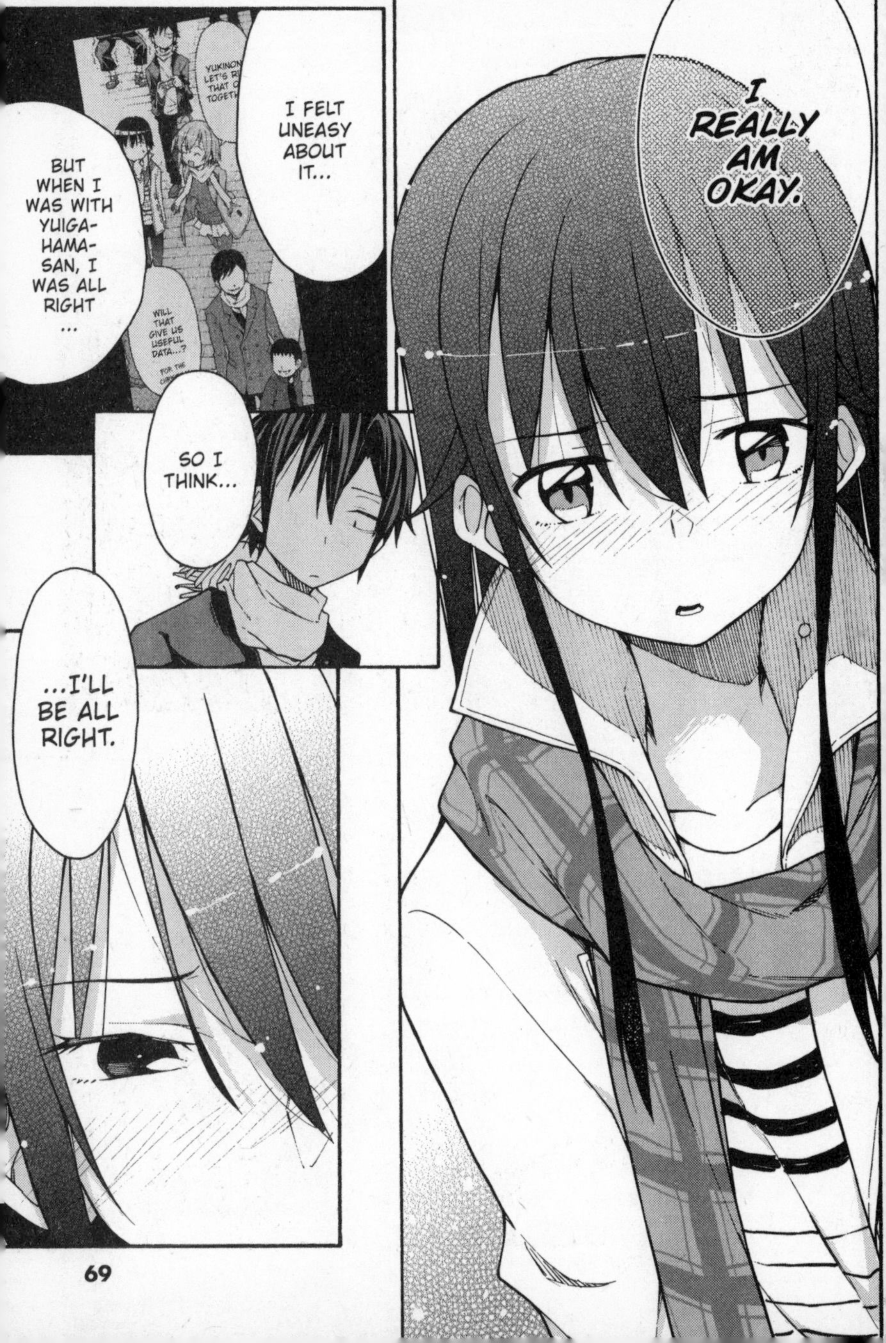
I REALLY AM OKAY.
I FELT UNEASY ABOUT IT...
BUT WHEN I WAS WITH YUIGA-HAMA-SAN, I WAS ALL RIGHT...
WILL THAT GIVE US USEFUL DATA...?
SO I THINK...
...I'LL BE ALL RIGHT.

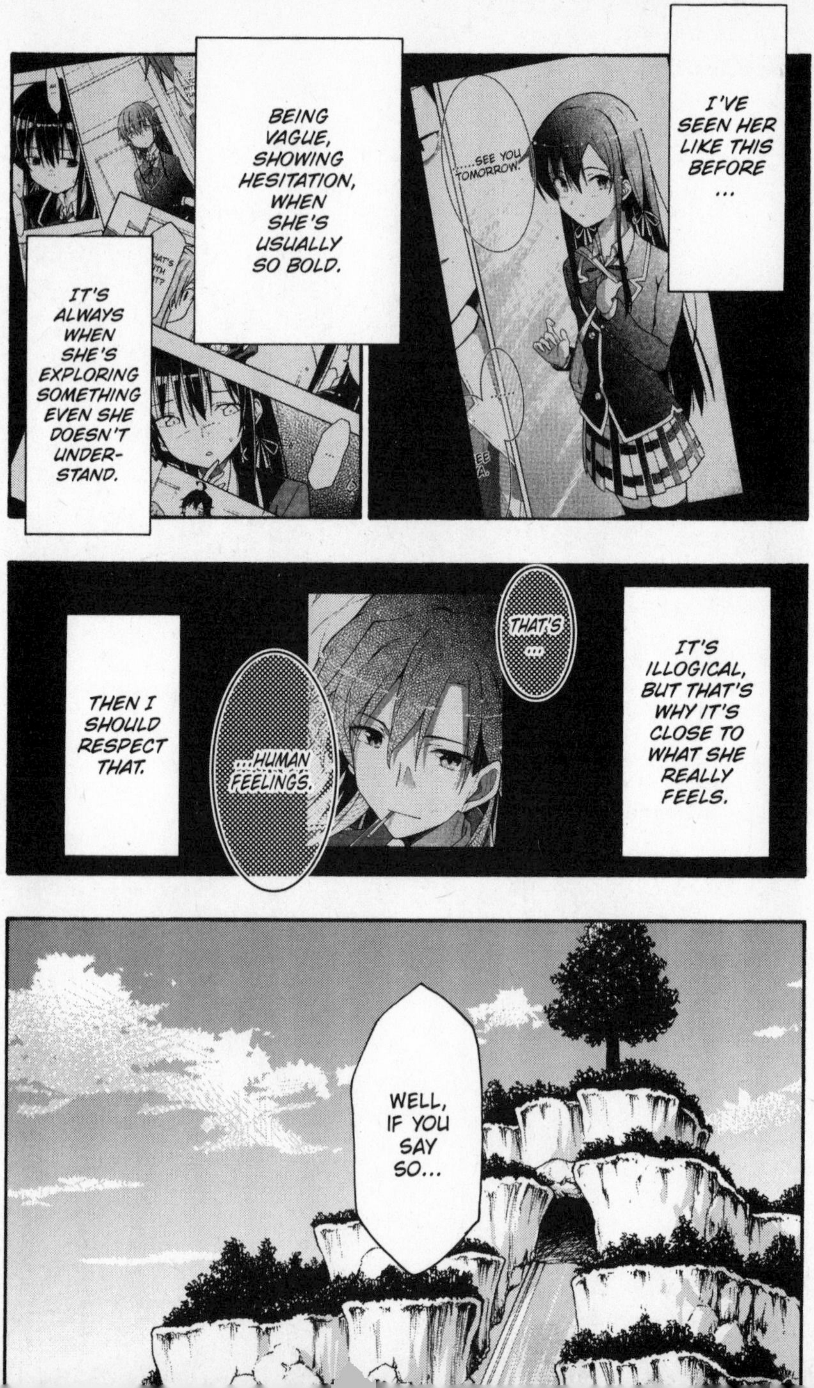
I'VE SEEN HER LIKE THIS BEFORE...
...SEE YOU TOMORROW.
BEING VAGUE, SHOWING HESITATION, WHEN SHE'S USUALLY SO BOLD.
IT'S ALWAYS WHEN SHE'S EXPLORING SOMETHING EVEN SHE DOESN'T UNDER-STAND.
IT'S ILLOGICAL, BUT THAT'S WHY IT'S CLOSE TO WHAT SHE REALLY FEELS.
THAT'S...
...HUMAN FEELINGS.
THEN I SHOULD RESPECT THAT.
WELL, IF YOU SAY SO...

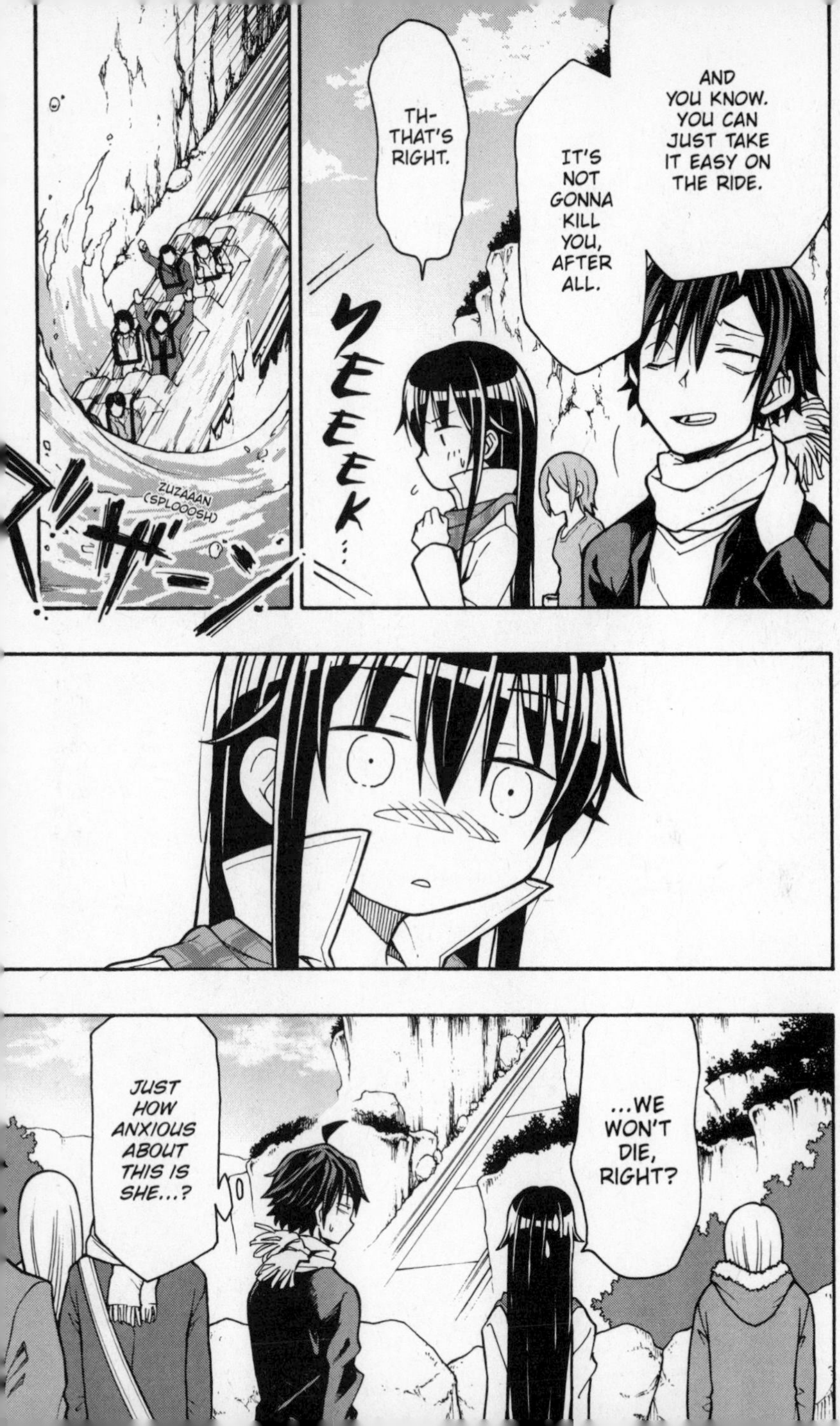
AND YOU KNOW. YOU CAN JUST TAKE IT EASY ON THE RIDE.
IT'S NOT GONNA KILL YOU, AFTER ALL.
TH-THAT'S RIGHT.
YEEEEK...
ZUZAAAN (SPLOOOSH)
...WE WON'T DIE, RIGHT?
JUST HOW ANXIOUS ABOUT THIS IS SHE...?

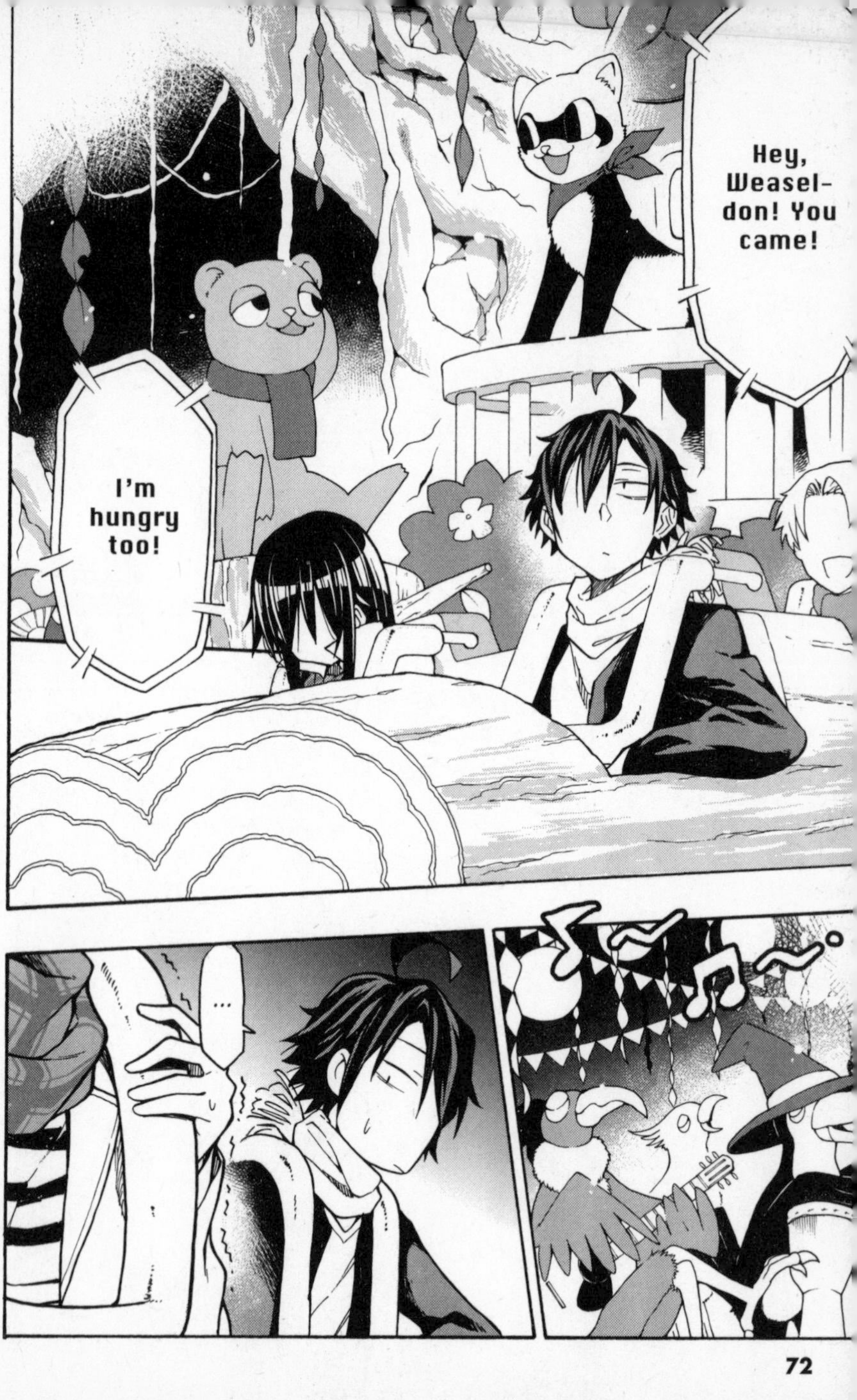
Hey, Weasel-don! You came!
I'm hungry too!
...

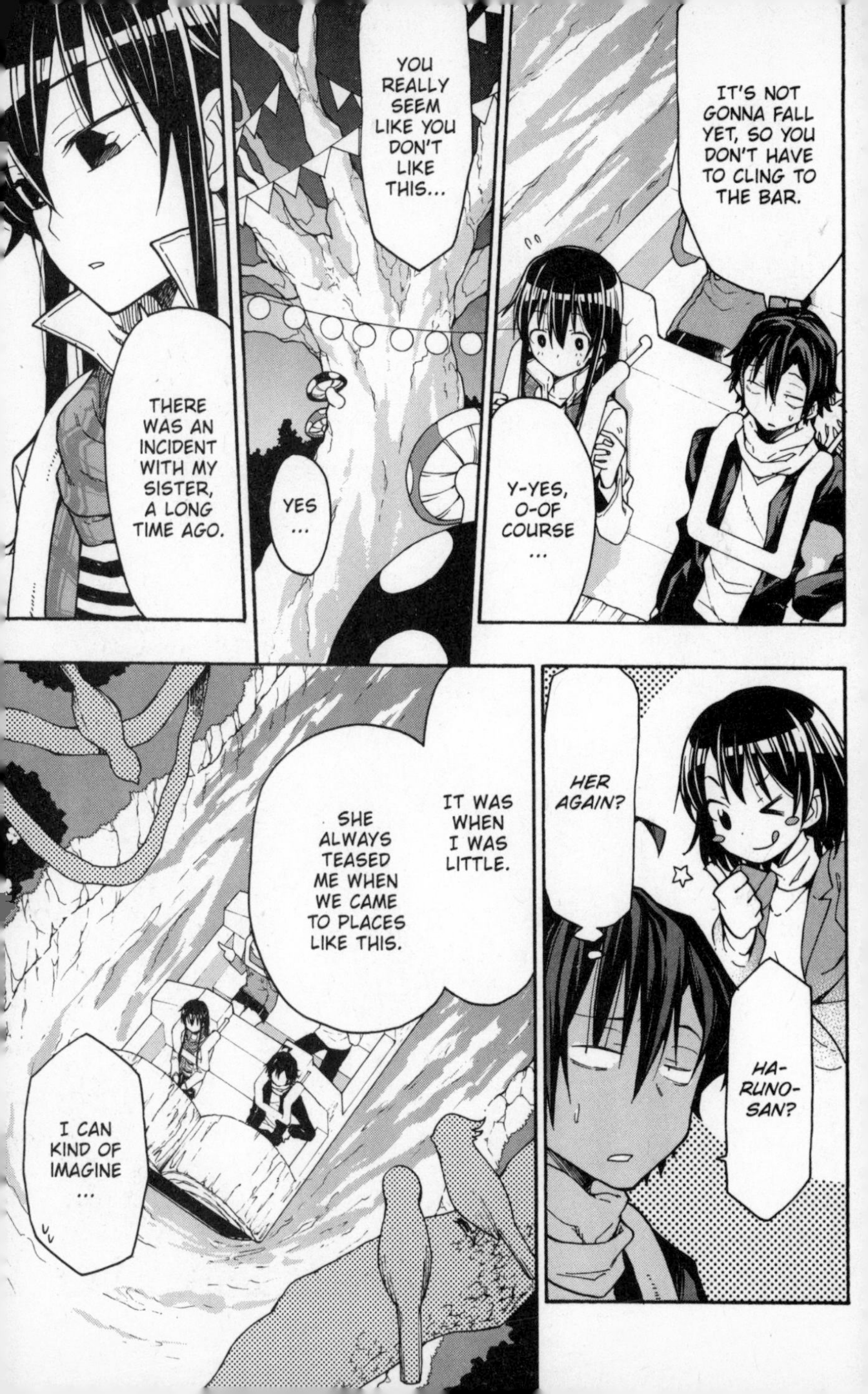
IT'S NOT GONNA FALL YET, SO YOU DON'T HAVE TO CLING TO THE BAR.
Y-YES, O-OF COURSE...
YOU REALLY SEEM LIKE YOU DON'T LIKE THIS...
YES...
THERE WAS AN INCIDENT WITH MY SISTER, A LONG TIME AGO.
HER AGAIN?
HA-RUNO-SAN?
IT WAS WHEN I WAS LITTLE.
SHE ALWAYS TEASED ME WHEN WE CAME TO PLACES LIKE THIS.
I CAN KIND OF IMAGINE...

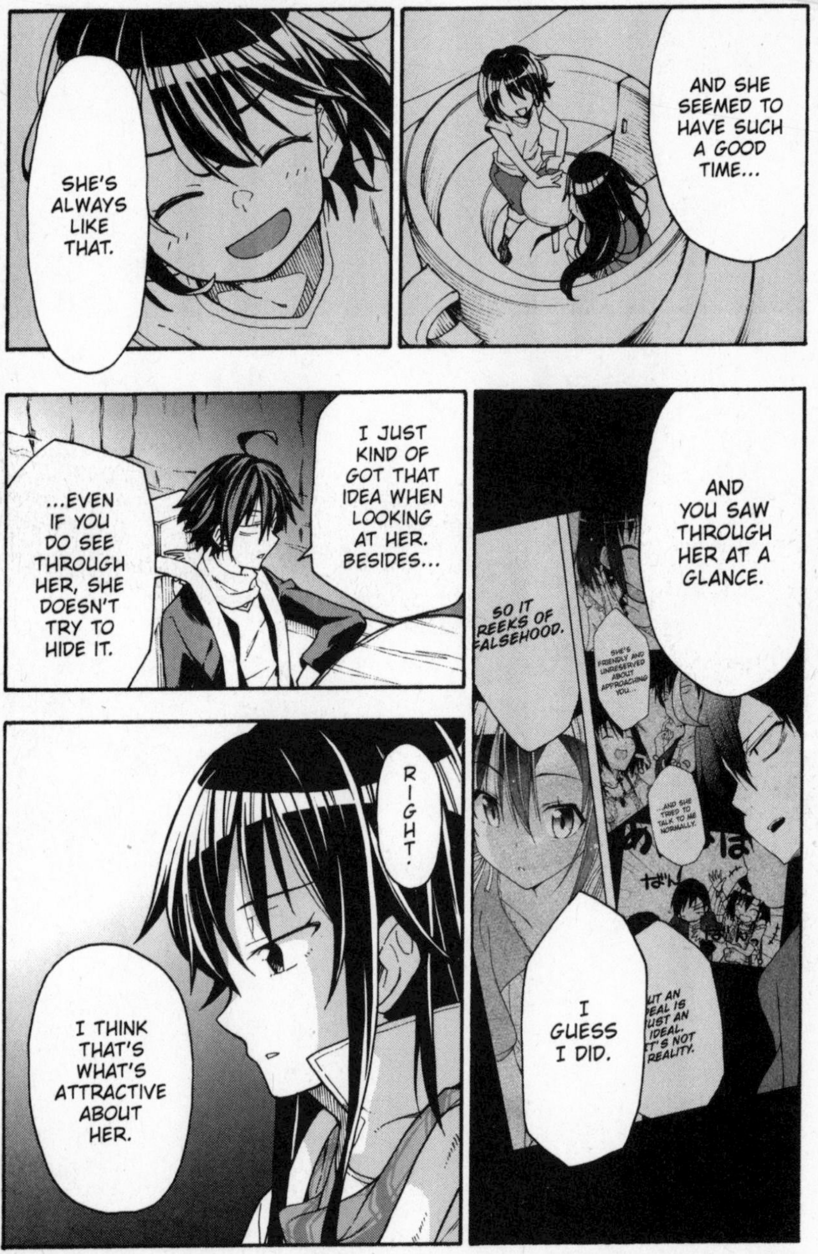
AND SHE SEEMED TO HAVE SUCH A GOOD TIME...
SHE'S ALWAYS LIKE THAT.
AND YOU SAW THROUGH HER AT A GLANCE.
SHE'S FRIENDLY AND UNRESERVED ABOUT APPROACHING YOU...
SO IT REEKS OF FALSEHOOD.
...AND SHE TRIED TO TALK TO ME NORMALLY.
UT AN DEAL IS UST AN IDEAL. T'S NOT REALITY.
I GUESS I DID.
I JUST KIND OF GOT THAT IDEA WHEN LOOKING AT HER. BESIDES...
...EVEN IF YOU DO SEE THROUGH HER, SHE DOESN'T TRY TO HIDE IT.
RIGHT.
I THINK THAT'S WHAT'S ATTRACTIVE ABOUT HER.

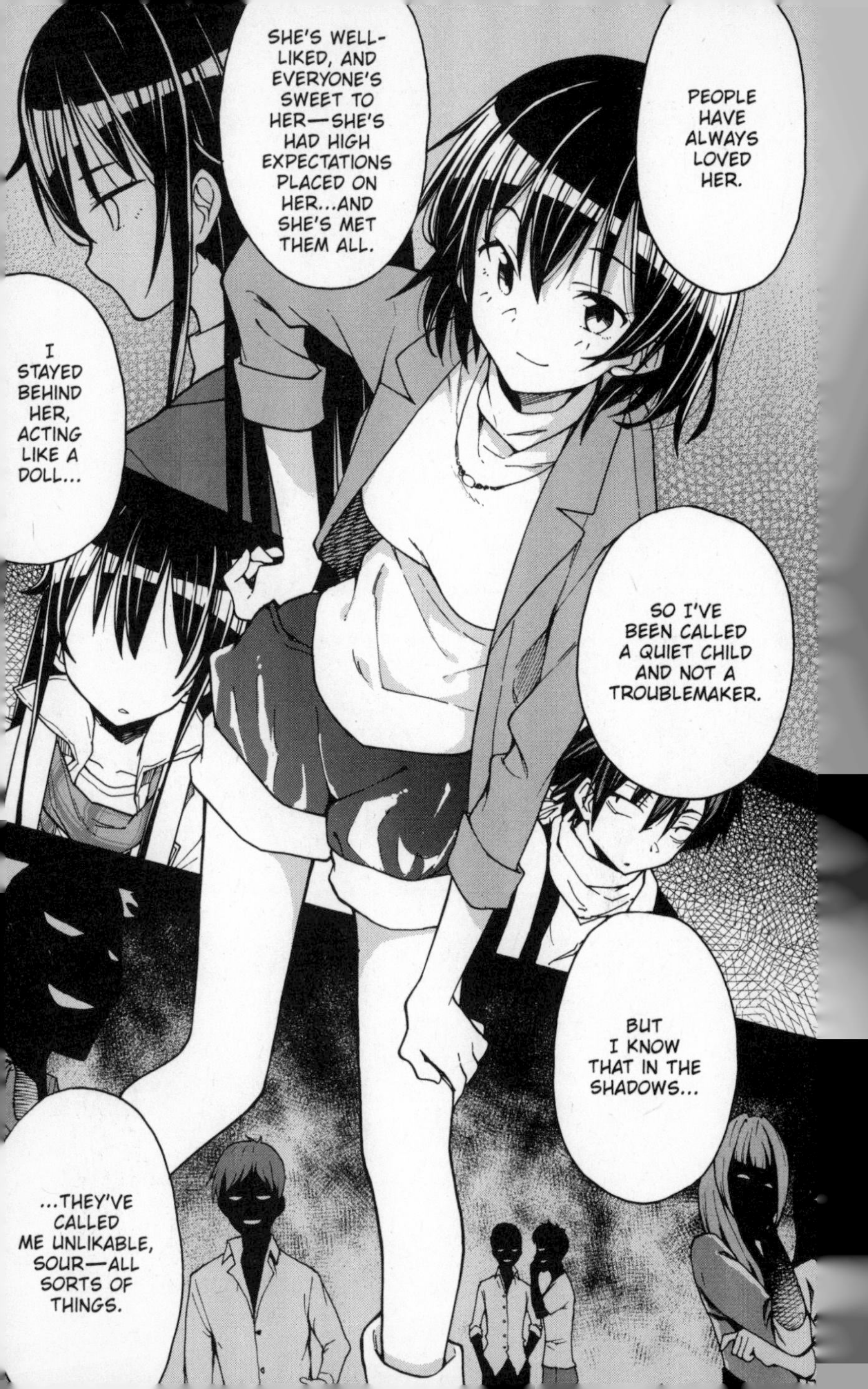
PEOPLE HAVE ALWAYS LOVED HER.
SHE'S WELL-LIKED, AND EVERYONE'S SWEET TO HER—SHE'S HAD HIGH EXPECTATIONS PLACED ON HER...AND SHE'S MET THEM ALL.
I STAYED BEHIND HER, ACTING LIKE A DOLL...
SO I'VE BEEN CALLED A QUIET CHILD AND NOT A TROUBLEMAKER.
BUT I KNOW THAT IN THE SHADOWS...
...THEY'VE CALLED ME UNLIKABLE, SOUR—ALL SORTS OF THINGS.

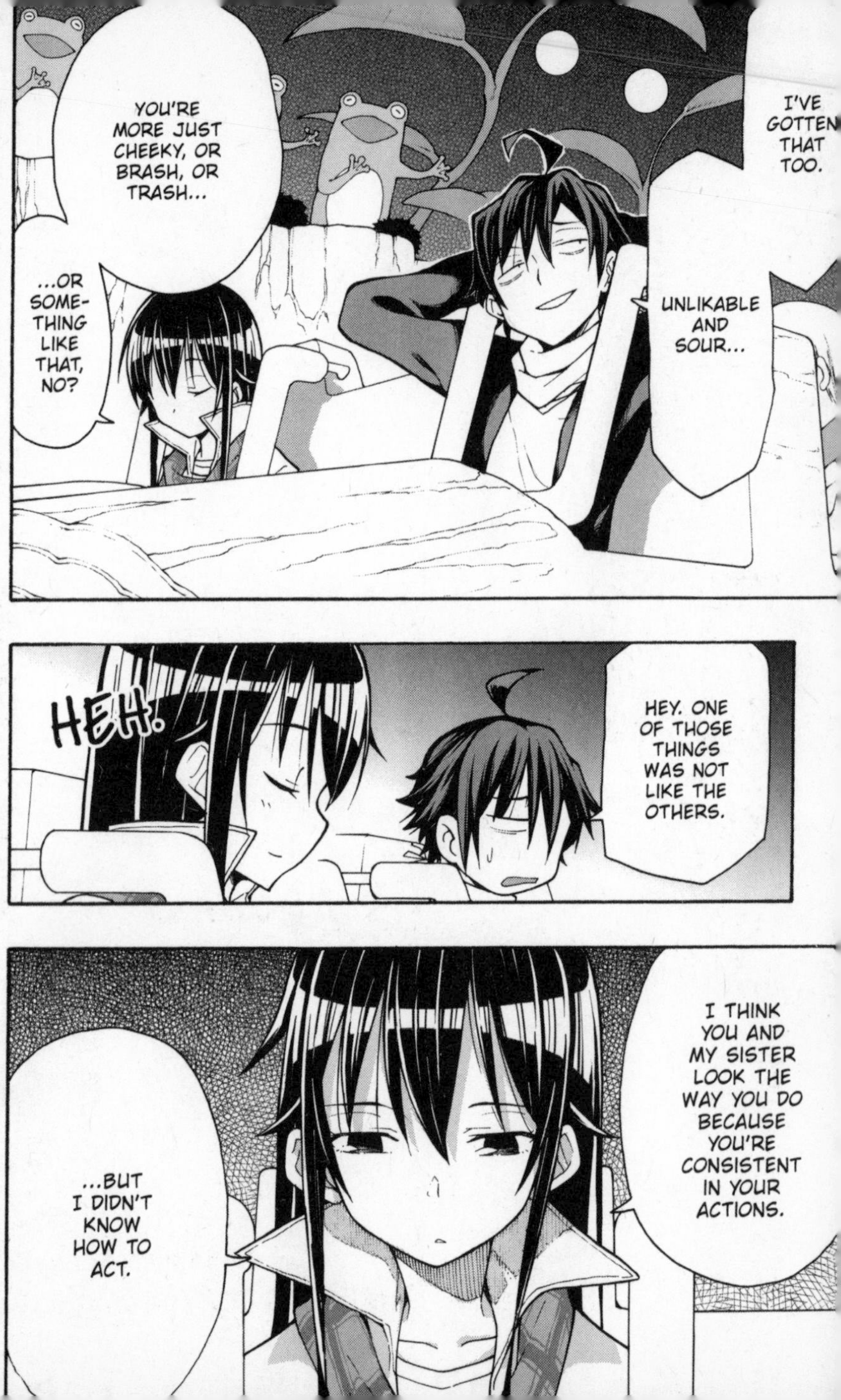
I'VE GOTTEN THAT TOO.
UNLIKABLE AND SOUR...
YOU'RE MORE JUST CHEEKY, OR BRASH, OR TRASH...
...OR SOMETHING LIKE THAT, NO?
HEY. ONE OF THOSE THINGS WAS NOT LIKE THE OTHERS.
HEH.
I THINK YOU AND MY SISTER LOOK THE WAY YOU DO BECAUSE YOU'RE CONSISTENT IN YOUR ACTIONS.
...BUT I DIDN'T KNOW HOW TO ACT.

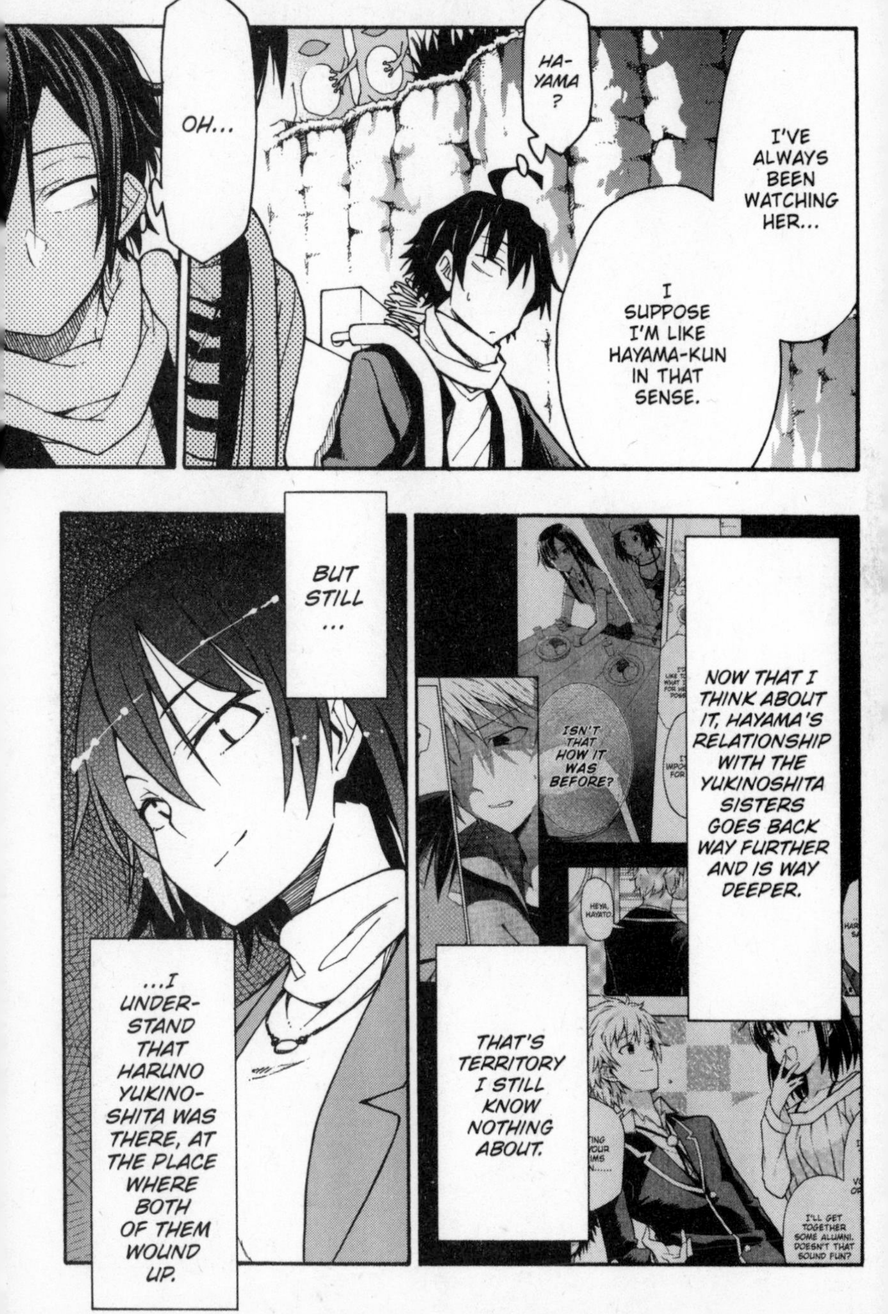
I'VE ALWAYS BEEN WATCHING HER...
I SUPPOSE I'M LIKE HAYAMA-KUN IN THAT SENSE.
HA-YAMA?
OH...
NOW THAT I THINK ABOUT IT, HAYAMA'S RELATIONSHIP WITH THE YUKINOSHITA SISTERS GOES BACK WAY FURTHER AND IS WAY DEEPER.
ISN'T THAT HOW IT WAS BEFORE?
HEYA, HAYATO.
I'LL GET TOGETHER SOME ALUMNI. DOESN'T THAT SOUND FUN?
THAT'S TERRITORY I STILL KNOW NOTHING ABOUT.
BUT STILL ...
...I UNDER-STAND THAT HARUNO YUKINO-SHITA WAS THERE, AT THE PLACE WHERE BOTH OF THEM WOUND UP.

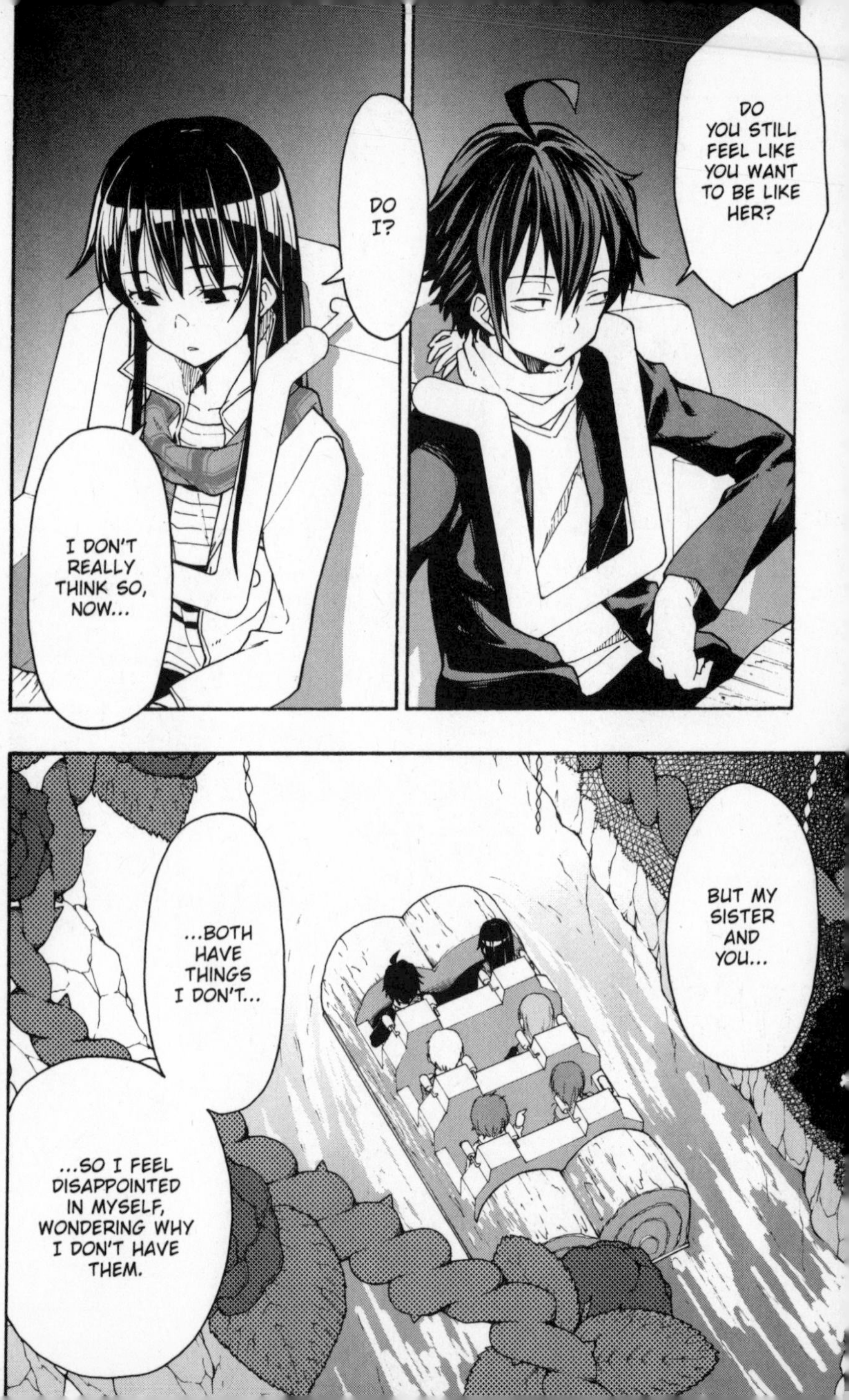
DO YOU STILL FEEL LIKE YOU WANT TO BE LIKE HER?
DO I?
I DON'T REALLY THINK SO, NOW...
BUT MY SISTER AND YOU...
...BOTH HAVE THINGS I DON'T...
...SO I FEEL DISAPPOINTED IN MYSELF, WONDERING WHY I DON'T HAVE THEM.

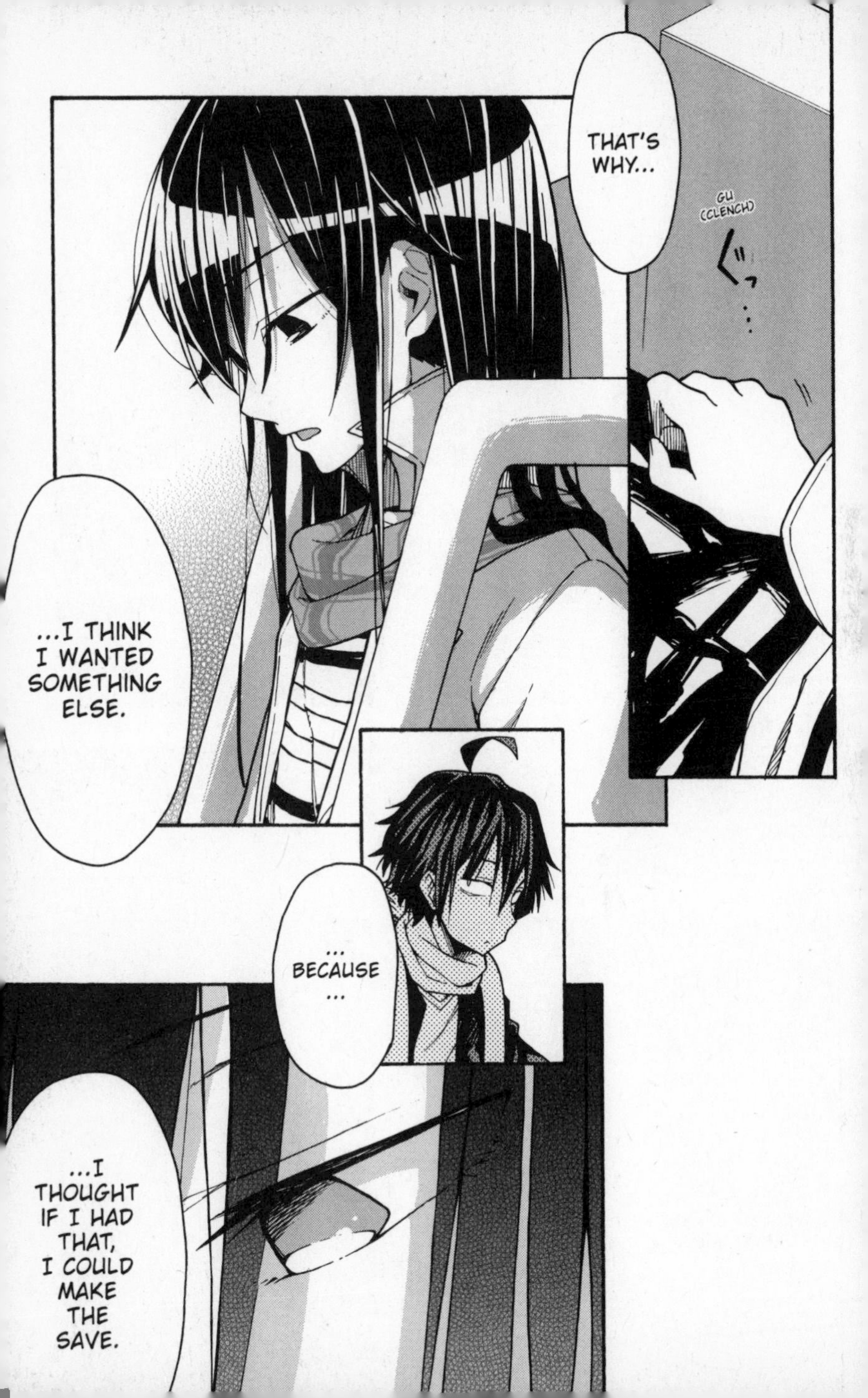
THAT'S WHY...
GU (CLENCH)
...I THINK I WANTED SOMETHING ELSE.
...BECAUSE...
...I THOUGHT IF I HAD THAT, I COULD MAKE THE SAVE.

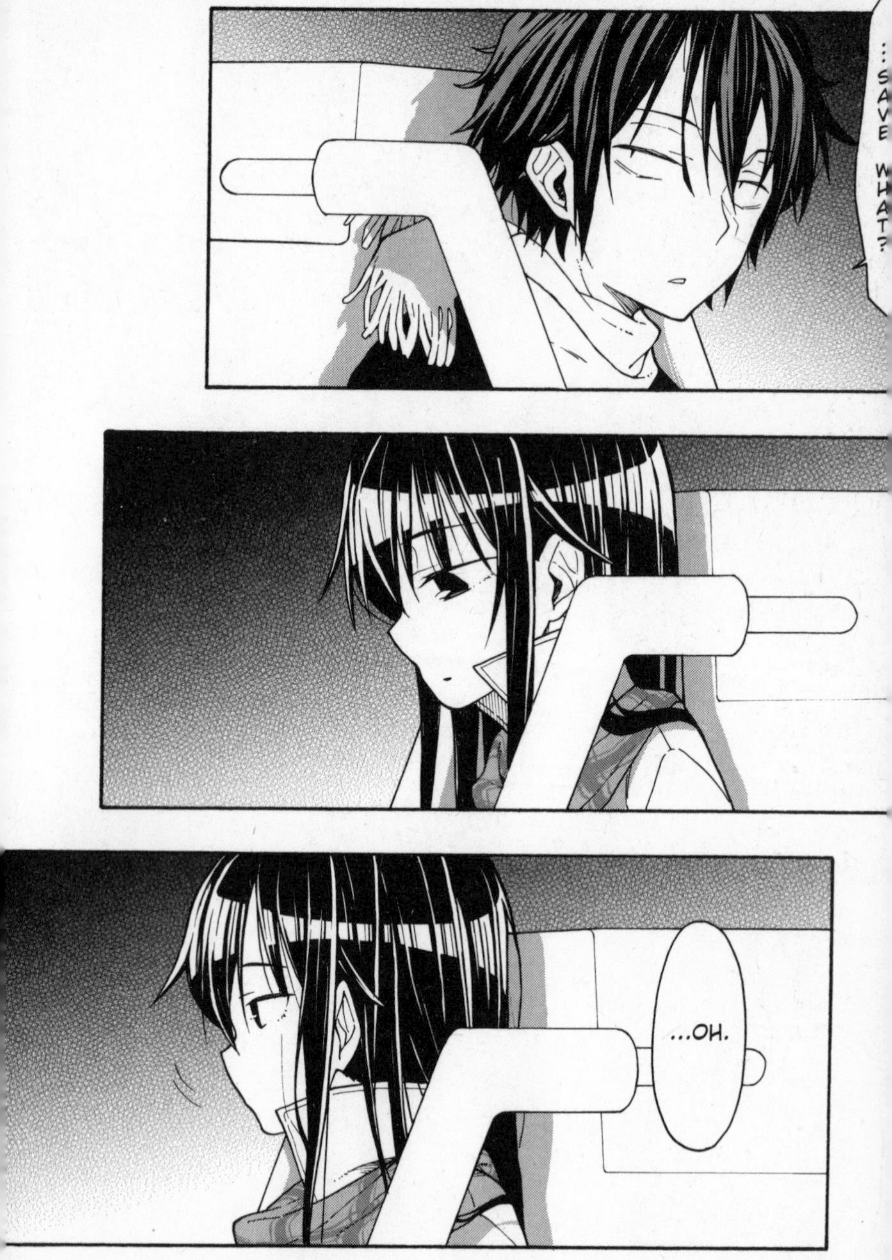
...SAVE WHAT?
...OH.

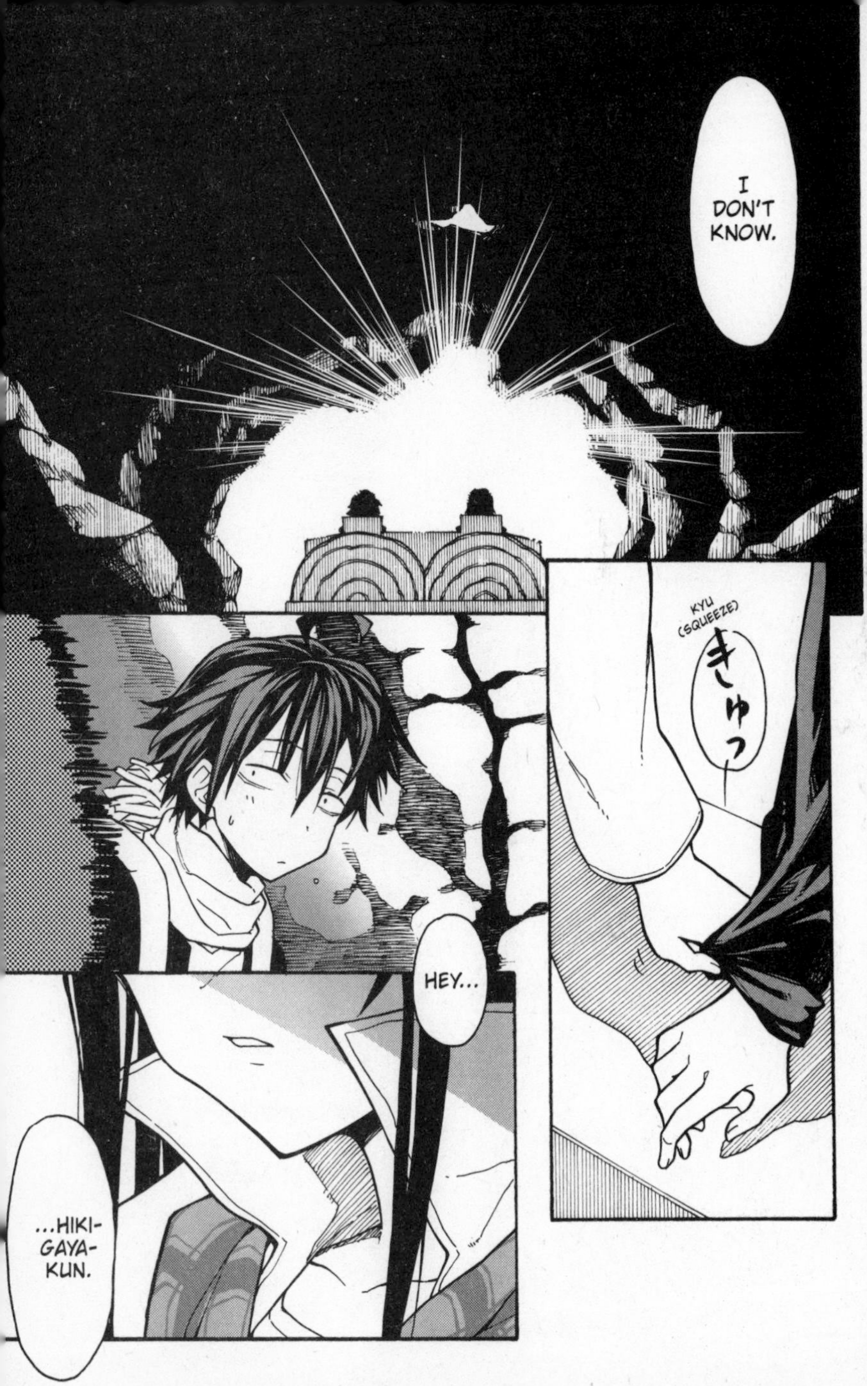
I DON'T KNOW.
KYU (SQUEEZE)
きゅっ
HEY...
...HIKI-GAYA-KUN.

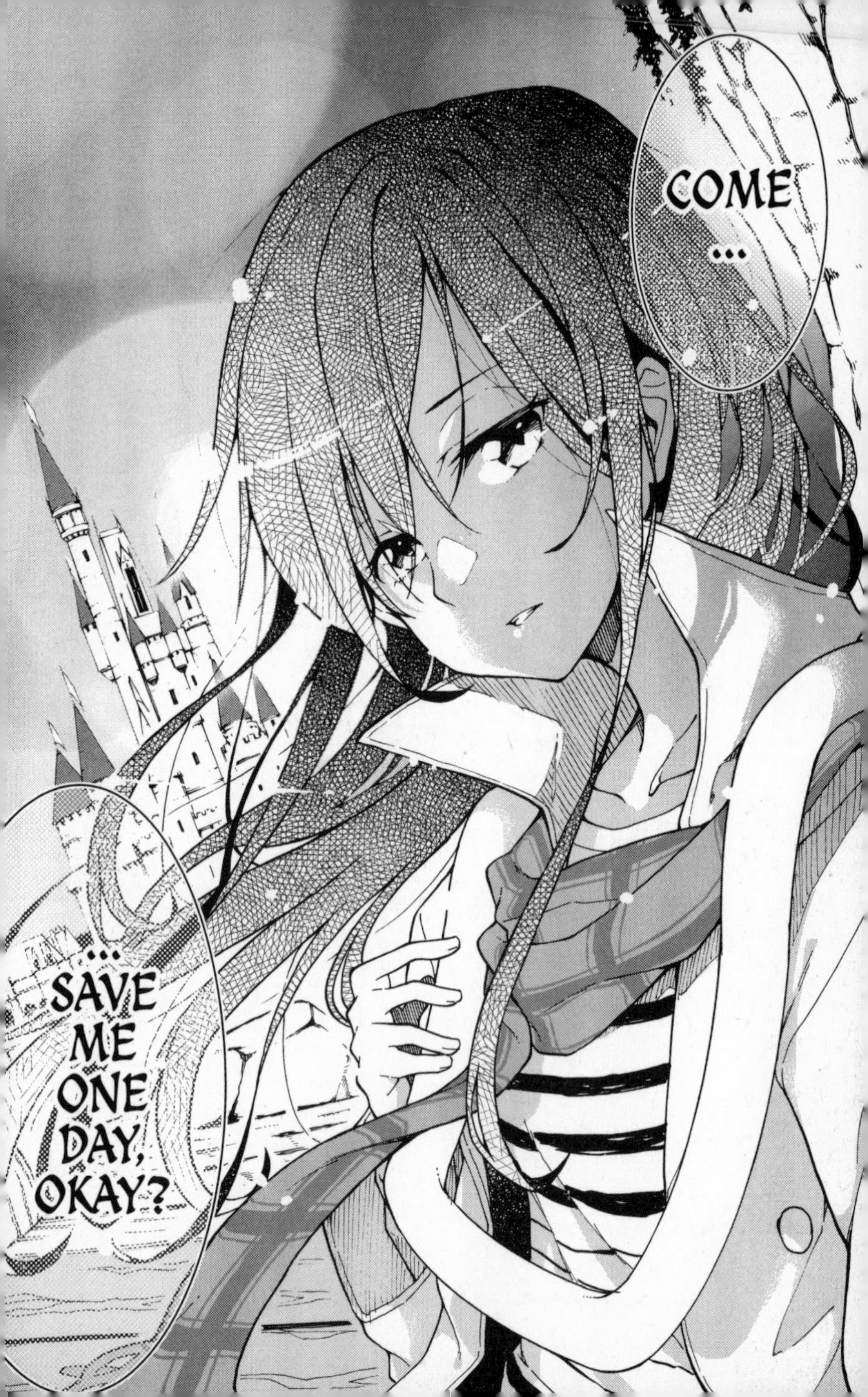
COME...
...SAVE ME ONE DAY, OKAY?

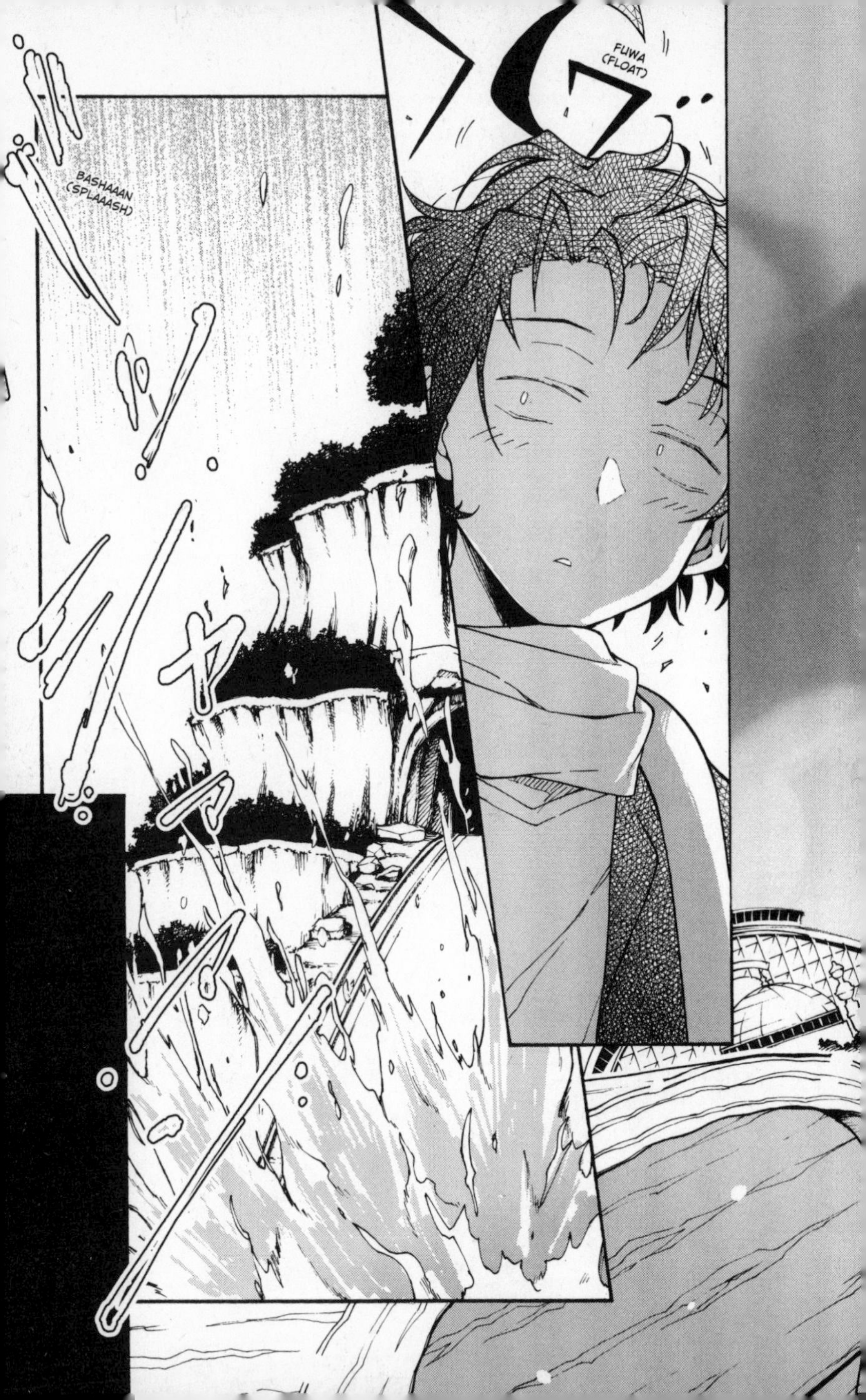
FUWA
(FLOAT)
BASHAAAN
(SPLAAASH)

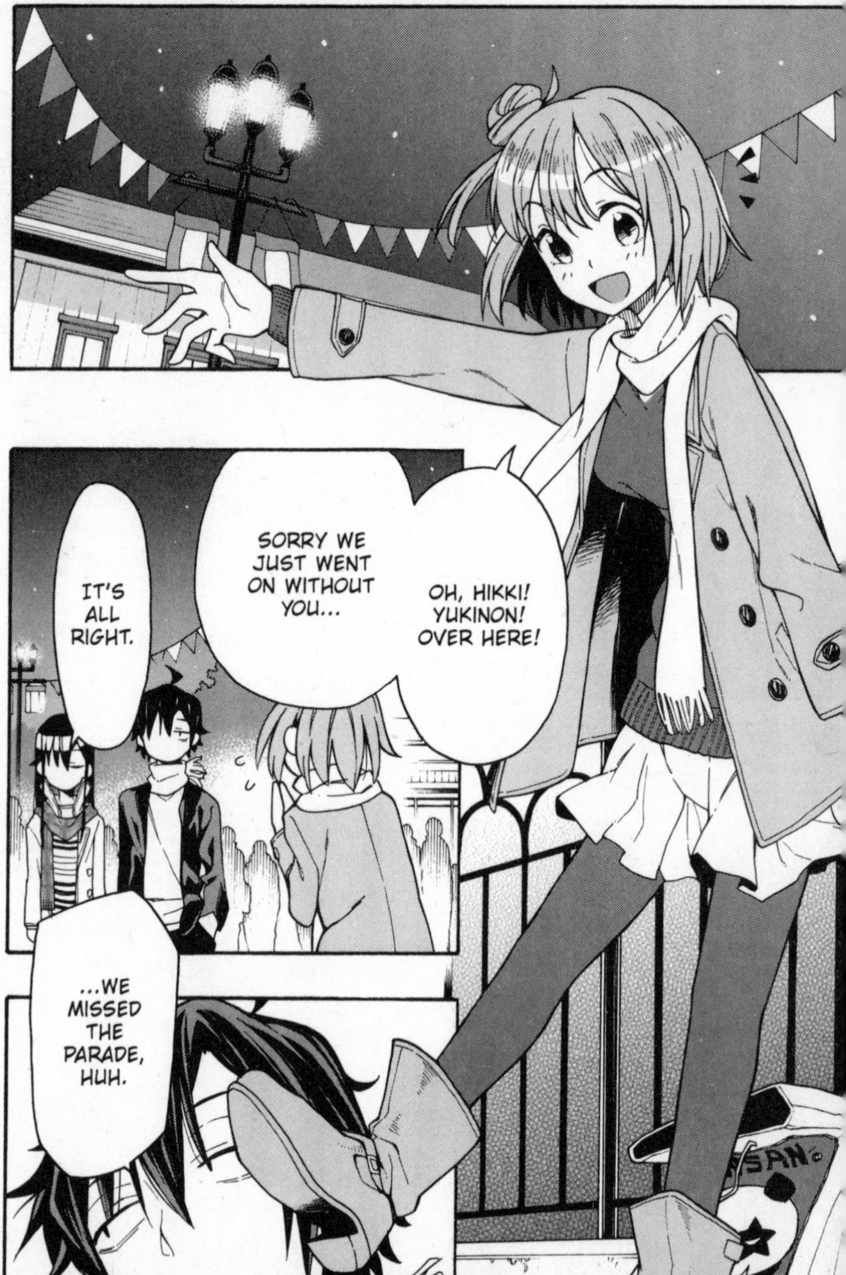
OH, HIKKI! YUKINON! OVER HERE!
SORRY WE JUST WENT ON WITHOUT YOU...
IT'S ALL RIGHT.
...WE MISSED THE PARADE, HUH.

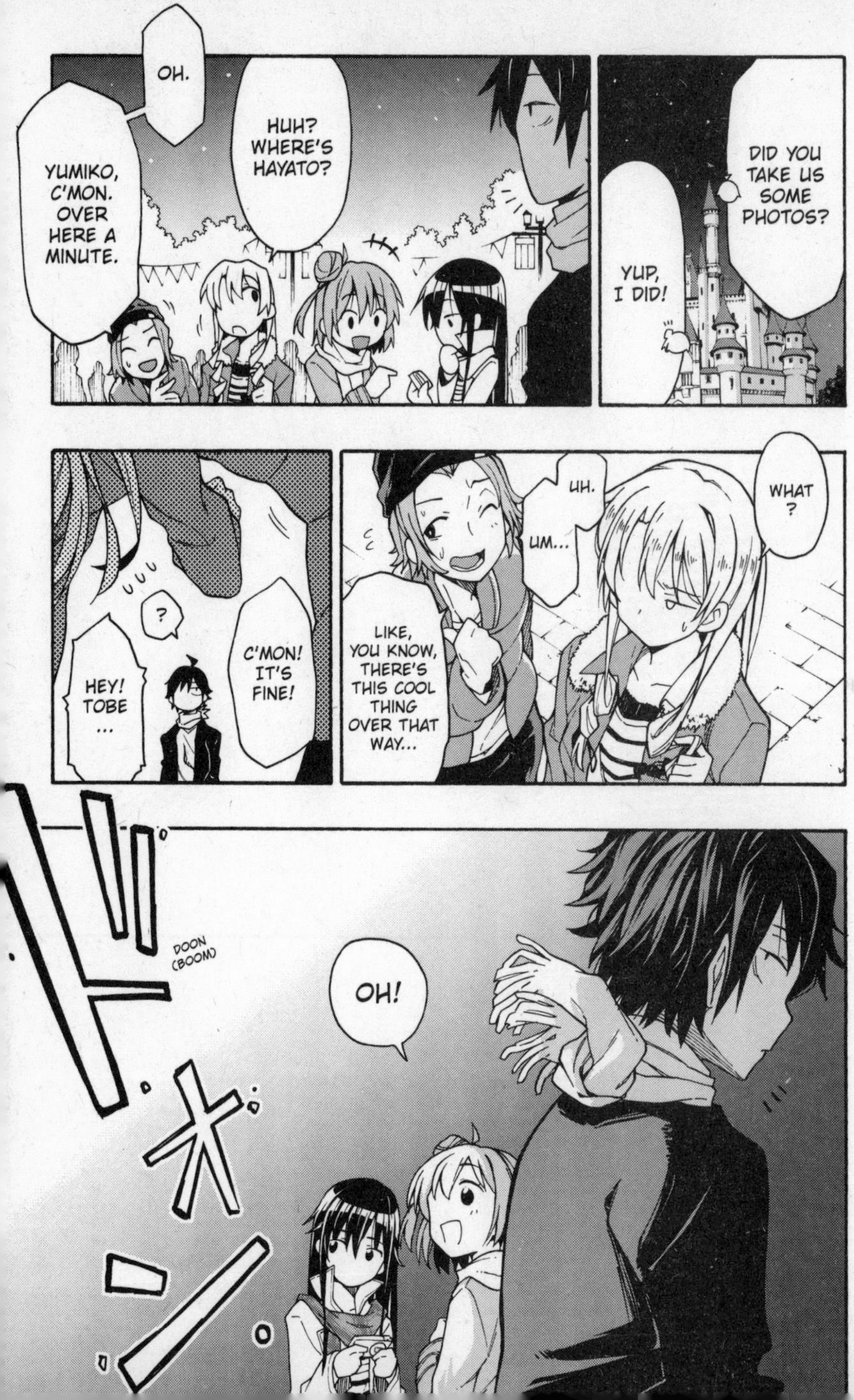
DID YOU TAKE US SOME PHOTOS?
YUP, I DID!
HUH? WHERE'S HAYATO?
OH.
YUMIKO, C'MON. OVER HERE A MINUTE.
WHAT?
UH.
UM...
LIKE, YOU KNOW, THERE'S THIS COOL THING OVER THAT WAY...
C'MON! IT'S FINE!
?
HEY! TOBE...
OH!
DOON (BOOM)

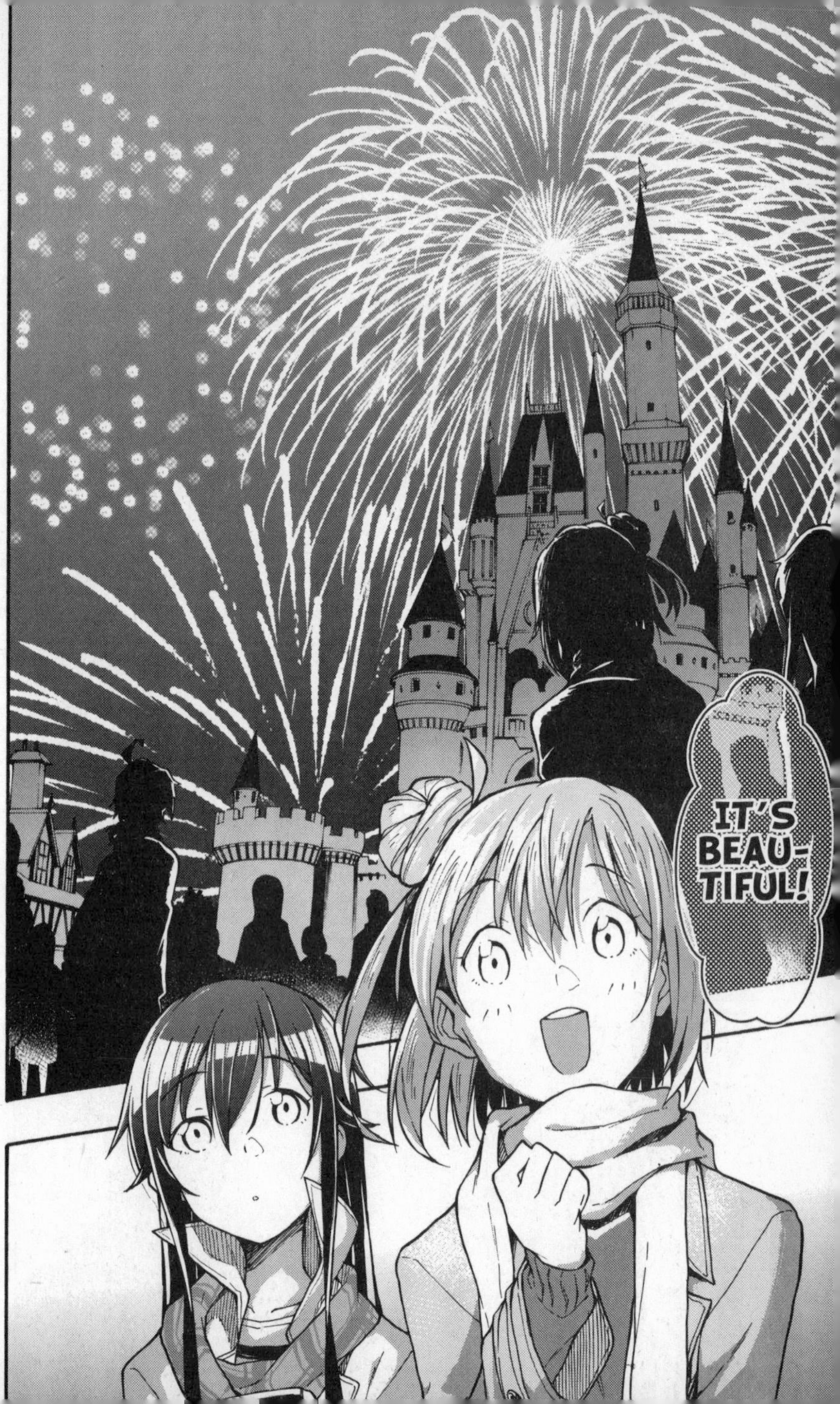
IT'S BEAU-TIFUL!

SHAAAA
(FSHHHHT)

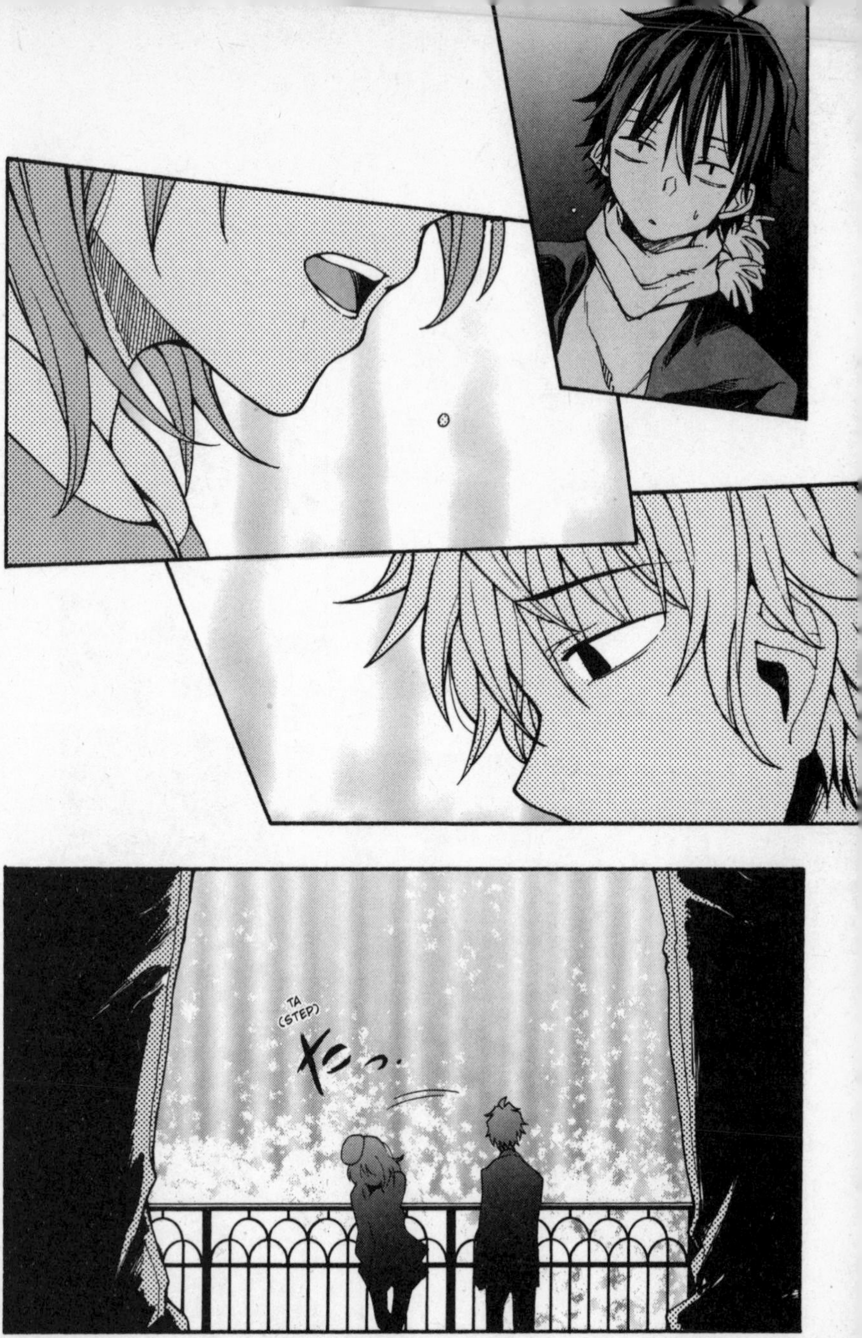
TA
(STEP)
たっ.

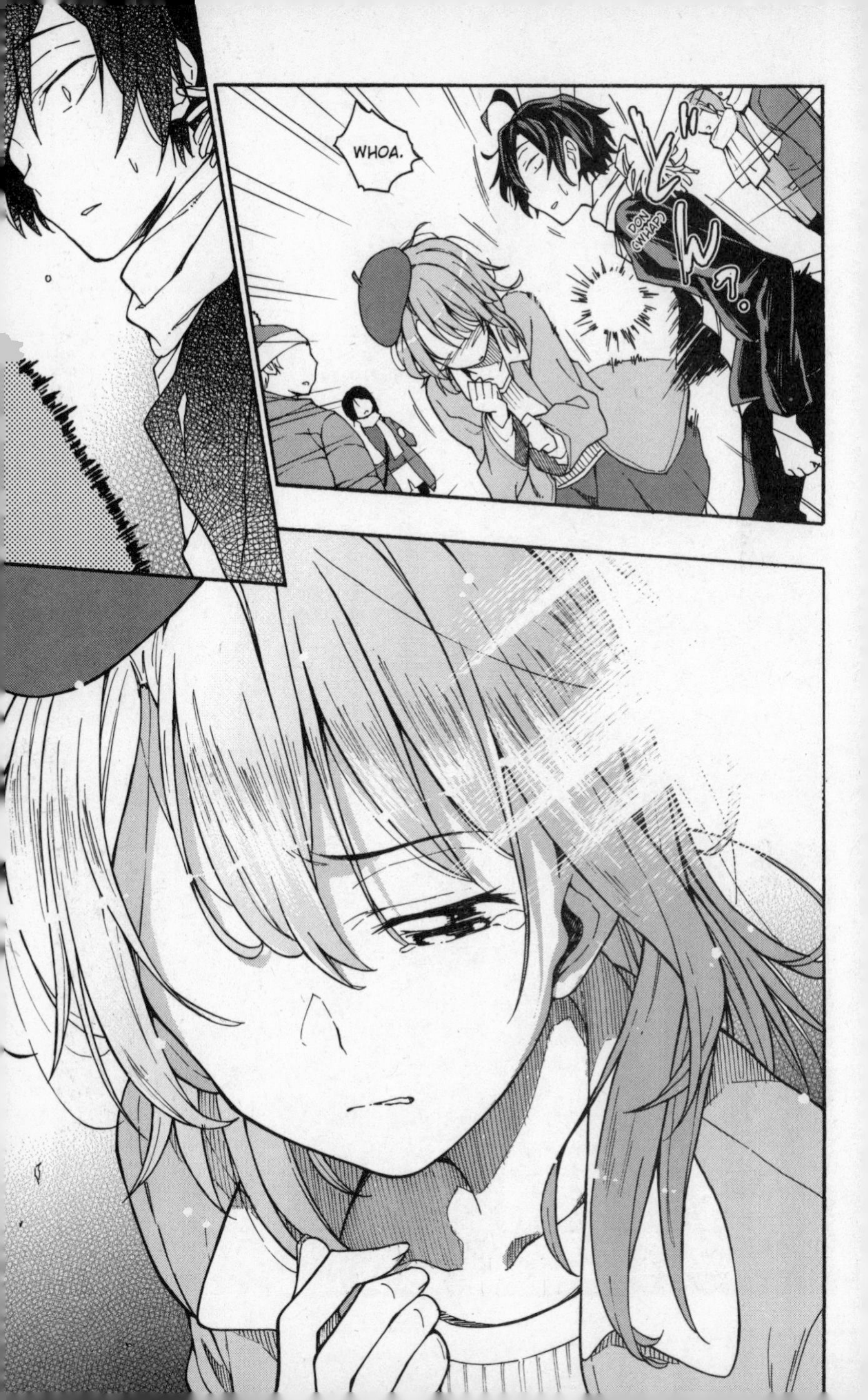
DON (WHAP)
WHOA.

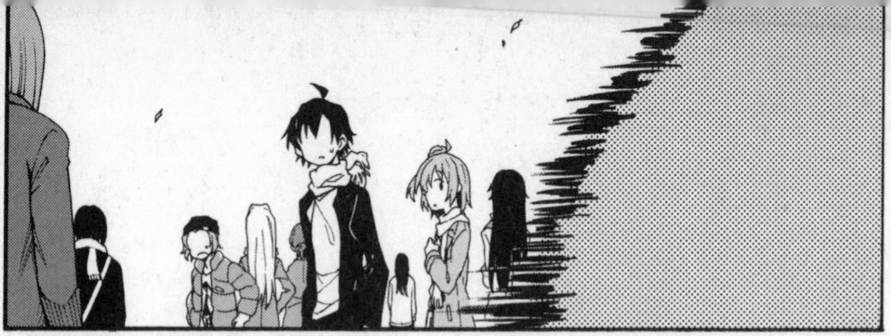

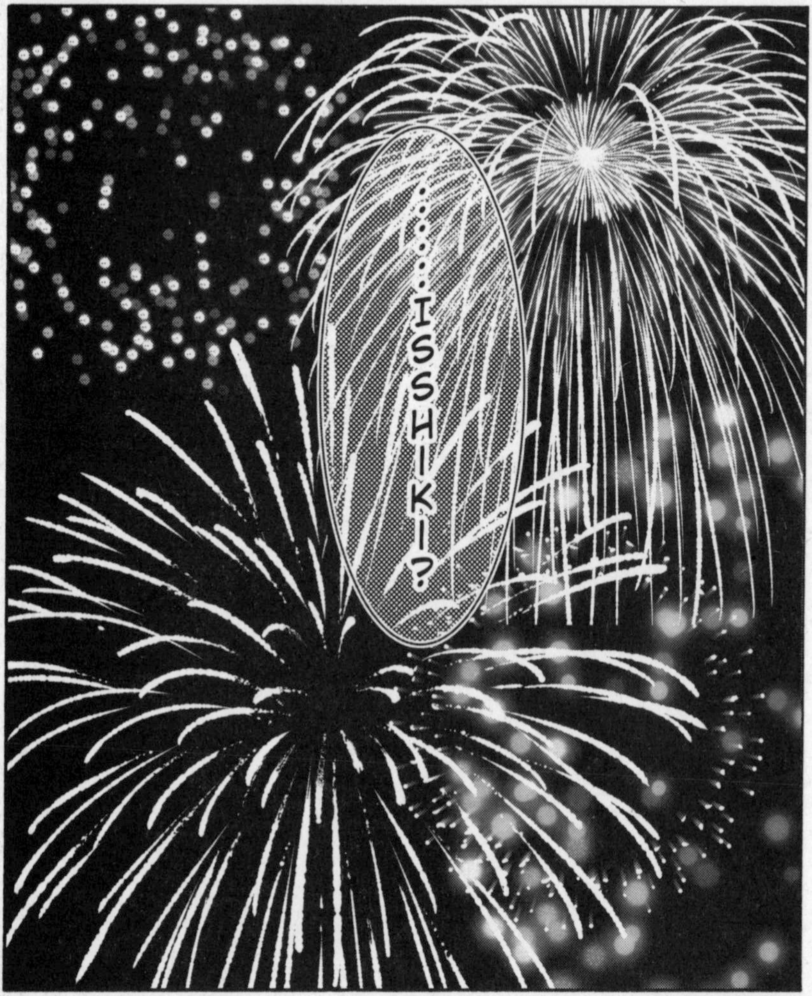
......ISSHIKI?

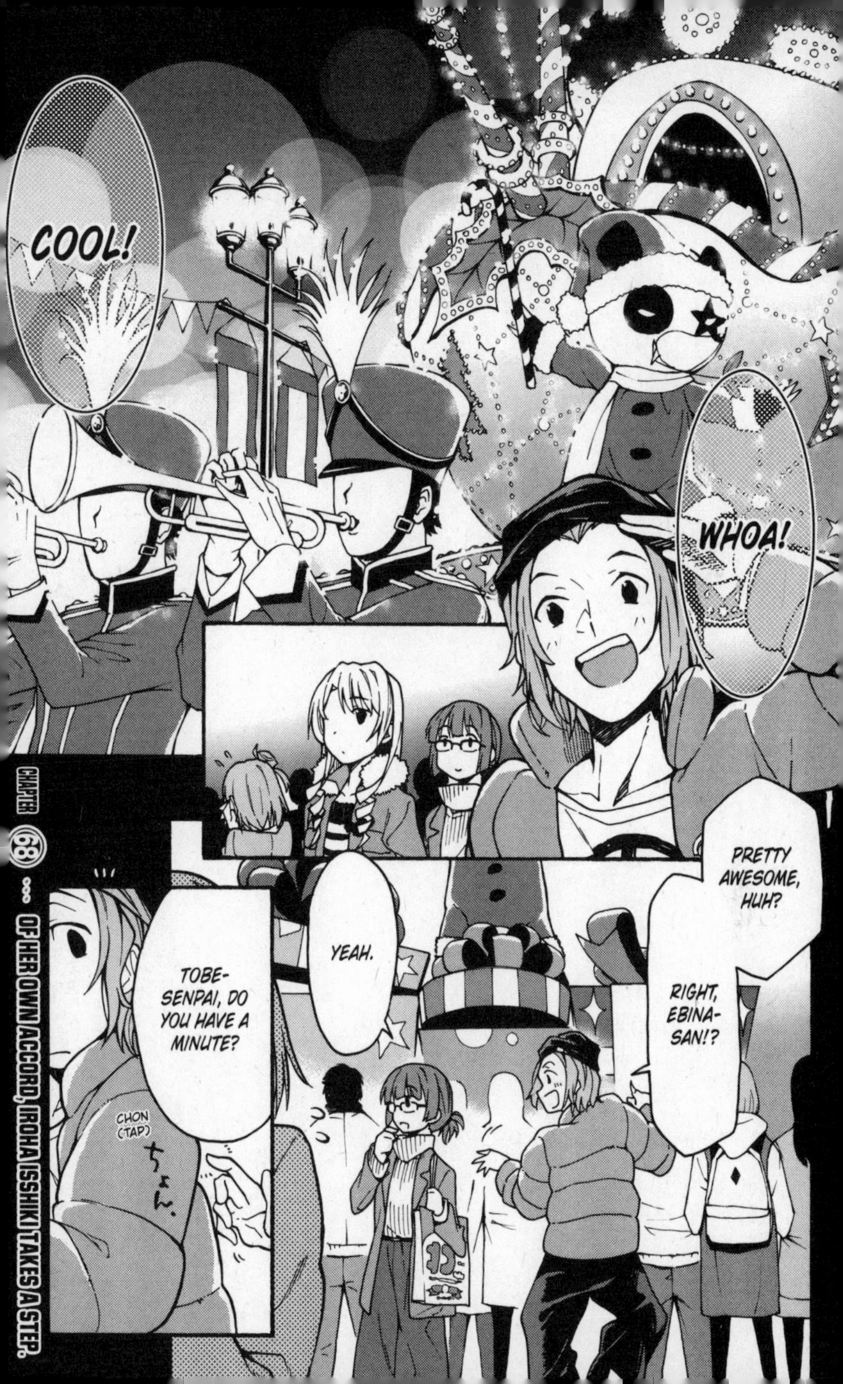

COOL!
WHOA!
PRETTY AWESOME, HUH?
RIGHT, EBINA-SAN!?
YEAH.
TOBE-SENPAI, DO YOU HAVE A MINUTE?
CHON (TAP)
ちょん。
CHAPTER 68 ... OF HER OWN ACCORD, IROHA ISSHIKI TAKES A STEP.

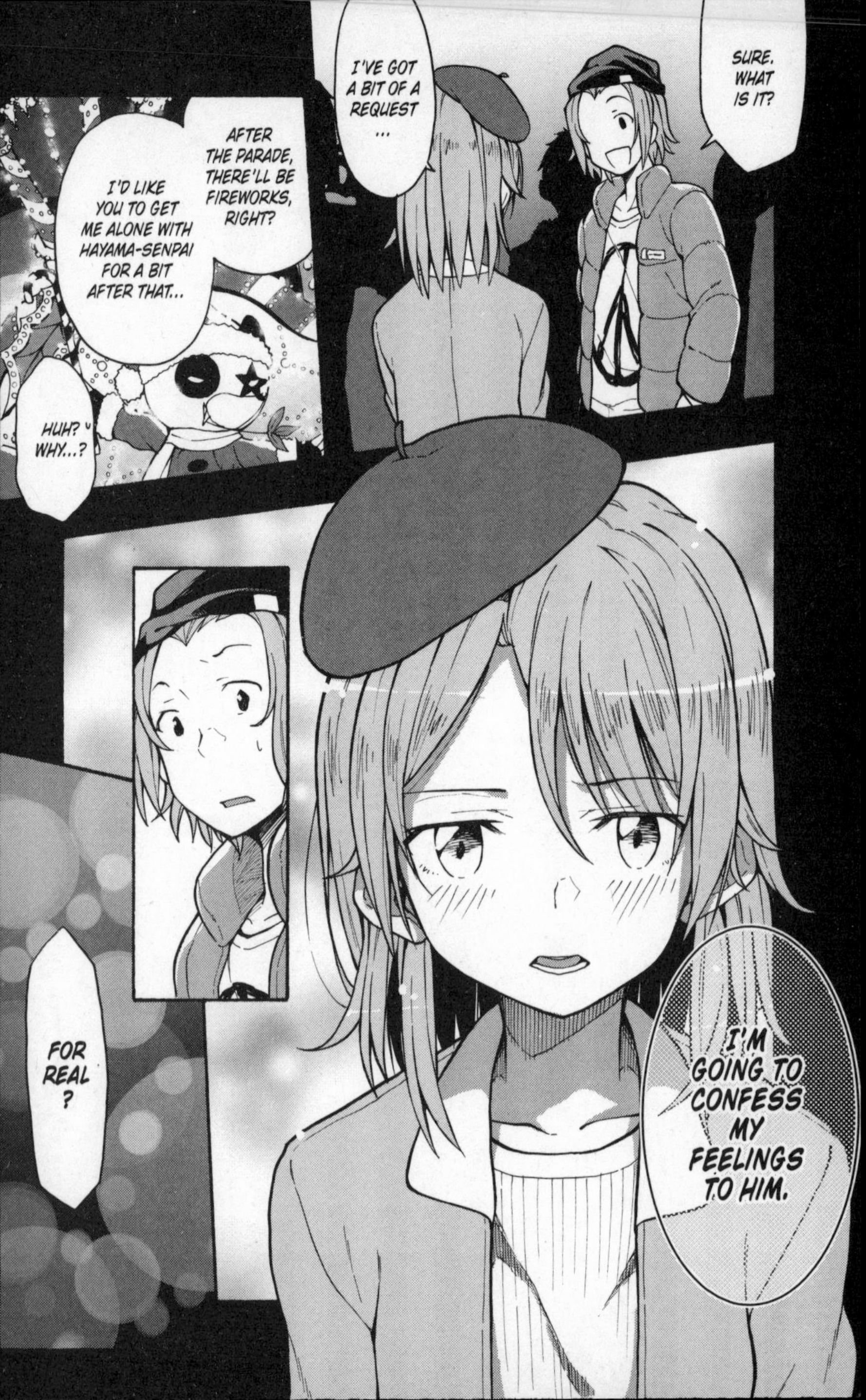
SURE. WHAT IS IT?
I'VE GOT A BIT OF A REQUEST ...
AFTER THE PARADE, THERE'LL BE FIREWORKS, RIGHT?
I'D LIKE YOU TO GET ME ALONE WITH HAYAMA-SENPAI FOR A BIT AFTER THAT...
HUH? WHY...?
I'M GOING TO CONFESS MY FEELINGS TO HIM.
FOR REAL?

CHAPTER 68 … OF HER OWN ACCORD, IROHA ISSHIKI TAKES A STEP.

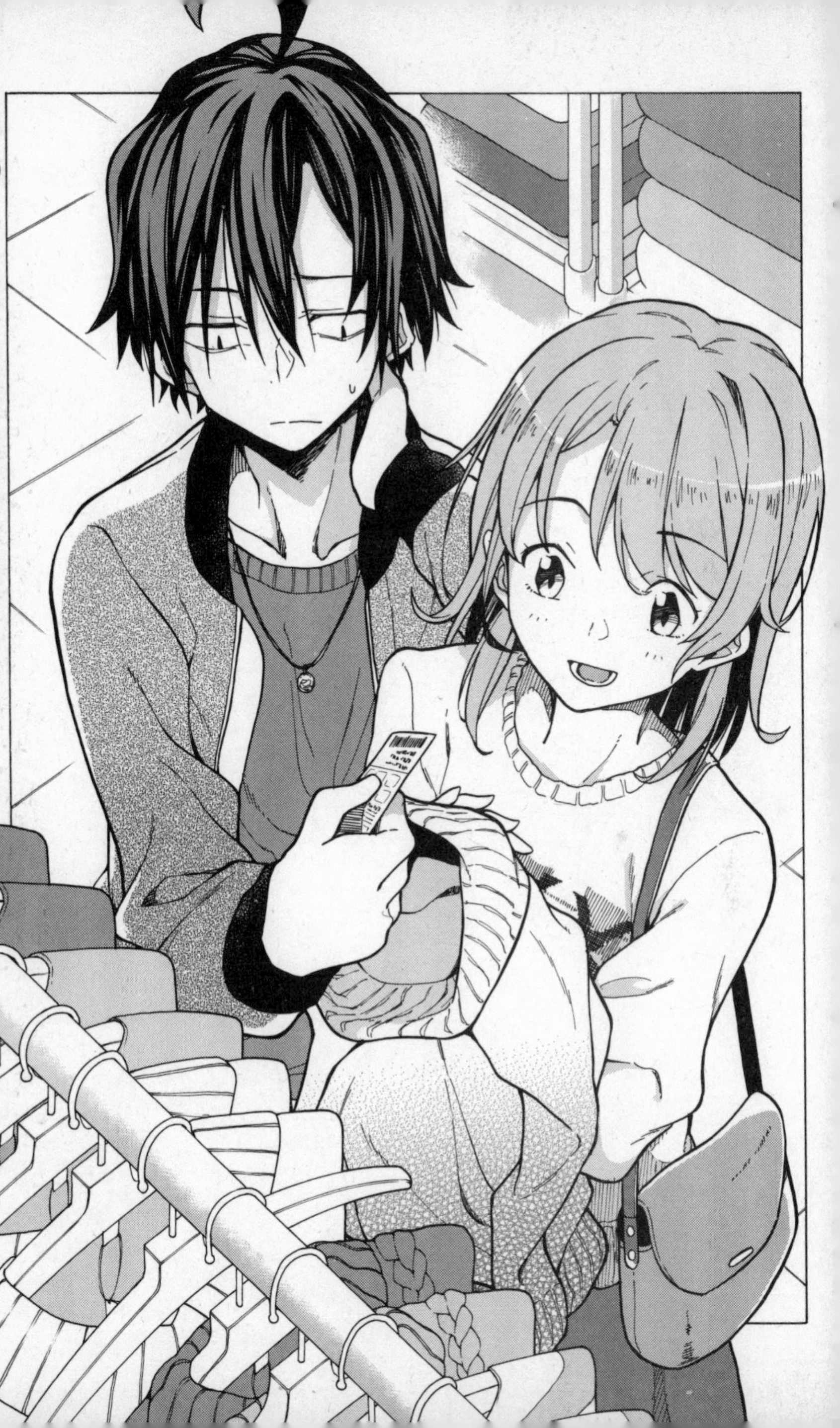

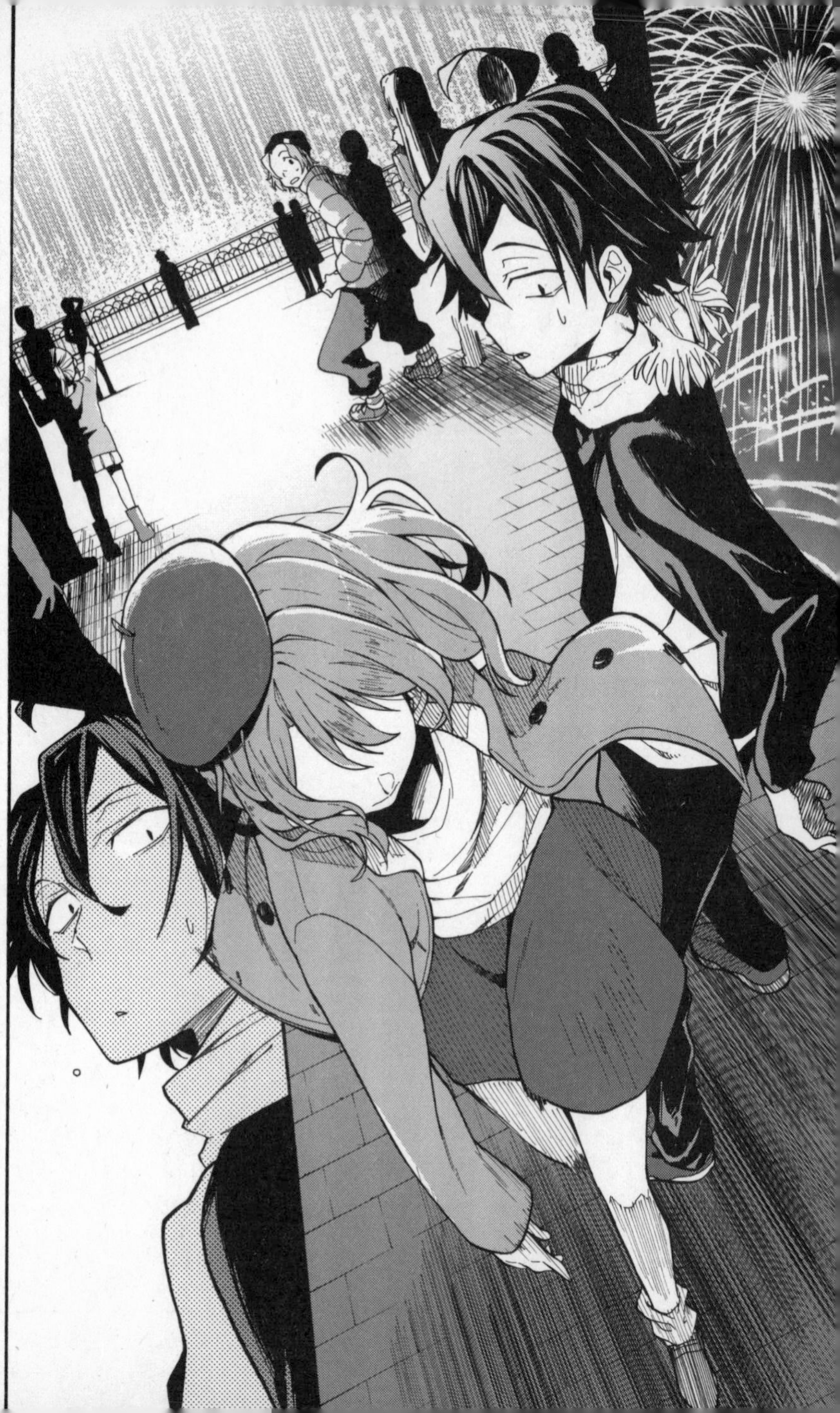

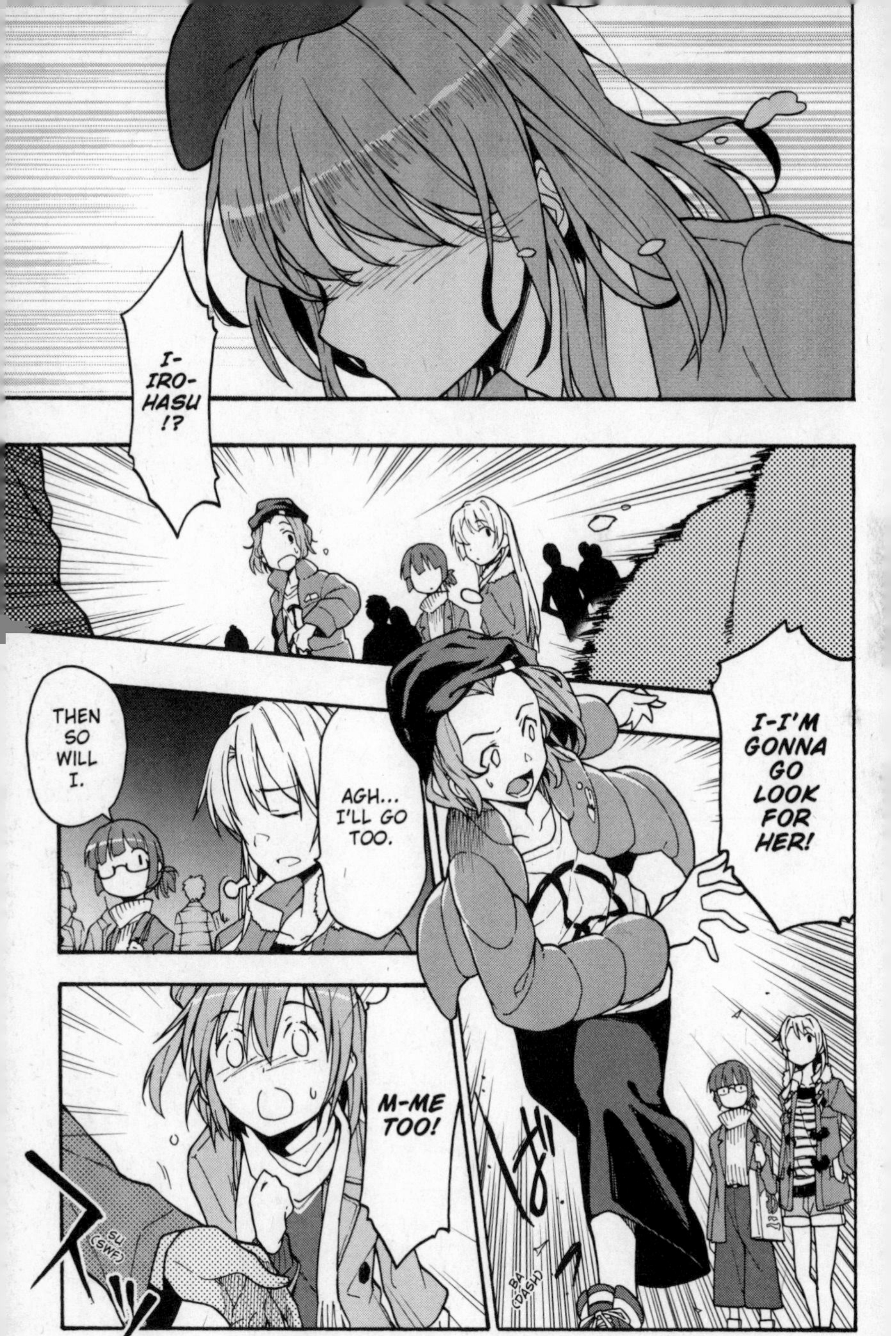
I-IRO-HASU!?
I-I'M GONNA GO LOOK FOR HER!
AGH... I'LL GO TOO.
THEN SO WILL I.
BA (DASH)
M-ME TOO!
SU (SWF)

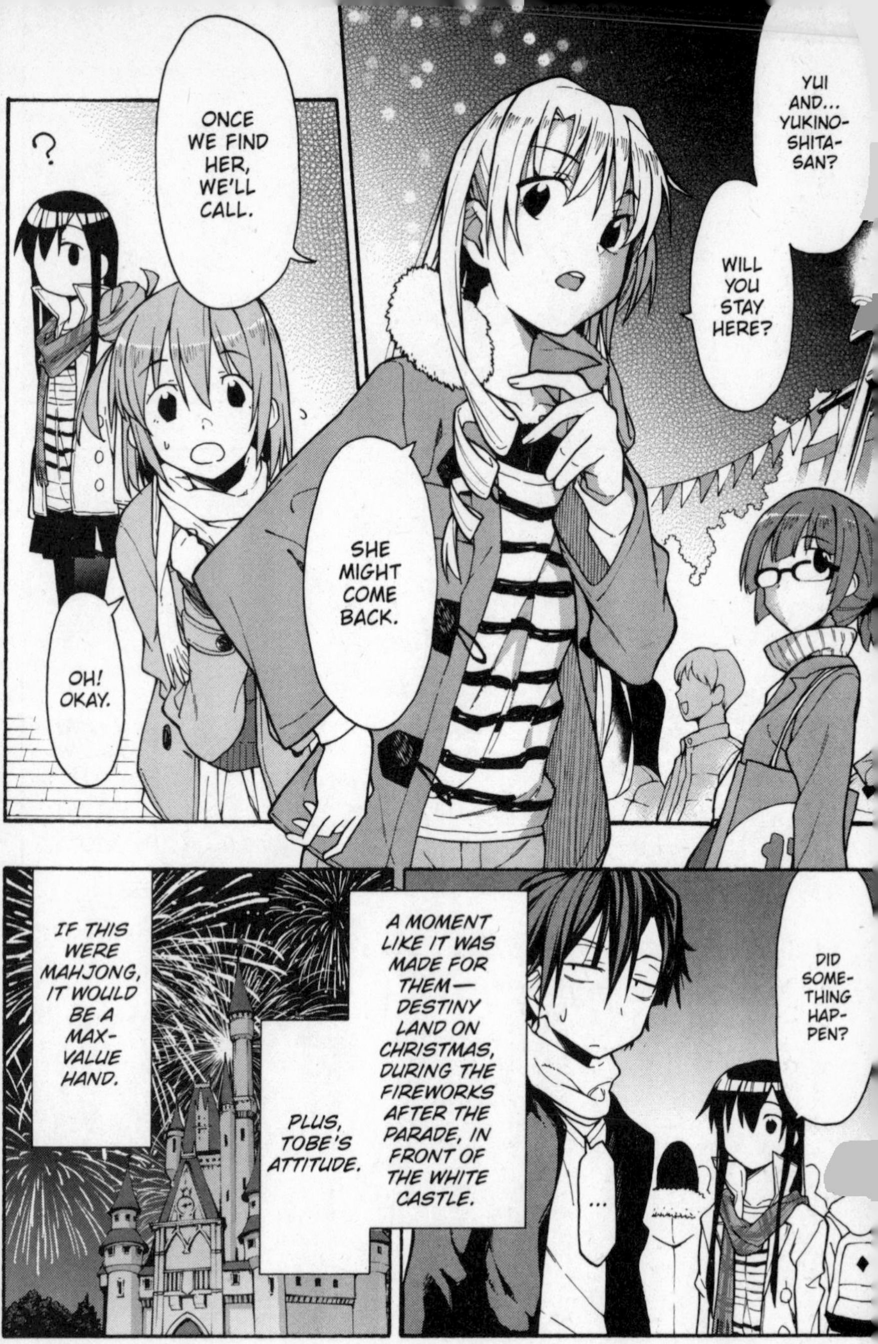
YUI AND... YUKINO-SHITA-SAN?
WILL YOU STAY HERE?
ONCE WE FIND HER, WE'LL CALL.
SHE MIGHT COME BACK.
?
OH! OKAY.
DID SOME-THING HAP-PEN?
...
A MOMENT LIKE IT WAS MADE FOR THEM—DESTINY LAND ON CHRISTMAS, DURING THE FIREWORKS AFTER THE PARADE, IN FRONT OF THE WHITE CASTLE.
PLUS, TOBE'S ATTITUDE.
IF THIS WERE MAHJONG, IT WOULD BE A MAX-VALUE HAND.

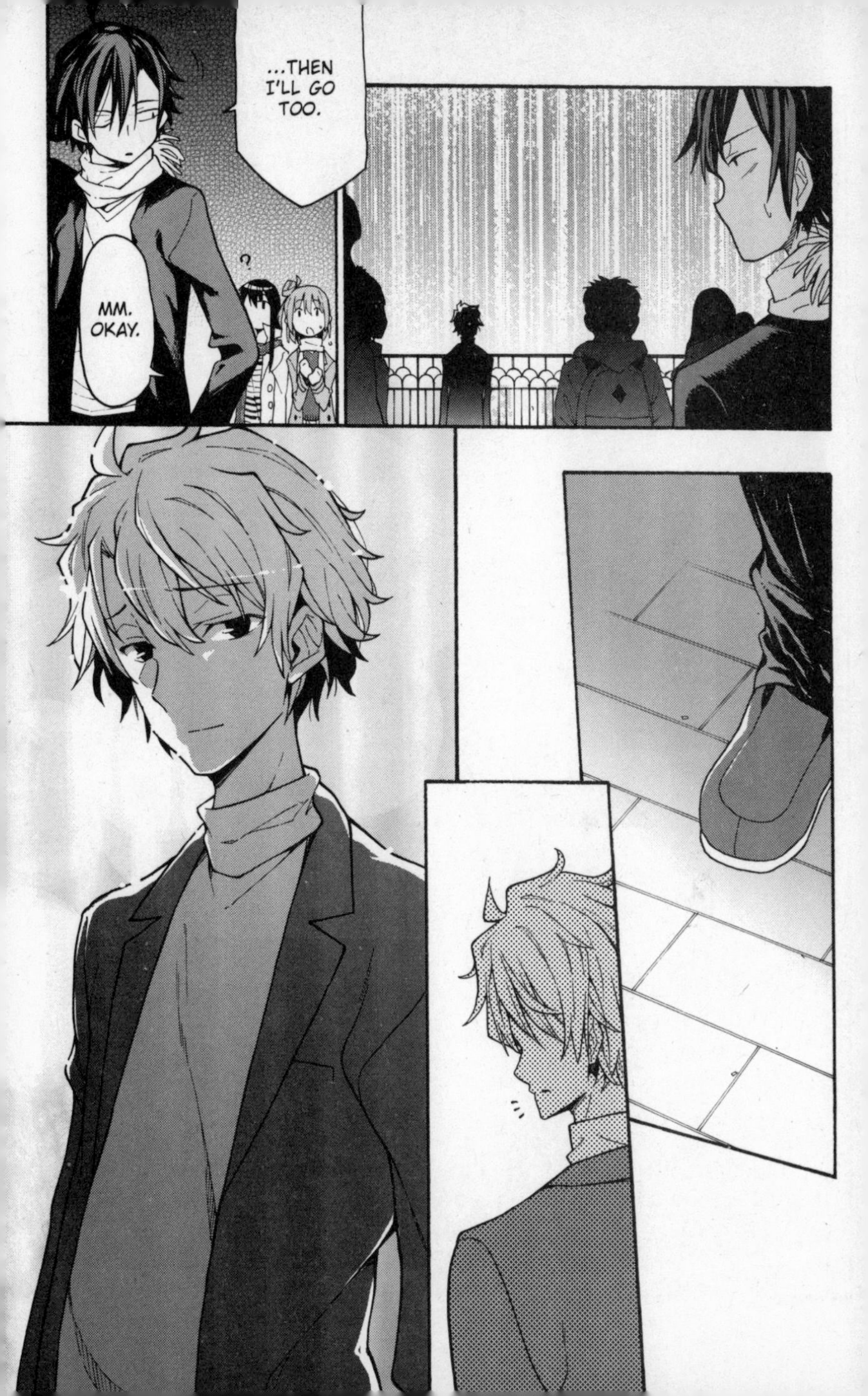
...THEN I'LL GO TOO.
MM. OKAY.
?

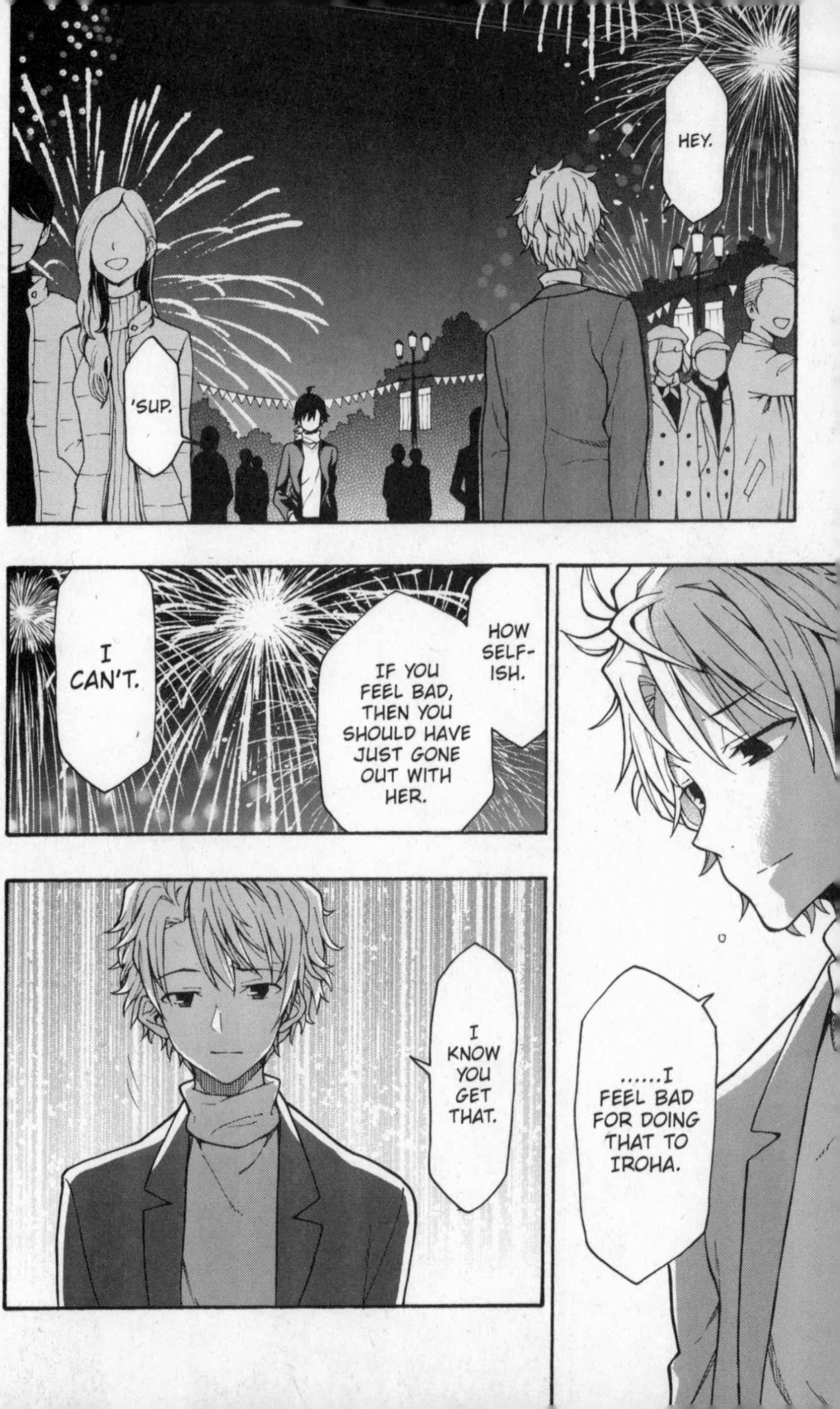
HEY.
'SUP.
......I FEEL BAD FOR DOING THAT TO IROHA.
HOW SELF-ISH.
IF YOU FEEL BAD, THEN YOU SHOULD HAVE JUST GONE OUT WITH HER.
I CAN'T.
I KNOW YOU GET THAT.

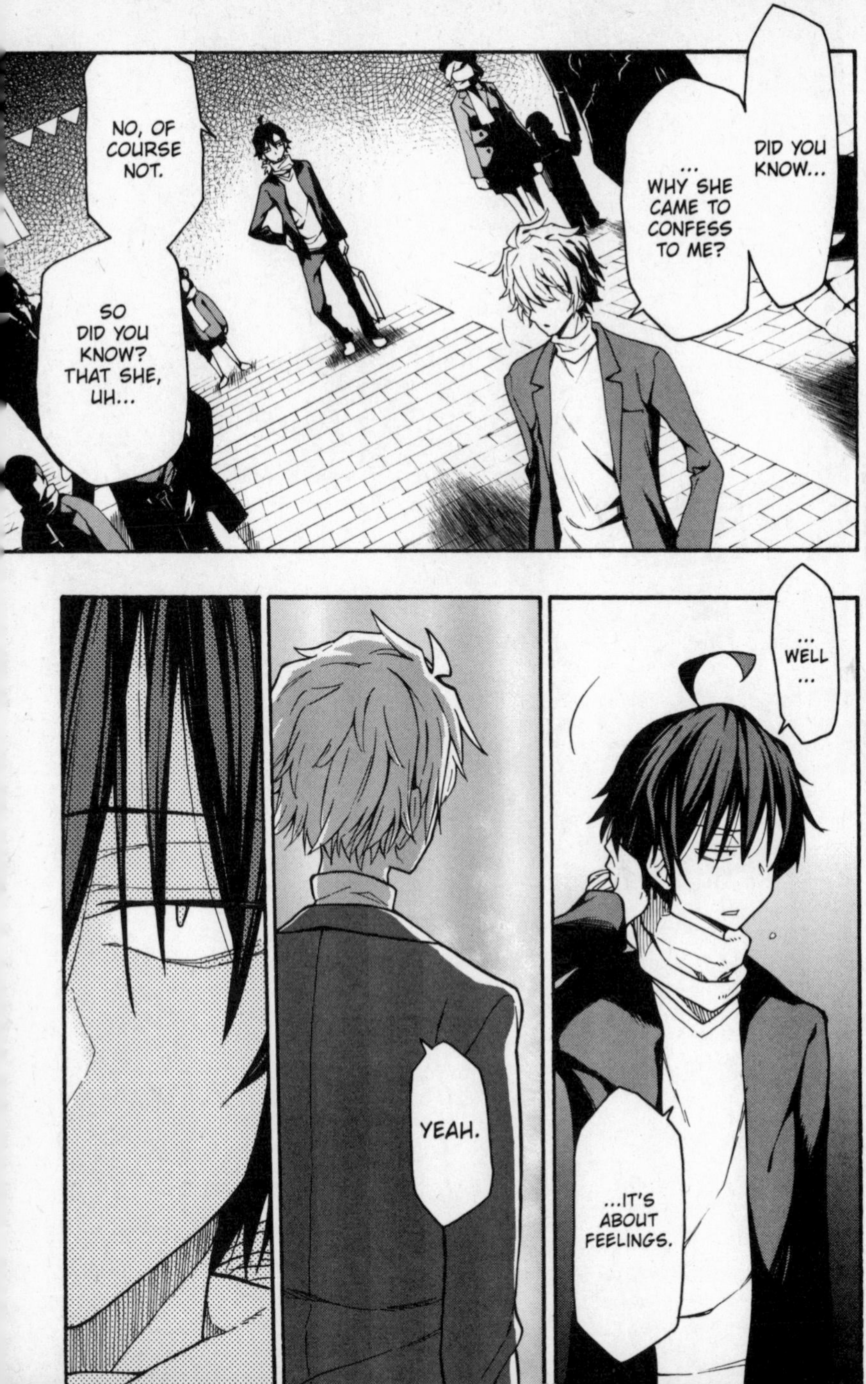
DID YOU KNOW...
... WHY SHE CAME TO CONFESS TO ME?
NO, OF COURSE NOT.
SO DID YOU KNOW? THAT SHE, UH...
... WELL ...
...IT'S ABOUT FEELINGS.
YEAH.

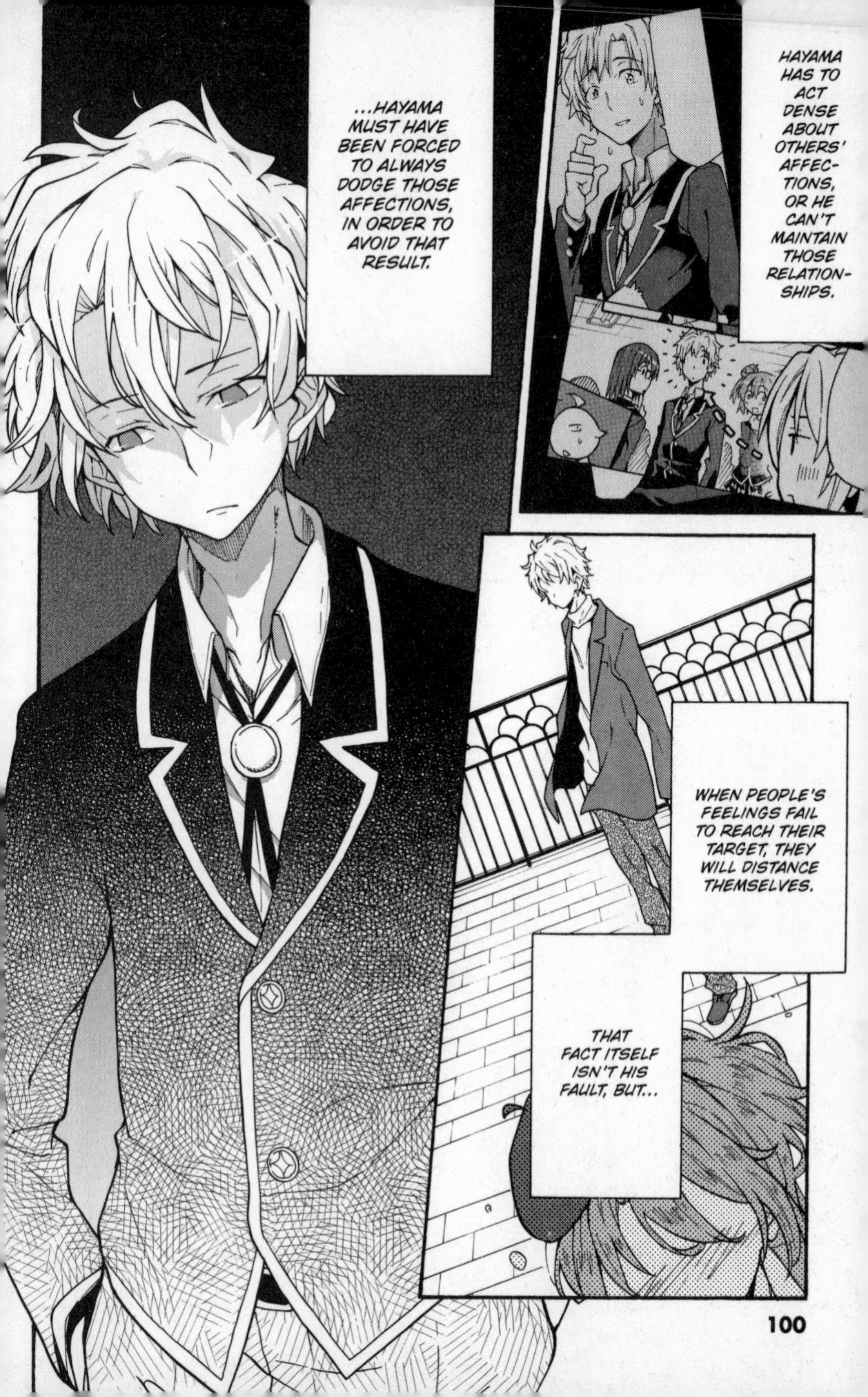
HAYAMA HAS TO ACT DENSE ABOUT OTHERS' AFFECTIONS, OR HE CAN'T MAINTAIN THOSE RELATIONSHIPS.
...HAYAMA MUST HAVE BEEN FORCED TO ALWAYS DODGE THOSE AFFECTIONS, IN ORDER TO AVOID THAT RESULT.
WHEN PEOPLE'S FEELINGS FAIL TO REACH THEIR TARGET, THEY WILL DISTANCE THEMSELVES.
THAT FACT ITSELF ISN'T HIS FAULT, BUT...

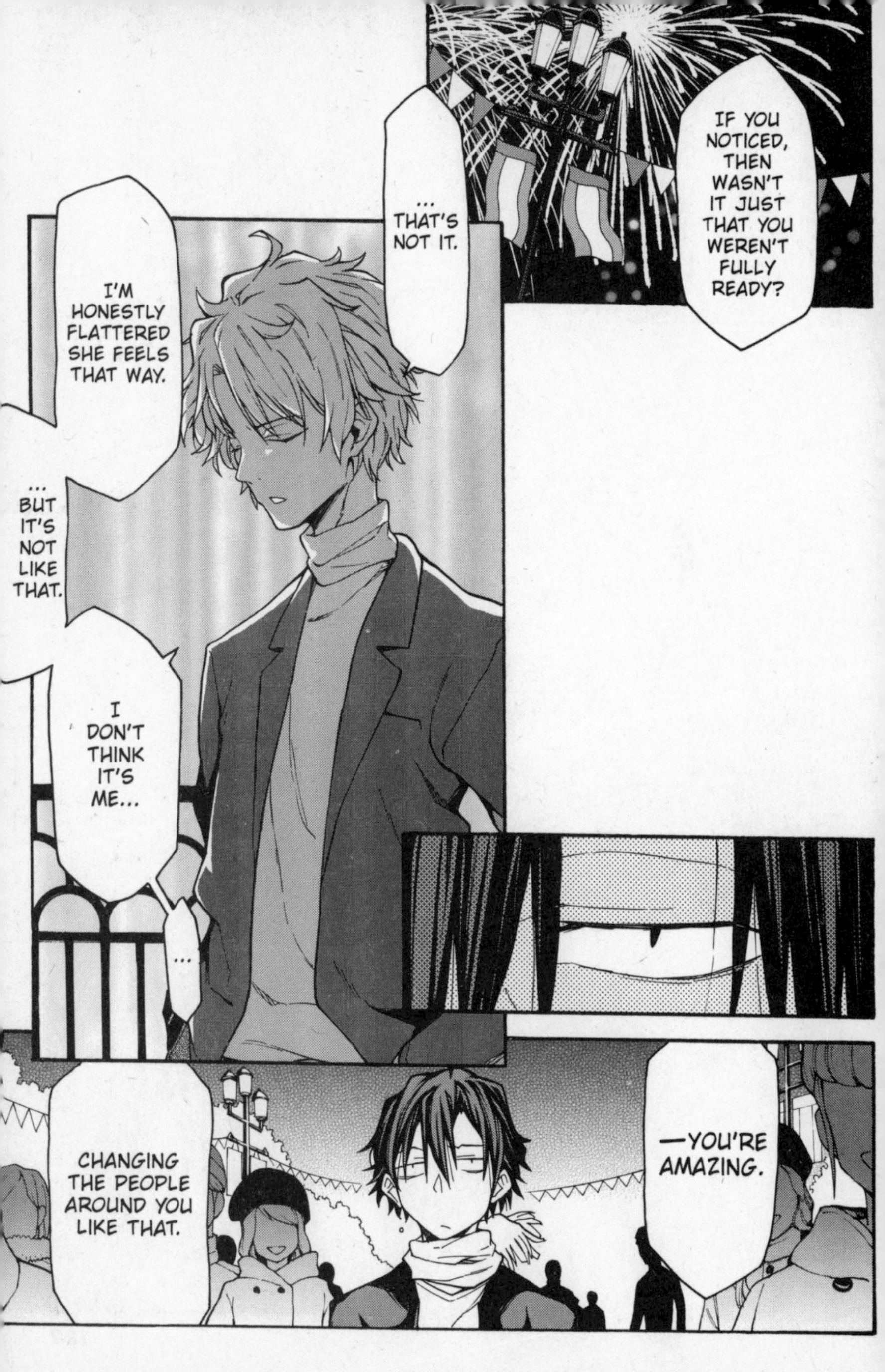
IF YOU NOTICED, THEN WASN'T IT JUST THAT YOU WEREN'T FULLY READY?
... THAT'S NOT IT.
I'M HONESTLY FLATTERED SHE FEELS THAT WAY.
... BUT IT'S NOT LIKE THAT.
I DON'T THINK IT'S ME...
...
—YOU'RE AMAZING.
CHANGING THE PEOPLE AROUND YOU LIKE THAT.

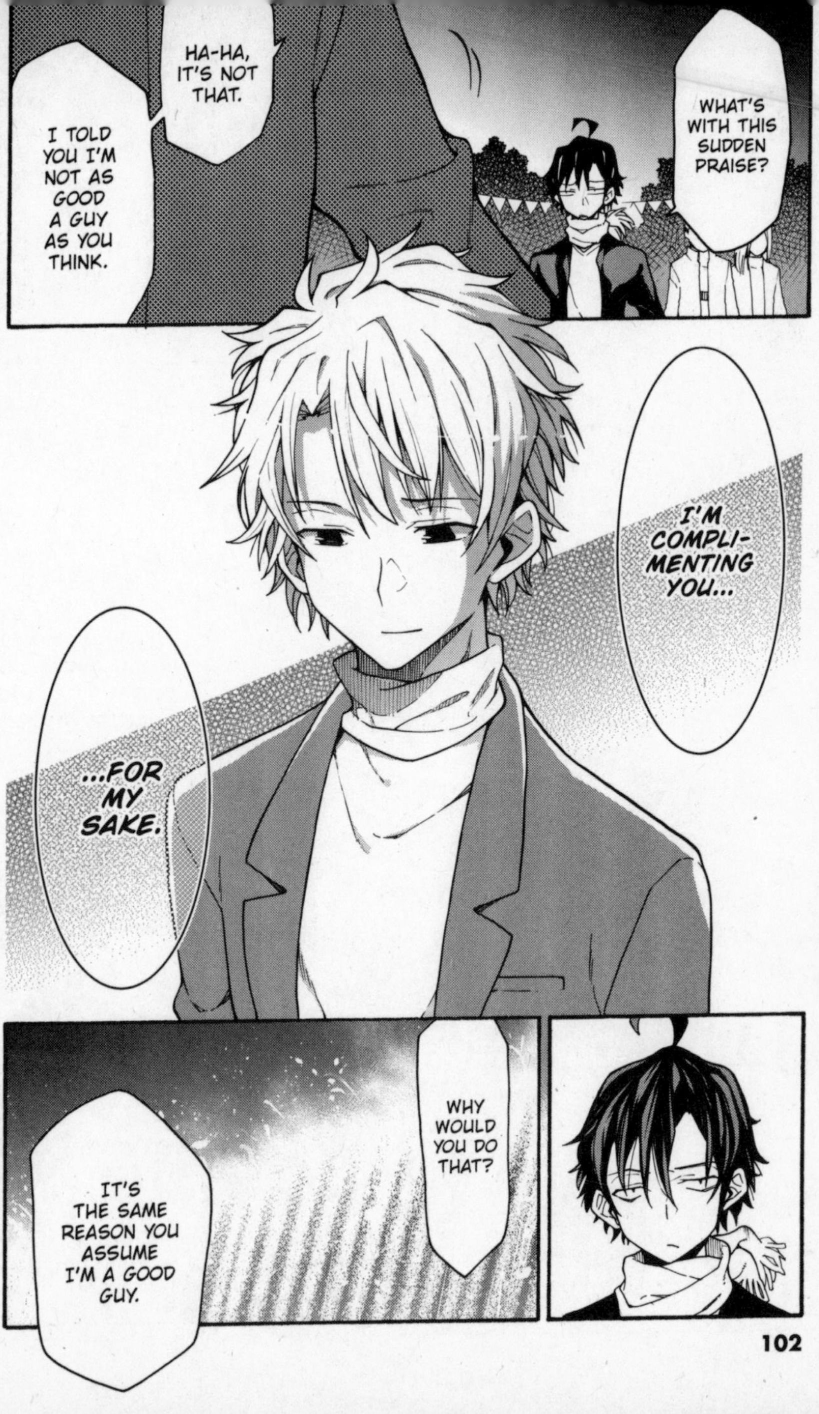
WHAT'S WITH THIS SUDDEN PRAISE?
HA-HA, IT'S NOT THAT.
I TOLD YOU I'M NOT AS GOOD A GUY AS YOU THINK.
I'M COMPLI-MENTING YOU...
...FOR MY SAKE.
WHY WOULD YOU DO THAT?
IT'S THE SAME REASON YOU ASSUME I'M A GOOD GUY.

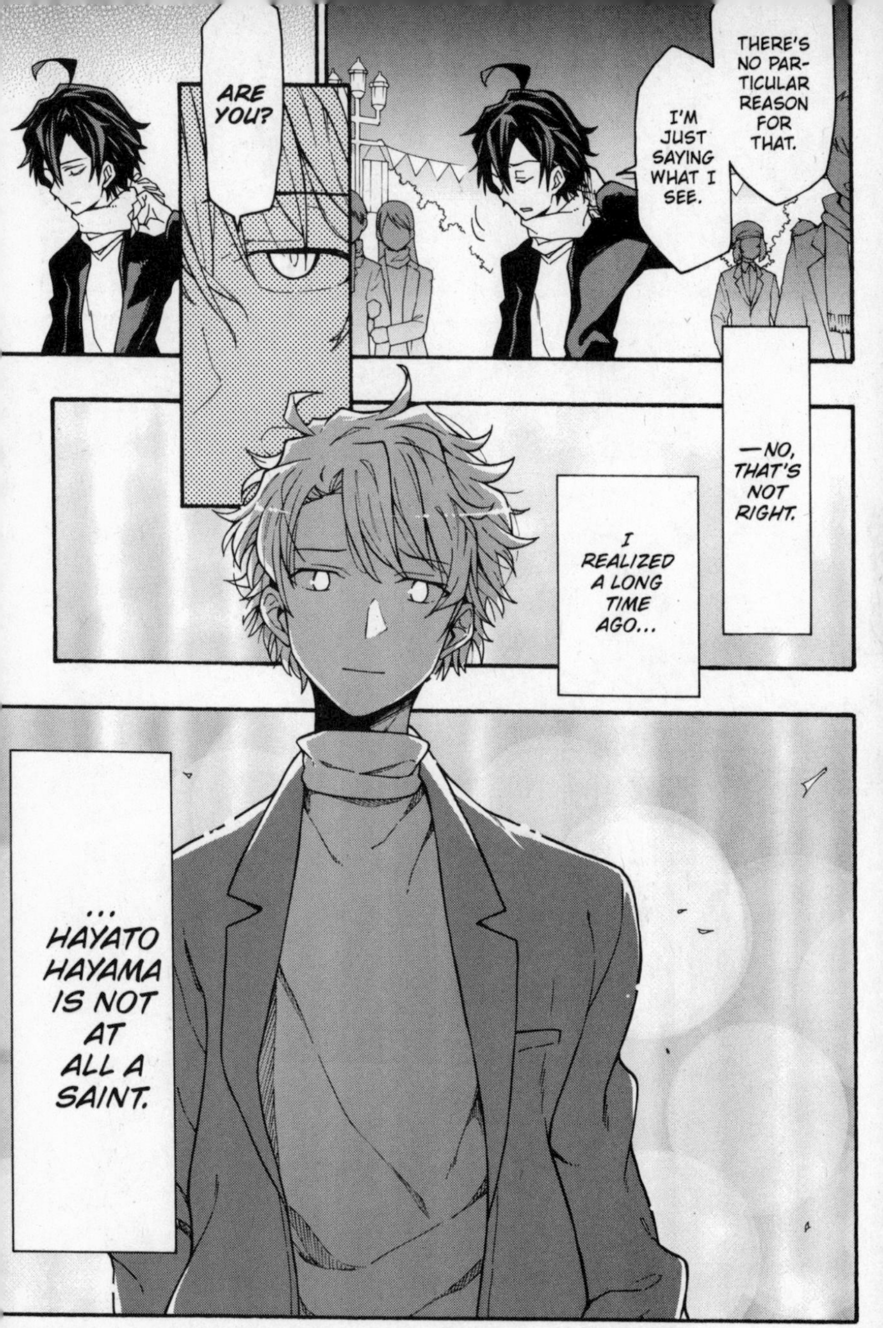
THERE'S NO PARTICULAR REASON FOR THAT.
I'M JUST SAYING WHAT I SEE.
ARE YOU?
—NO, THAT'S NOT RIGHT.
I REALIZED A LONG TIME AGO...
...HAYATO HAYAMA IS NOT AT ALL A SAINT.

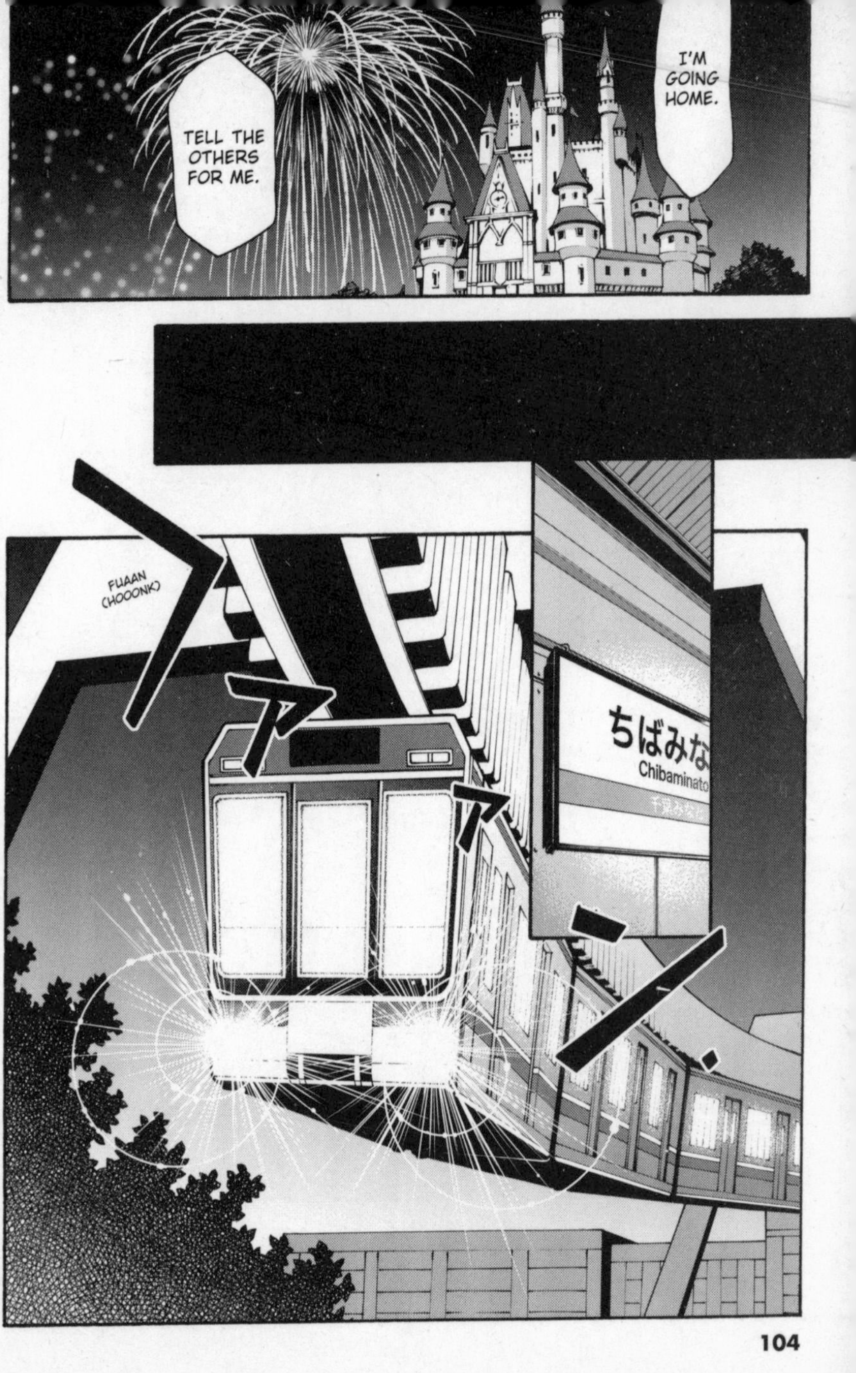
I'M GOING HOME.
TELL THE OTHERS FOR ME.
FUAAN (HOOONK)
ちばみな
Chibaminato

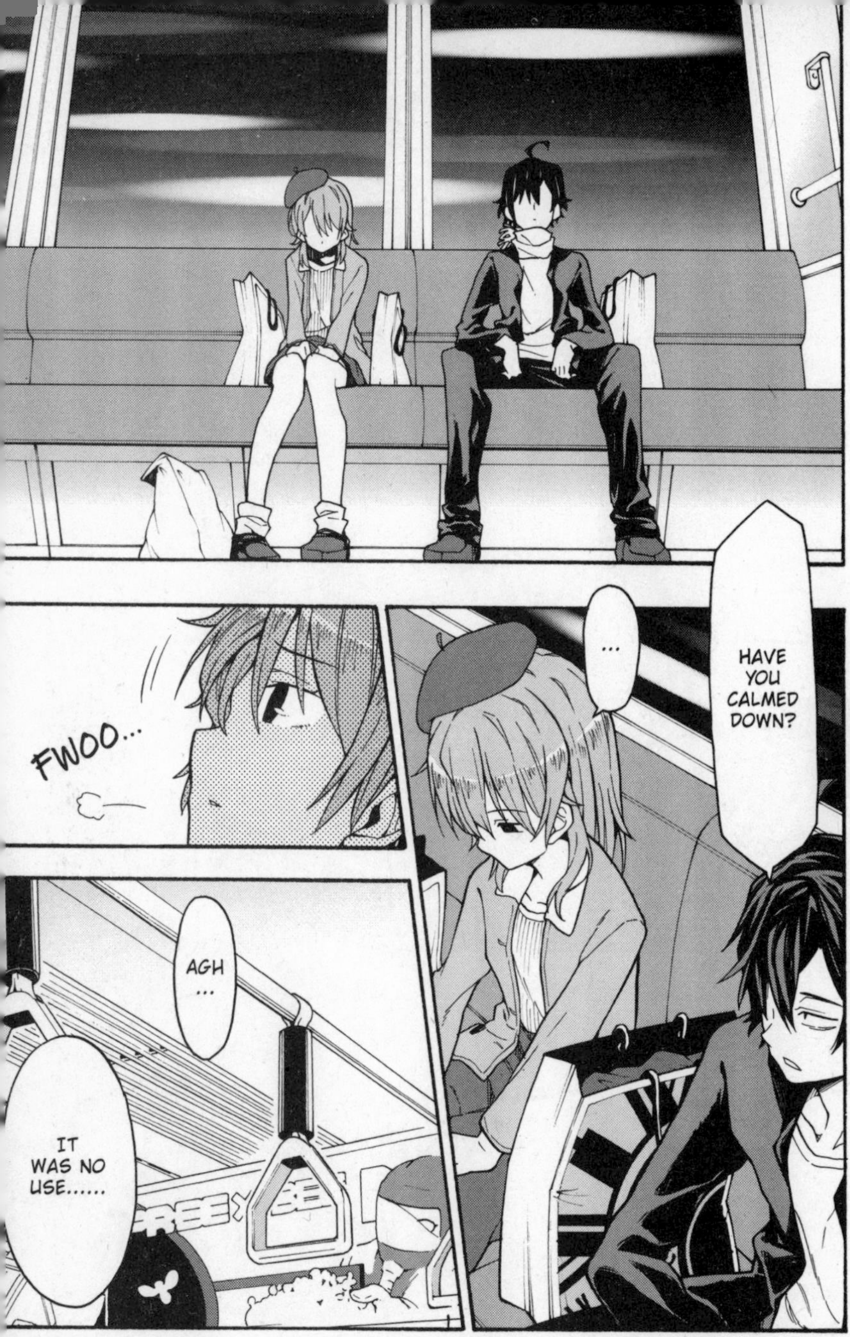
HAVE YOU CALMED DOWN?
...
FWOO...
AGH...
IT WAS NO USE......

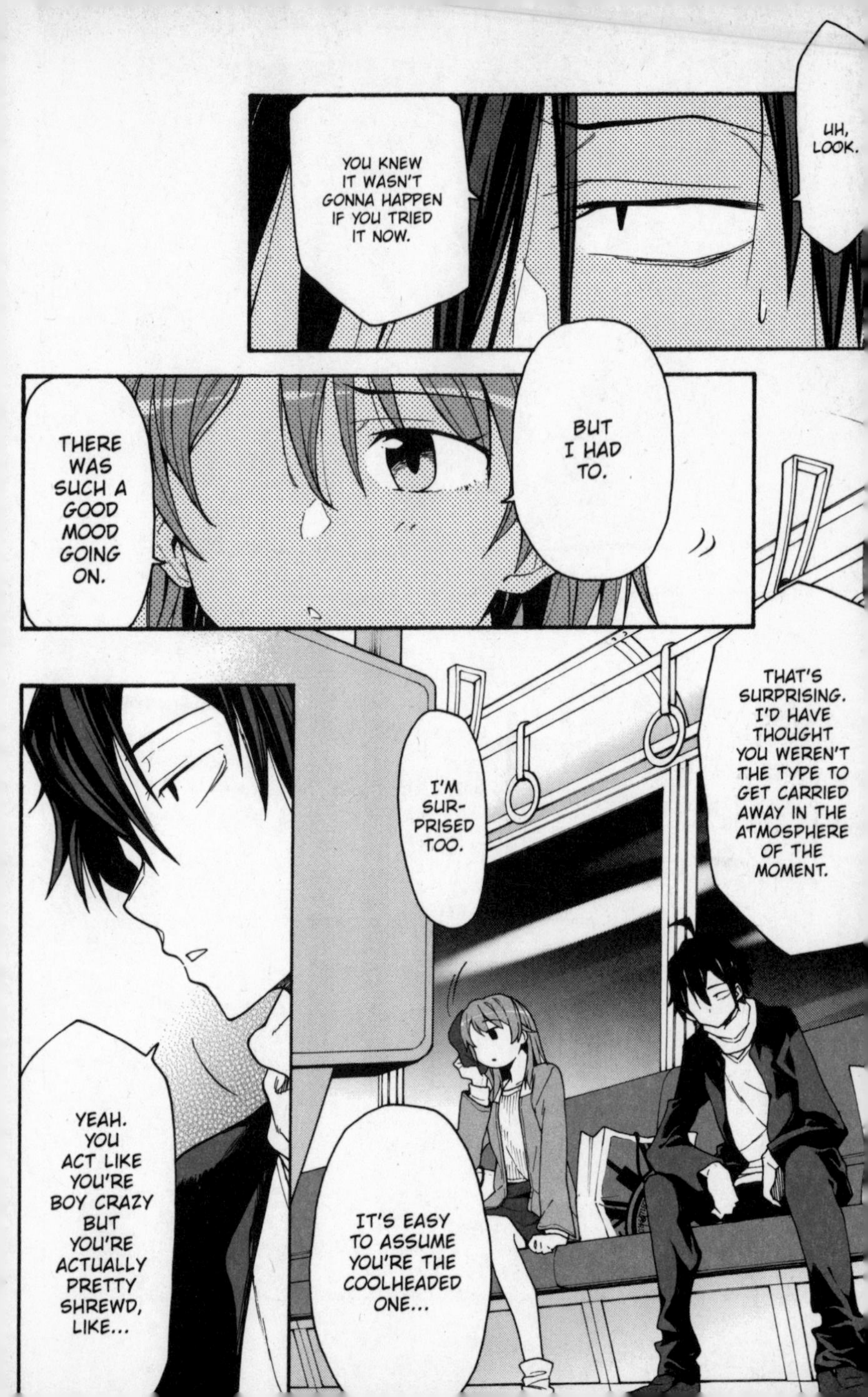
UH, LOOK.
YOU KNEW IT WASN'T GONNA HAPPEN IF YOU TRIED IT NOW.
BUT I HAD TO.
THERE WAS SUCH A GOOD MOOD GOING ON.
THAT'S SURPRISING. I'D HAVE THOUGHT YOU WEREN'T THE TYPE TO GET CARRIED AWAY IN THE ATMOSPHERE OF THE MOMENT.
I'M SUR-PRISED TOO.
IT'S EASY TO ASSUME YOU'RE THE COOLHEADED ONE...
YEAH. YOU ACT LIKE YOU'RE BOY CRAZY BUT YOU'RE ACTUALLY PRETTY SHREWD, LIKE...

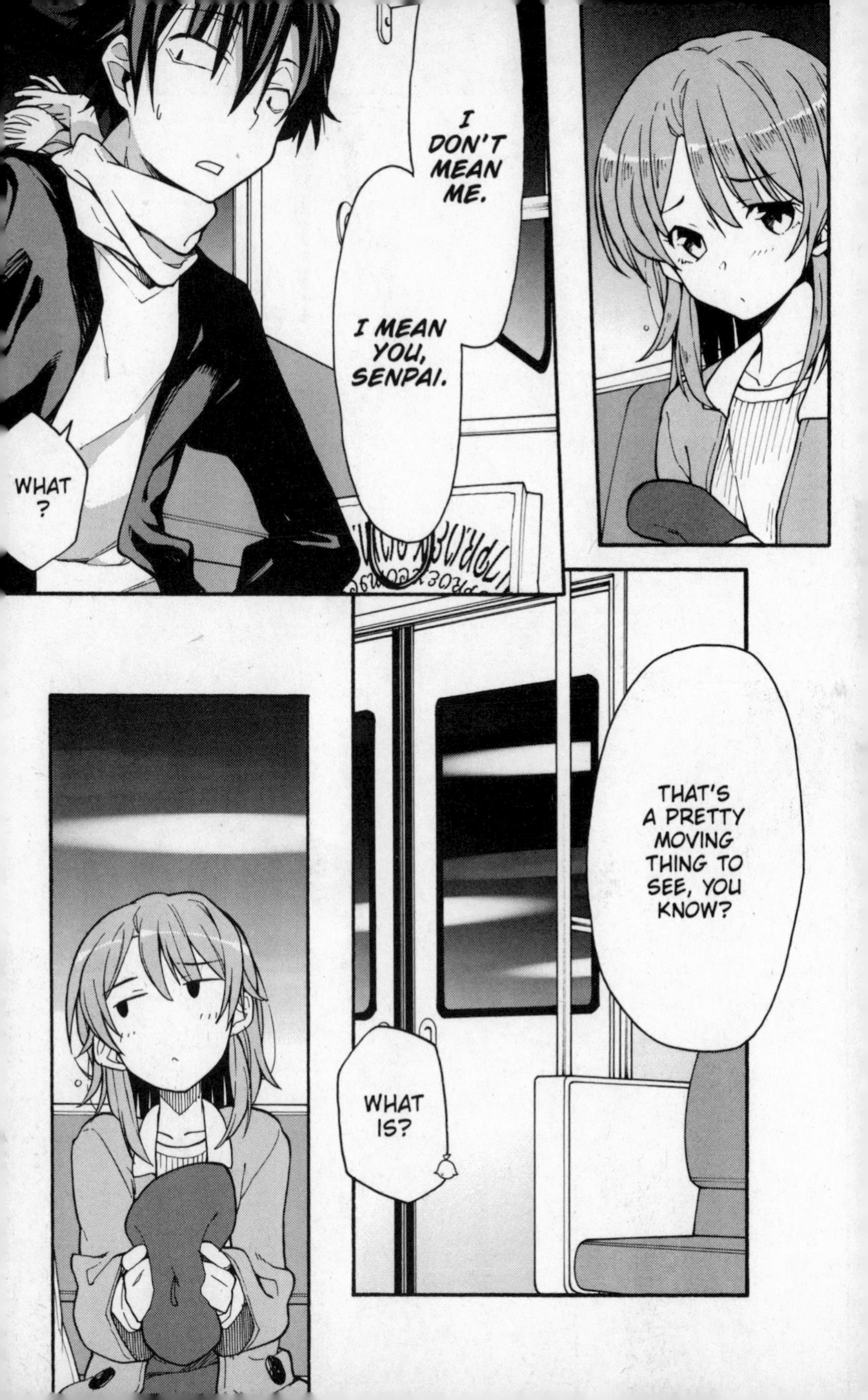
I DON'T MEAN ME.
I MEAN YOU, SENPAI.
WHAT?
THAT'S A PRETTY MOVING THING TO SEE, YOU KNOW?
WHAT IS?

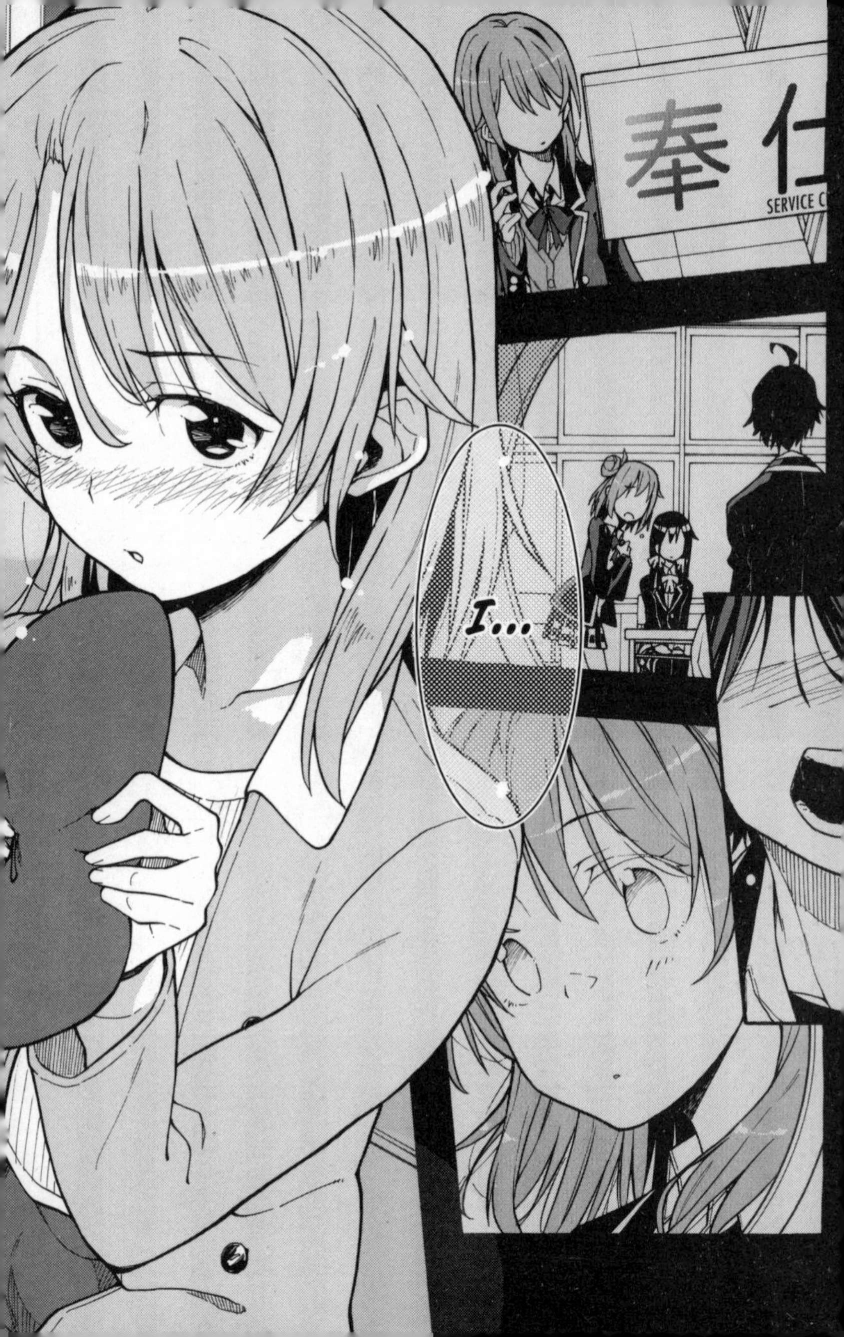
奉仕
SERVICE C
I...

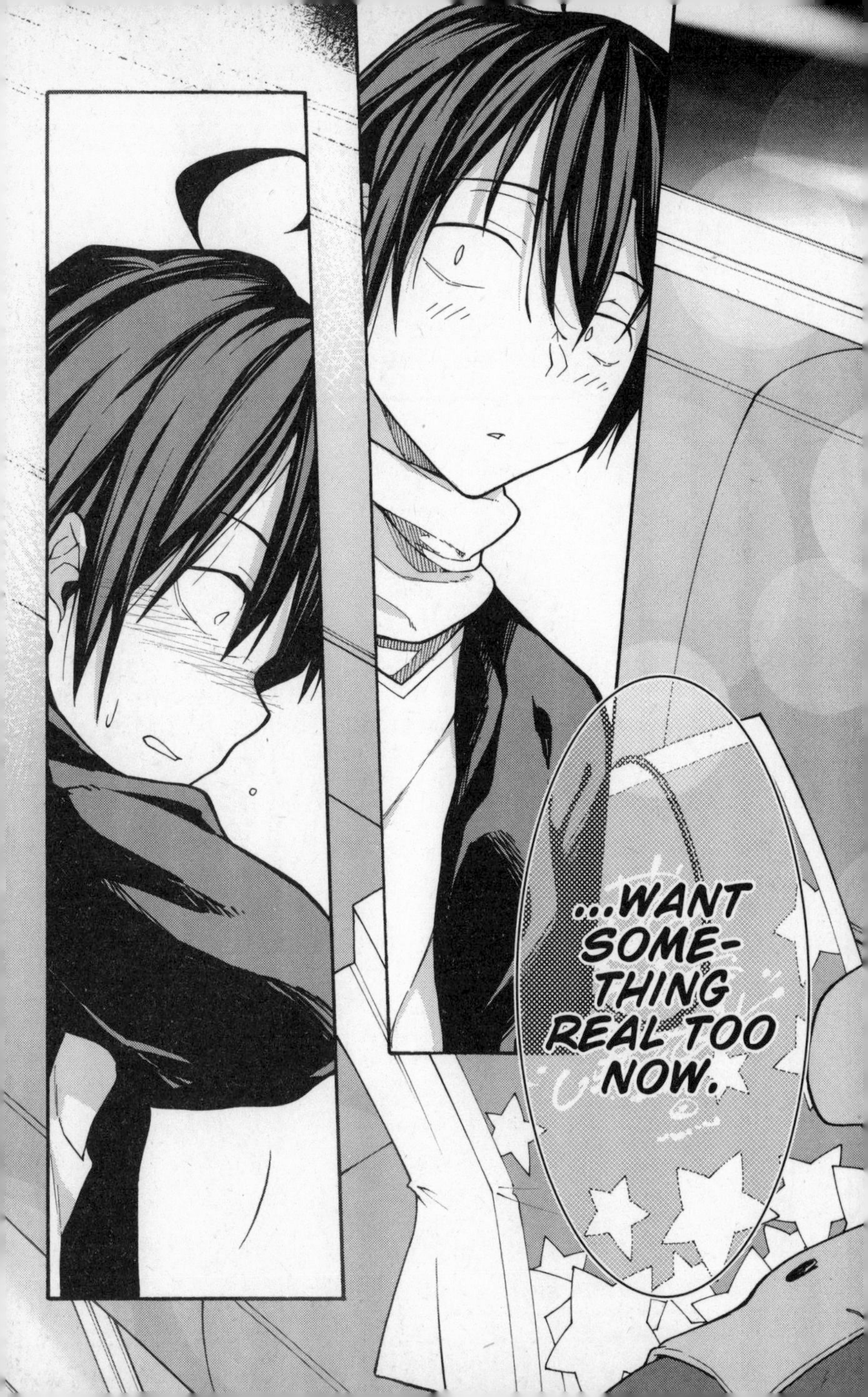
...WANT SOME-THING REAL TOO NOW.

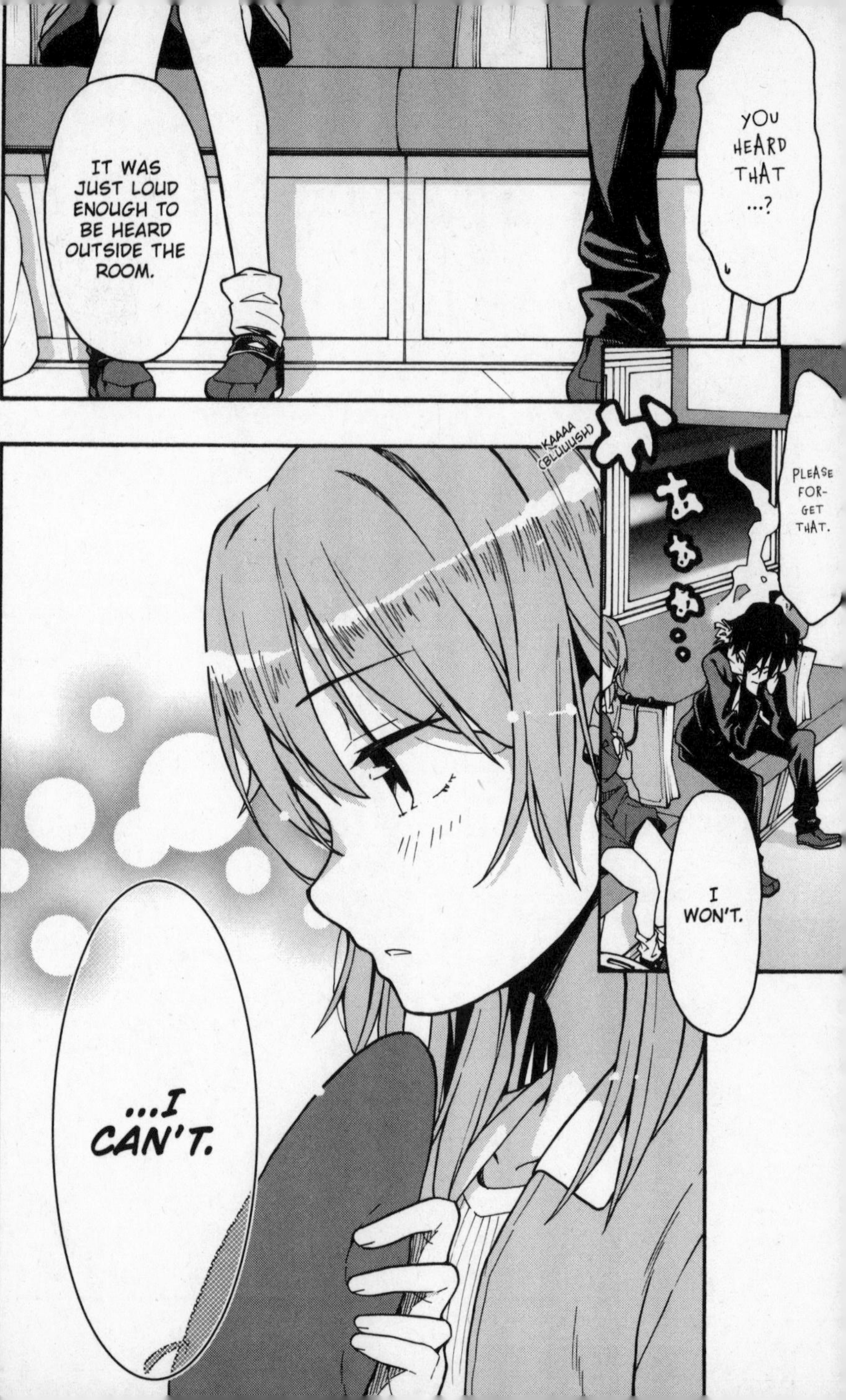
YOU HEARD THAT ...?
IT WAS JUST LOUD ENOUGH TO BE HEARD OUTSIDE THE ROOM.
KAAAA (BLUUUSH)
PLEASE FOR-GET THAT.
I WON'T.
...I CAN'T.

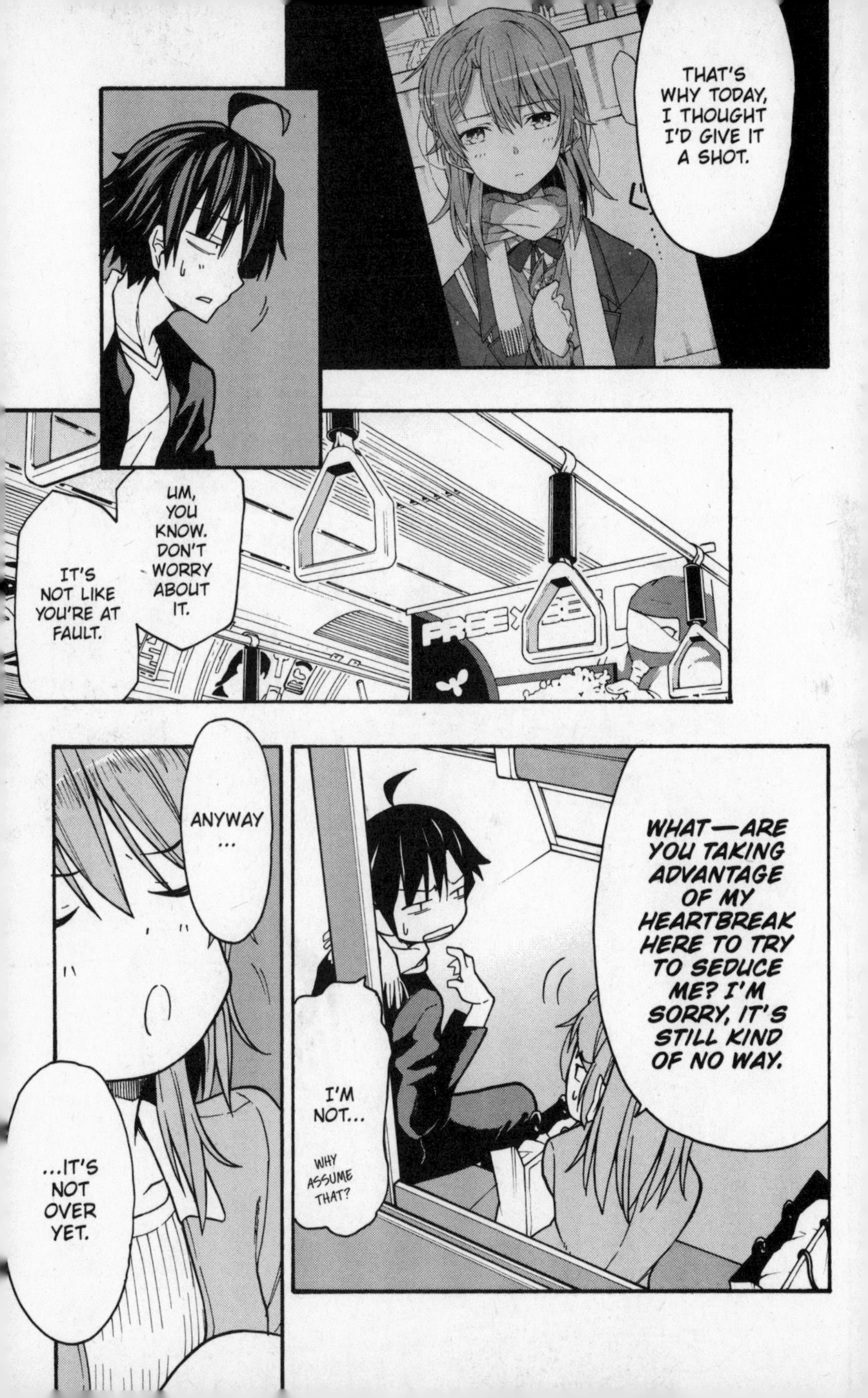
THAT'S WHY TODAY, I THOUGHT I'D GIVE IT A SHOT.
UM, YOU KNOW. DON'T WORRY ABOUT IT.
IT'S NOT LIKE YOU'RE AT FAULT.
WHAT—ARE YOU TAKING ADVANTAGE OF MY HEARTBREAK HERE TO TRY TO SEDUCE ME? I'M SORRY, IT'S STILL KIND OF NO WAY.
I'M NOT...
WHY ASSUME THAT?
ANYWAY...
...IT'S NOT OVER YET.

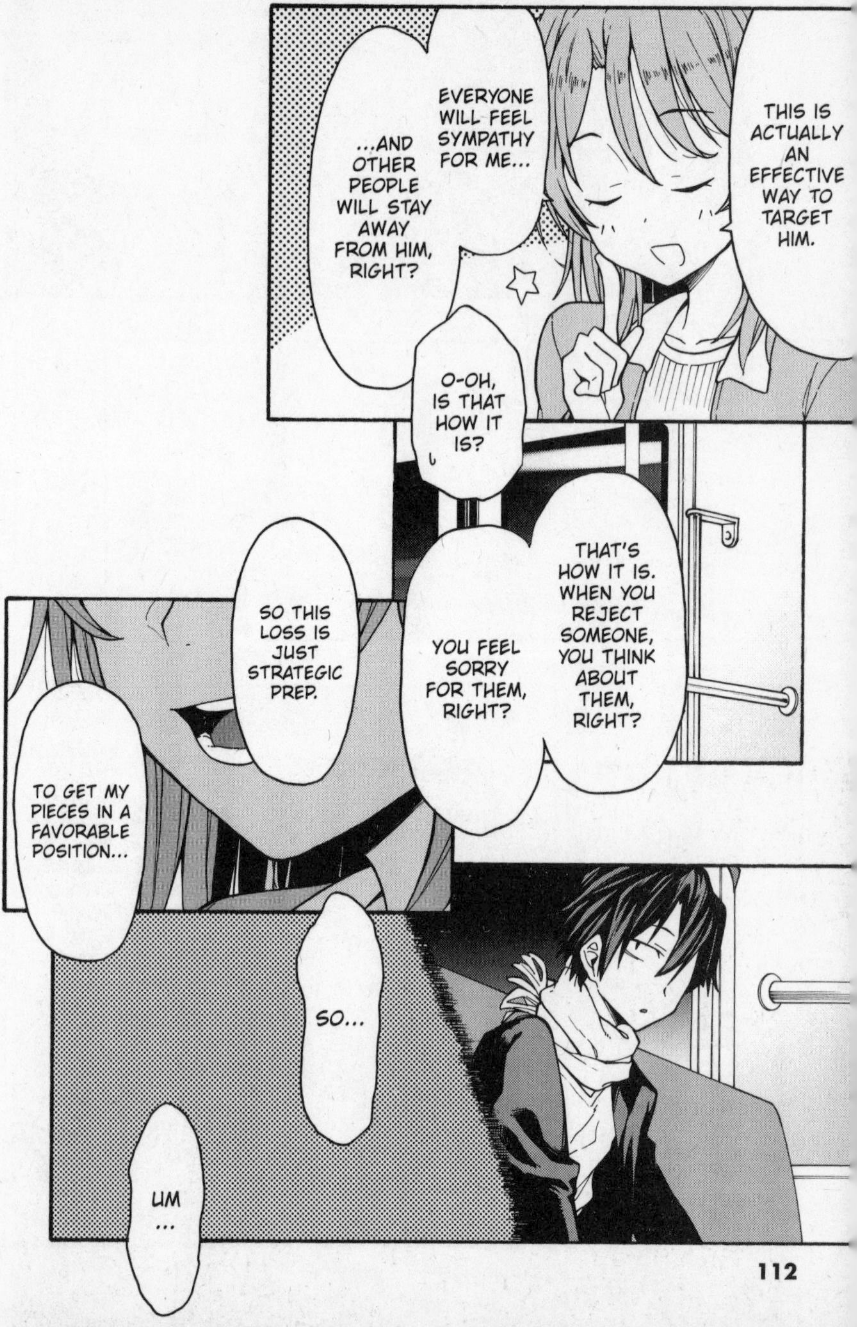
THIS IS ACTUALLY AN EFFECTIVE WAY TO TARGET HIM.
EVERYONE WILL FEEL SYMPATHY FOR ME...
...AND OTHER PEOPLE WILL STAY AWAY FROM HIM, RIGHT?
O-OH, IS THAT HOW IT IS?
THAT'S HOW IT IS. WHEN YOU REJECT SOMEONE, YOU THINK ABOUT THEM, RIGHT?
YOU FEEL SORRY FOR THEM, RIGHT?
SO THIS LOSS IS JUST STRATEGIC PREP.
TO GET MY PIECES IN A FAVORABLE POSITION...
SO...
UM ...

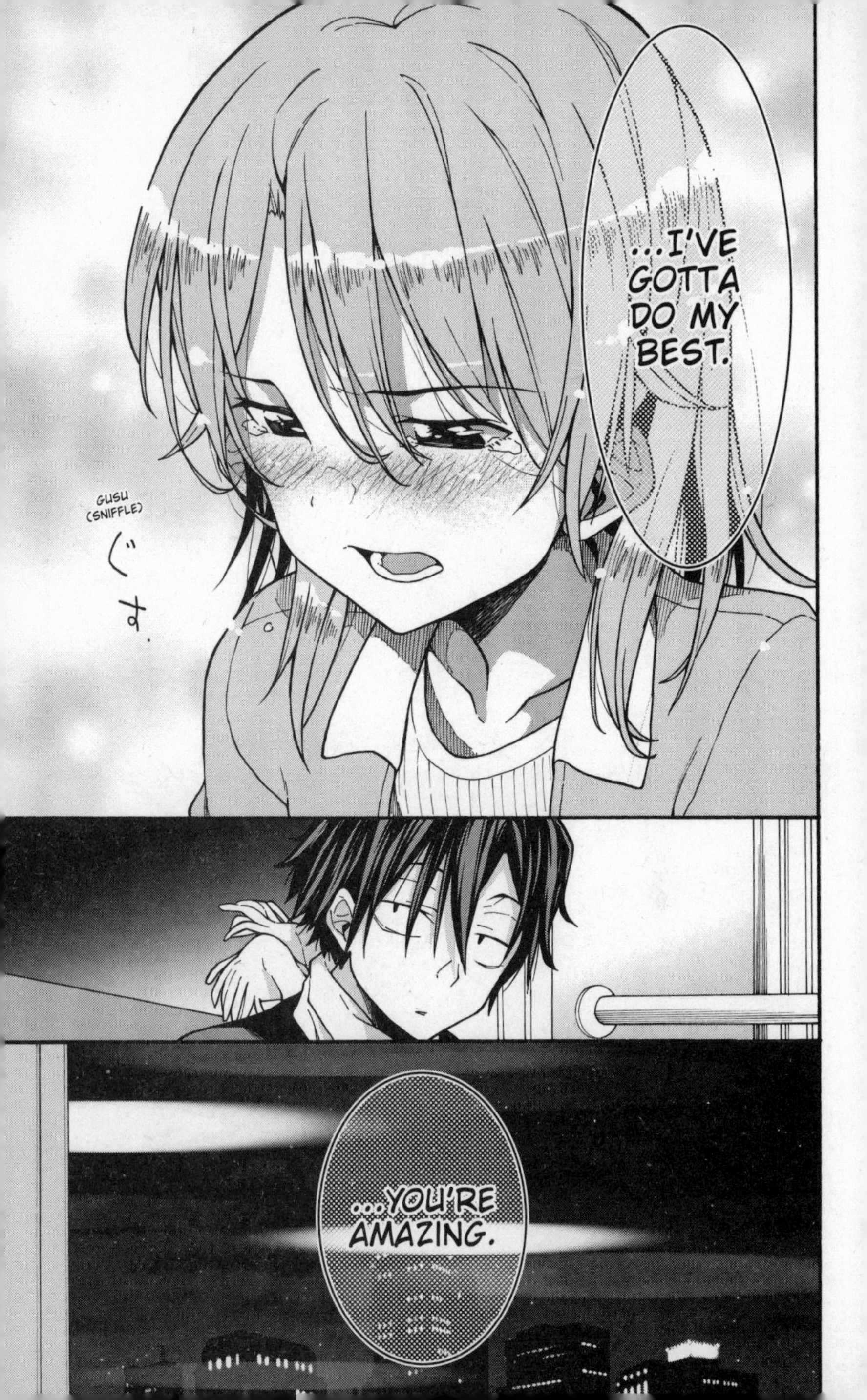
...I'VE GOTTA DO MY BEST.
GUSU (SNIFFLE)
ぐす.
...YOU'RE AMAZING.

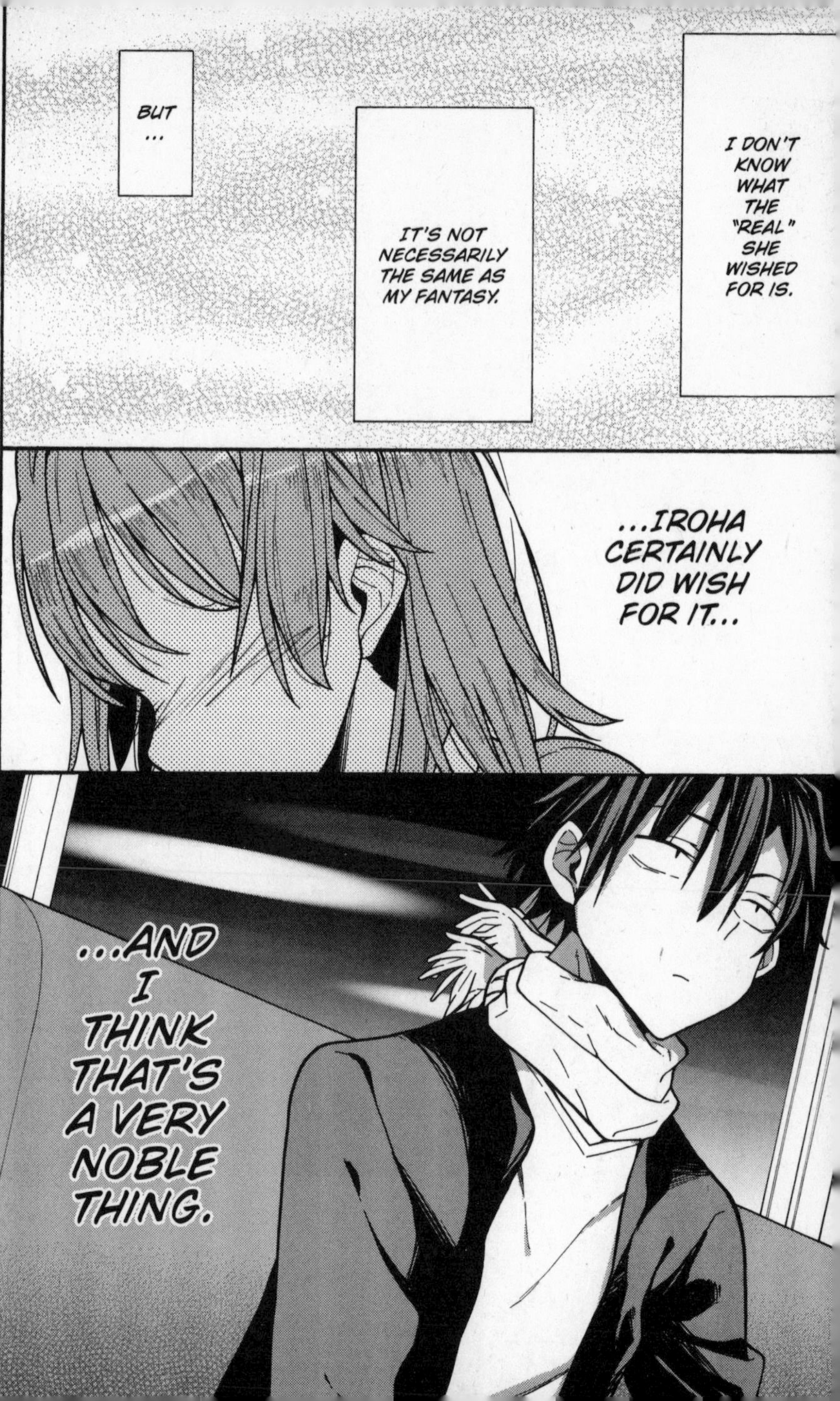
I DON'T KNOW WHAT THE "REAL" SHE WISHED FOR IS.
IT'S NOT NECESSARILY THE SAME AS MY FANTASY.
BUT...
...IROHA CERTAINLY DID WISH FOR IT...
...AND I THINK THAT'S A VERY NOBLE THING.

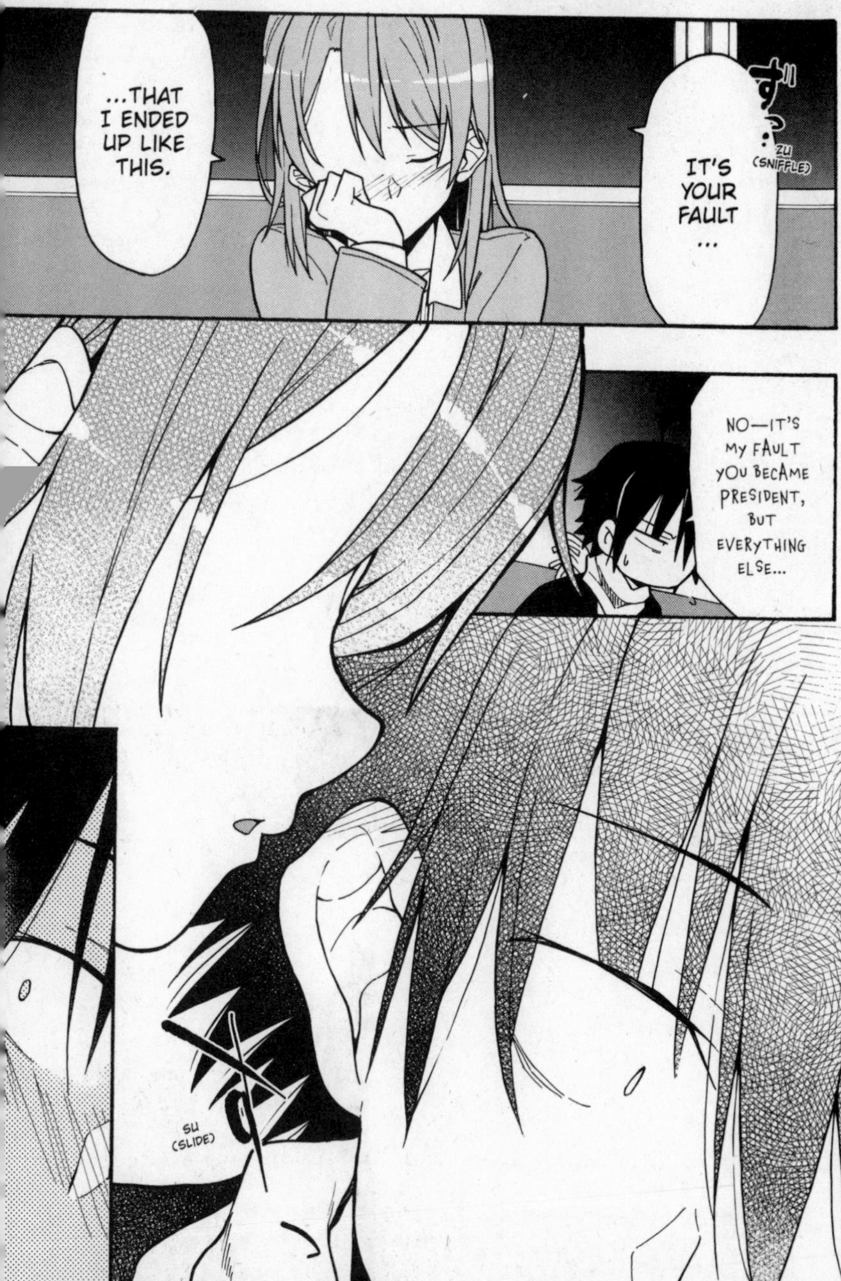
IT'S YOUR FAULT...
ずっ
ZU (SNIFFLE)
...THAT I ENDED UP LIKE THIS.
NO—IT'S MY FAULT YOU BECAME PRESIDENT, BUT EVERYTHING ELSE...
SU (SLIDE)

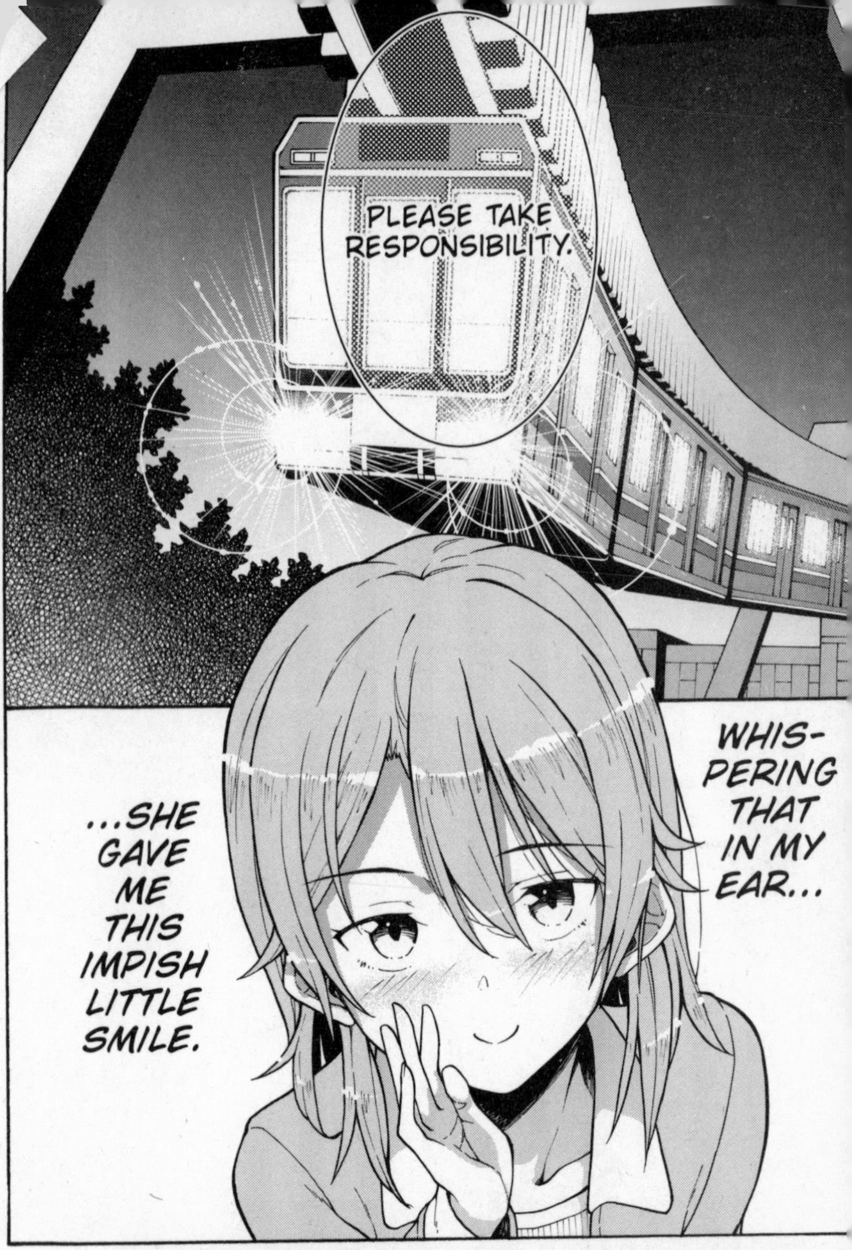
PLEASE TAKE RESPONSIBILITY.
WHISPERING THAT IN MY EAR...
...SHE GAVE ME THIS IMPISH LITTLE SMILE.

CHAPTER 69 … AND SO THIS NONFUNCTIONING MEETING ENDS UP…

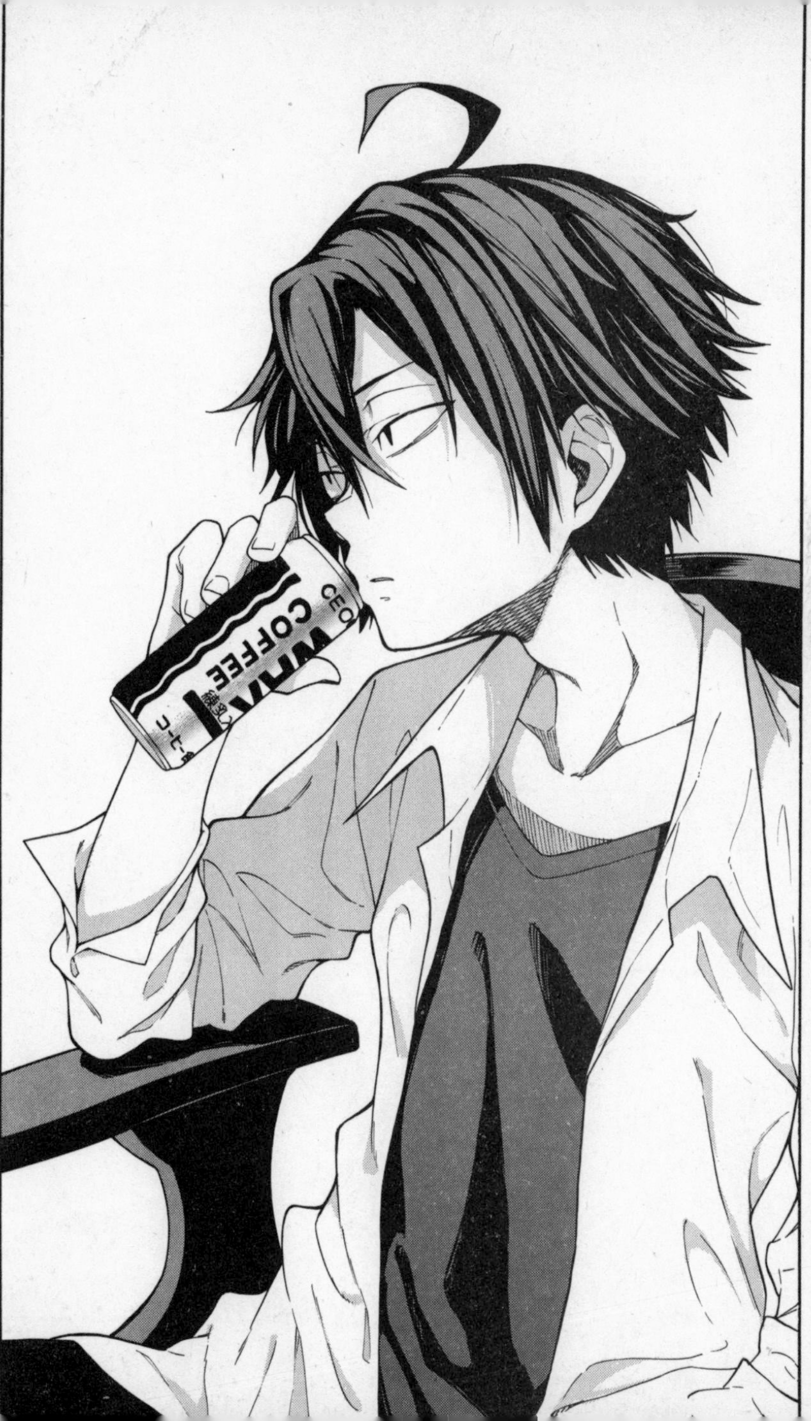
CEO
COFFEE

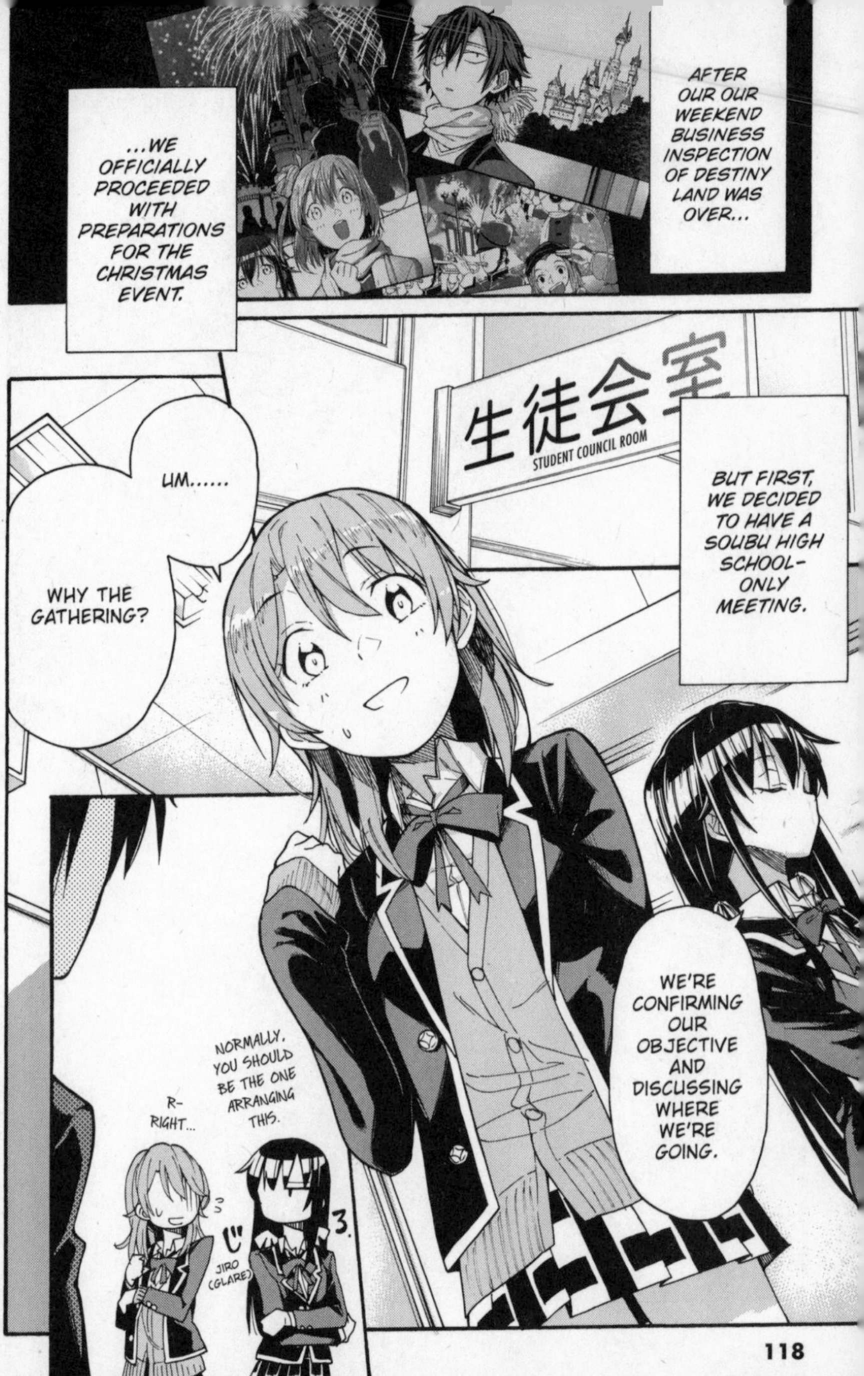
AFTER OUR OUR WEEKEND BUSINESS INSPECTION OF DESTINY LAND WAS OVER...
...WE OFFICIALLY PROCEEDED WITH PREPARATIONS FOR THE CHRISTMAS EVENT.
生徒会室
STUDENT COUNCIL ROOM
BUT FIRST, WE DECIDED TO HAVE A SOUBU HIGH SCHOOL-ONLY MEETING.
UM......
WHY THE GATHERING?
WE'RE CONFIRMING OUR OBJECTIVE AND DISCUSSING WHERE WE'RE GOING.
NORMALLY, YOU SHOULD BE THE ONE ARRANGING THIS.
R-RIGHT...
じ
JIRO (GLARE)

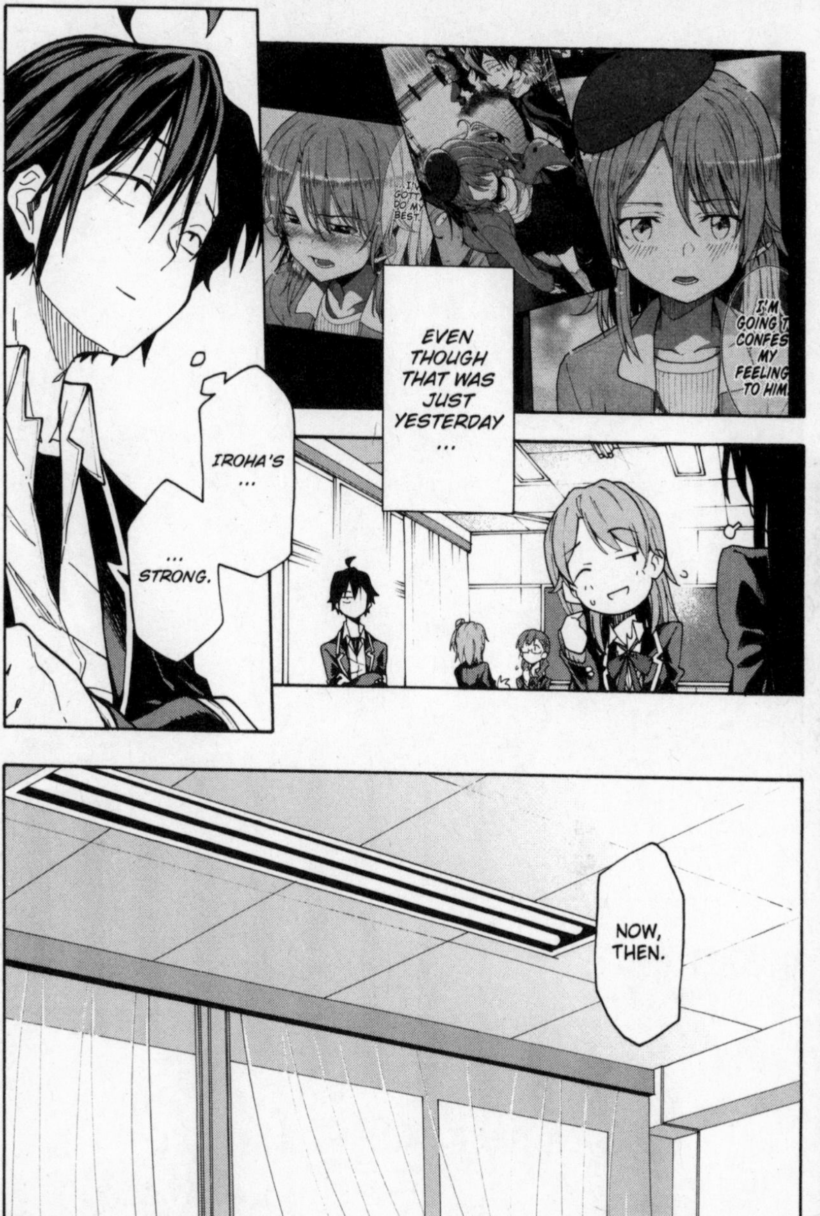
I'M GOING T CONFES MY FEELING TO HIM
...I'V GOTT DO MY BEST.
EVEN THOUGH THAT WAS JUST YESTERDAY ...
IROHA'S ...
... STRONG.
NOW, THEN.

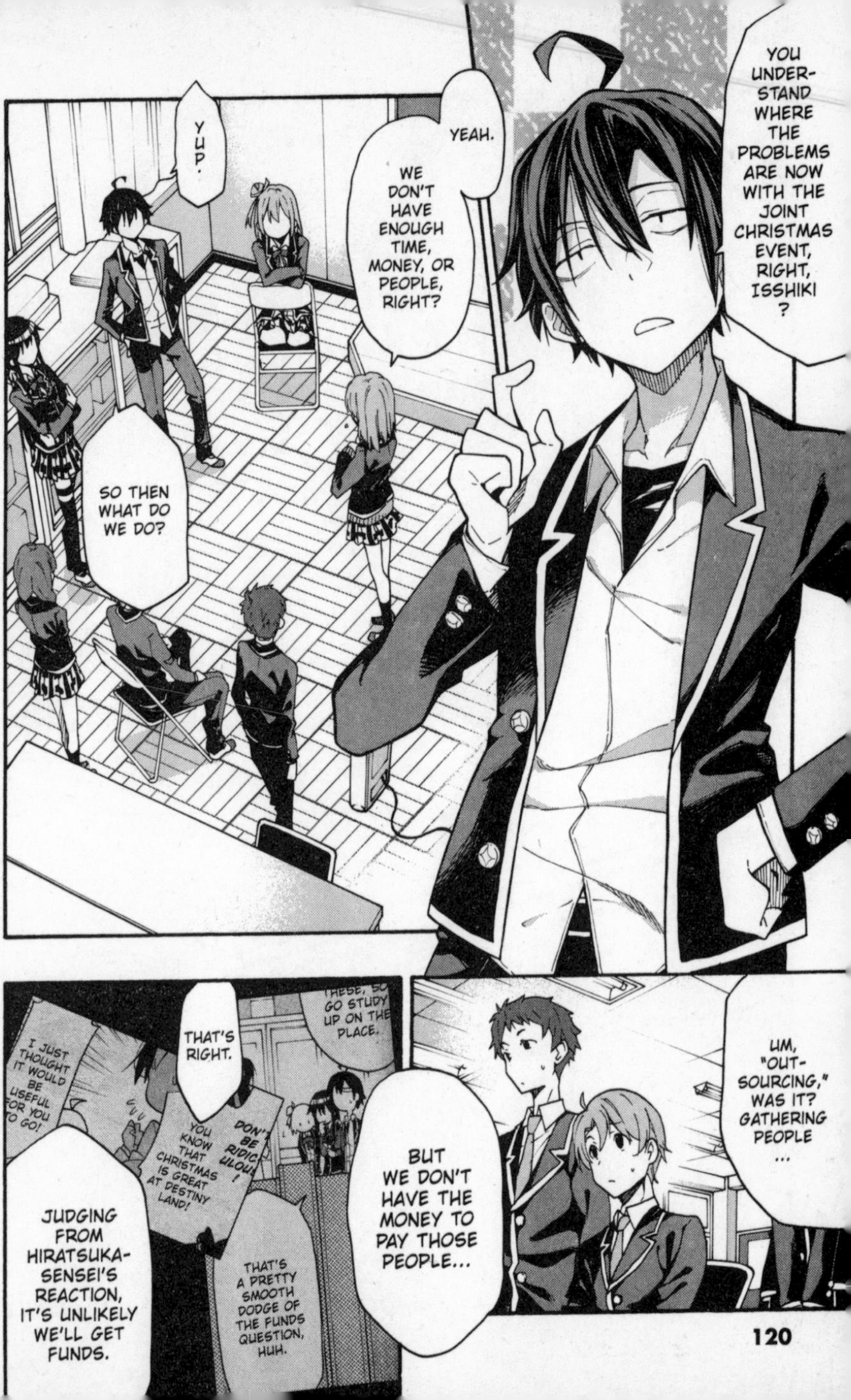
YOU UNDERSTAND WHERE THE PROBLEMS ARE NOW WITH THE JOINT CHRISTMAS EVENT, RIGHT, ISSHIKI?
YEAH.
WE DON'T HAVE ENOUGH TIME, MONEY, OR PEOPLE, RIGHT?
YUP.
SO THEN WHAT DO WE DO?
UM, "OUTSOURCING," WAS IT? GATHERING PEOPLE...
BUT WE DON'T HAVE THE MONEY TO PAY THOSE PEOPLE...
THAT'S RIGHT.
THESE, SO GO STUDY UP ON THE PLACE.
I JUST THOUGHT IT WOULD BE USEFUL FOR YOU TO GO!
DON'T BE RIDICULOU!
YOU KNOW THAT CHRISTMAS IS GREAT AT DESTINY LAND!
THAT'S A PRETTY SMOOTH DODGE OF THE FUNDS QUESTION, HUH.
JUDGING FROM HIRATSUKA-SENSEI'S REACTION, IT'S UNLIKELY WE'LL GET FUNDS.

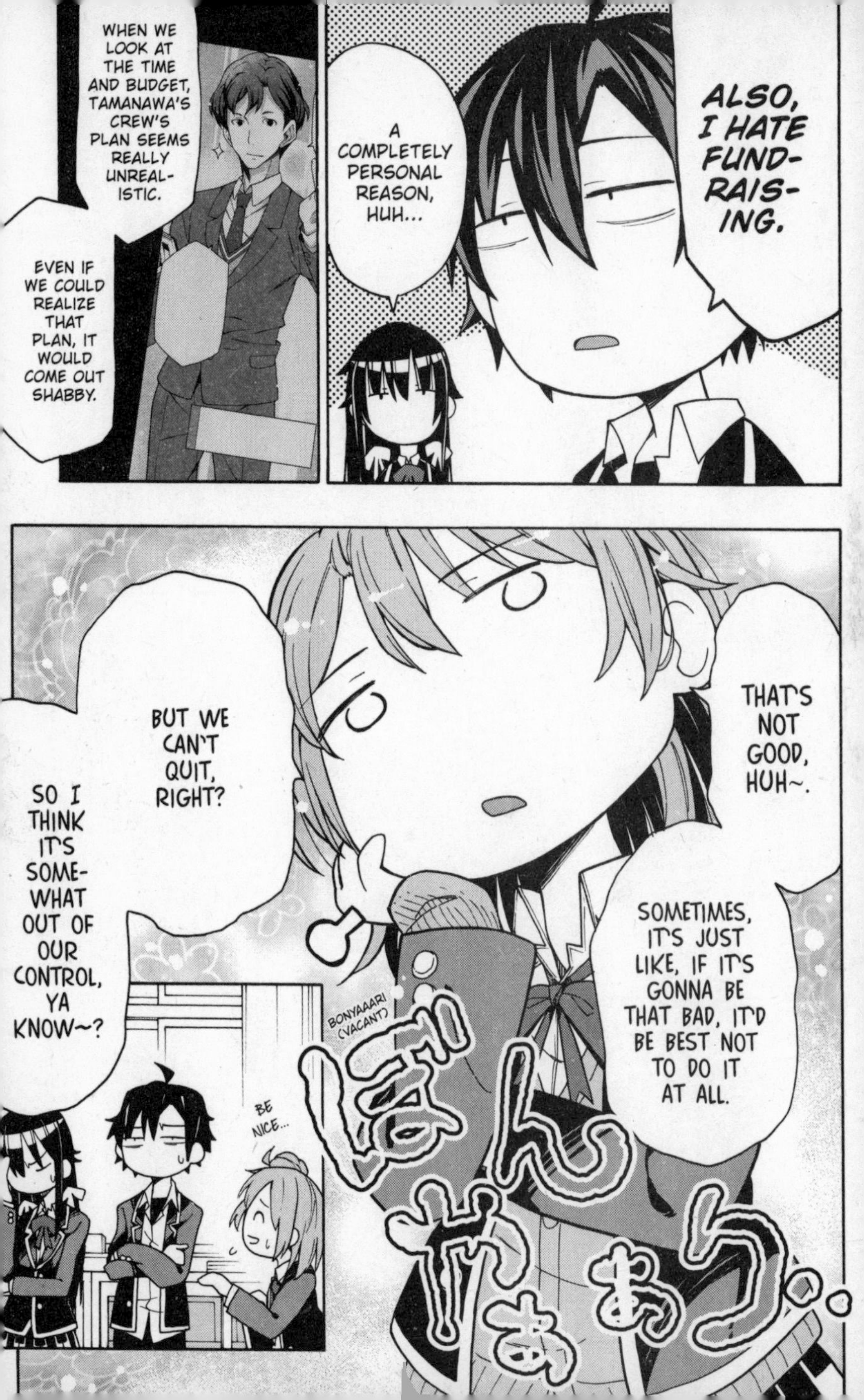
ALSO, I HATE FUND-RAISING.
A COMPLETELY PERSONAL REASON, HUH...
WHEN WE LOOK AT THE TIME AND BUDGET, TAMANAWA'S CREW'S PLAN SEEMS REALLY UNREALISTIC.
EVEN IF WE COULD REALIZE THAT PLAN, IT WOULD COME OUT SHABBY.
THAT'S NOT GOOD, HUH~.
SOMETIMES, IT'S JUST LIKE, IF IT'S GONNA BE THAT BAD, IT'D BE BEST NOT TO DO IT AT ALL.
BONYAAARI (VACANT)
BUT WE CAN'T QUIT, RIGHT?
SO I THINK IT'S SOMEWHAT OUT OF OUR CONTROL, YA KNOW~?
BE NICE...

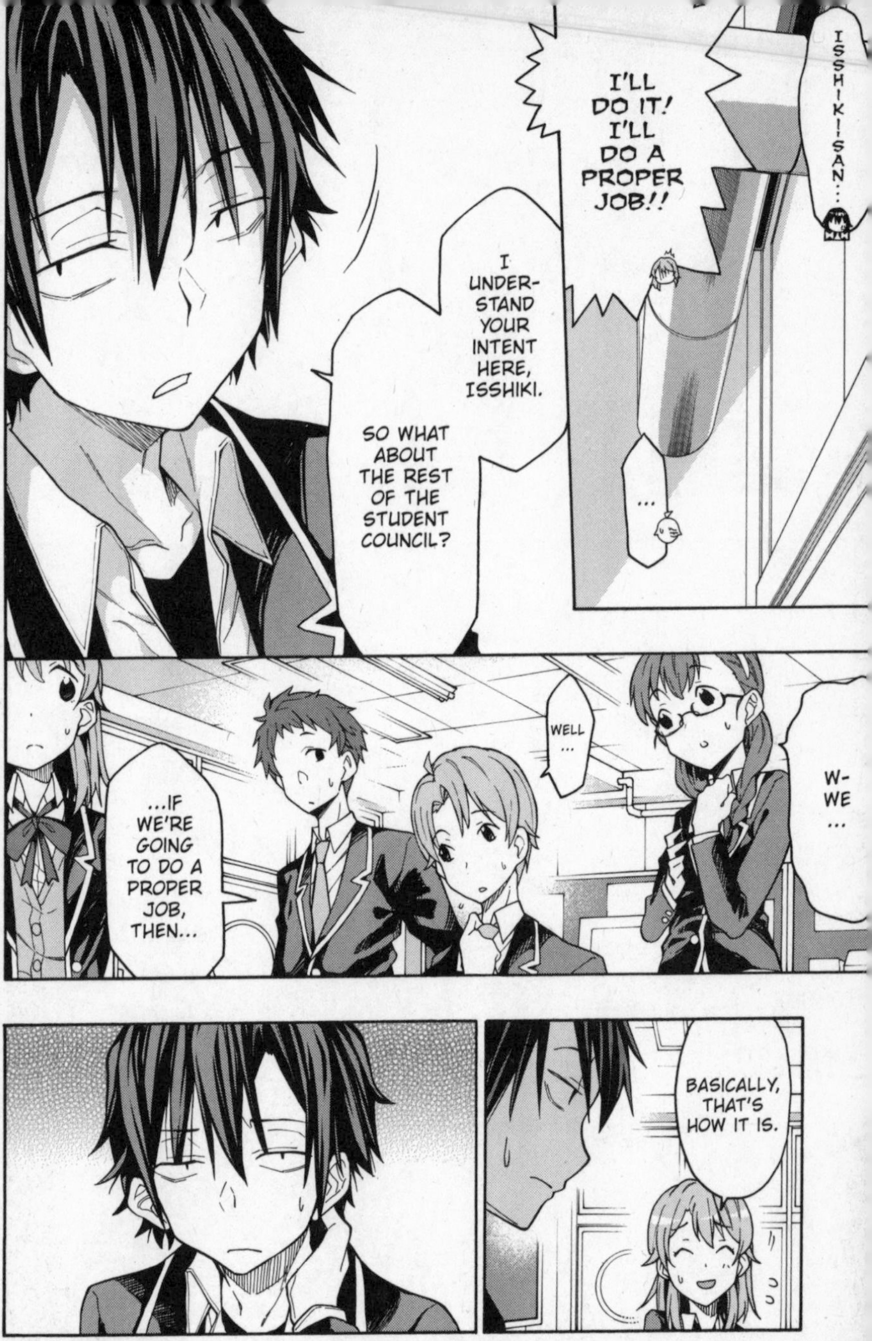
ISSHIKI-SAN...
I'LL DO IT! I'LL DO A PROPER JOB!!
...
I UNDERSTAND YOUR INTENT HERE, ISSHIKI.
SO WHAT ABOUT THE REST OF THE STUDENT COUNCIL?
W-WE...
WELL...
...IF WE'RE GOING TO DO A PROPER JOB, THEN...
BASICALLY, THAT'S HOW IT IS.

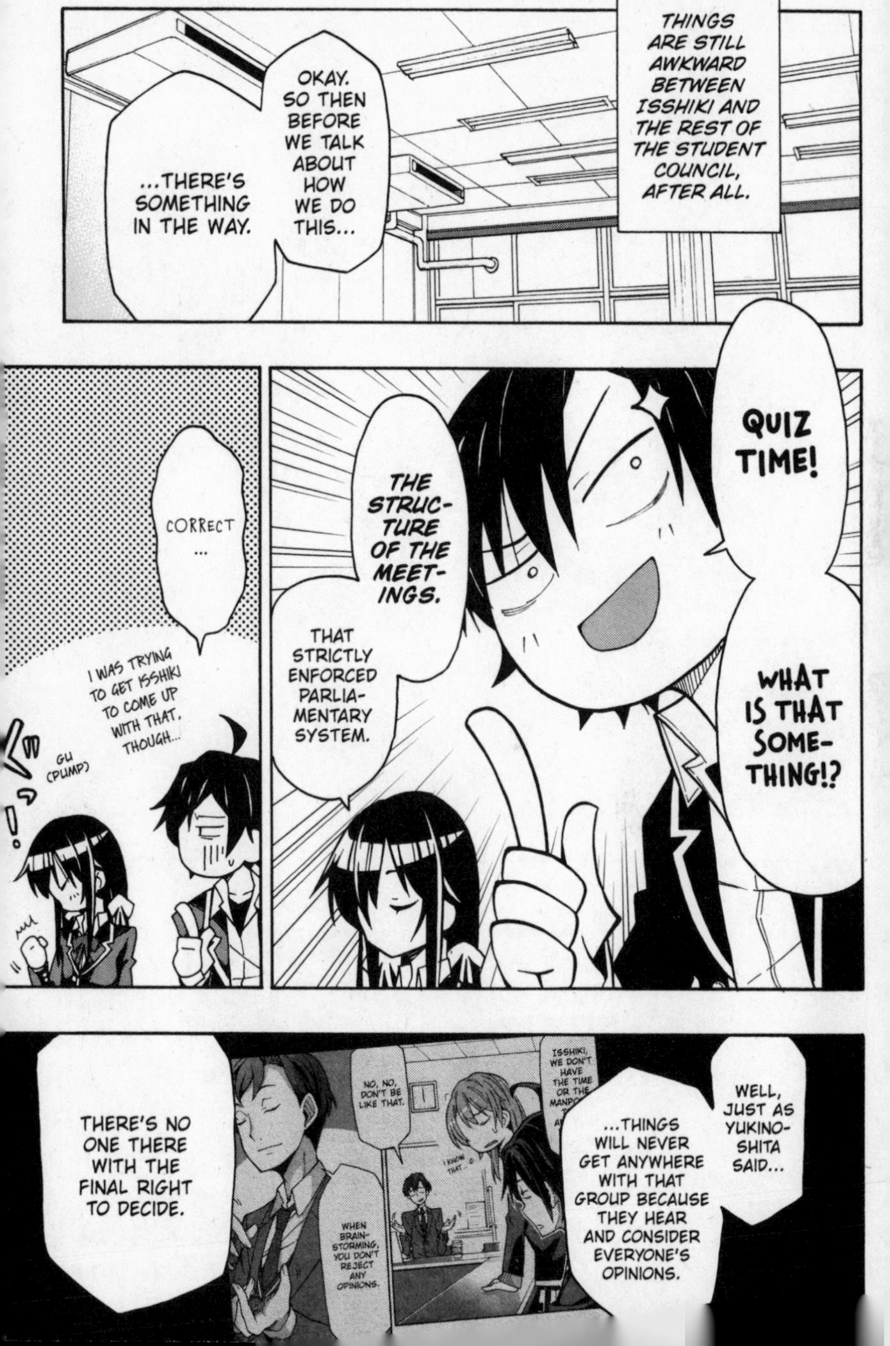
THINGS ARE STILL AWKWARD BETWEEN ISSHIKI AND THE REST OF THE STUDENT COUNCIL, AFTER ALL.
OKAY. SO THEN BEFORE WE TALK ABOUT HOW WE DO THIS...
...THERE'S SOMETHING IN THE WAY.
QUIZ TIME!
WHAT IS THAT SOMETHING!?
THE STRUCTURE OF THE MEETINGS.
THAT STRICTLY ENFORCED PARLIAMENTARY SYSTEM.
CORRECT...
I WAS TRYING TO GET ISSHIKI TO COME UP WITH THAT, THOUGH...
GU (PUMP)
WELL, JUST AS YUKINOSHITA SAID...
...THINGS WILL NEVER GET ANYWHERE WITH THAT GROUP BECAUSE THEY HEAR AND CONSIDER EVERYONE'S OPINIONS.
ISSHIKI, WE DON'T HAVE THE TIME OR THE
NO, NO, DON'T BE LIKE THAT.
I KNOW THAT...
WHEN BRAINSTORMING, YOU DON'T REJECT ANY OPINIONS.
THERE'S NO ONE THERE WITH THE FINAL RIGHT TO DECIDE.

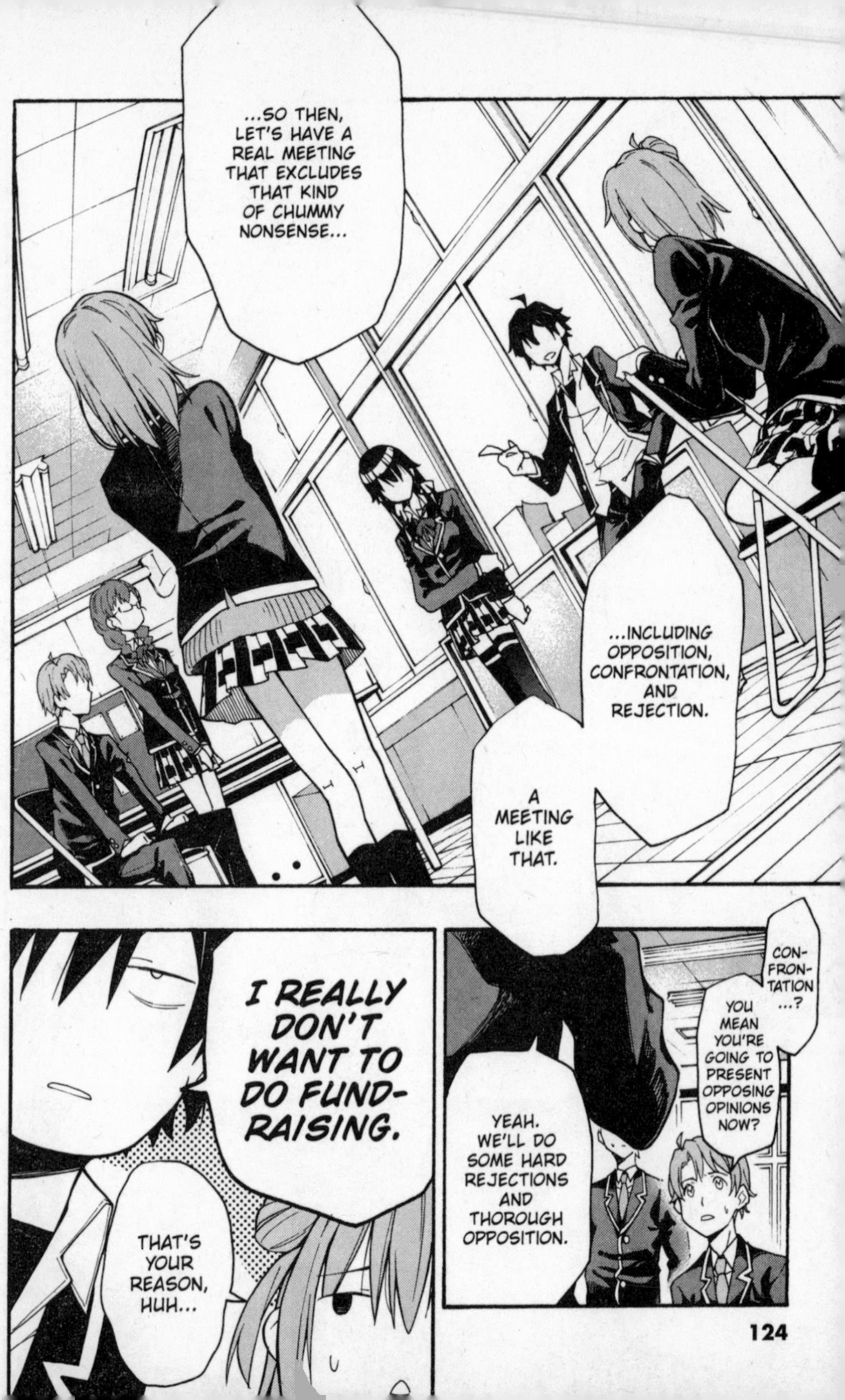
...SO THEN, LET'S HAVE A REAL MEETING THAT EXCLUDES THAT KIND OF CHUMMY NONSENSE...
...INCLUDING OPPOSITION, CONFRONTATION, AND REJECTION.
A MEETING LIKE THAT.
CON-FRON-TATION ...?
YOU MEAN YOU'RE GOING TO PRESENT OPPOSING OPINIONS NOW?
YEAH. WE'LL DO SOME HARD REJECTIONS AND THOROUGH OPPOSITION.
I REALLY DON'T WANT TO DO FUND-RAISING.
THAT'S YOUR REASON, HUH...

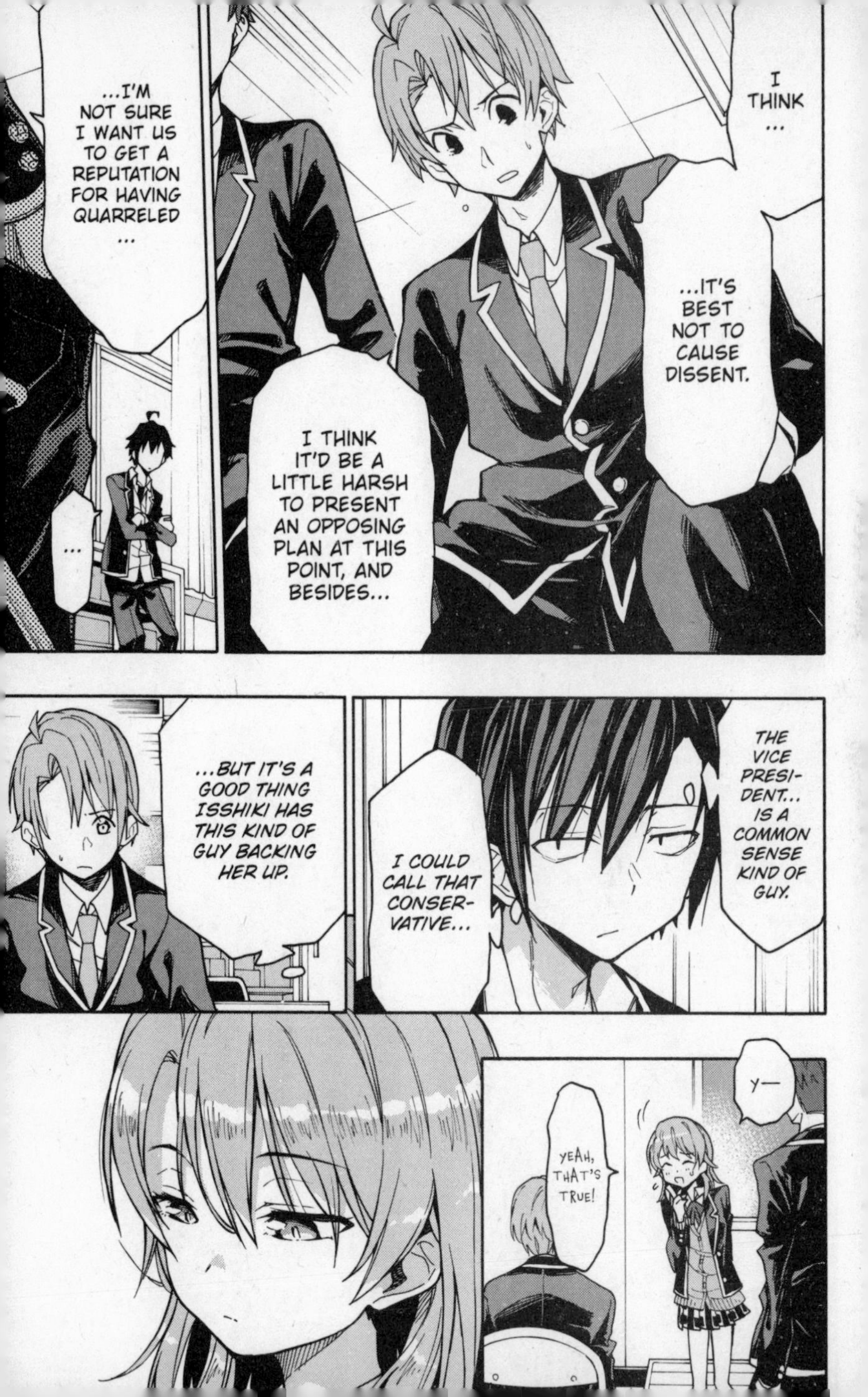
I THINK...
...IT'S BEST NOT TO CAUSE DISSENT.
I THINK IT'D BE A LITTLE HARSH TO PRESENT AN OPPOSING PLAN AT THIS POINT, AND BESIDES...
...I'M NOT SURE I WANT US TO GET A REPUTATION FOR HAVING QUARRELED...
...
THE VICE PRESI-DENT... IS A COMMON SENSE KIND OF GUY.
I COULD CALL THAT CONSER-VATIVE...
...BUT IT'S A GOOD THING ISSHIKI HAS THIS KIND OF GUY BACKING HER UP.
Y—
YEAH, THAT'S TRUE!

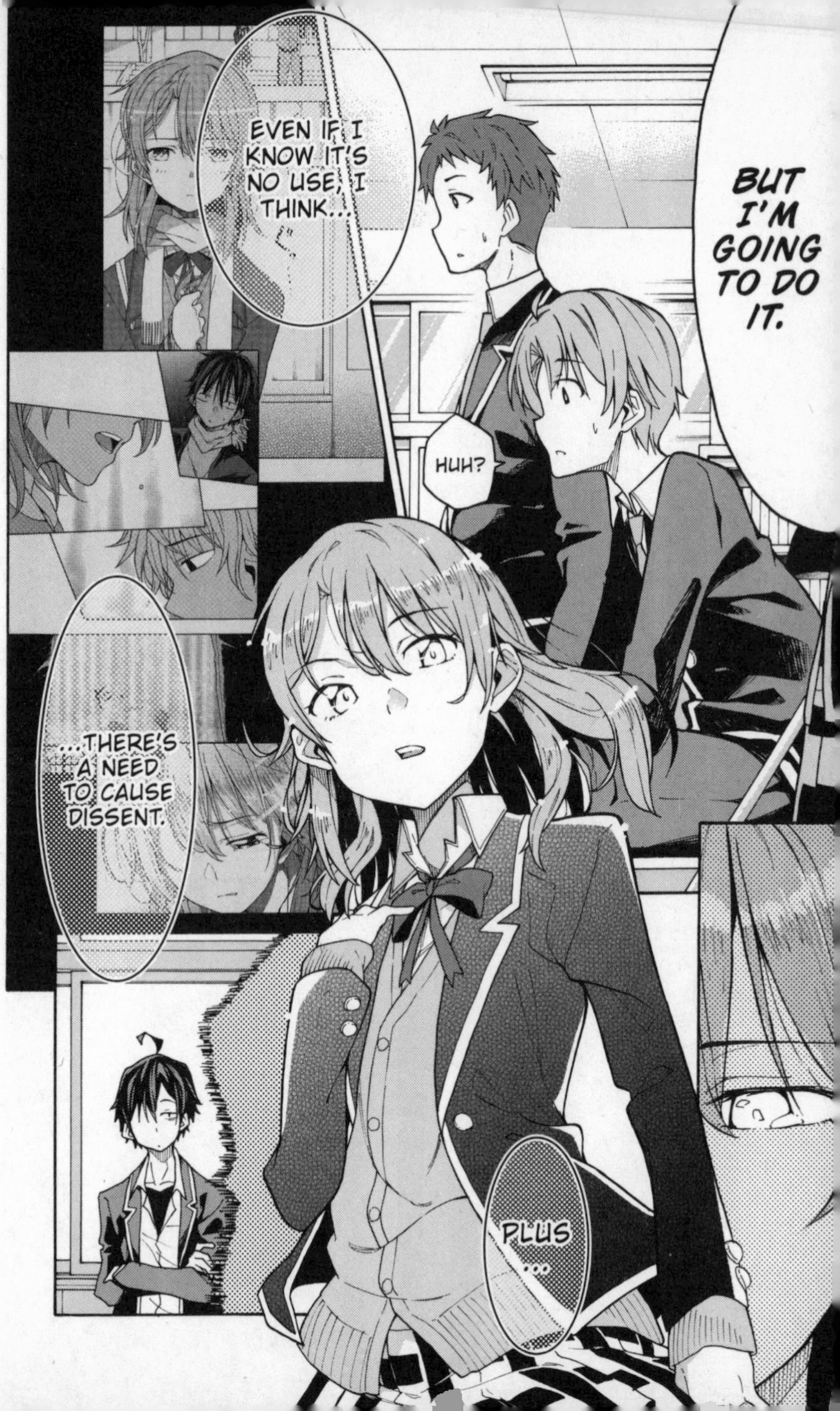
BUT I'M GOING TO DO IT.
HUH?
EVEN IF I KNOW IT'S NO USE, I THINK...
...THERE'S A NEED TO CAUSE DISSENT.
PLUS...

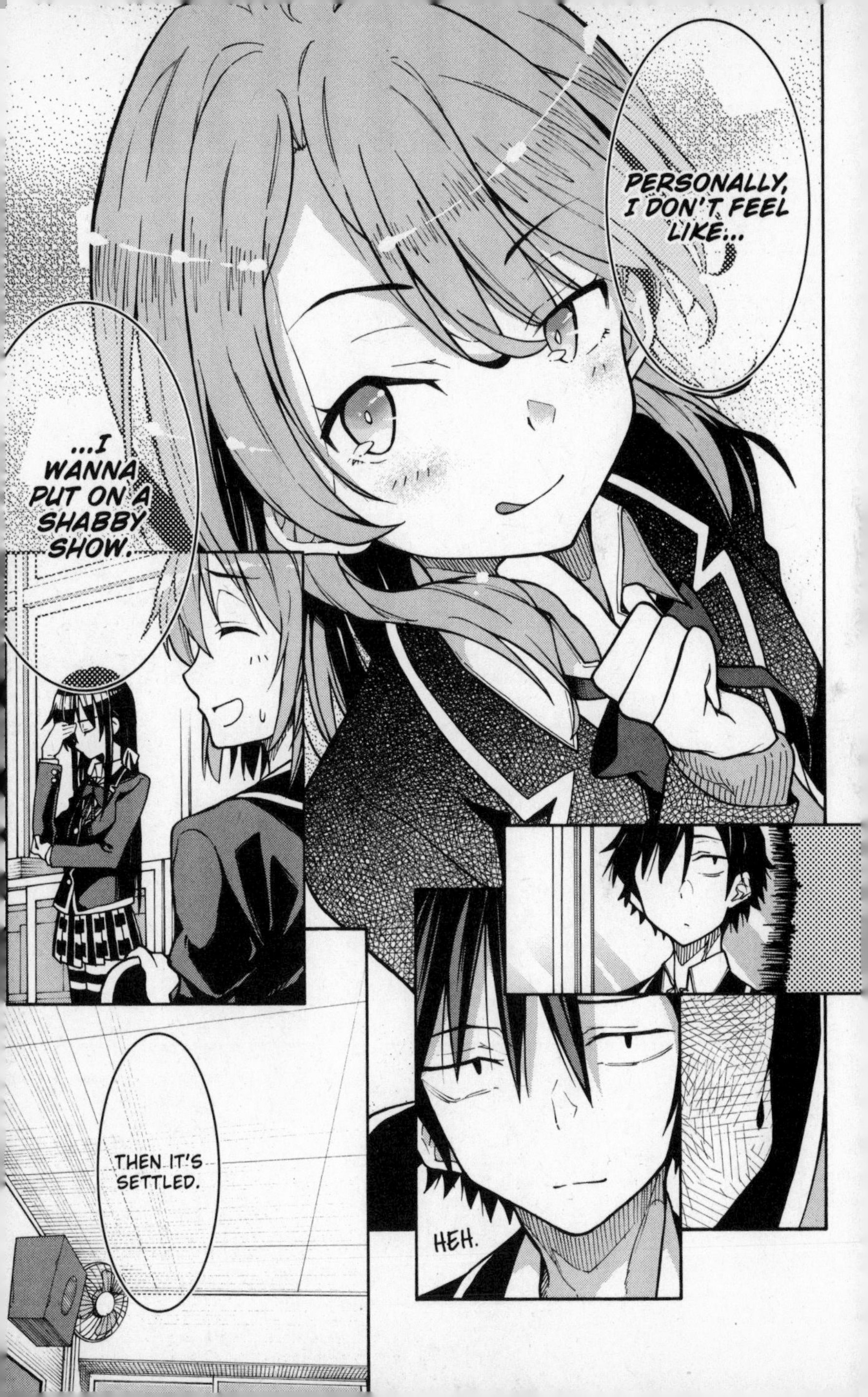
PERSONALLY, I DON'T FEEL LIKE...
...I WANNA PUT ON A SHABBY SHOW.
HEH.
THEN IT'S SETTLED.

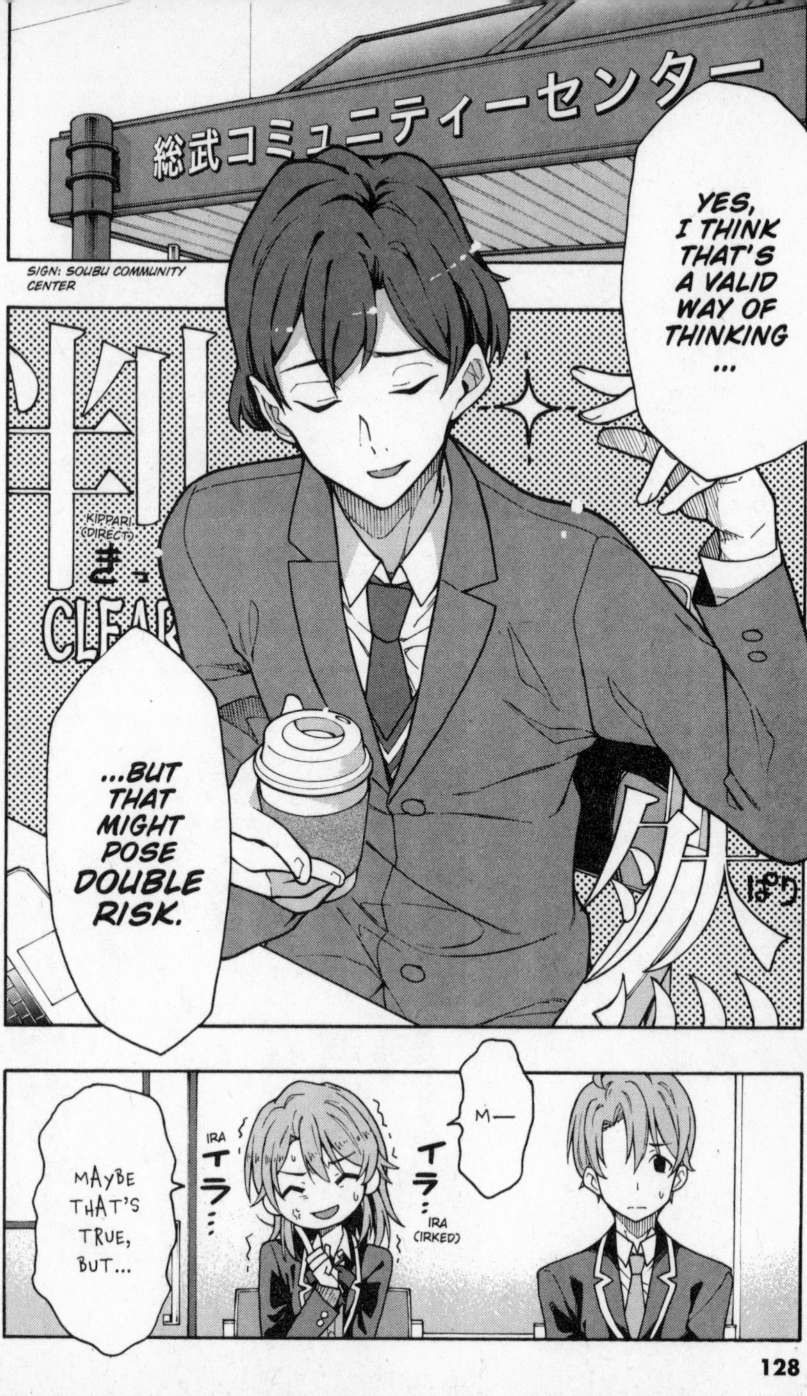
総武コミュニティーセンター
SIGN: SOUBU COMMUNITY CENTER
YES, I THINK THAT'S A VALID WAY OF THINKING ...
きっ
KIPPARI (DIRECT)
CLEAR
ぱり
...BUT THAT MIGHT POSE DOUBLE RISK.
M—
イラ
IRA (IRKED)
イラ
IRA
MAYBE THAT'S TRUE, BUT...

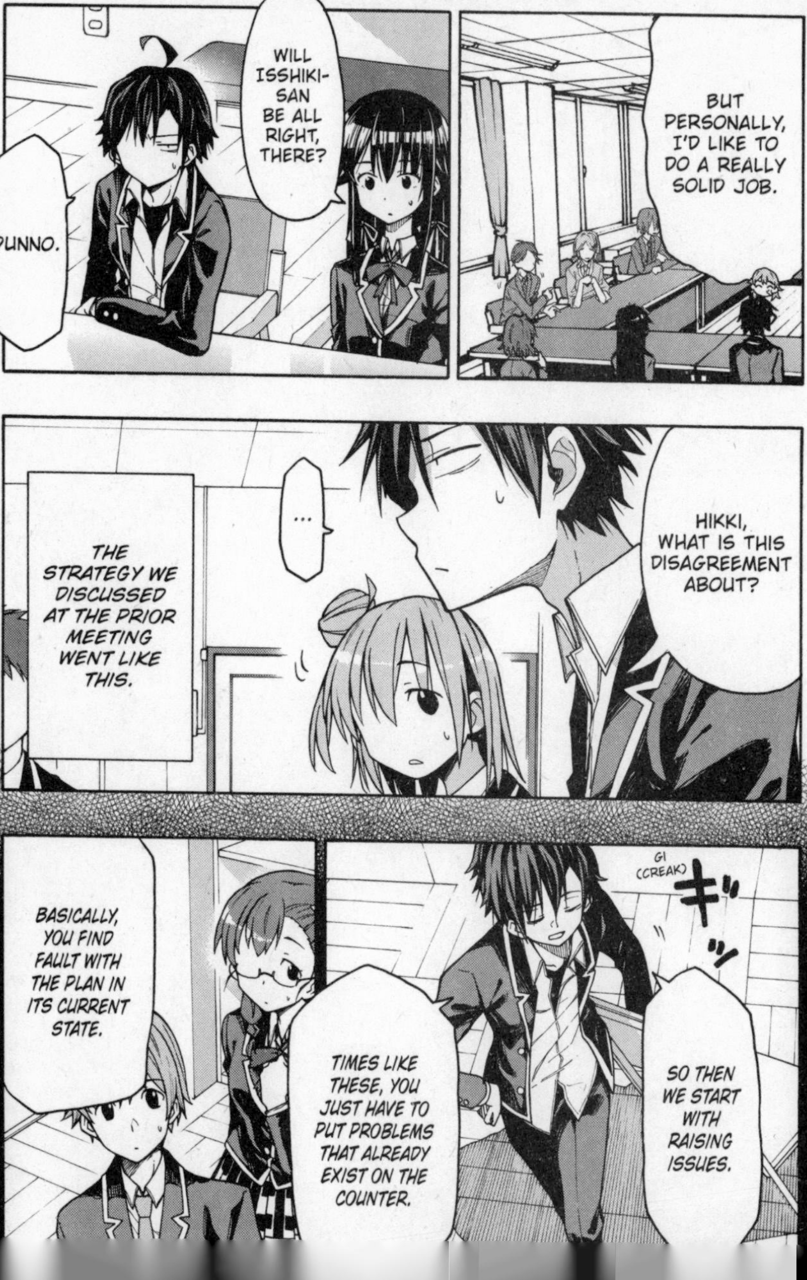
BUT PERSONALLY, I'D LIKE TO DO A REALLY SOLID JOB.
WILL ISSHIKI-SAN BE ALL RIGHT, THERE?
DUNNO.
HIKKI, WHAT IS THIS DISAGREEMENT ABOUT?
...
THE STRATEGY WE DISCUSSED AT THE PRIOR MEETING WENT LIKE THIS.
GI (CREAK)
SO THEN WE START WITH RAISING ISSUES.
TIMES LIKE THESE, YOU JUST HAVE TO PUT PROBLEMS THAT ALREADY EXIST ON THE COUNTER.
BASICALLY, YOU FIND FAULT WITH THE PLAN IN ITS CURRENT STATE.

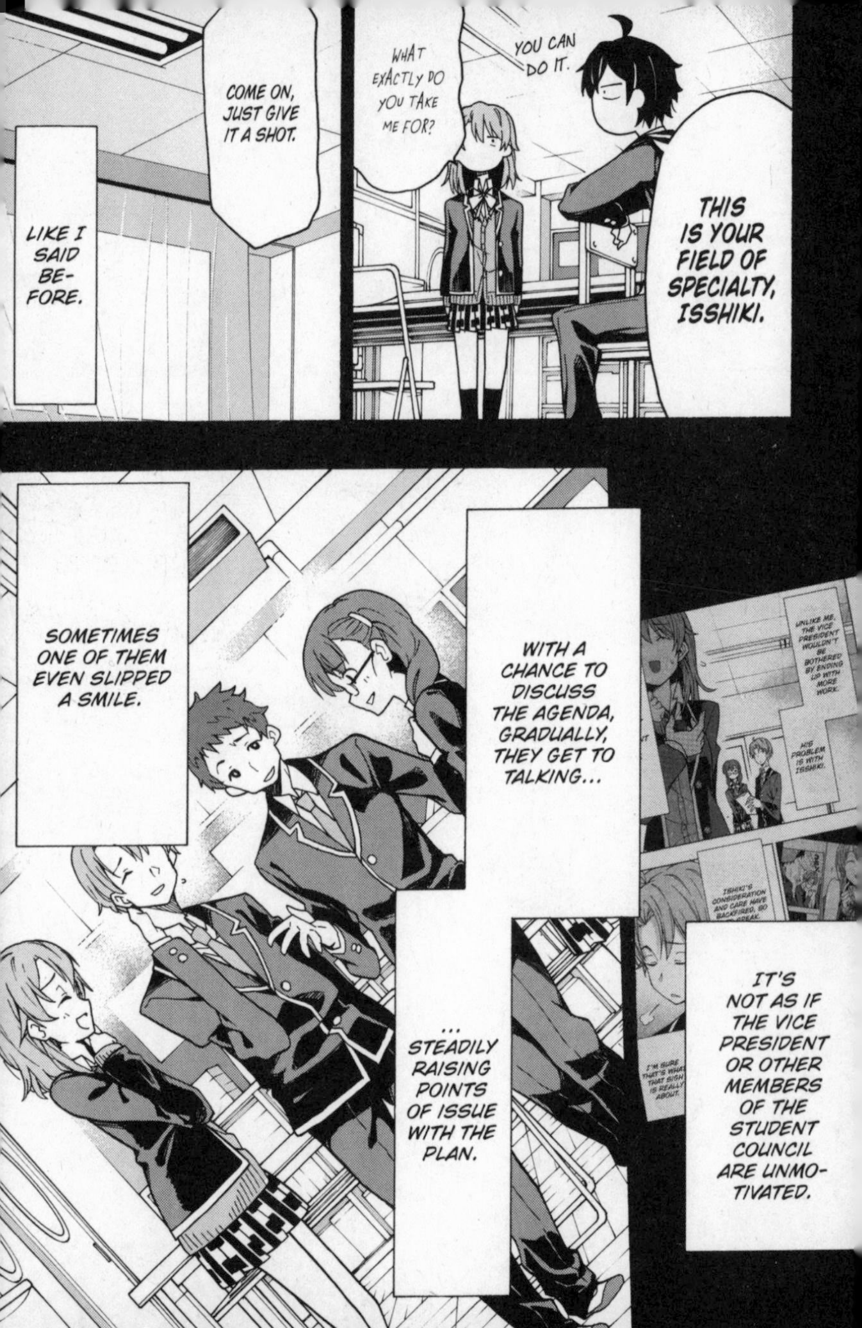
YOU CAN DO IT.
THIS IS YOUR FIELD OF SPECIALTY, ISSHIKI.
WHAT EXACTLY DO YOU TAKE ME FOR?
COME ON, JUST GIVE IT A SHOT.
LIKE I SAID BEFORE.
UNLIKE ME, THE VICE PRESIDENT WOULDN'T BE BOTHERED BY ENDING UP WITH MORE WORK.
HIS PROBLEM IS WITH ISSHIKI.
I'M SURE THAT'S WHAT THAT SIGH IS REALLY ABOUT.
IT'S NOT AS IF THE VICE PRESIDENT OR OTHER MEMBERS OF THE STUDENT COUNCIL ARE UNMOTIVATED.
WITH A CHANCE TO DISCUSS THE AGENDA, GRADUALLY, THEY GET TO TALKING...
...STEADILY RAISING POINTS OF ISSUE WITH THE PLAN.
SOMETIMES ONE OF THEM EVEN SLIPPED A SMILE.

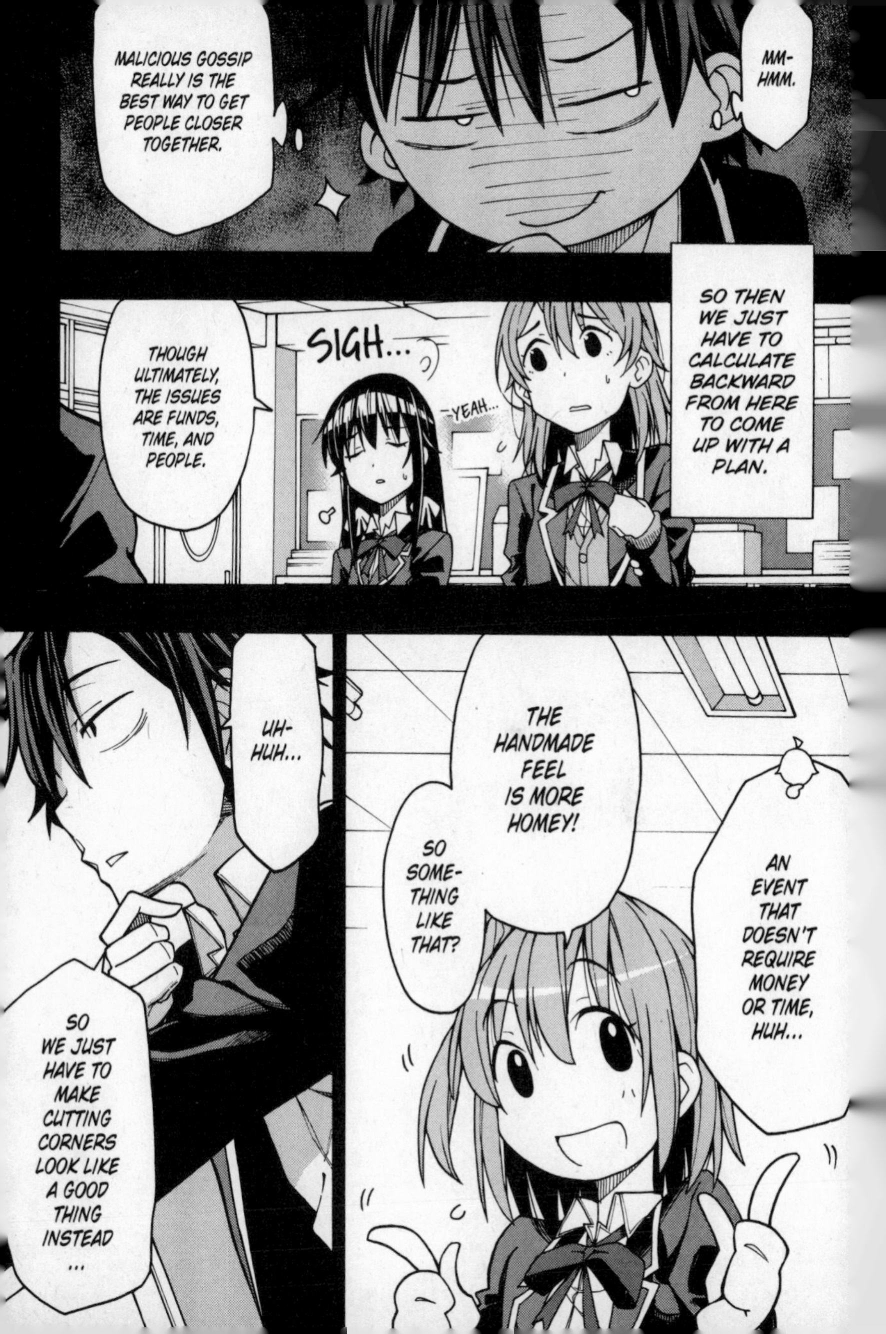
MM-HMM.
MALICIOUS GOSSIP REALLY IS THE BEST WAY TO GET PEOPLE CLOSER TOGETHER.
SO THEN WE JUST HAVE TO CALCULATE BACKWARD FROM HERE TO COME UP WITH A PLAN.
THOUGH ULTIMATELY, THE ISSUES ARE FUNDS, TIME, AND PEOPLE.
SIGH...
YEAH...
AN EVENT THAT DOESN'T REQUIRE MONEY OR TIME, HUH...
THE HANDMADE FEEL IS MORE HOMEY!
SO SOME-THING LIKE THAT?
UH-HUH...
SO WE JUST HAVE TO MAKE CUTTING CORNERS LOOK LIKE A GOOD THING INSTEAD...

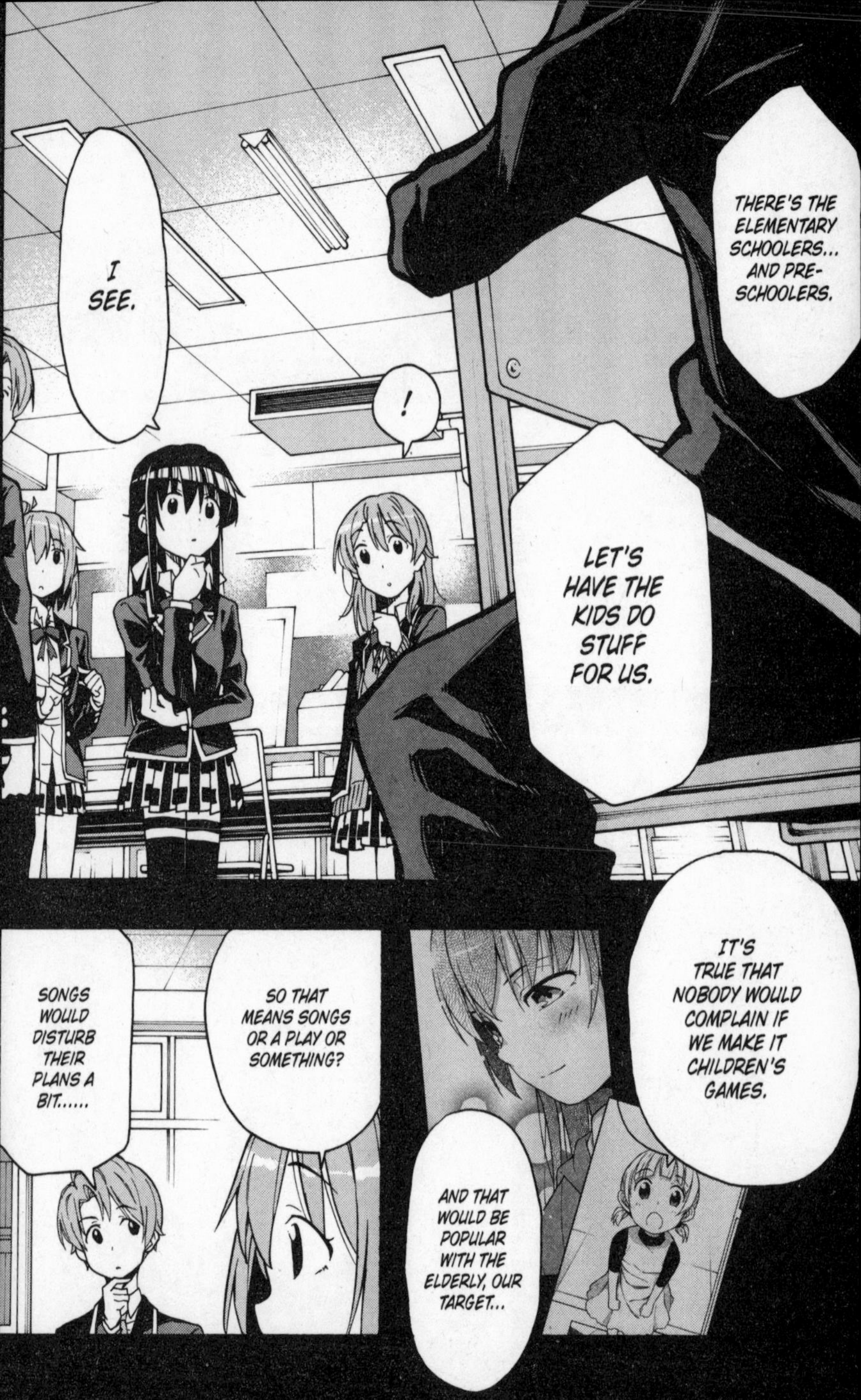
THERE'S THE ELEMENTARY SCHOOLERS... AND PRE-SCHOOLERS.
LET'S HAVE THE KIDS DO STUFF FOR US.
!
I SEE.
IT'S TRUE THAT NOBODY WOULD COMPLAIN IF WE MAKE IT CHILDREN'S GAMES.
AND THAT WOULD BE POPULAR WITH THE ELDERLY, OUR TARGET...
SO THAT MEANS SONGS OR A PLAY OR SOMETHING?
SONGS WOULD DISTURB THEIR PLANS A BIT......

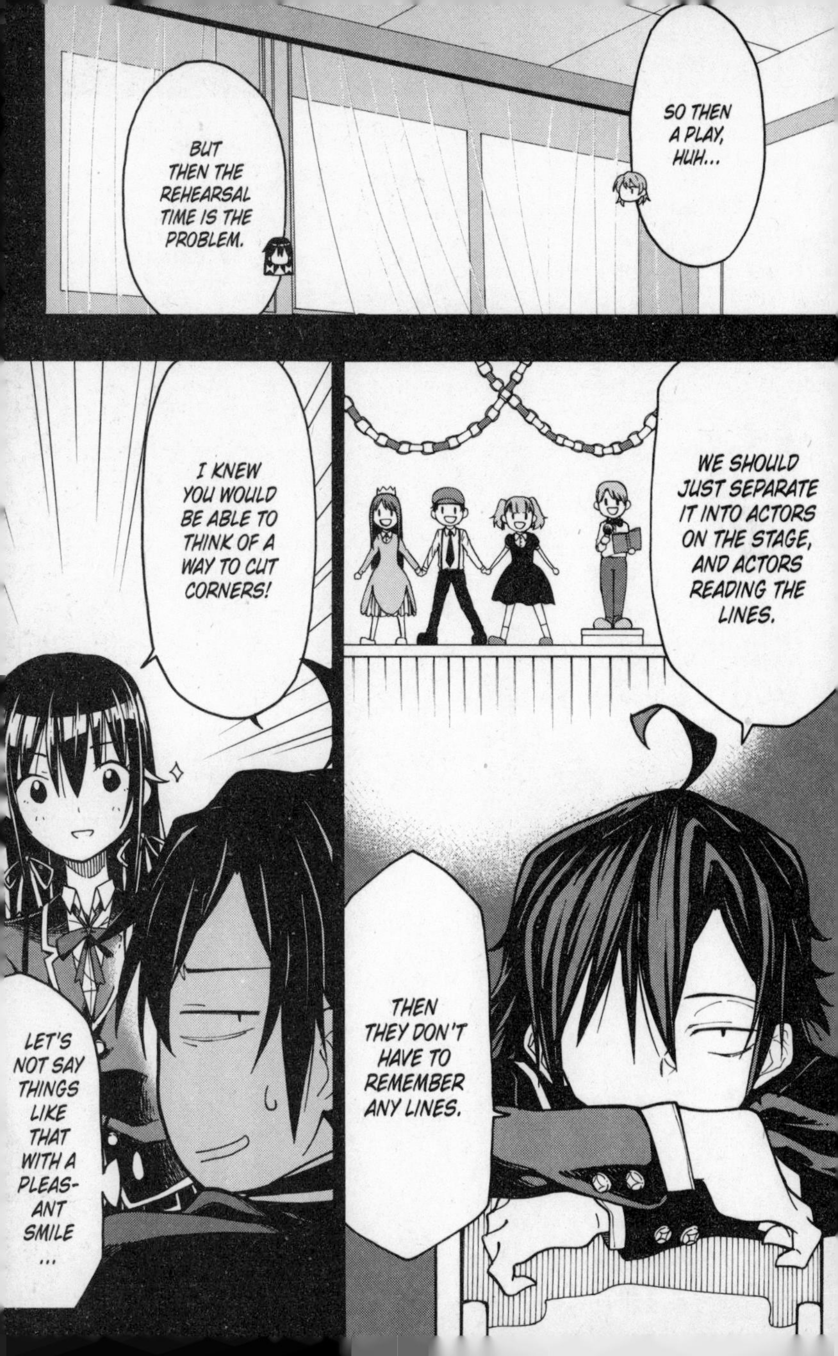
SO THEN A PLAY, HUH...
BUT THEN THE REHEARSAL TIME IS THE PROBLEM.
WE SHOULD JUST SEPARATE IT INTO ACTORS ON THE STAGE, AND ACTORS READING THE LINES.
THEN THEY DON'T HAVE TO REMEMBER ANY LINES.
I KNEW YOU WOULD BE ABLE TO THINK OF A WAY TO CUT CORNERS!
LET'S NOT SAY THINGS LIKE THAT WITH A PLEAS-ANT SMILE ...

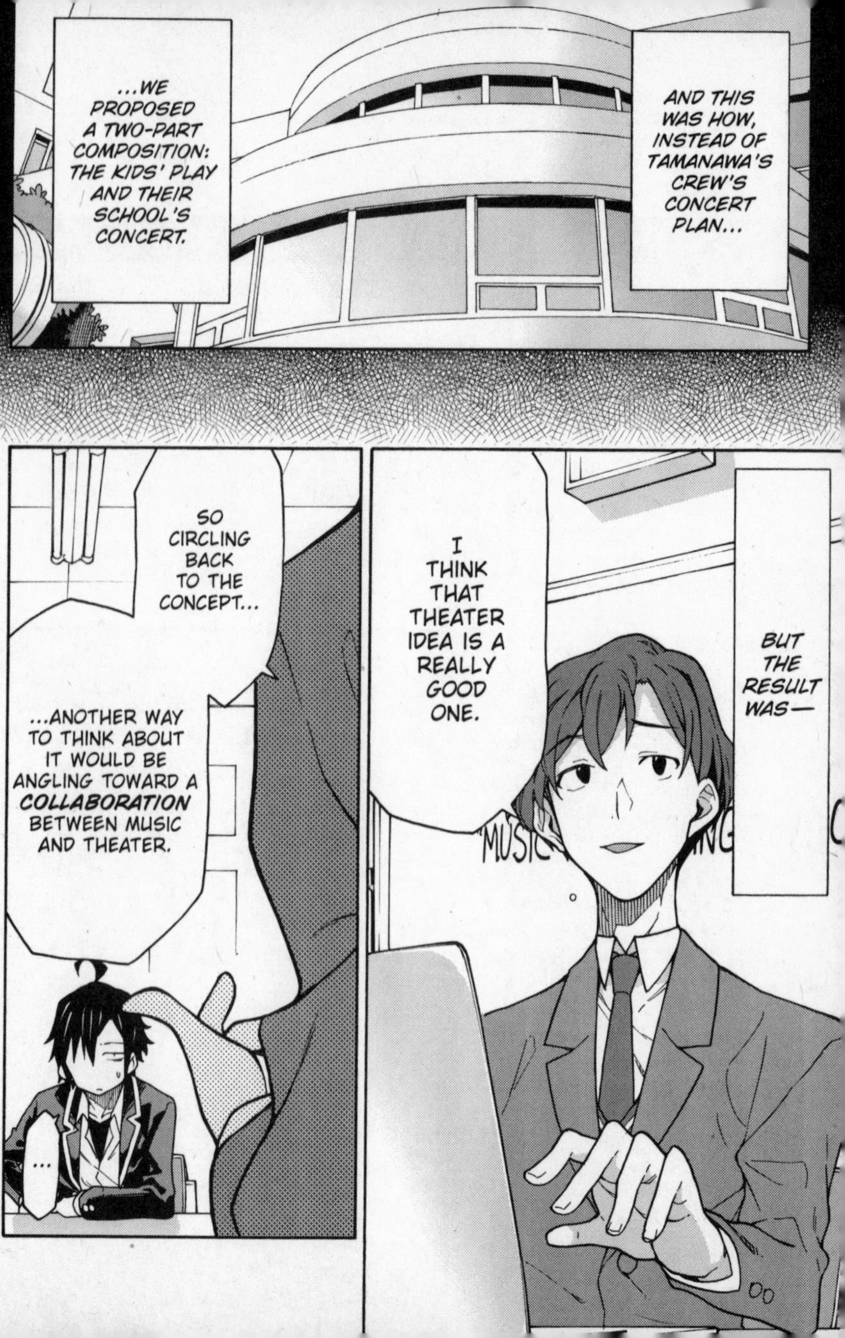
AND THIS WAS HOW, INSTEAD OF TAMANAWA'S CREW'S CONCERT PLAN...
...WE PROPOSED A TWO-PART COMPOSITION: THE KIDS' PLAY AND THEIR SCHOOL'S CONCERT.
BUT THE RESULT WAS—
I THINK THAT THEATER IDEA IS A REALLY GOOD ONE.
SO CIRCLING BACK TO THE CONCEPT...
...ANOTHER WAY TO THINK ABOUT IT WOULD BE ANGLING TOWARD A **COLLABORATION** BETWEEN MUSIC AND THEATER.
...

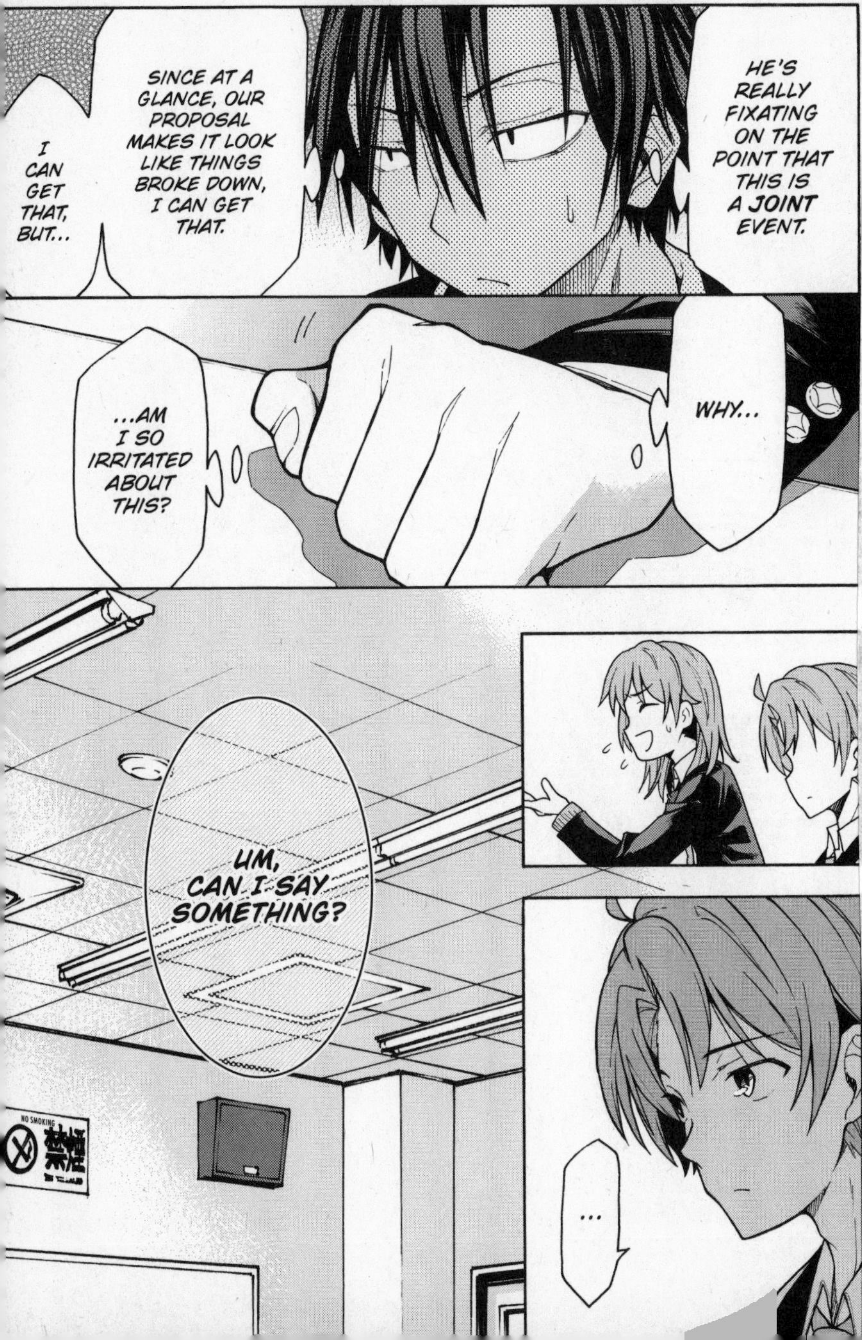
HE'S REALLY FIXATING ON THE POINT THAT THIS IS A JOINT EVENT.
SINCE AT A GLANCE, OUR PROPOSAL MAKES IT LOOK LIKE THINGS BROKE DOWN, I CAN GET THAT.
I CAN GET THAT, BUT...
WHY...
...AM I SO IRRITATED ABOUT THIS?
...
UM, CAN I SAY SOMETHING?
NO SMOKING
禁煙

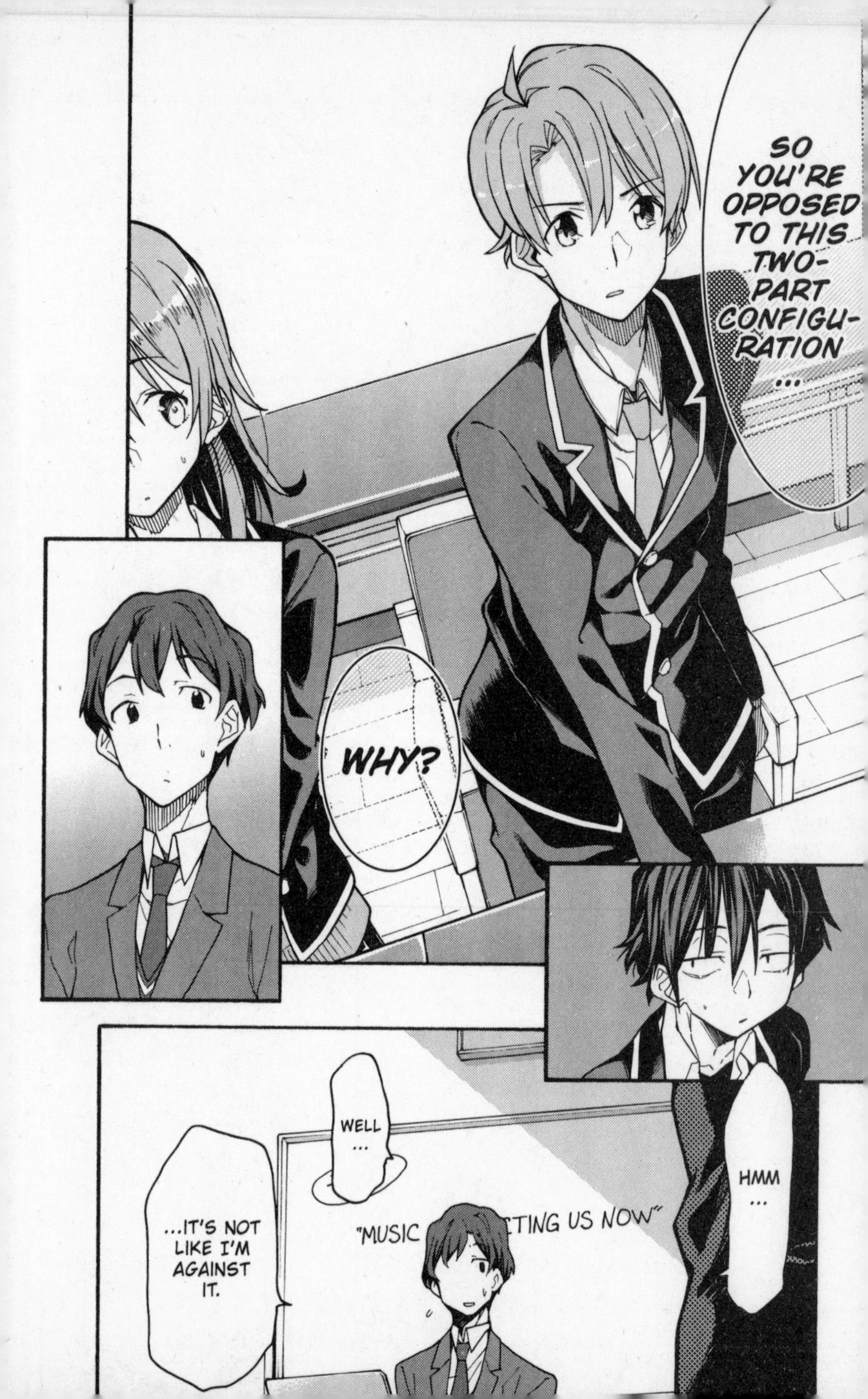
SO YOU'RE OPPOSED TO THIS TWO-PART CONFIGURATION...
WHY?
HMM...
WELL...
...IT'S NOT LIKE I'M AGAINST IT.

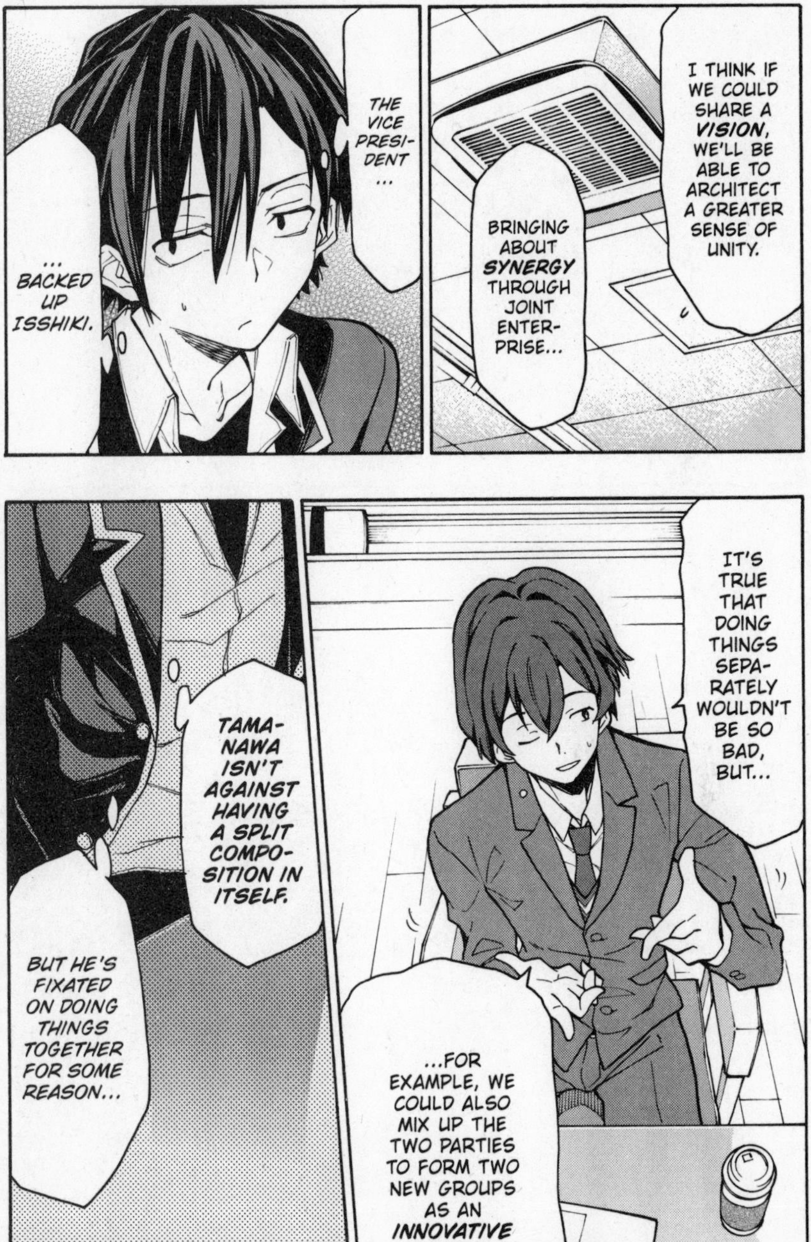
I THINK IF WE COULD SHARE A VISION, WE'LL BE ABLE TO ARCHITECT A GREATER SENSE OF UNITY.
BRINGING ABOUT SYNERGY THROUGH JOINT ENTER-PRISE...
THE VICE PRESI-DENT...
...BACKED UP ISSHIKI.
IT'S TRUE THAT DOING THINGS SEPA-RATELY WOULDN'T BE SO BAD, BUT...
...FOR EXAMPLE, WE COULD ALSO MIX UP THE TWO PARTIES TO FORM TWO NEW GROUPS AS AN INNOVATIVE SOLUTION.
TAMA-NAWA ISN'T AGAINST HAVING A SPLIT COMPO-SITION IN ITSELF.
BUT HE'S FIXATED ON DOING THINGS TOGETHER FOR SOME REASON...

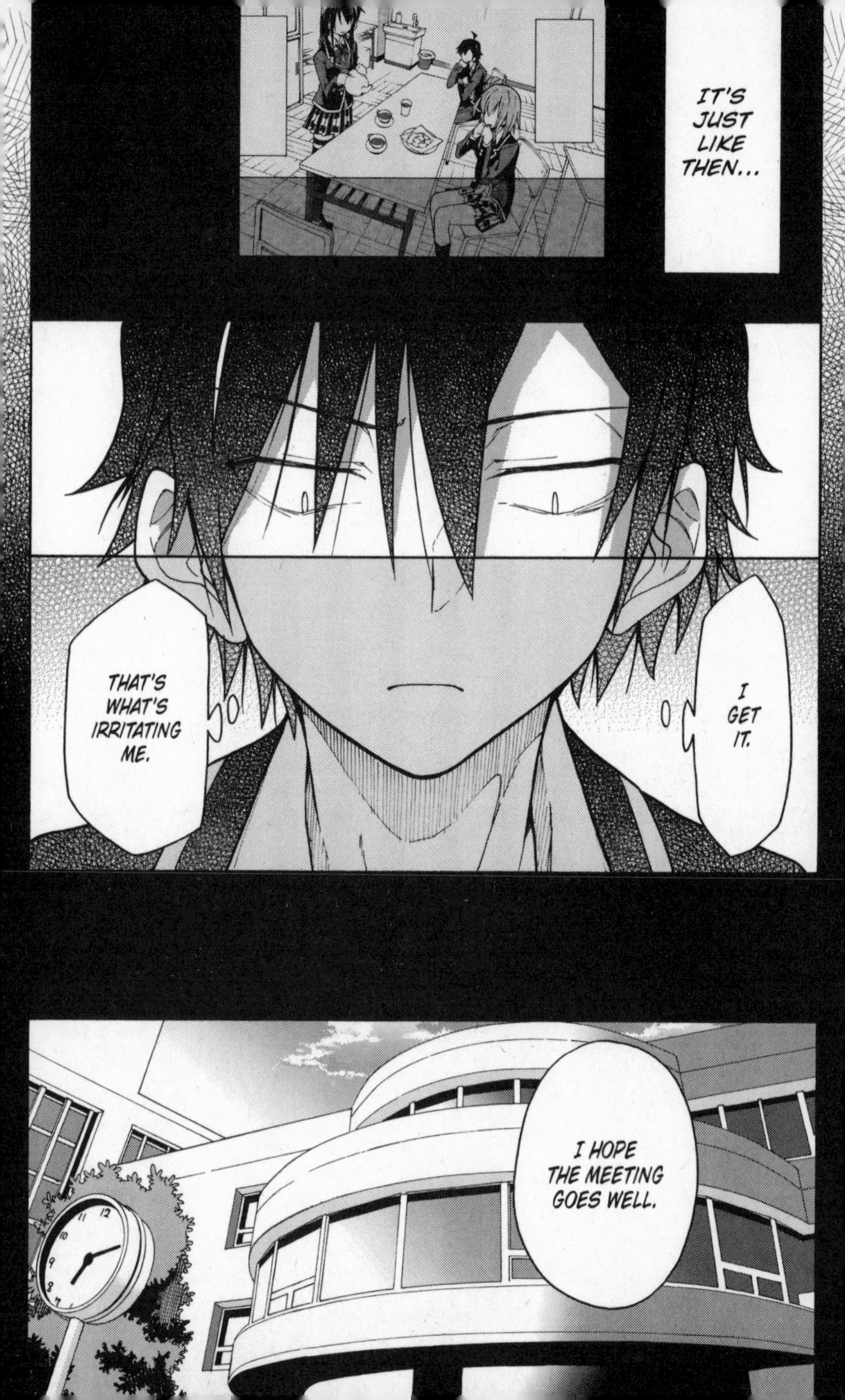
IT'S JUST LIKE THEN...
I GET IT.
THAT'S WHAT'S IRRITATING ME.
I HOPE THE MEETING GOES WELL.

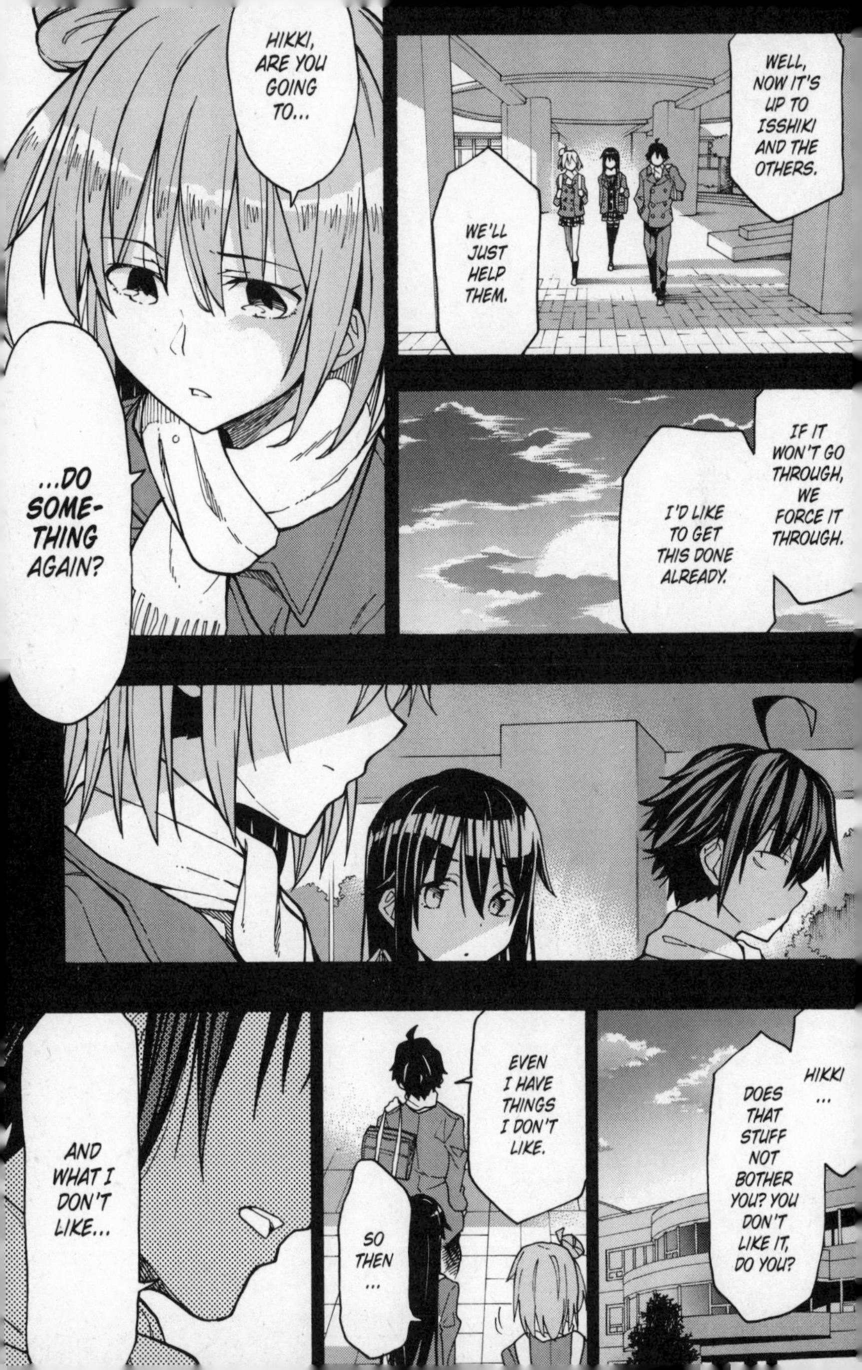
WELL, NOW IT'S UP TO ISSHIKI AND THE OTHERS.
WE'LL JUST HELP THEM.
IF IT WON'T GO THROUGH, WE FORCE IT THROUGH.
I'D LIKE TO GET THIS DONE ALREADY.
HIKKI, ARE YOU GOING TO...
...DO SOME-THING AGAIN?
HIKKI ...
DOES THAT STUFF NOT BOTHER YOU? YOU DON'T LIKE IT, DO YOU?
EVEN I HAVE THINGS I DON'T LIKE.
SO THEN ...
AND WHAT I DON'T LIKE...

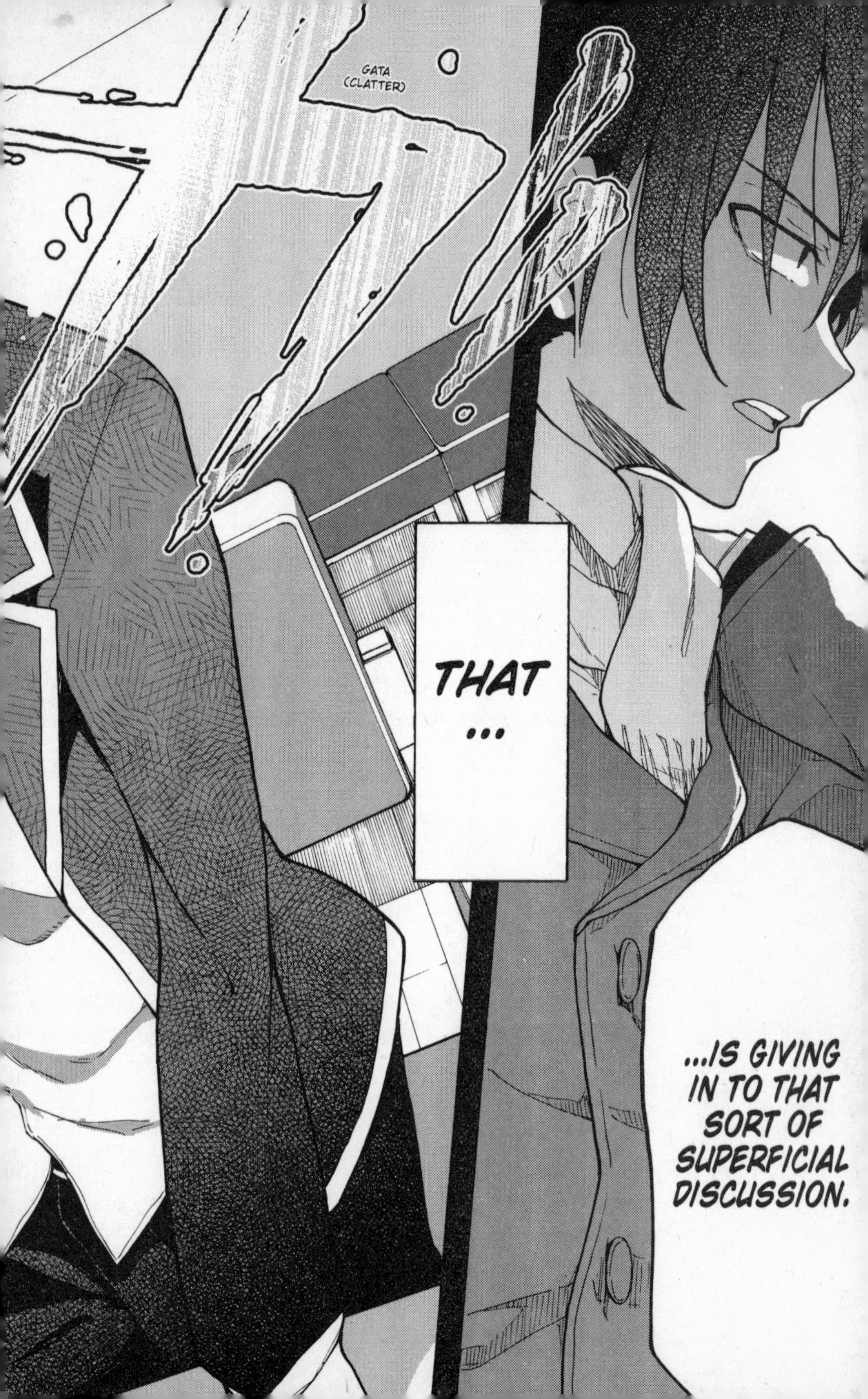
GATA (CLATTER)
THAT ...
...IS GIVING IN TO THAT SORT OF SUPERFICIAL DISCUSSION.

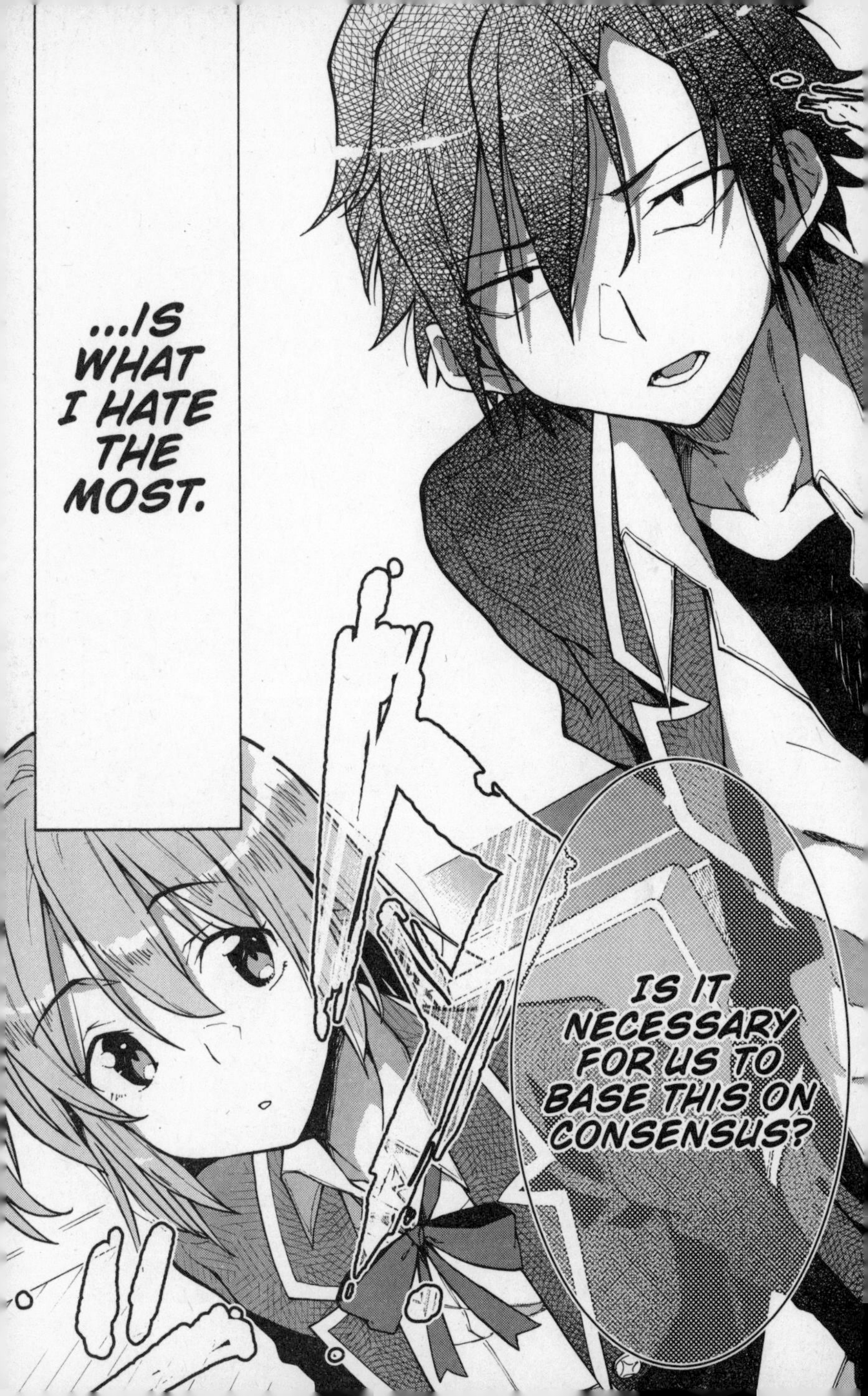
IS IT NECESSARY FOR US TO BASE THIS ON CONSENSUS?
...IS WHAT I HATE THE MOST.

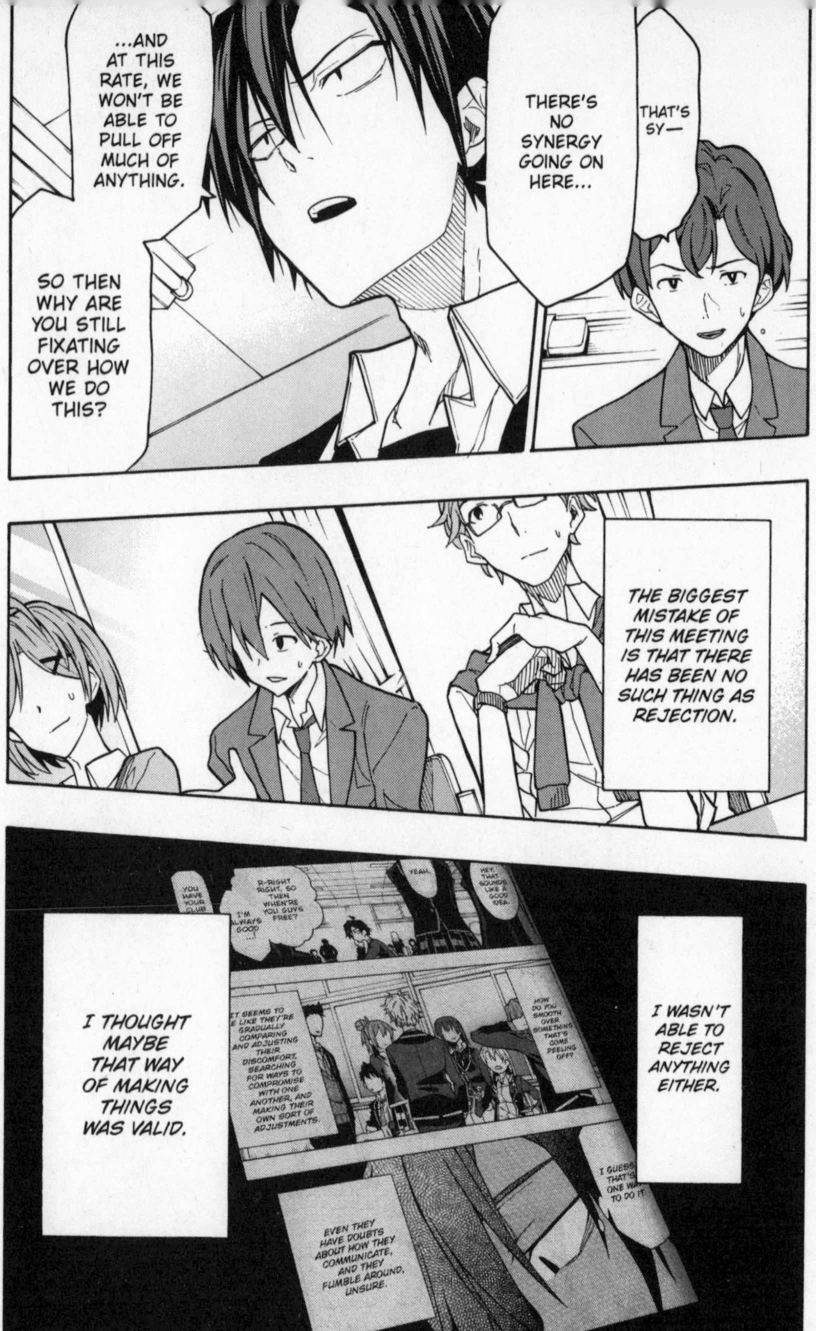
THAT'S SY—
THERE'S NO SYNERGY GOING ON HERE...
...AND AT THIS RATE, WE WON'T BE ABLE TO PULL OFF MUCH OF ANYTHING.
SO THEN WHY ARE YOU STILL FIXATING OVER HOW WE DO THIS?
THE BIGGEST MISTAKE OF THIS MEETING IS THAT THERE HAS BEEN NO SUCH THING AS REJECTION.
I WASN'T ABLE TO REJECT ANYTHING EITHER.
HEY, THAT SOUNDS LIKE A GOOD IDEA.
YEAH.
R-RIGHT RIGHT, SO THEN WHEN'RE YOU GUYS FREE?
I'M ALWAYS GOOD ...!
YOU HAVE YOUR CLUB
HOW DO YOU SMOOTH OVER SOMETHING THAT'S COME PEELING OFF?
EVEN THEY HAVE DOUBTS ABOUT HOW THEY COMMUNICATE, AND THEY FUMBLE AROUND, UNSURE.
I THOUGHT MAYBE THAT WAY OF MAKING THINGS WAS VALID.

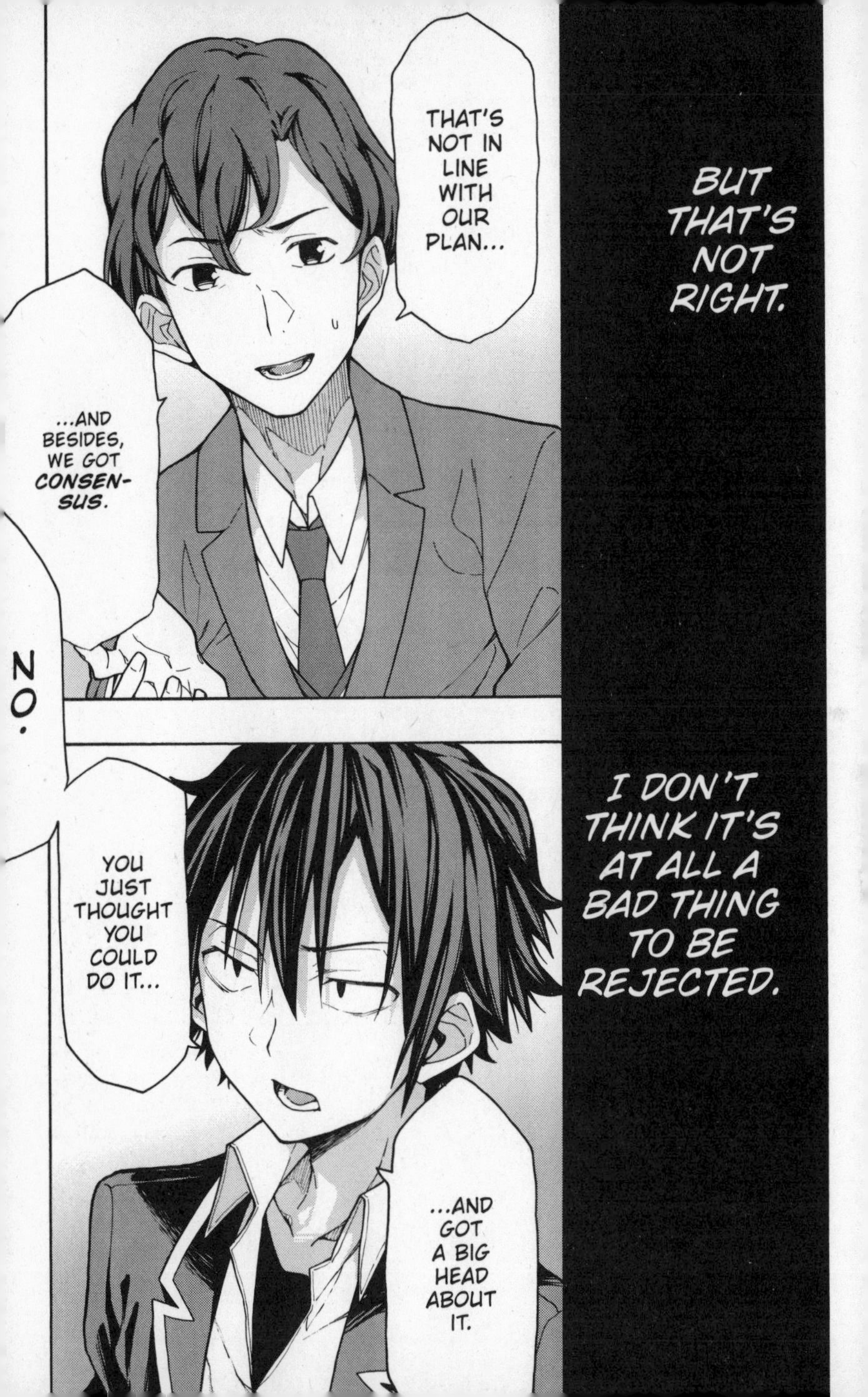
BUT THAT'S NOT RIGHT.
I DON'T THINK IT'S AT ALL A BAD THING TO BE REJECTED.
THAT'S NOT IN LINE WITH OUR PLAN...
...AND BESIDES, WE GOT CONSENSUS.
NO.
YOU JUST THOUGHT YOU COULD DO IT...
...AND GOT A BIG HEAD ABOUT IT.

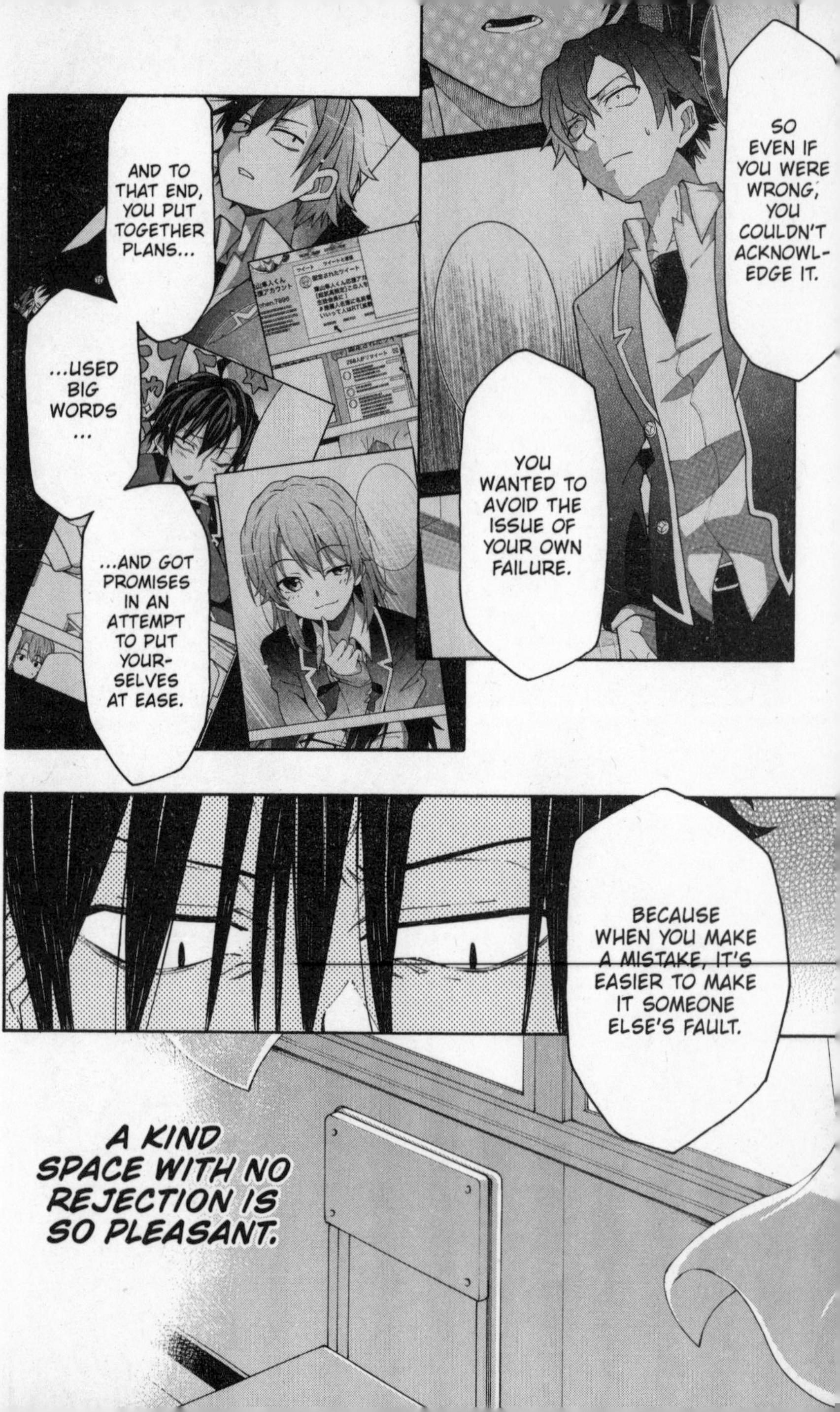
SO EVEN IF YOU WERE WRONG, YOU COULDN'T ACKNOWL-EDGE IT.
YOU WANTED TO AVOID THE ISSUE OF YOUR OWN FAILURE.
AND TO THAT END, YOU PUT TOGETHER PLANS...
...USED BIG WORDS...
...AND GOT PROMISES IN AN ATTEMPT TO PUT YOUR-SELVES AT EASE.
BECAUSE WHEN YOU MAKE A MISTAKE, IT'S EASIER TO MAKE IT SOMEONE ELSE'S FAULT.
A KIND SPACE WITH NO REJECTION IS SO PLEASANT.

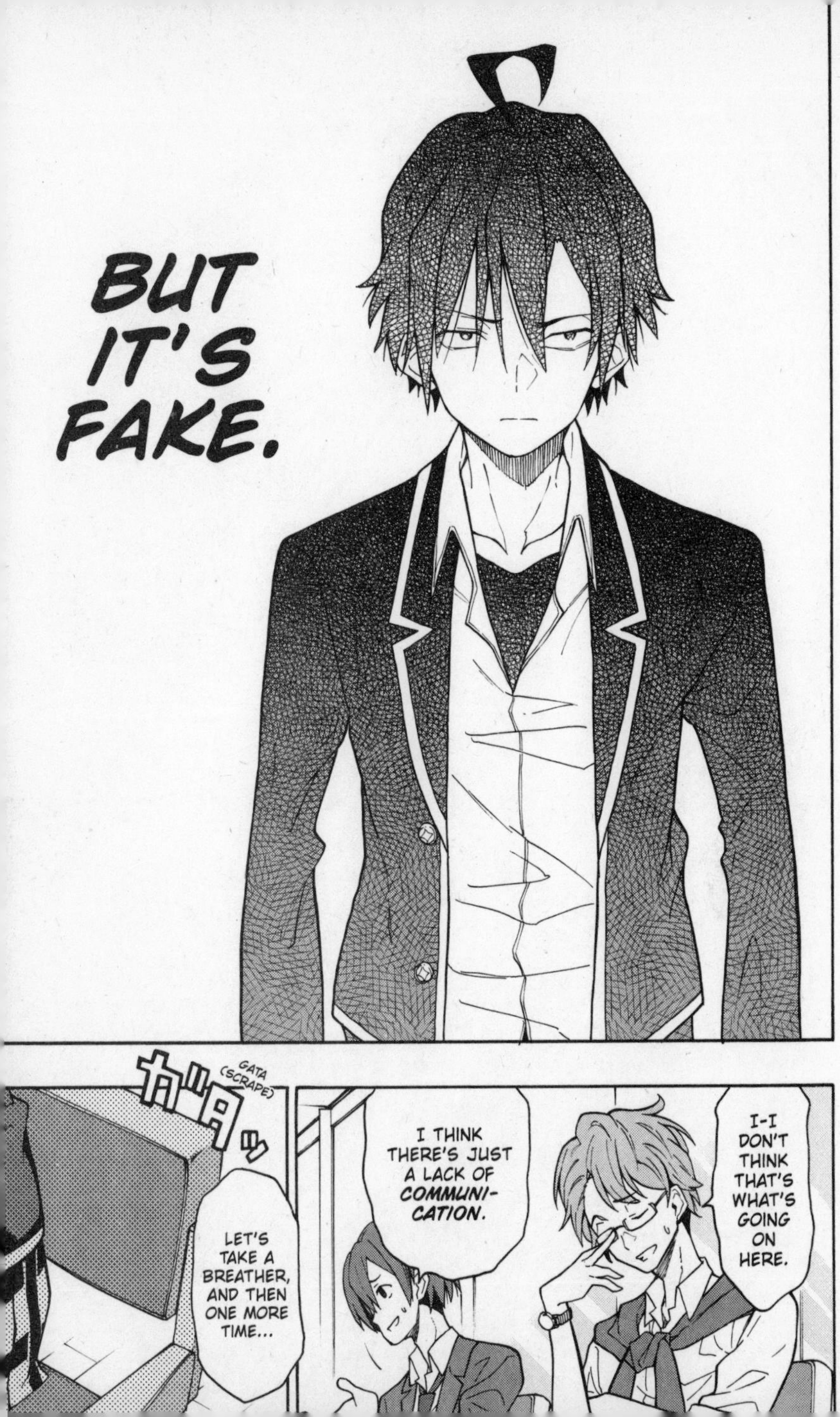
BUT IT'S FAKE.
I-I DON'T THINK THAT'S WHAT'S GOING ON HERE.
I THINK THERE'S JUST A LACK OF ***COMMUNICATION***.
カタッ
GATA (SCRAPE)
LET'S TAKE A BREATHER, AND THEN ONE MORE TIME...

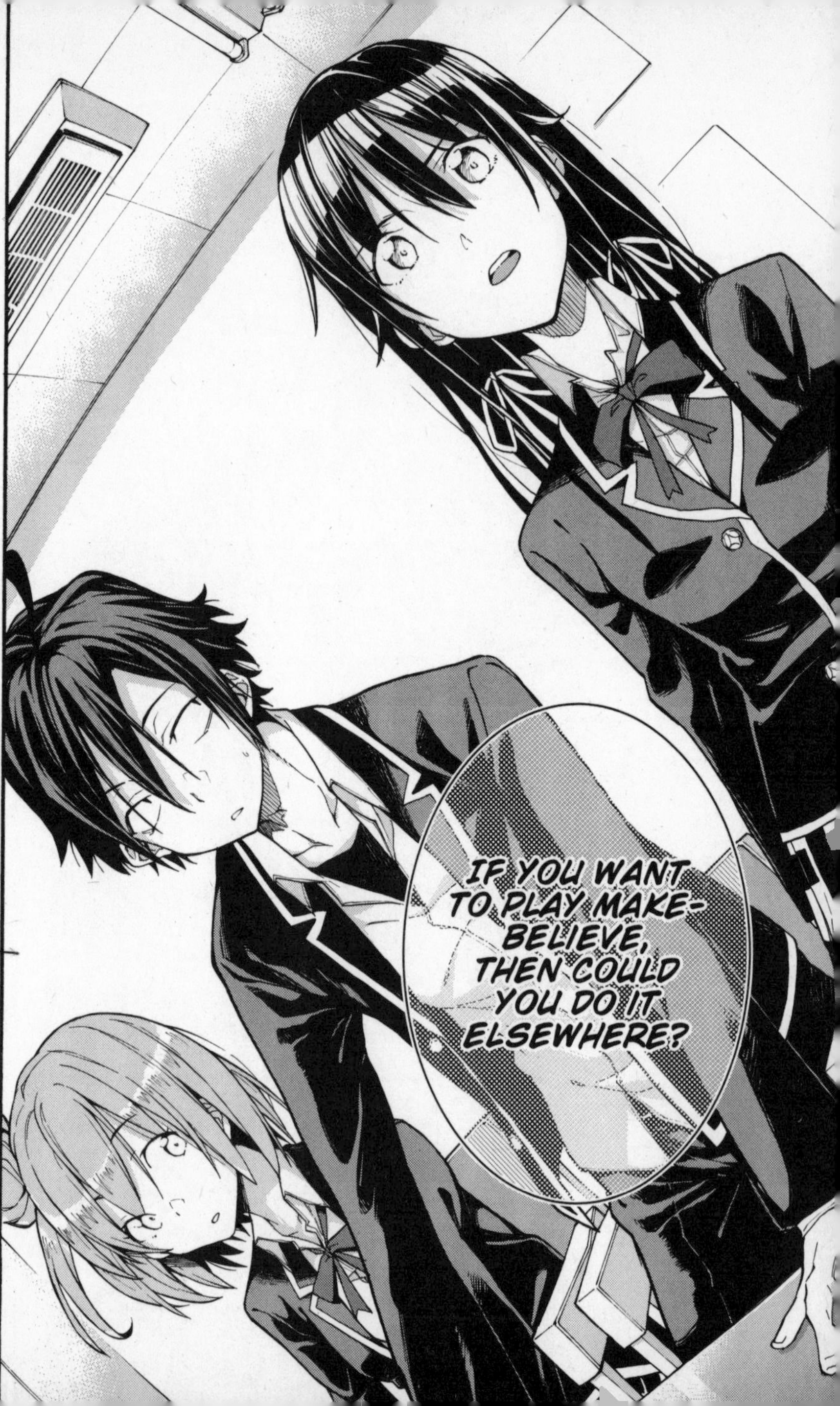
IF YOU WANT TO PLAY MAKE-BELIEVE, THEN COULD YOU DO IT ELSEWHERE?

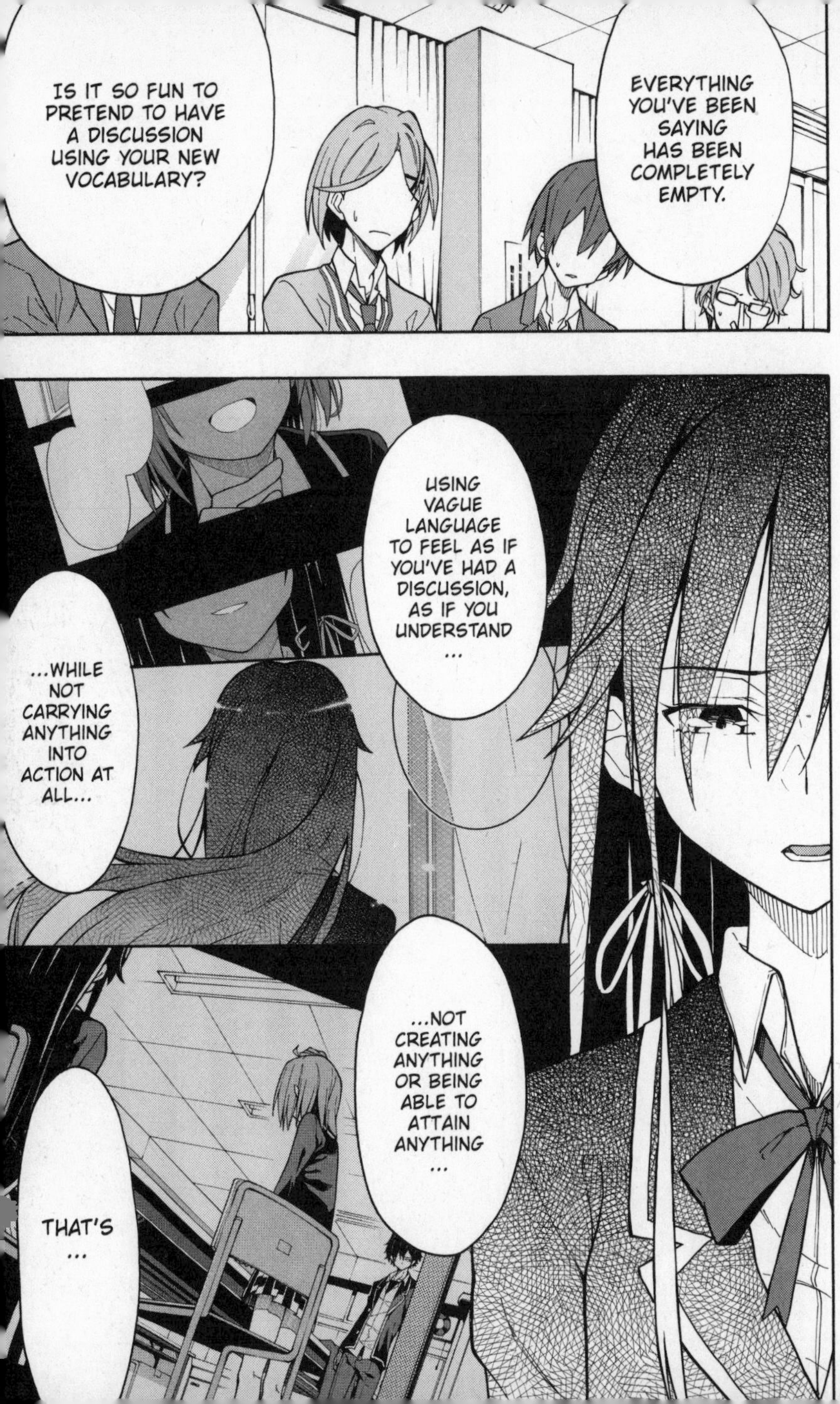
EVERYTHING YOU'VE BEEN SAYING HAS BEEN COMPLETELY EMPTY.
IS IT SO FUN TO PRETEND TO HAVE A DISCUSSION USING YOUR NEW VOCABULARY?
USING VAGUE LANGUAGE TO FEEL AS IF YOU'VE HAD A DISCUSSION, AS IF YOU UNDERSTAND ...
...WHILE NOT CARRYING ANYTHING INTO ACTION AT ALL...
...NOT CREATING ANYTHING OR BEING ABLE TO ATTAIN ANYTHING ...
THAT'S ...

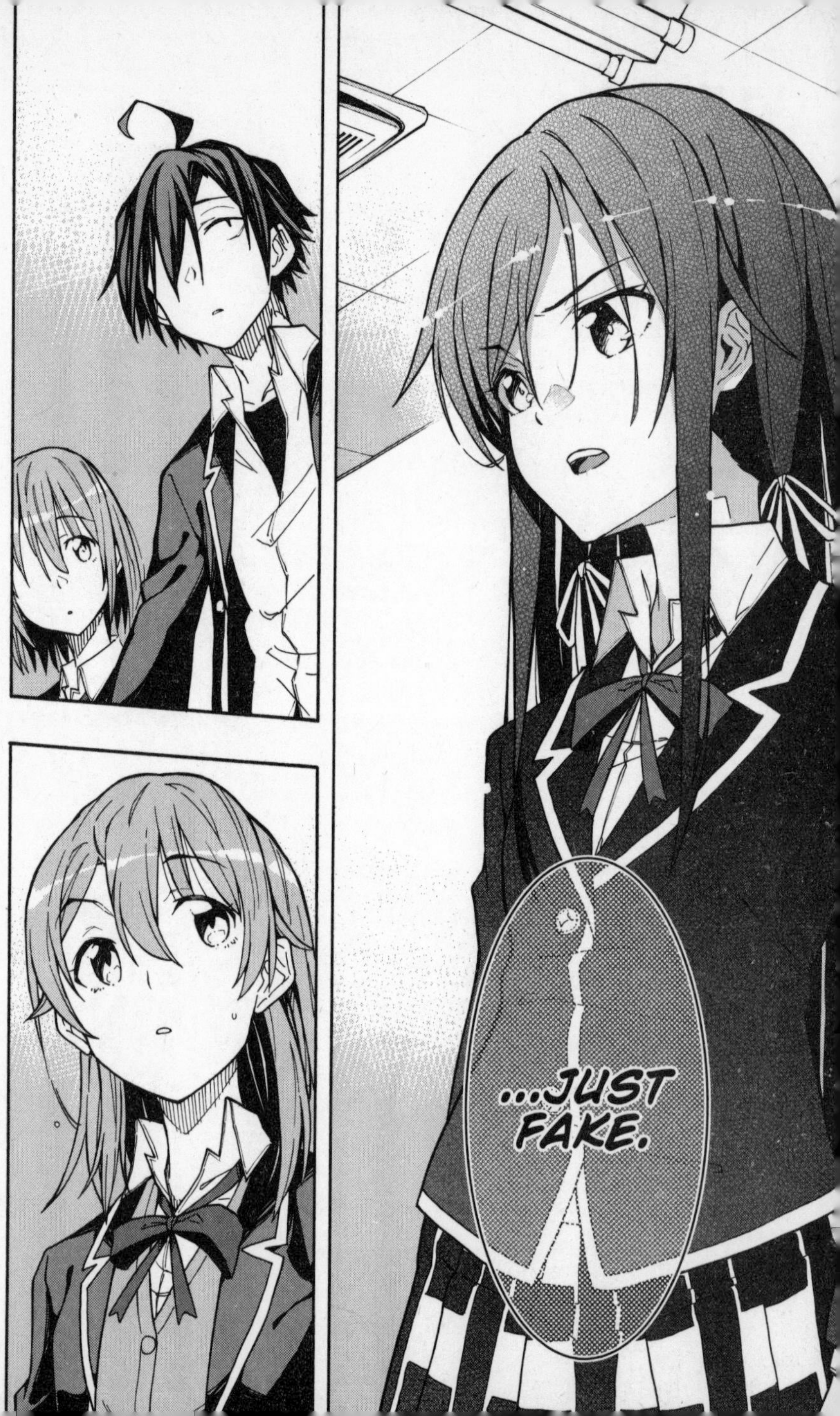
...JUST FAKE.

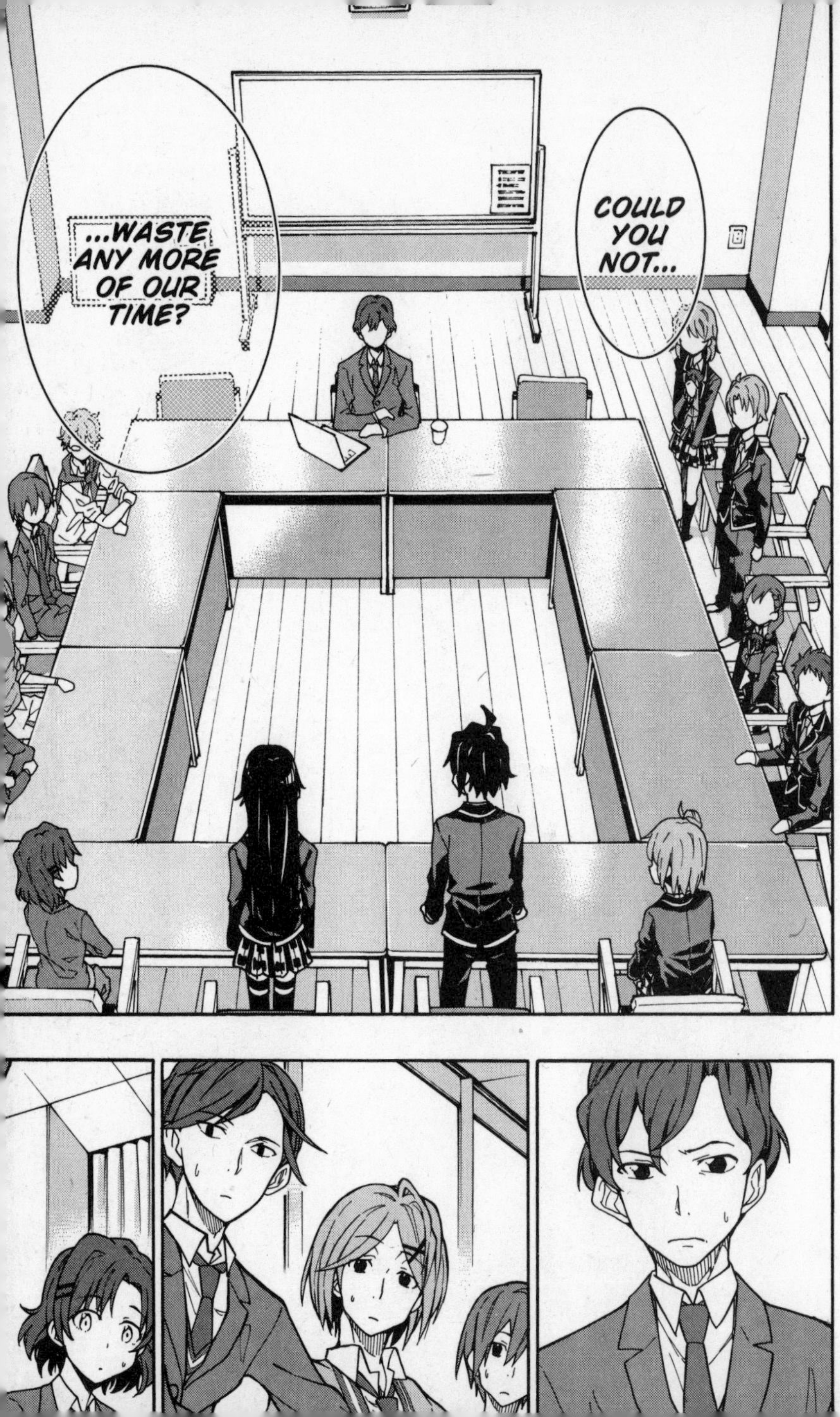
COULD YOU NOT...
...WASTE ANY MORE OF OUR TIME?

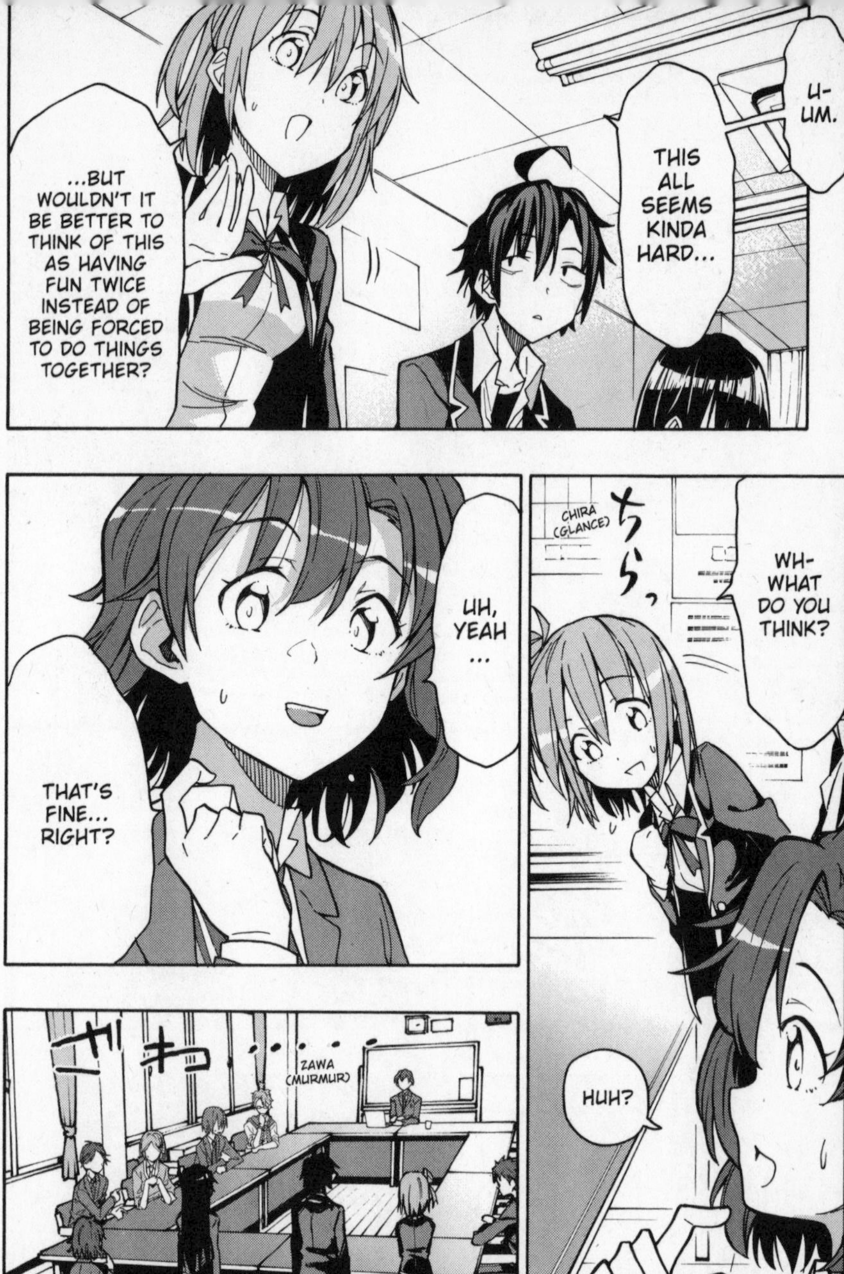
U-UM.
THIS ALL SEEMS KINDA HARD...
...BUT WOULDN'T IT BE BETTER TO THINK OF THIS AS HAVING FUN TWICE INSTEAD OF BEING FORCED TO DO THINGS TOGETHER?
ちらっ
CHIRA (GLANCE)
WH-WHAT DO YOU THINK?
HUH?
UH, YEAH...
THAT'S FINE... RIGHT?
ZAWA (MURMUR)

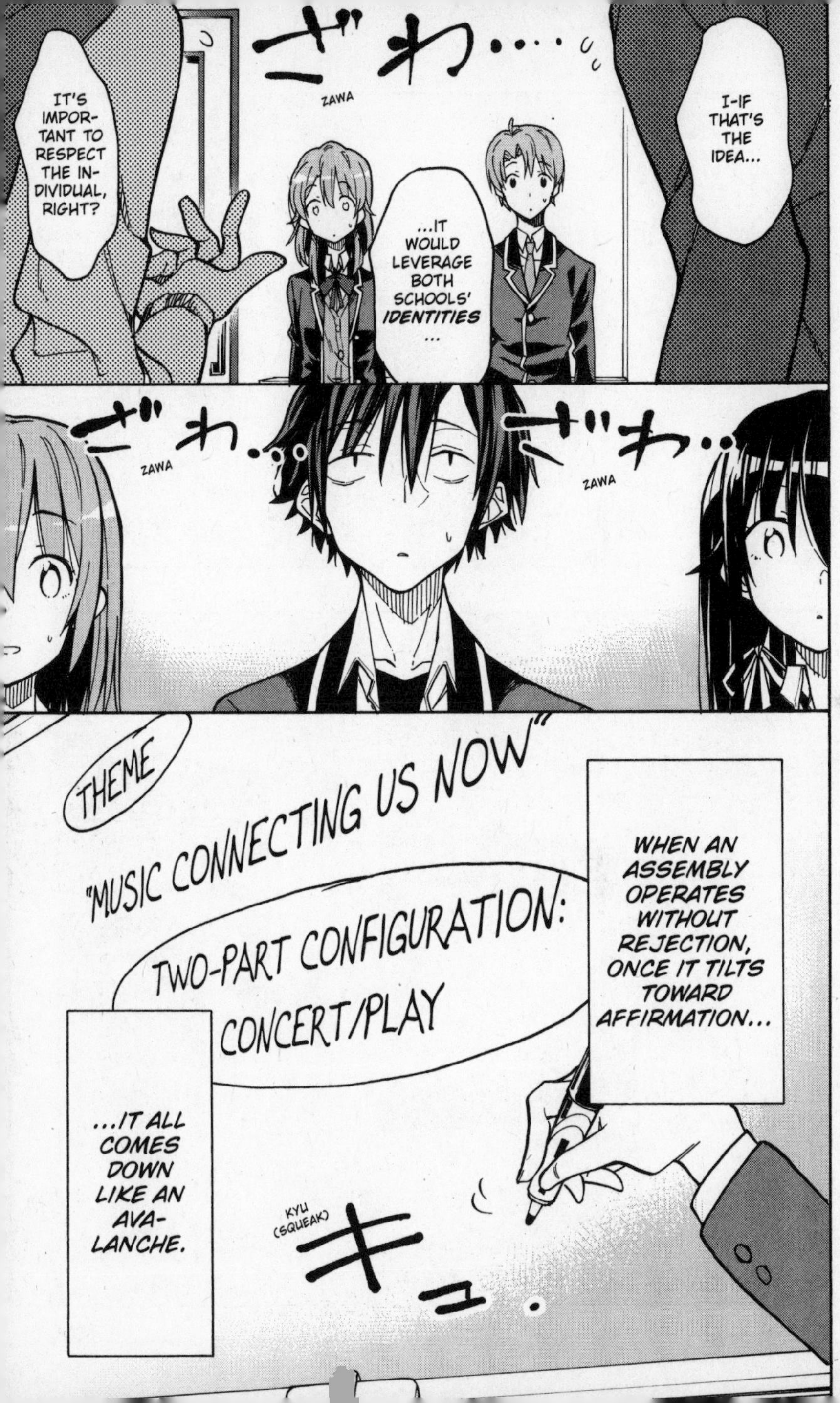
I-IF THAT'S THE IDEA...
ざわ…
ZAWA
IT'S IMPORTANT TO RESPECT THE INDIVIDUAL, RIGHT?
...IT WOULD LEVERAGE BOTH SCHOOLS' *IDENTITIES*...
ざわ…
ZAWA
ざわ…
ZAWA
WHEN AN ASSEMBLY OPERATES WITHOUT REJECTION, ONCE IT TILTS TOWARD AFFIRMATION...
THEME
"MUSIC CONNECTING US NOW"
TWO-PART CONFIGURATION:
CONCERT/PLAY
KYU (SQUEAK)
キュ
...IT ALL COMES DOWN LIKE AN AVALANCHE.

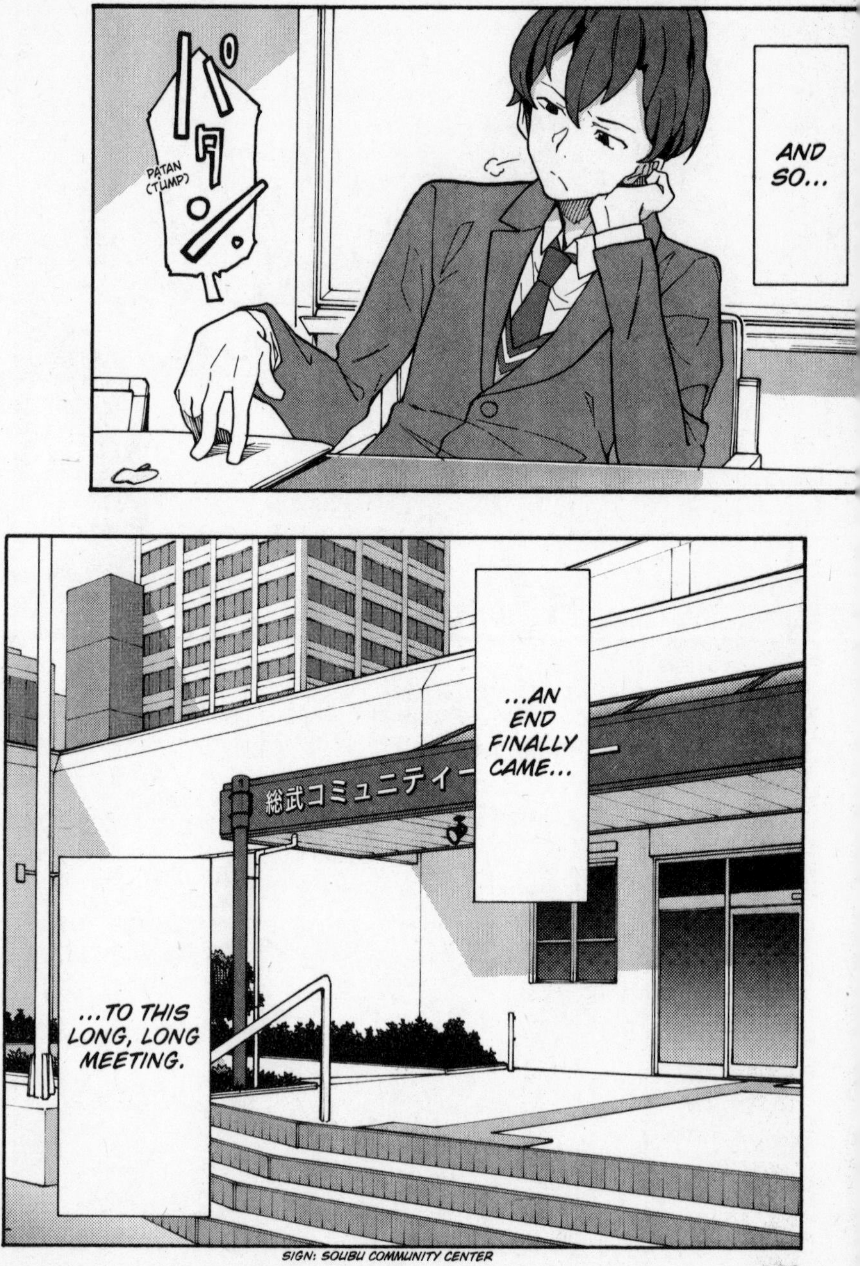
AND SO...
パタン
PATAN (TUMP)
...AN END FINALLY CAME...
...TO THIS LONG, LONG MEETING.
総武コミュニティー
SIGN: SOUBU COMMUNITY CENTER

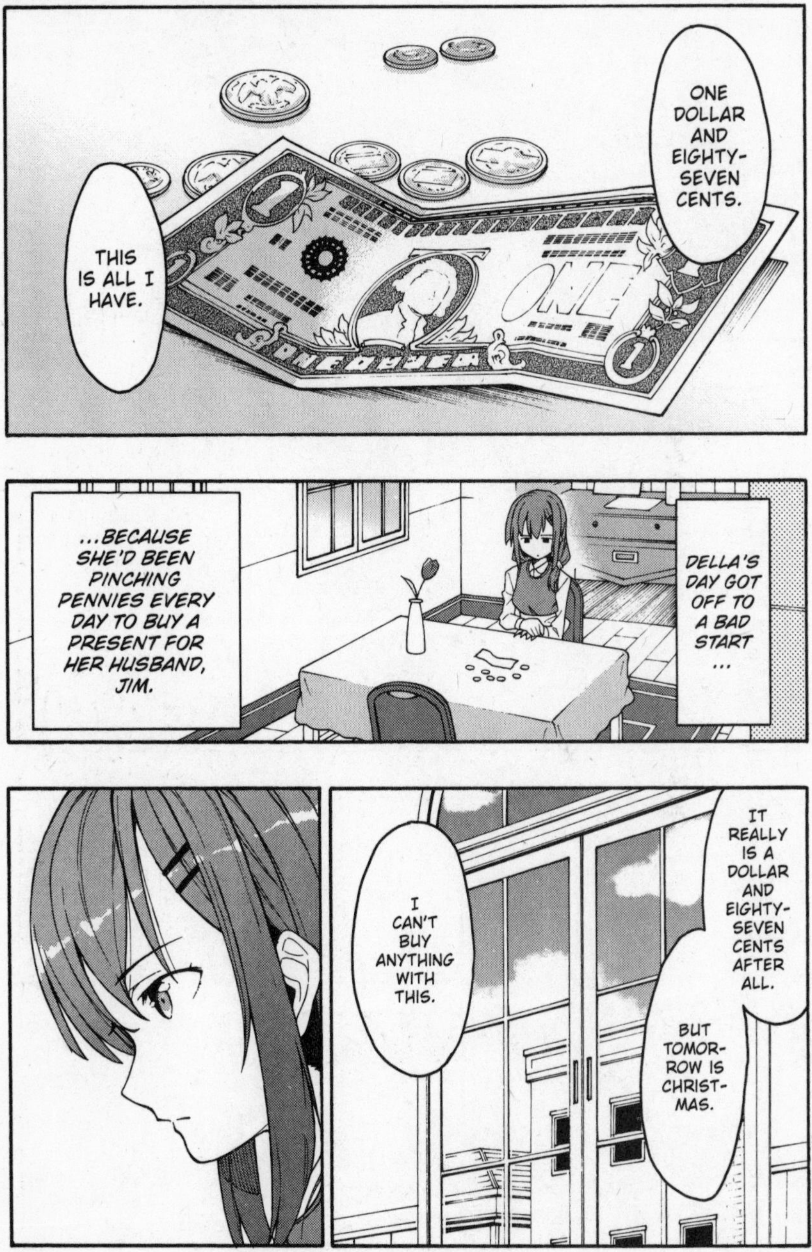
ONE DOLLAR AND EIGHTY-SEVEN CENTS.
THIS IS ALL I HAVE.
DELLA'S DAY GOT OFF TO A BAD START ...
...BECAUSE SHE'D BEEN PINCHING PENNIES EVERY DAY TO BUY A PRESENT FOR HER HUSBAND, JIM.
IT REALLY IS A DOLLAR AND EIGHTY-SEVEN CENTS AFTER ALL.
BUT TOMORROW IS CHRISTMAS.
I CAN'T BUY ANYTHING WITH THIS.

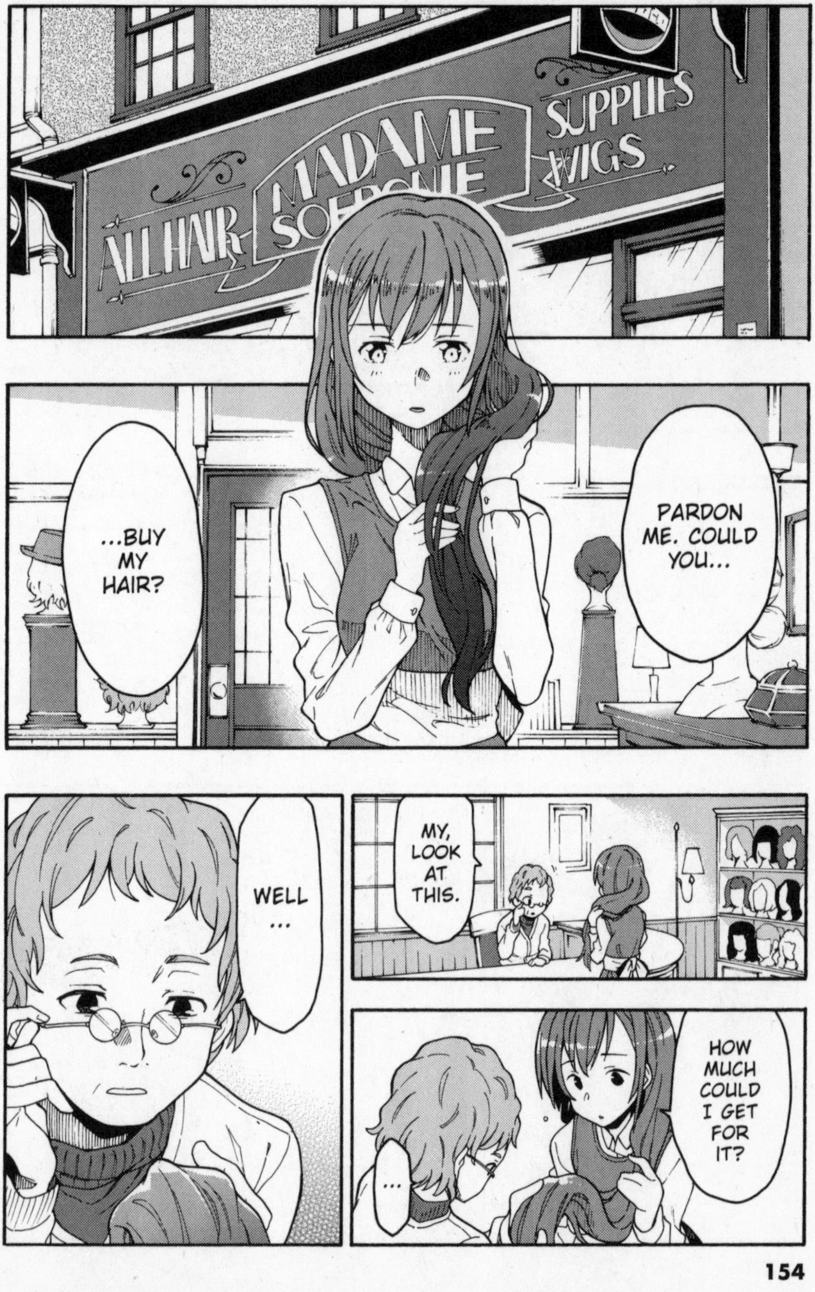
SUPPLIES
WIGS
MADAME
ALL HAIR
PARDON ME. COULD YOU...
...BUY MY HAIR?
MY, LOOK AT THIS.
HOW MUCH COULD I GET FOR IT?
...
WELL ...

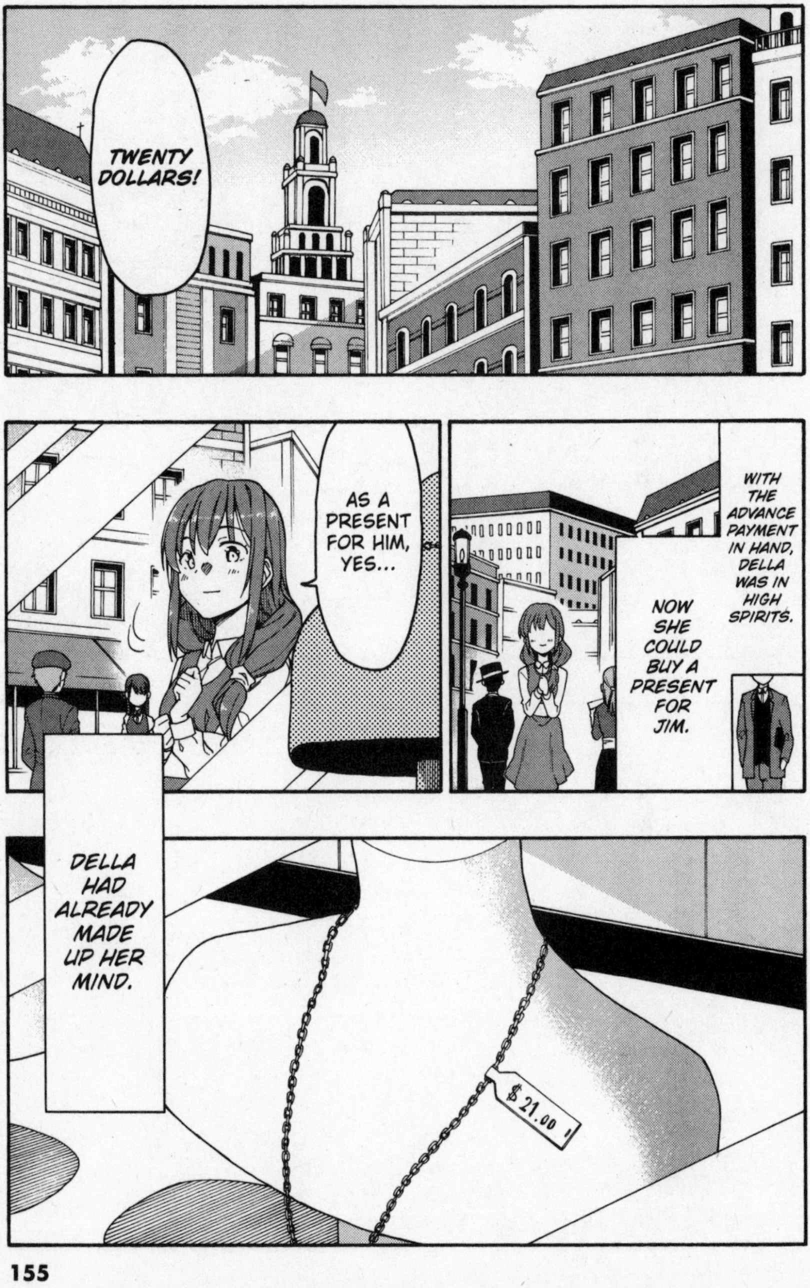
TWENTY DOLLARS!
WITH THE ADVANCE PAYMENT IN HAND, DELLA WAS IN HIGH SPIRITS.
NOW SHE COULD BUY A PRESENT FOR JIM.
AS A PRESENT FOR HIM, YES...
DELLA HAD ALREADY MADE UP HER MIND.
$ 21.00

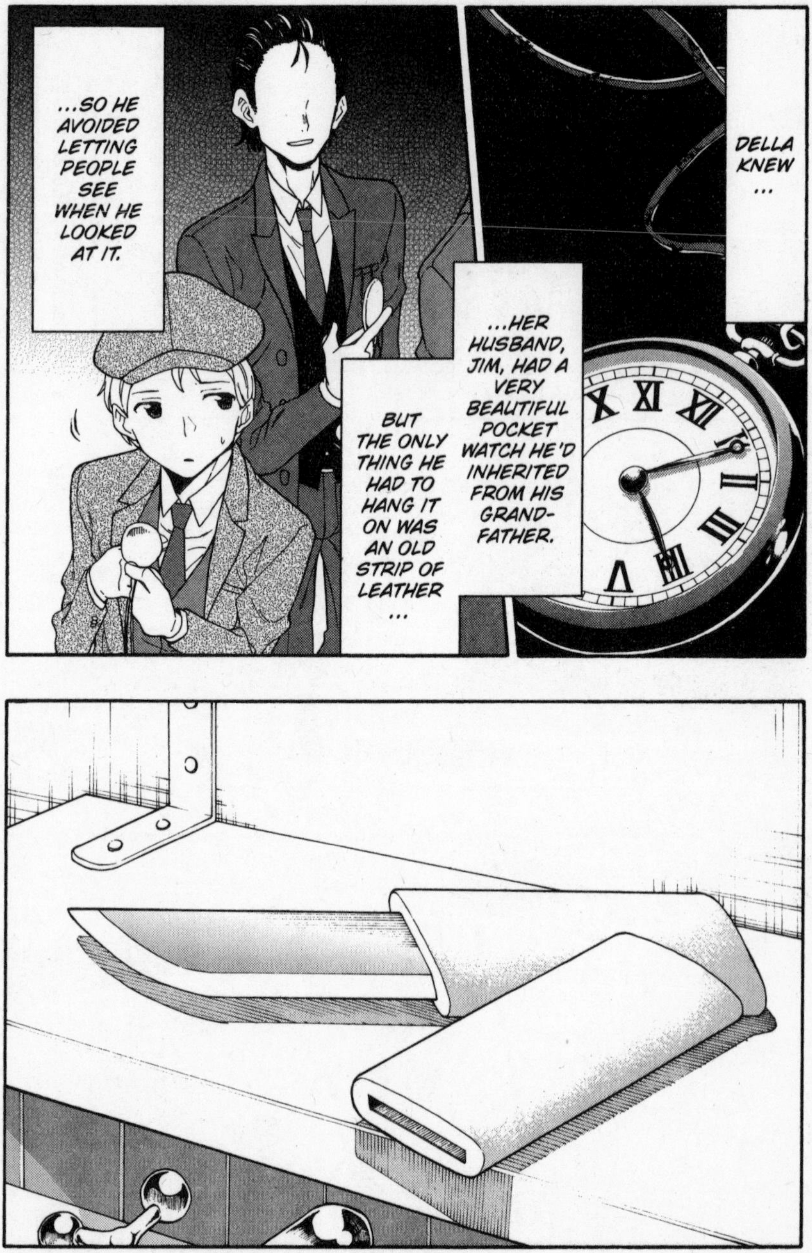
DELLA KNEW ...
...HER HUSBAND, JIM, HAD A VERY BEAUTIFUL POCKET WATCH HE'D INHERITED FROM HIS GRAND-FATHER.
BUT THE ONLY THING HE HAD TO HANG IT ON WAS AN OLD STRIP OF LEATHER ...
...SO HE AVOIDED LETTING PEOPLE SEE WHEN HE LOOKED AT IT.

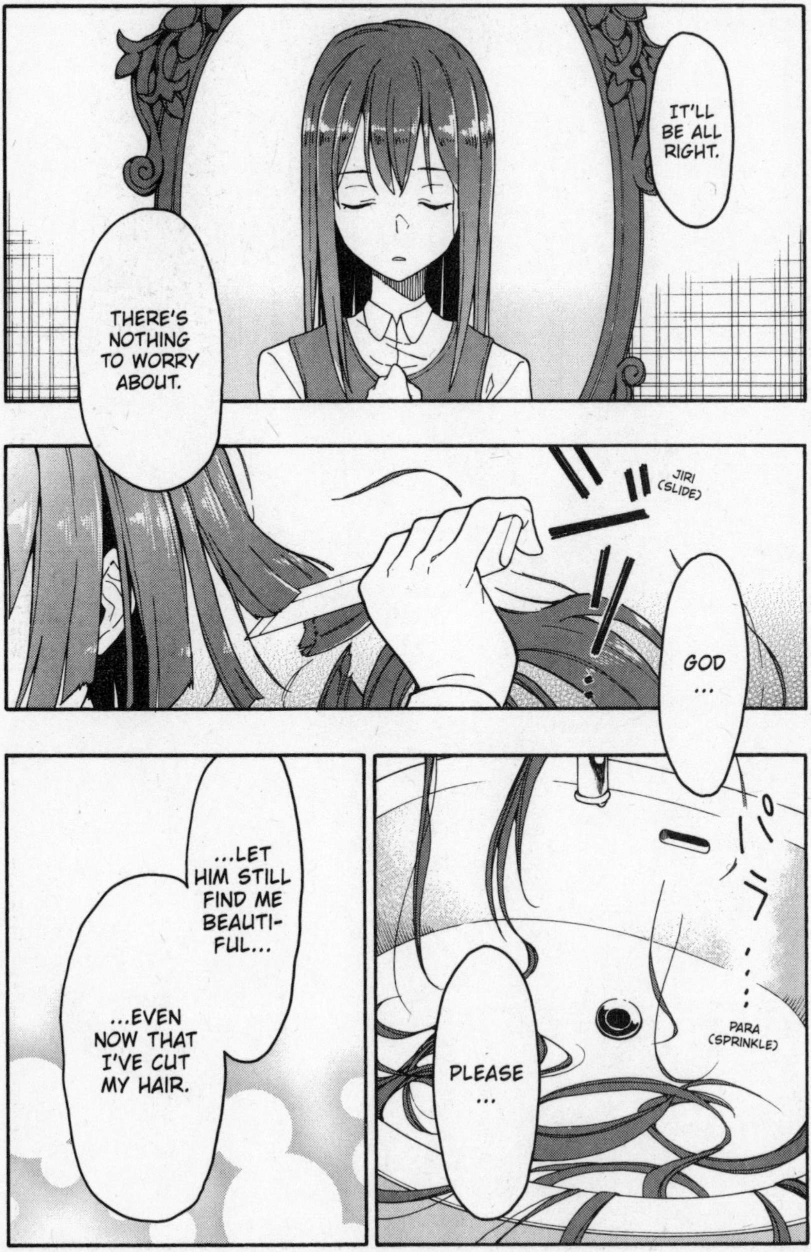
IT'LL BE ALL RIGHT.
THERE'S NOTHING TO WORRY ABOUT.
JIRI (SLIDE)
GOD ...
PARA (SPRINKLE)
PLEASE ...
...LET HIM STILL FIND ME BEAUTI-FUL...
...EVEN NOW THAT I'VE CUT MY HAIR.

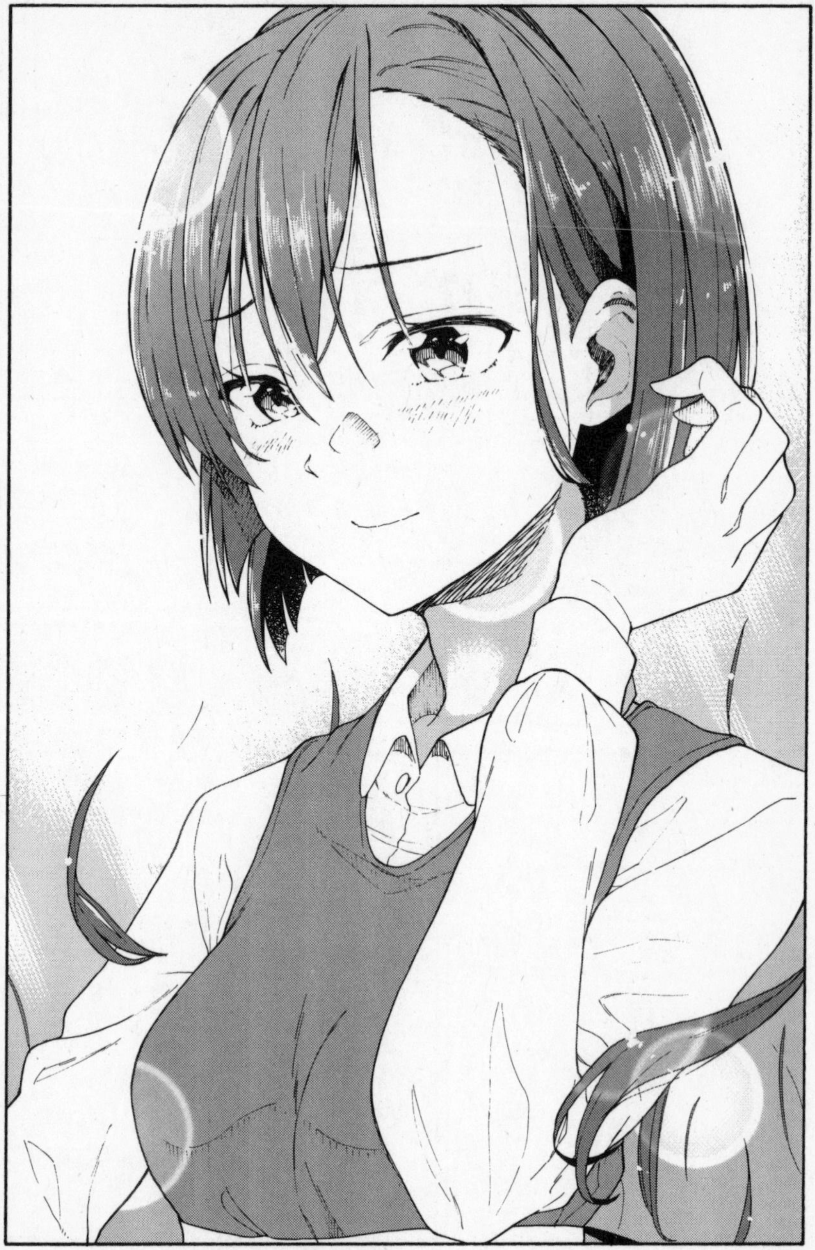

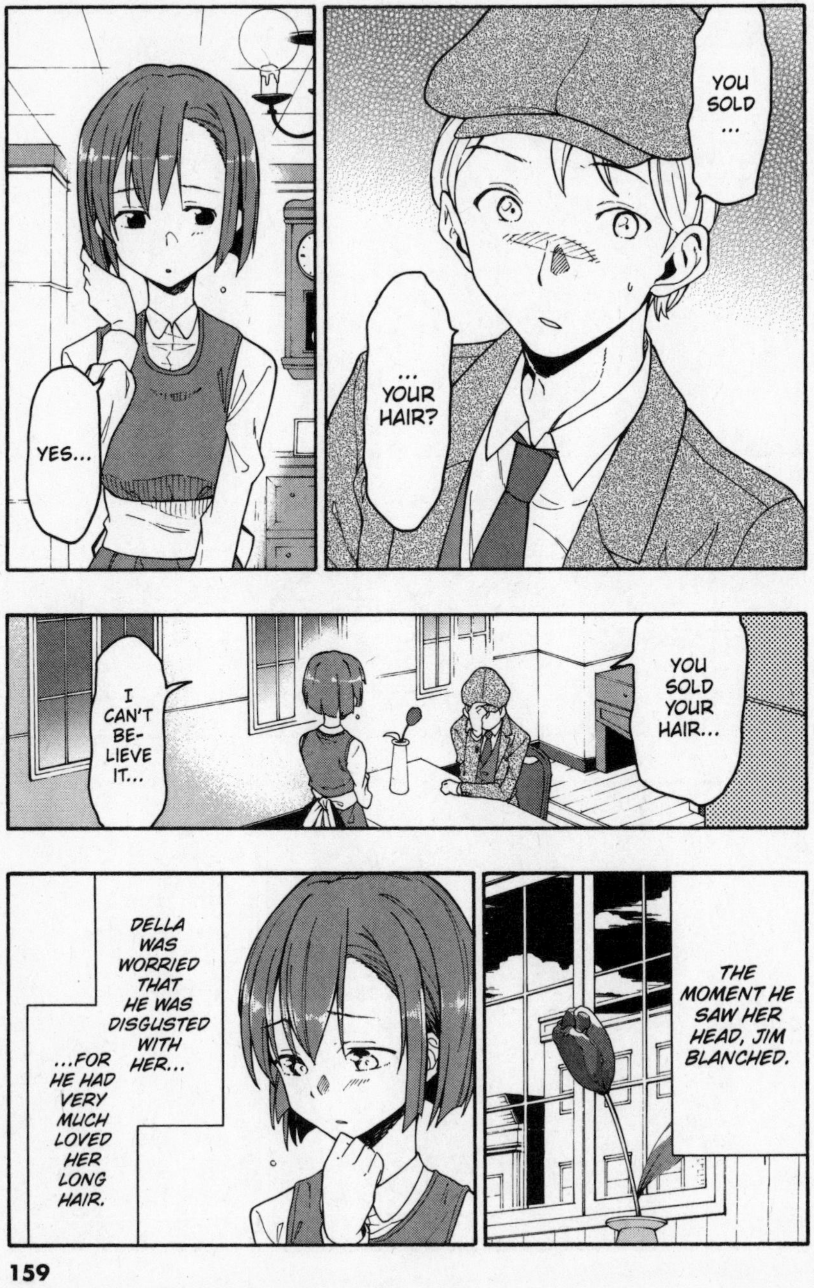
YOU SOLD ...
... YOUR HAIR?
YES...
YOU SOLD YOUR HAIR...
I CAN'T BE-LIEVE IT...
THE MOMENT HE SAW HER HEAD, JIM BLANCHED.
DELLA WAS WORRIED THAT HE WAS DISGUSTED WITH HER...
...FOR HE HAD VERY MUCH LOVED HER LONG HAIR.

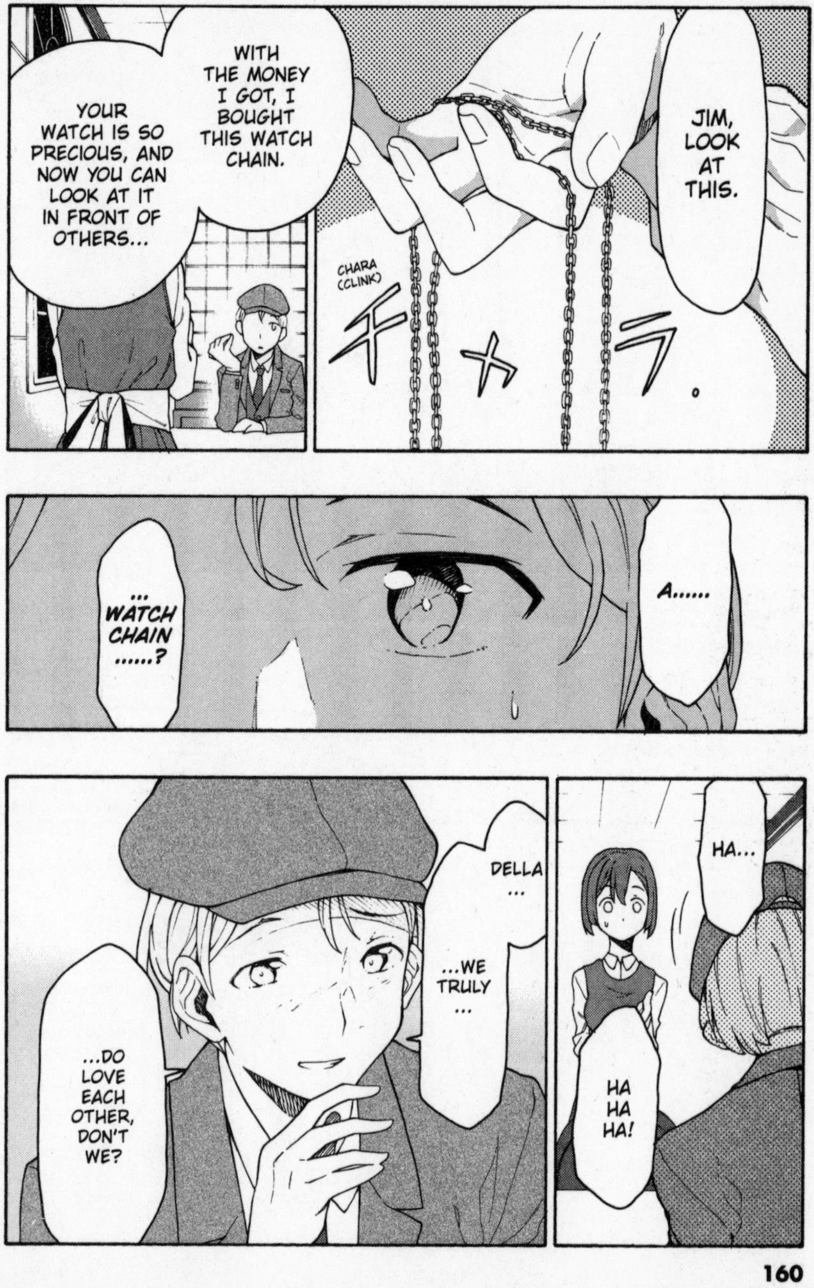
JIM, LOOK AT THIS.
CHARA (CLINK)
チャラ。
WITH THE MONEY I GOT, I BOUGHT THIS WATCH CHAIN.
YOUR WATCH IS SO PRECIOUS, AND NOW YOU CAN LOOK AT IT IN FRONT OF OTHERS...
A......
...*WATCH CHAIN*......?
HA...
HA HA HA!
DELLA...
...WE TRULY...
...DO LOVE EACH OTHER, DON'T WE?

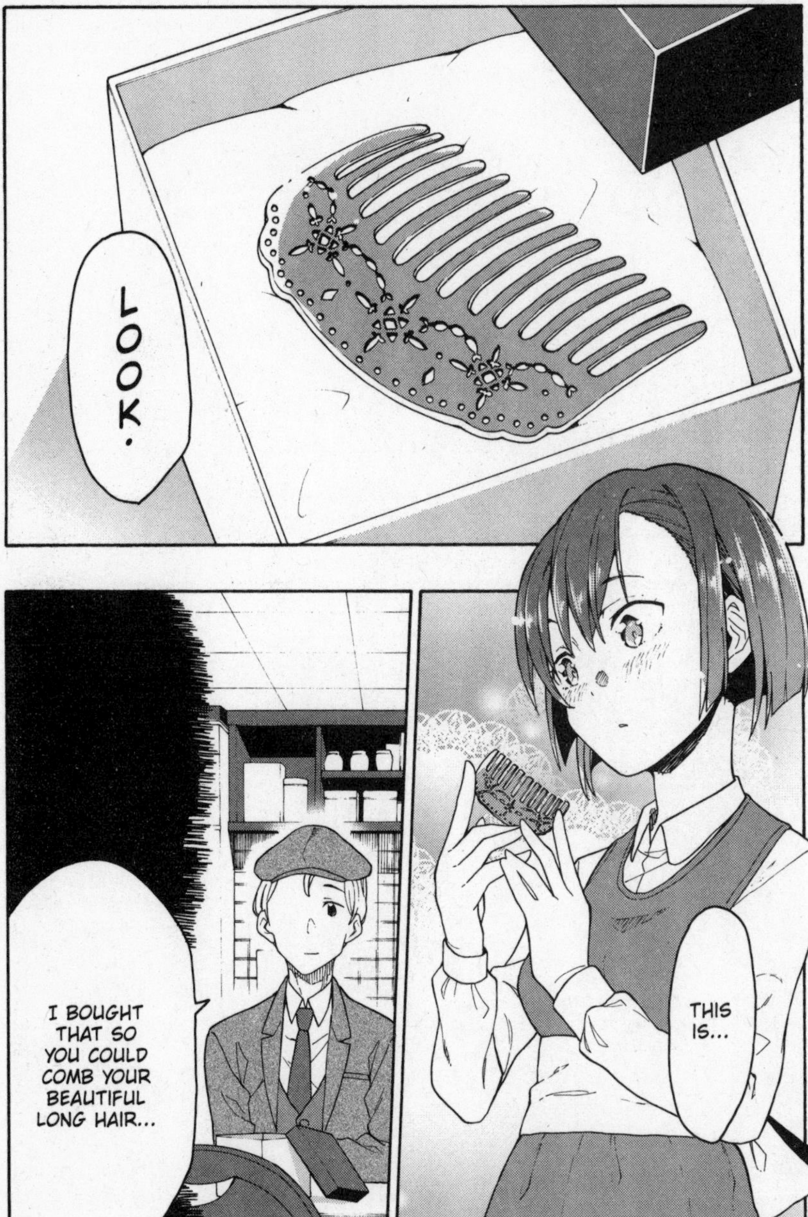
LOOK.
THIS IS...
I BOUGHT THAT SO YOU COULD COMB YOUR BEAUTIFUL LONG HAIR...

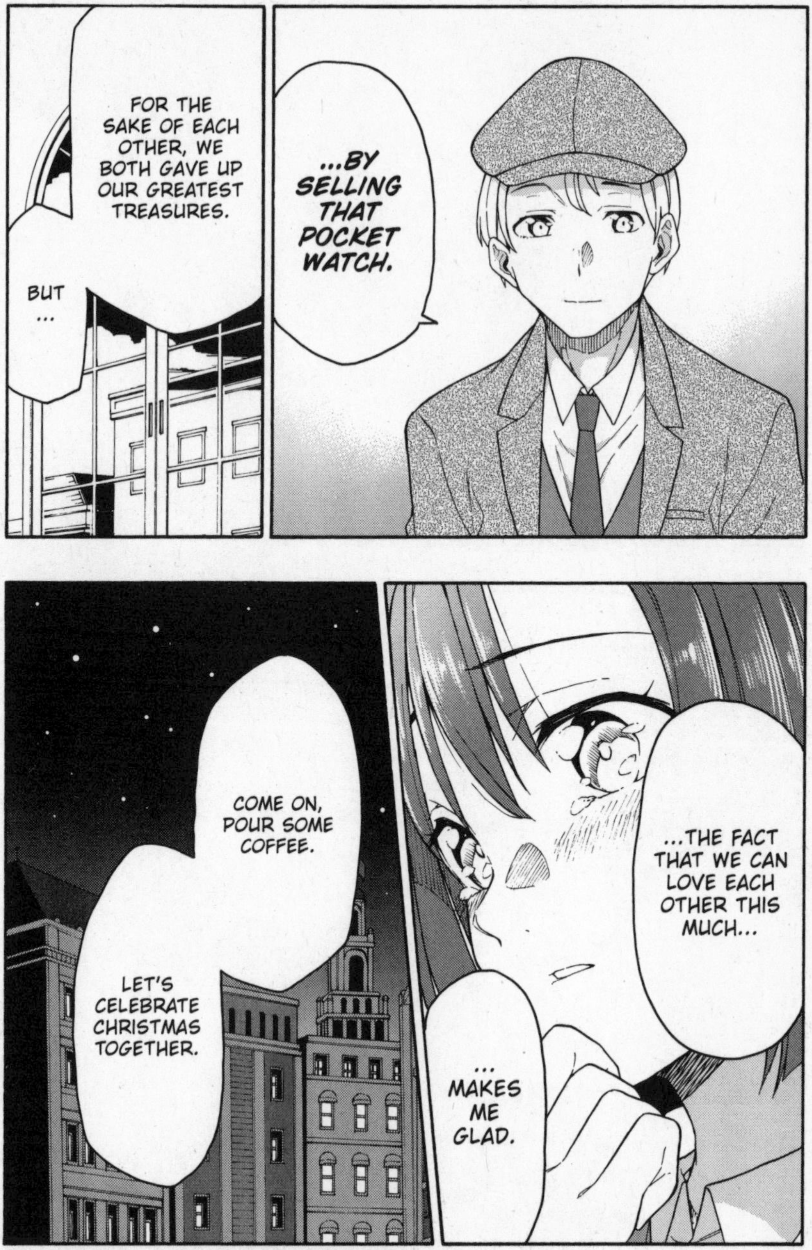
...BY SELLING THAT POCKET WATCH.
FOR THE SAKE OF EACH OTHER, WE BOTH GAVE UP OUR GREATEST TREASURES.
BUT ...
...THE FACT THAT WE CAN LOVE EACH OTHER THIS MUCH...
... MAKES ME GLAD.
COME ON, POUR SOME COFFEE.
LET'S CELEBRATE CHRISTMAS TOGETHER.

SPECIAL EXTRA ··· THE GIFT OF THE MAGI END

CHAPTER 70 ∘∘∘ WHAT THE LIGHTS IN EACH OF THEIR PALMS ILLUMINATES

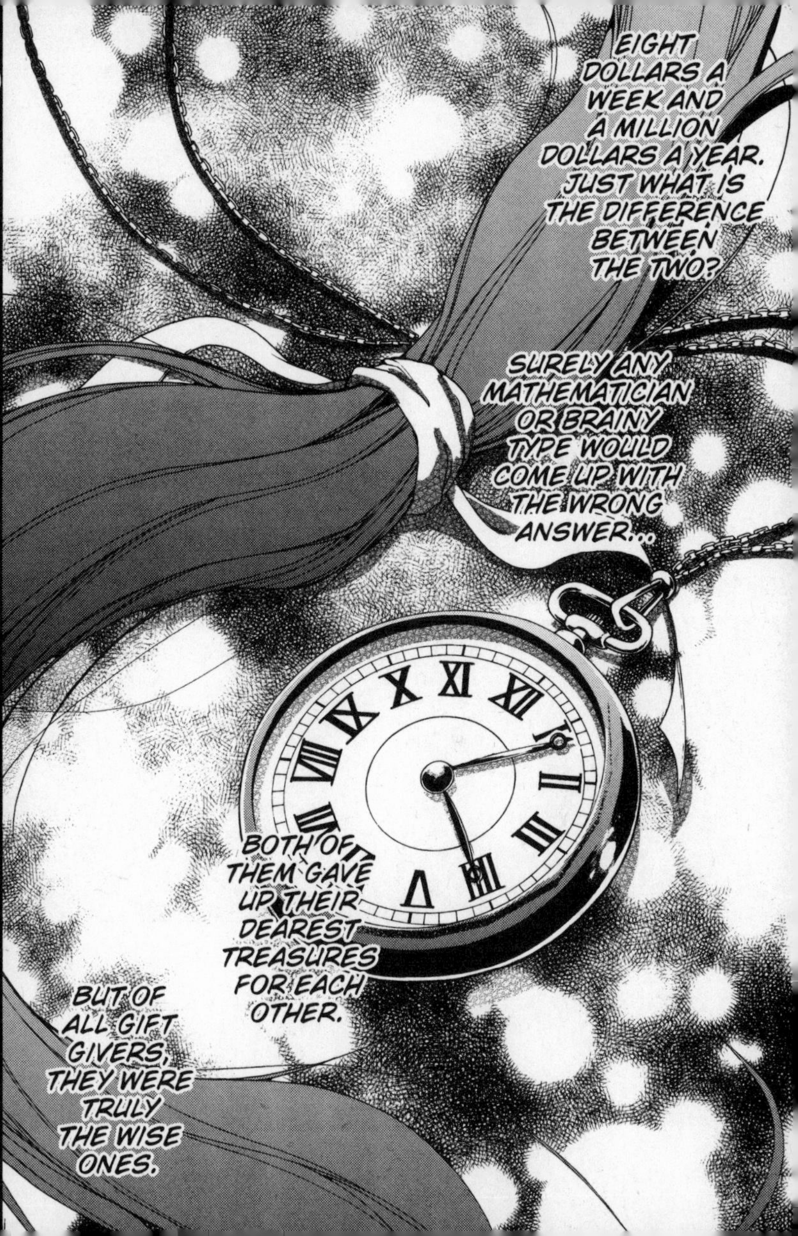
EIGHT DOLLARS A WEEK AND A MILLION DOLLARS A YEAR. JUST WHAT IS THE DIFFERENCE BETWEEN THE TWO?
SURELY ANY MATHEMATICIAN OR BRAINY TYPE WOULD COME UP WITH THE WRONG ANSWER...
BOTH OF THEM GAVE UP THEIR DEAREST TREASURES FOR EACH OTHER.
BUT OF ALL GIFT GIVERS, THEY WERE TRULY THE WISE ONES.

CHAPTER ··· **WHAT THE LIGHTS IN EACH OF THEIR PALMS ILLUMINATES.**

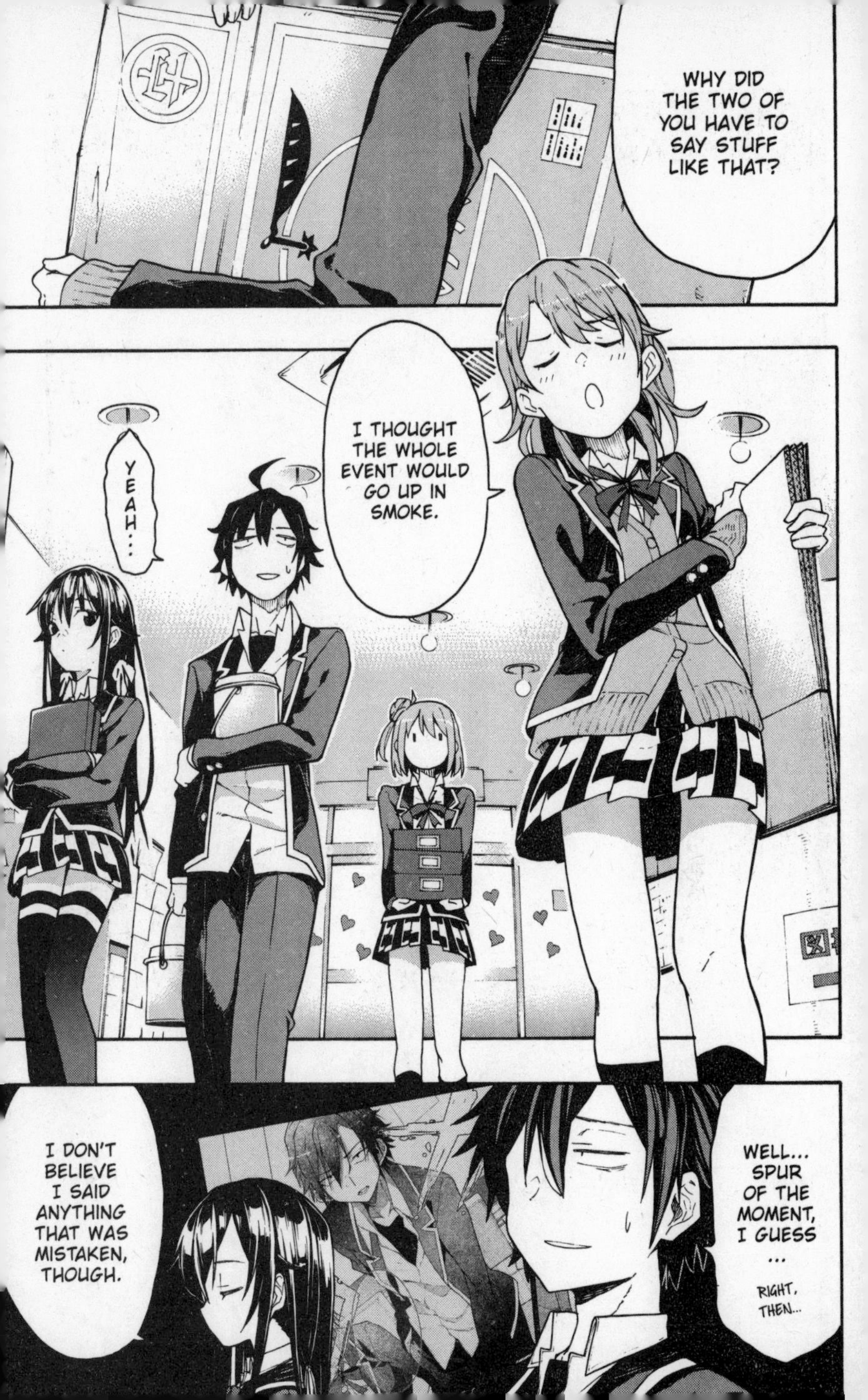
WHY DID THE TWO OF YOU HAVE TO SAY STUFF LIKE THAT?
I THOUGHT THE WHOLE EVENT WOULD GO UP IN SMOKE.
YEAH...
WELL... SPUR OF THE MOMENT, I GUESS...
I DON'T BELIEVE I SAID ANYTHING THAT WAS MISTAKEN, THOUGH.
RIGHT, THEN...

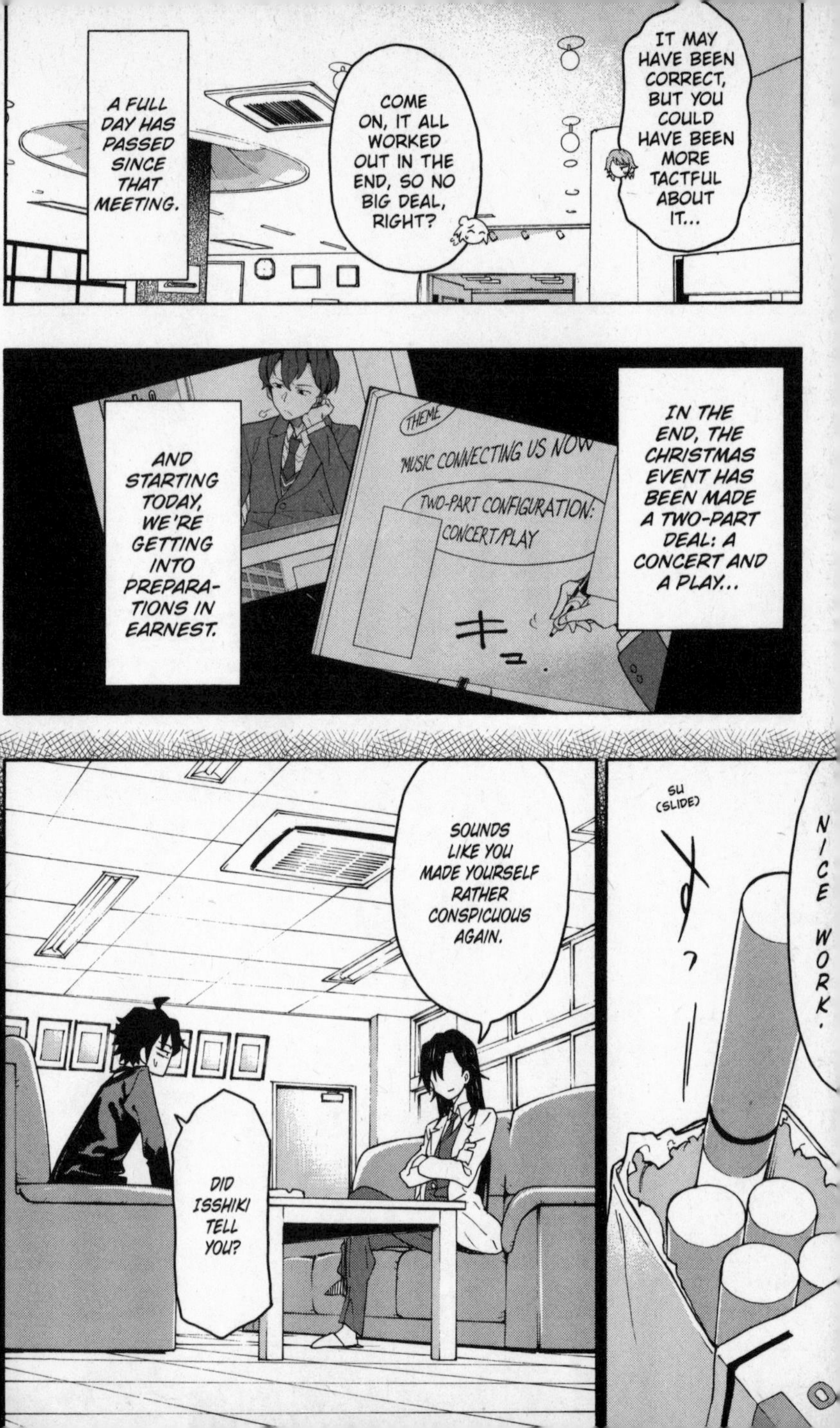
IT MAY HAVE BEEN CORRECT, BUT YOU COULD HAVE BEEN MORE TACTFUL ABOUT IT...
COME ON, IT ALL WORKED OUT IN THE END, SO NO BIG DEAL, RIGHT?
A FULL DAY HAS PASSED SINCE THAT MEETING.
IN THE END, THE CHRISTMAS EVENT HAS BEEN MADE A TWO-PART DEAL: A CONCERT AND A PLAY...
THEME
"MUSIC CONNECTING US NOW"
TWO-PART CONFIGURATION: CONCERT/PLAY
キュ
AND STARTING TODAY, WE'RE GETTING INTO PREPARATIONS IN EARNEST.
NICE WORK.
SU (SLIDE)
SOUNDS LIKE YOU MADE YOURSELF RATHER CONSPICUOUS AGAIN.
DID ISSHIKI TELL YOU?

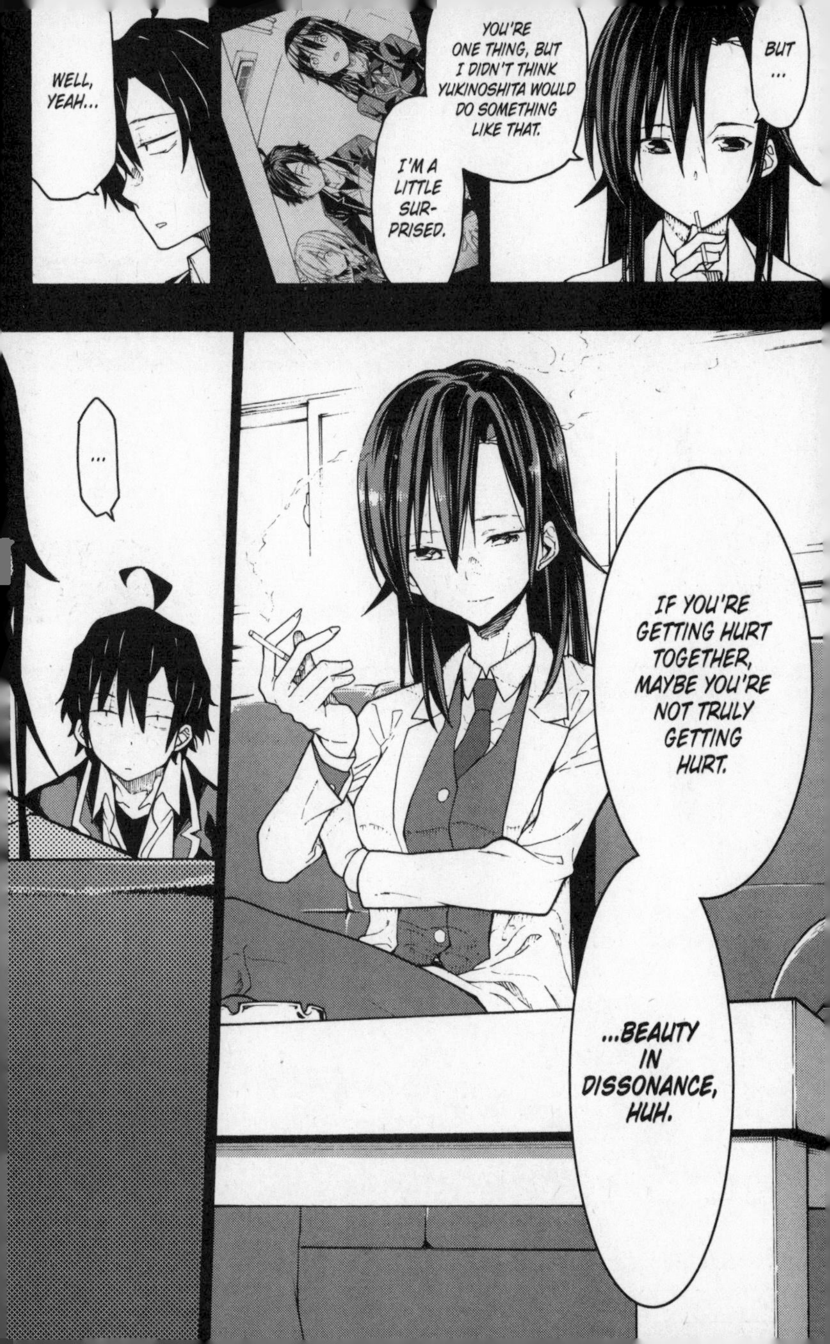
BUT ...
YOU'RE ONE THING, BUT I DIDN'T THINK YUKINOSHITA WOULD DO SOMETHING LIKE THAT.
I'M A LITTLE SUR-PRISED.
WELL, YEAH...
IF YOU'RE GETTING HURT TOGETHER, MAYBE YOU'RE NOT TRULY GETTING HURT.
...BEAUTY IN DISSONANCE, HUH.
...

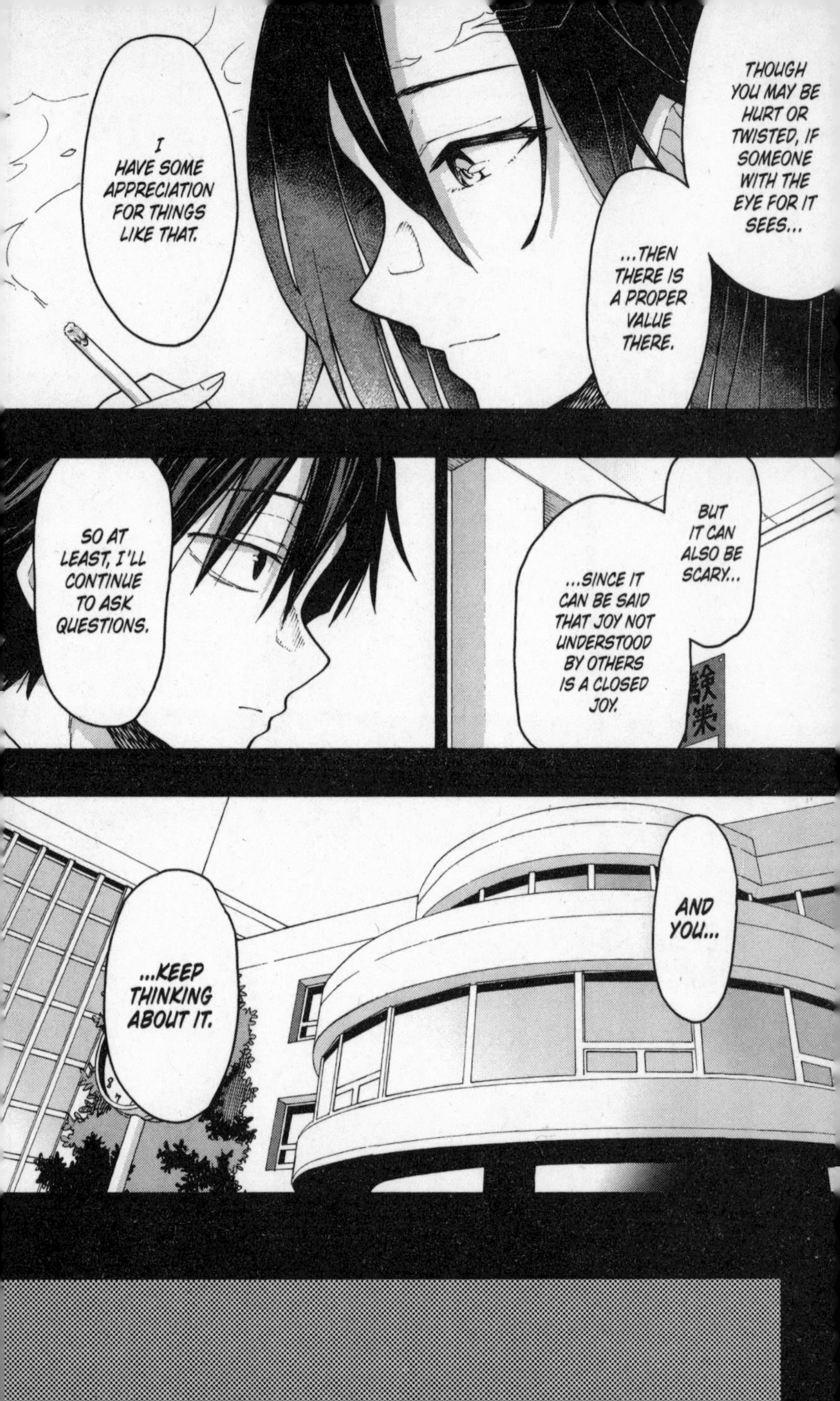
THOUGH YOU MAY BE HURT OR TWISTED, IF SOMEONE WITH THE EYE FOR IT SEES...
...THEN THERE IS A PROPER VALUE THERE.
I HAVE SOME APPRECIATION FOR THINGS LIKE THAT.
BUT IT CAN ALSO BE SCARY...
...SINCE IT CAN BE SAID THAT JOY NOT UNDERSTOOD BY OTHERS IS A CLOSED JOY.
SO AT LEAST, I'LL CONTINUE TO ASK QUESTIONS.
AND YOU...
...KEEP THINKING ABOUT IT.

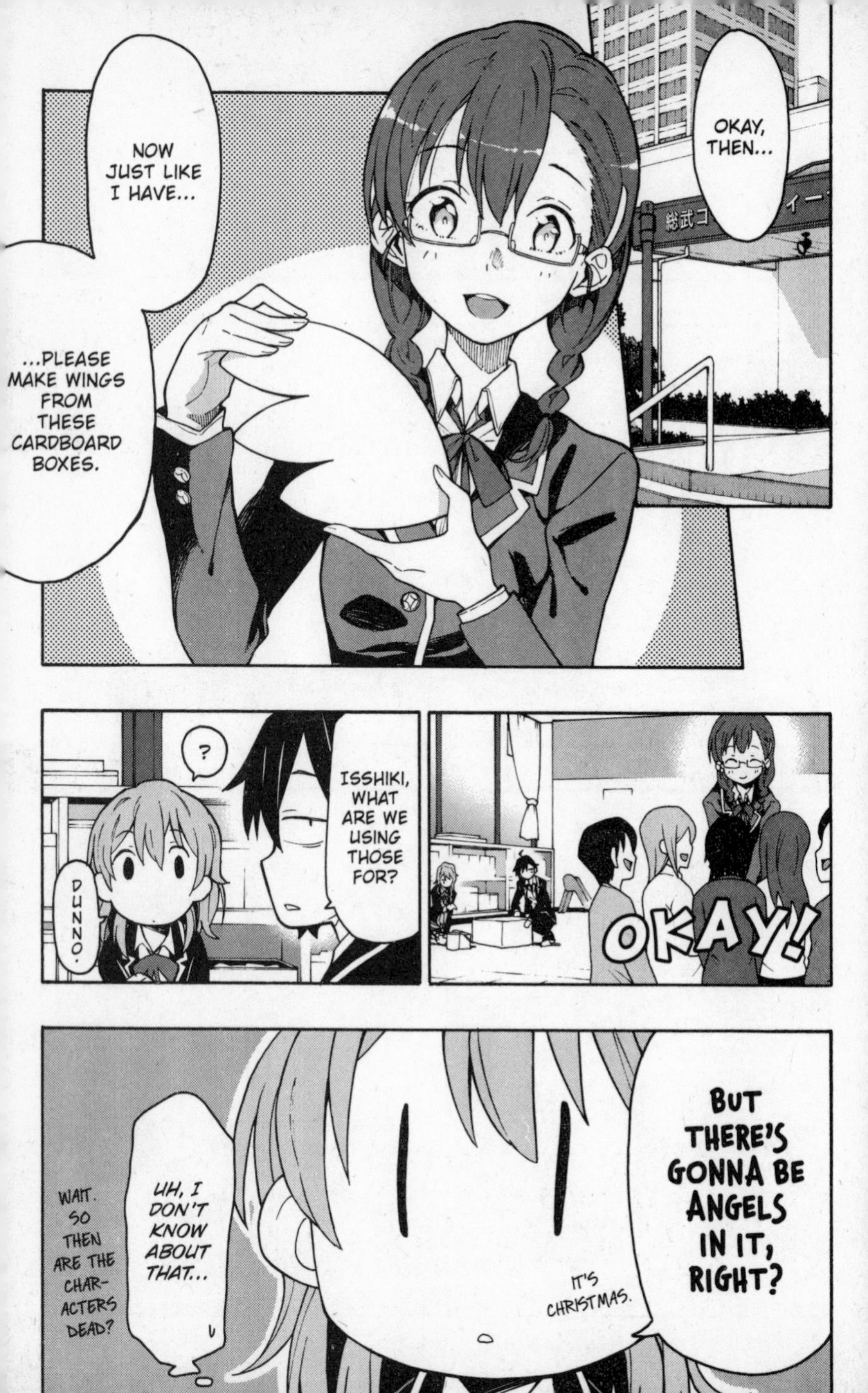
OKAY, THEN...
NOW JUST LIKE I HAVE...
...PLEASE MAKE WINGS FROM THESE CARDBOARD BOXES.
OKAY!
ISSHIKI, WHAT ARE WE USING THOSE FOR?
?
DUNNO.
BUT THERE'S GONNA BE ANGELS IN IT, RIGHT?
IT'S CHRISTMAS.
UH, I DON'T KNOW ABOUT THAT...
WAIT. SO THEN ARE THE CHAR-ACTERS DEAD?

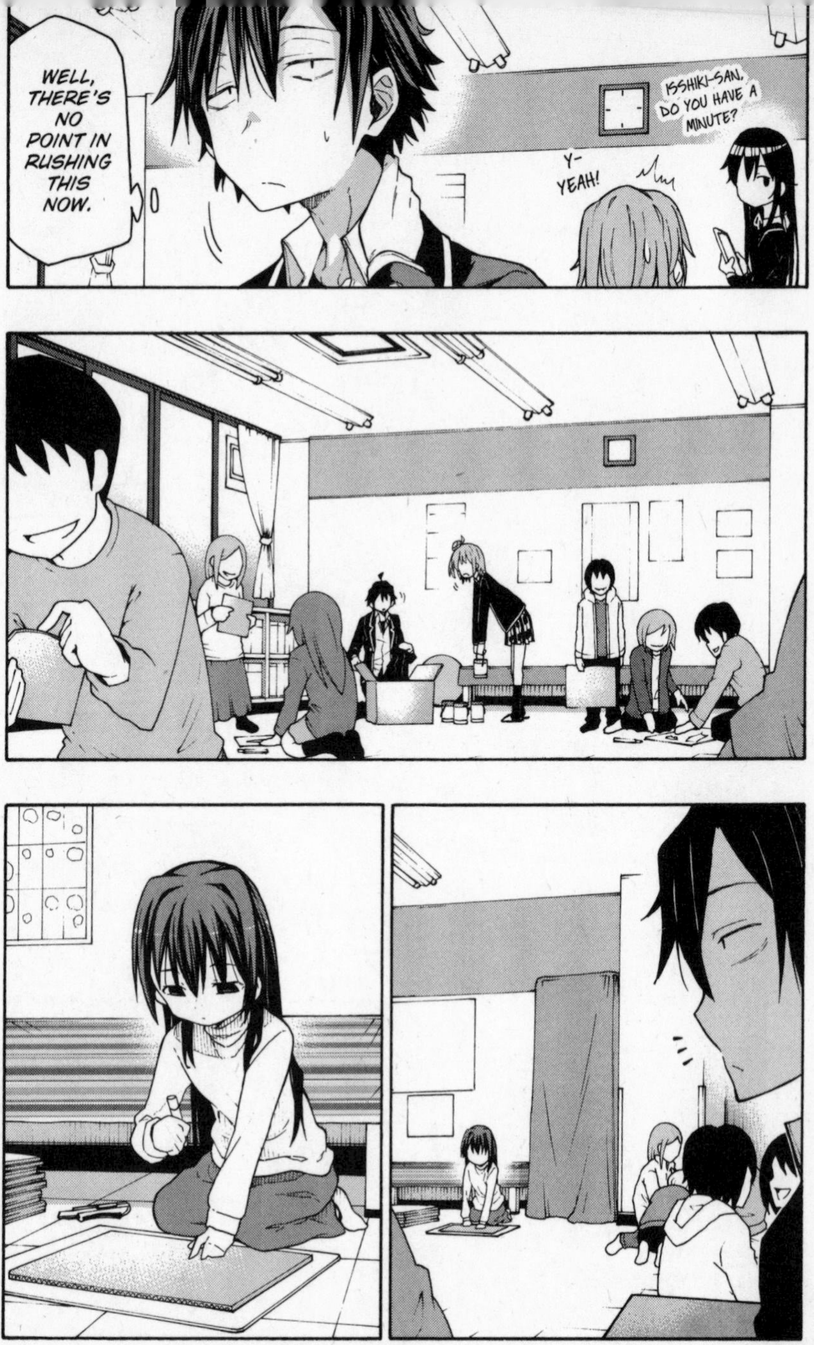
ISSHIKI-SAN, DO YOU HAVE A MINUTE?
Y-YEAH!
WELL, THERE'S NO POINT IN RUSHING THIS NOW.

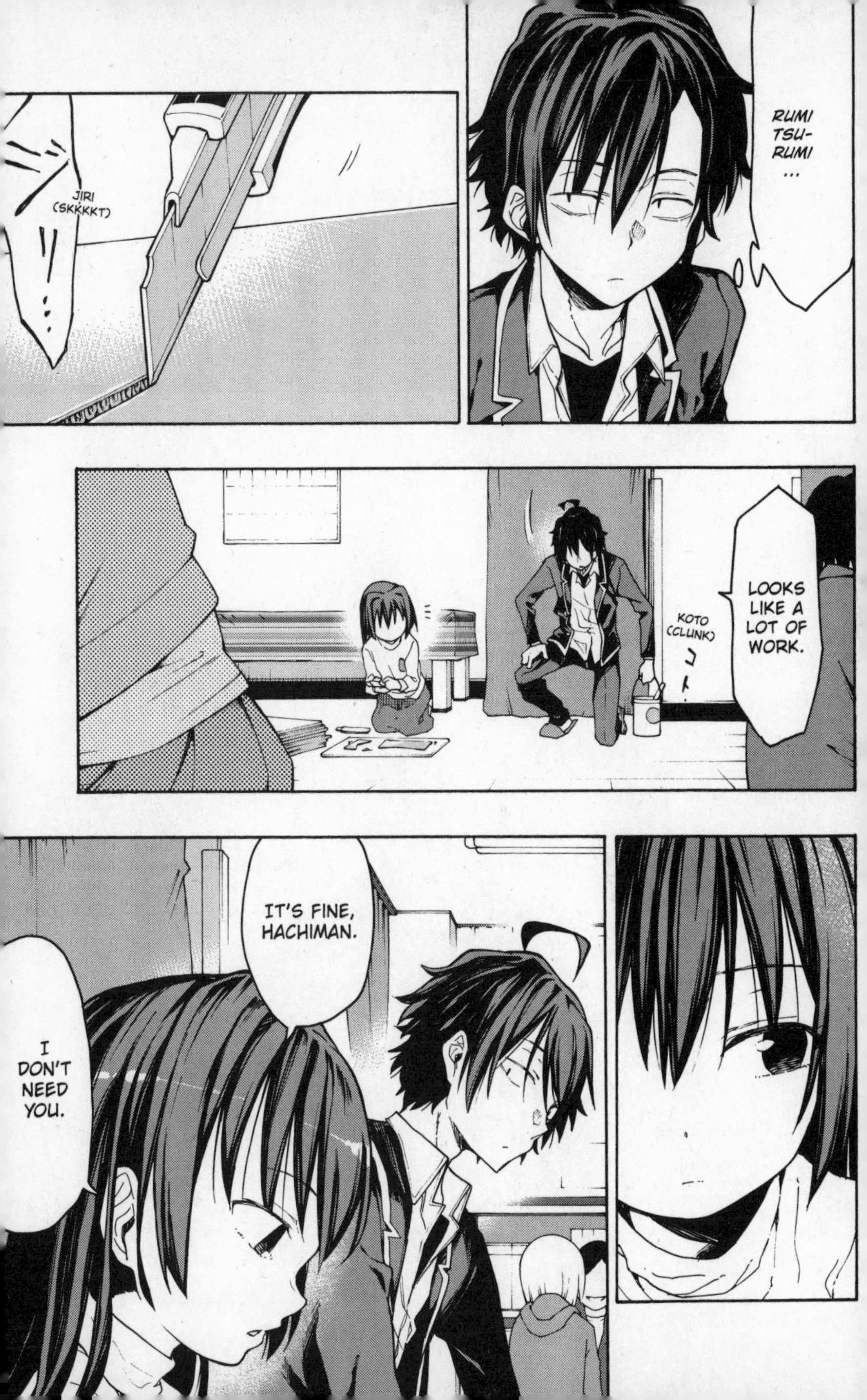
RUMI TSU-RUMI ...
JIRI (SKKKKT)
LOOKS LIKE A LOT OF WORK.
KOTO (CLUNK)
IT'S FINE, HACHIMAN.
I DON'T NEED YOU.

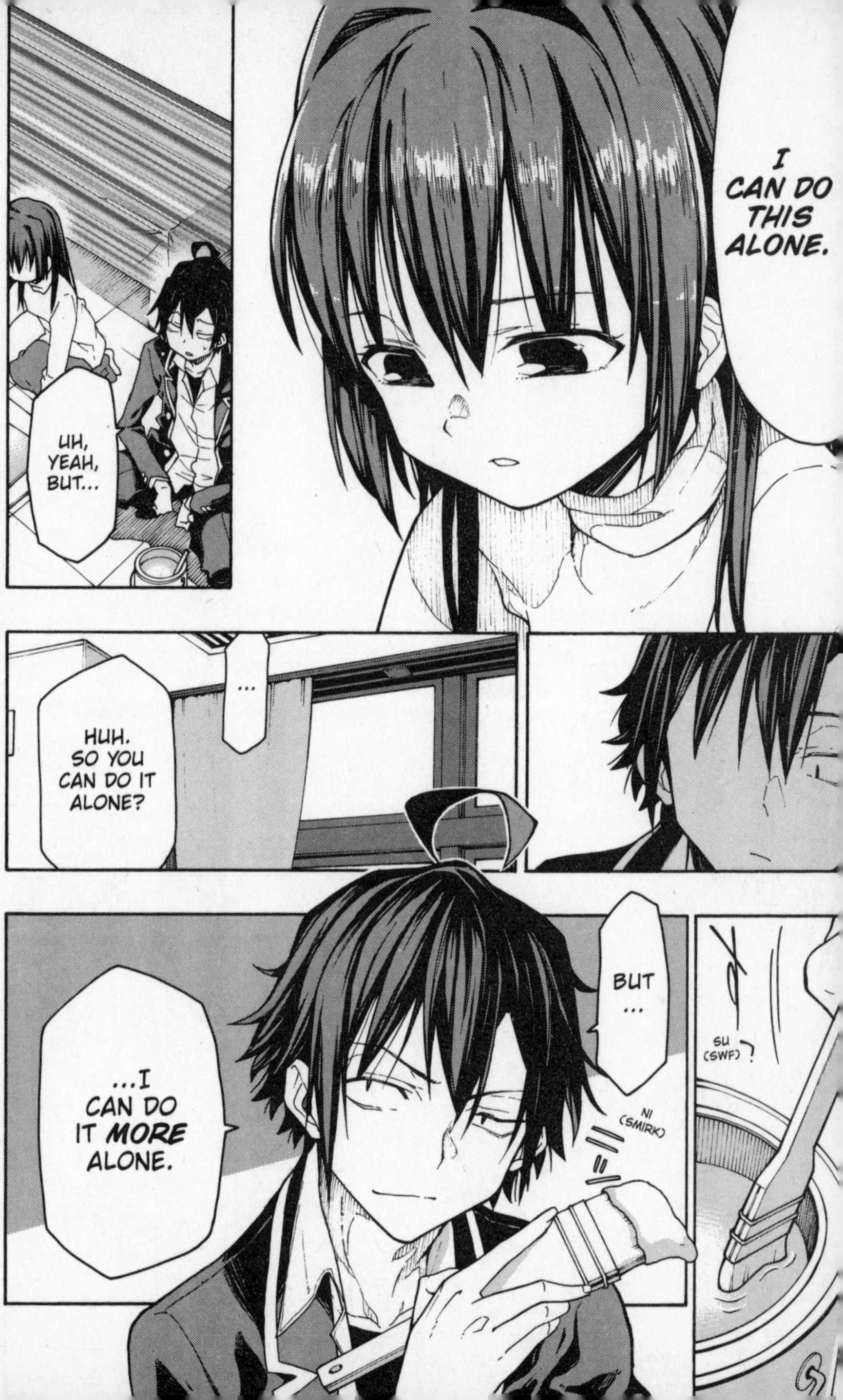
I CAN DO THIS ALONE.
UH, YEAH, BUT...
...
HUH. SO YOU CAN DO IT ALONE?
SU (SWF)
BUT ...
NI (SMIRK)
...I CAN DO IT **MORE** ALONE.

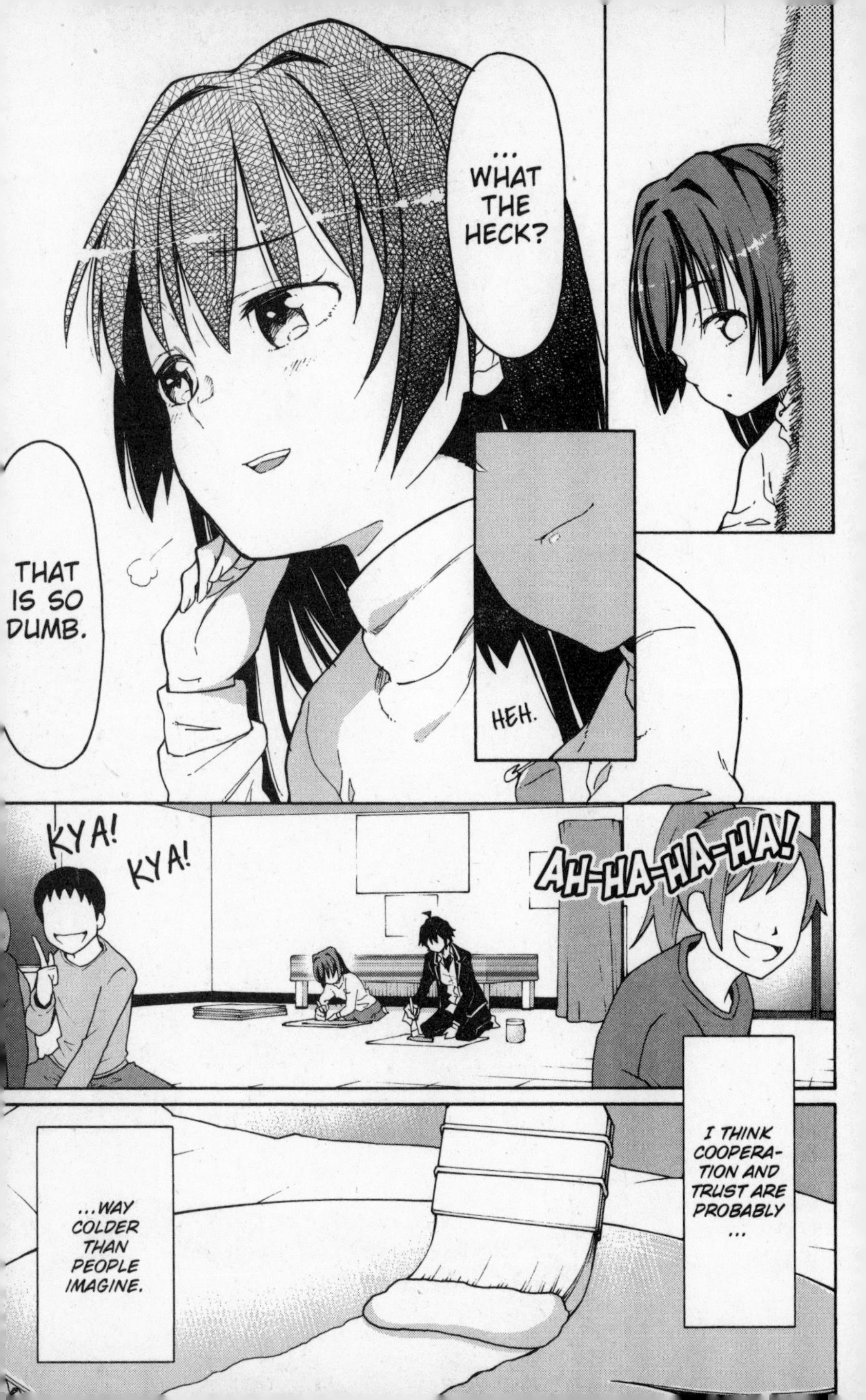
...WHAT THE HECK?
THAT IS SO DUMB.
HEH.
AH-HA-HA-HA!
KYA! KYA!
I THINK COOPERATION AND TRUST ARE PROBABLY ...
...WAY COLDER THAN PEOPLE IMAGINE.

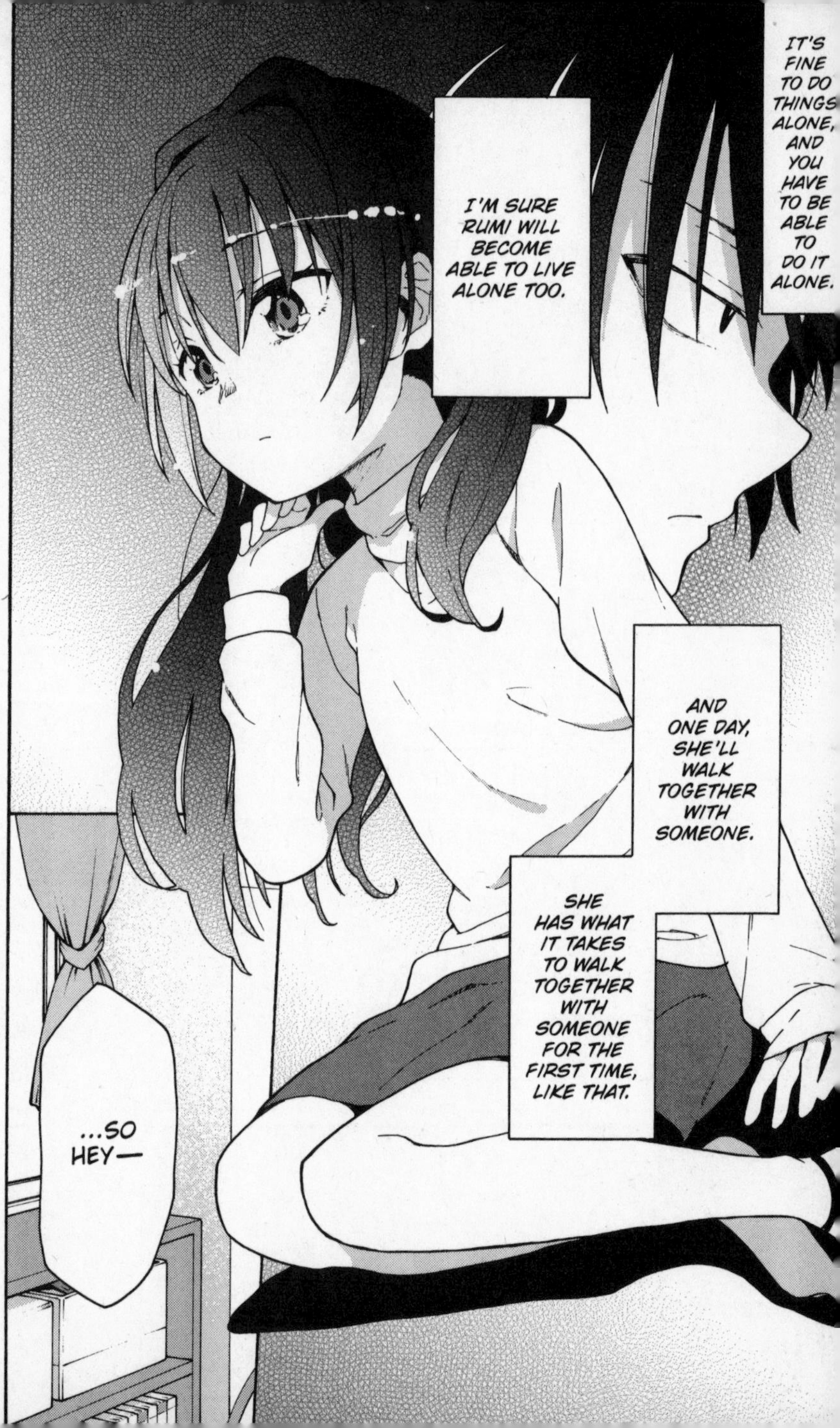
IT'S FINE TO DO THINGS ALONE, AND YOU HAVE TO BE ABLE TO DO IT ALONE.
I'M SURE RUMI WILL BECOME ABLE TO LIVE ALONE TOO.
AND ONE DAY, SHE'LL WALK TOGETHER WITH SOMEONE.
SHE HAS WHAT IT TAKES TO WALK TOGETHER WITH SOMEONE FOR THE FIRST TIME, LIKE THAT.
...SO HEY—

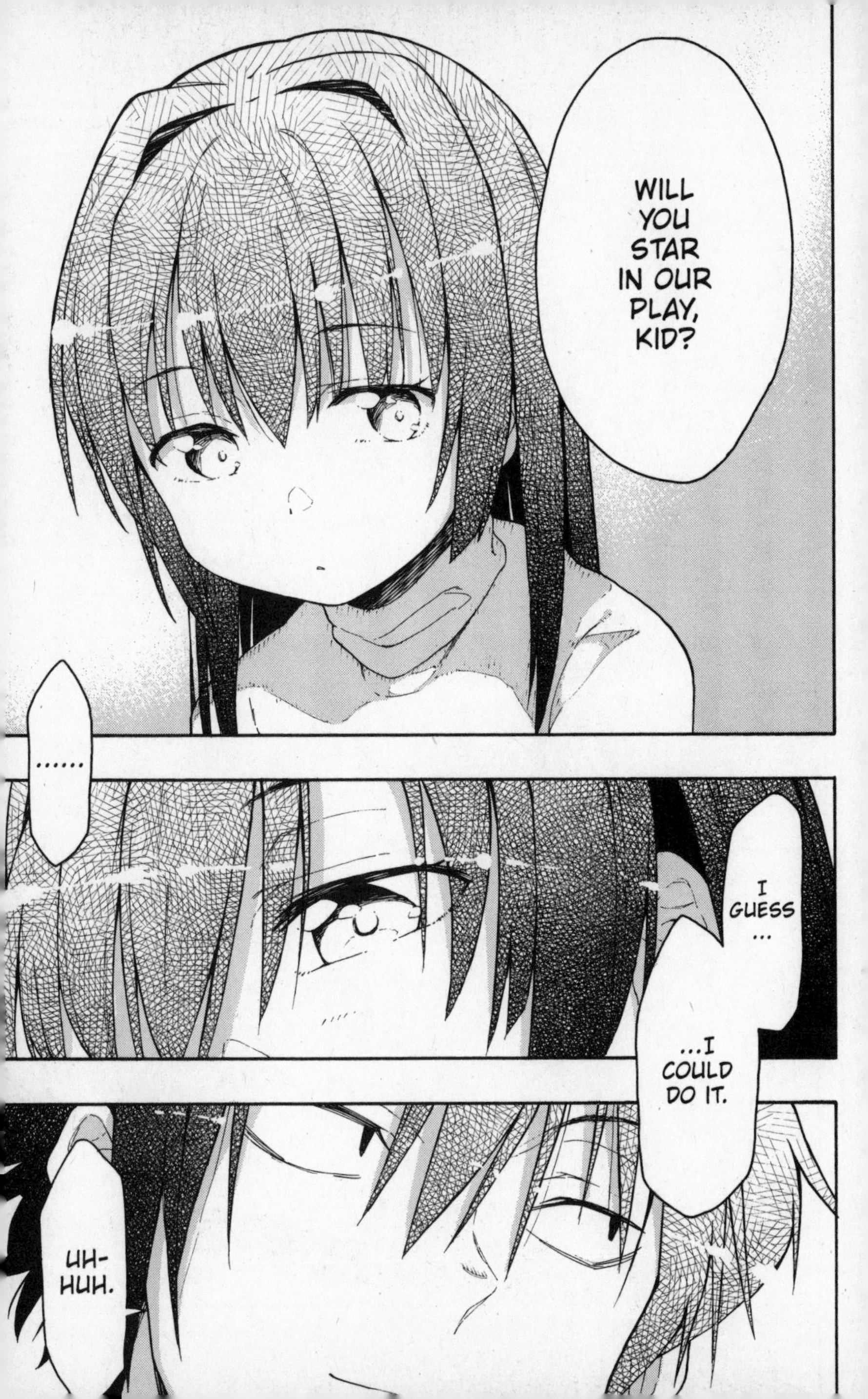
WILL YOU STAR IN OUR PLAY, KID?
......
I GUESS...
...I COULD DO IT.
UH-HUH.

...IT'S NOT...

..."KID."

...IT'S RUMI.

BUT, HACHI-MAN...

UH-HUH.

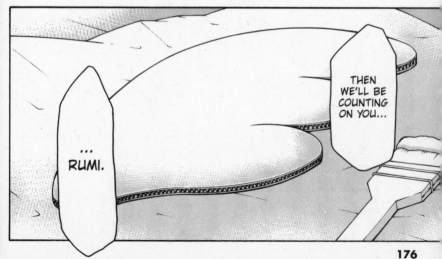

THEN WE'LL BE COUNTING ON YOU...

...RUMI.

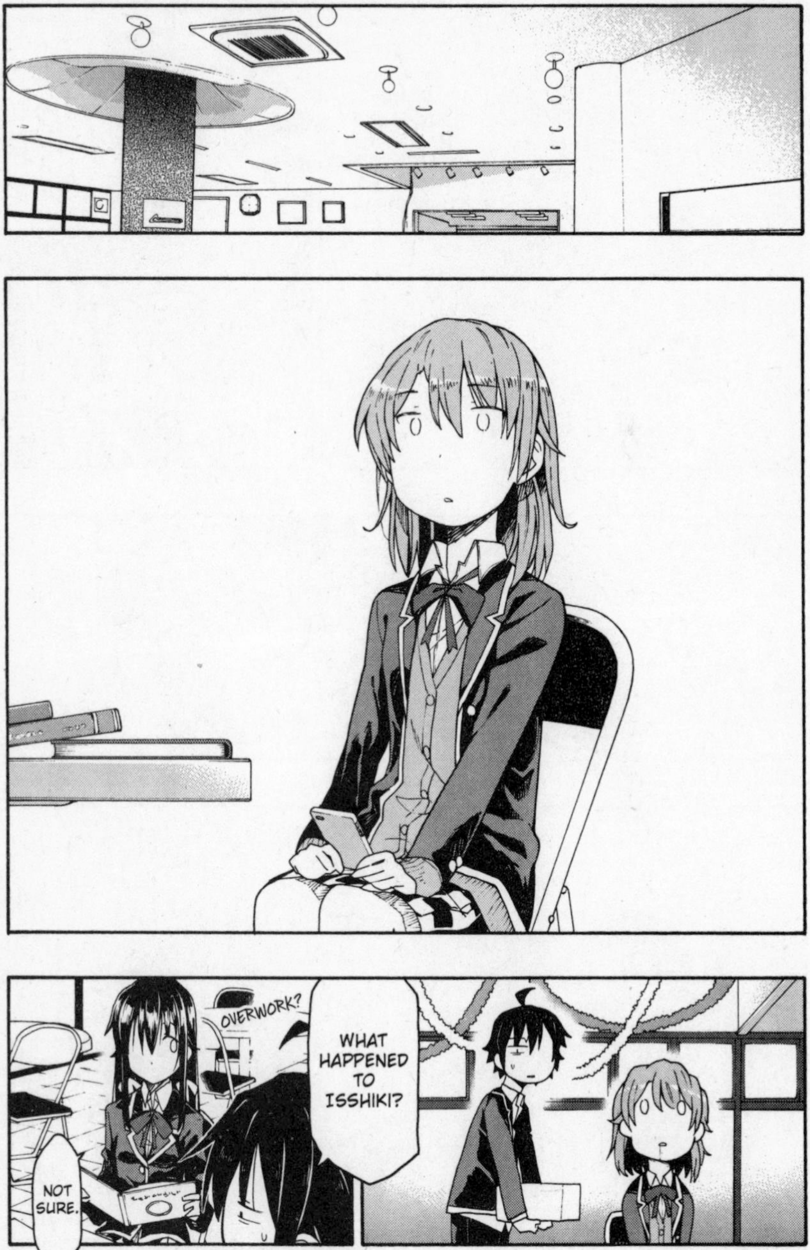
WHAT HAPPENED TO ISSHIKI?
OVERWORK?
NOT SURE.

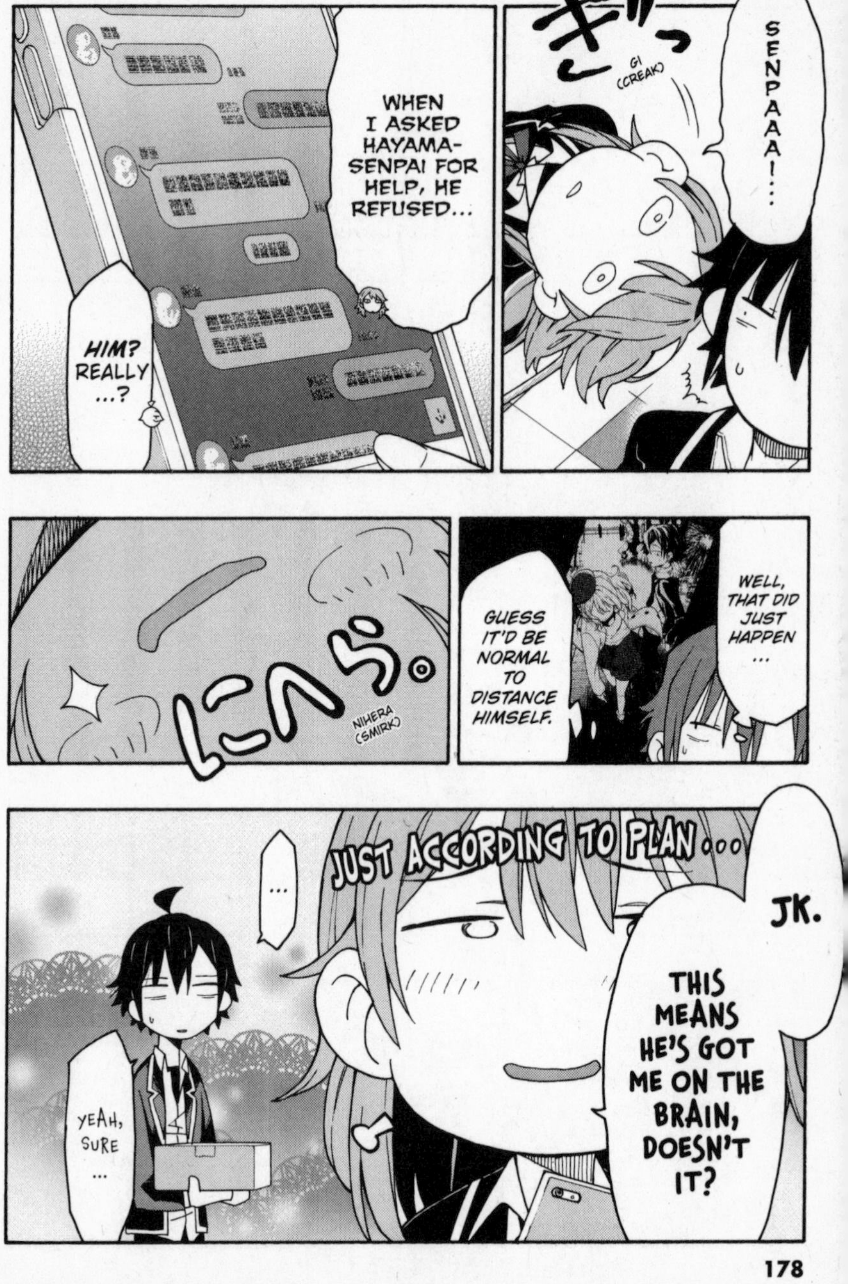
ぎっ
GI (CREAK)
SENPAAAI!...
WHEN I ASKED HAYAMA-SENPAI FOR HELP, HE REFUSED...
HIM? REALLY ...?
WELL, THAT DID JUST HAPPEN ...
GUESS IT'D BE NORMAL TO DISTANCE HIMSELF.
にへらっ
NIHERA (SMIRK)
JUST ACCORDING TO PLAN...
JK.
THIS MEANS HE'S GOT ME ON THE BRAIN, DOESN'T IT?
...
YEAH, SURE ...

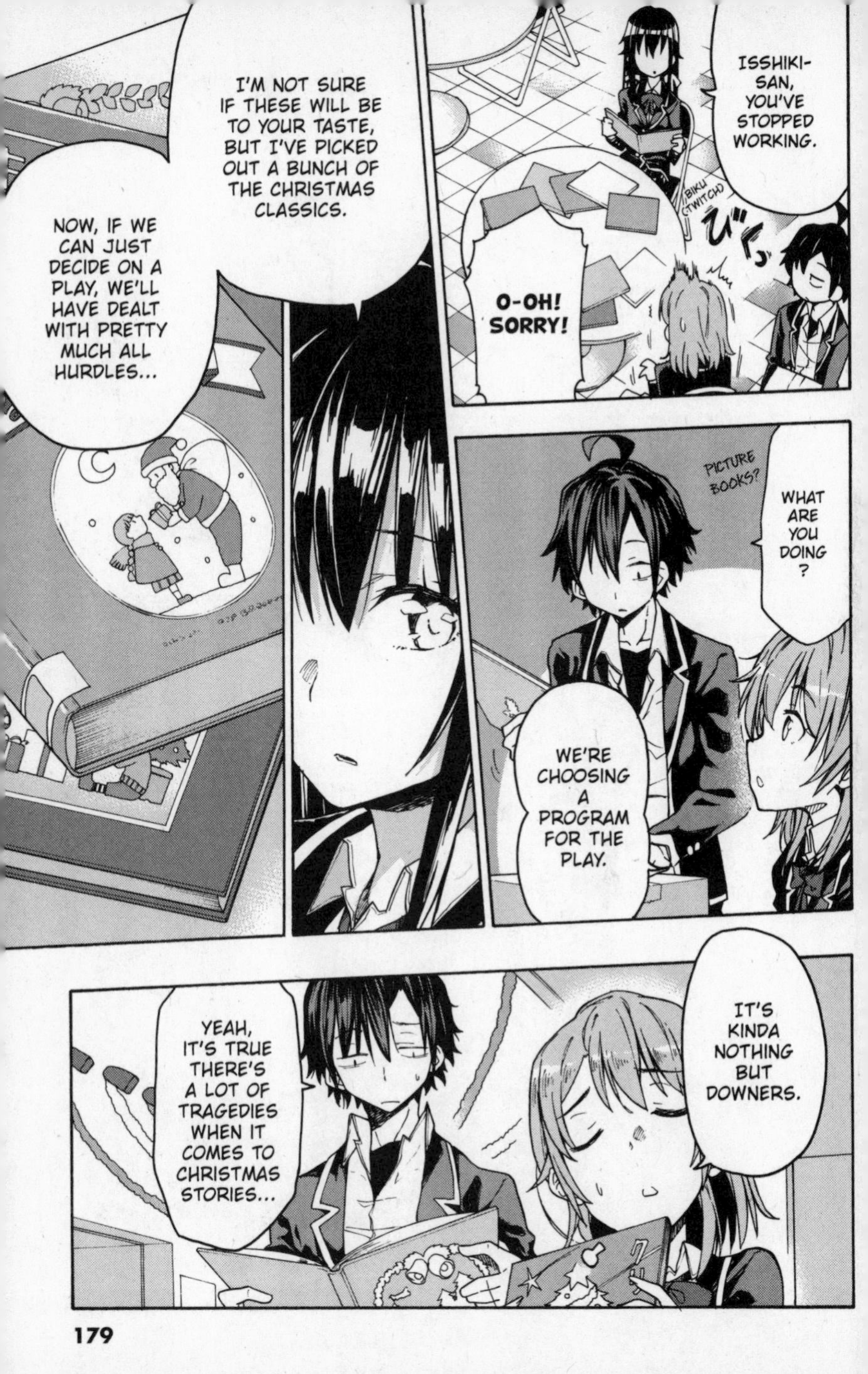
ISSHIKI-SAN, YOU'VE STOPPED WORKING.
BIKU (TWITCH)
O-OH! SORRY!
PICTURE BOOKS?
WHAT ARE YOU DOING?
WE'RE CHOOSING A PROGRAM FOR THE PLAY.
I'M NOT SURE IF THESE WILL BE TO YOUR TASTE, BUT I'VE PICKED OUT A BUNCH OF THE CHRISTMAS CLASSICS.
NOW, IF WE CAN JUST DECIDE ON A PLAY, WE'LL HAVE DEALT WITH PRETTY MUCH ALL HURDLES...
IT'S KINDA NOTHING BUT DOWNERS.
YEAH, IT'S TRUE THERE'S A LOT OF TRAGEDIES WHEN IT COMES TO CHRISTMAS STORIES...

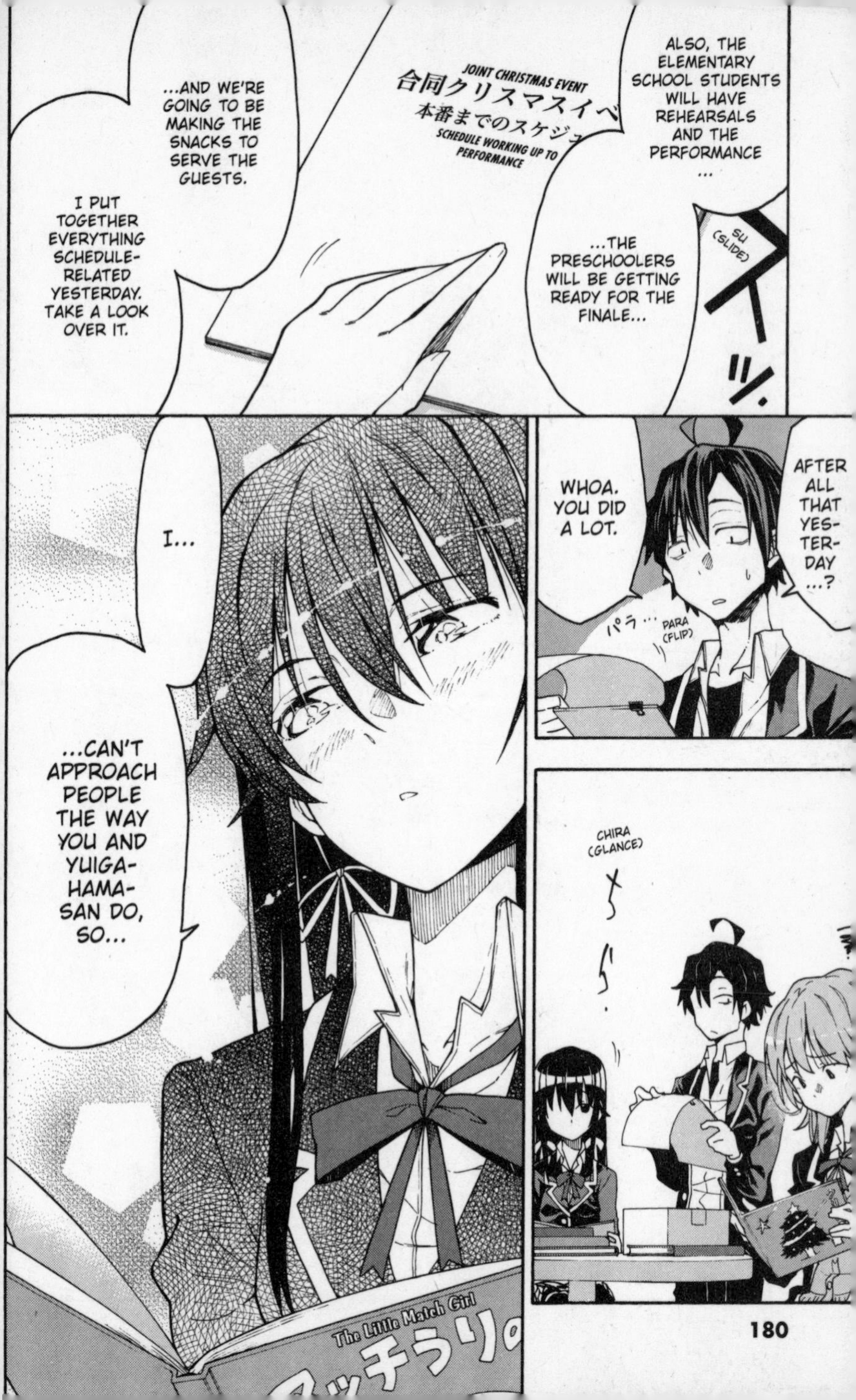
ALSO, THE ELEMENTARY SCHOOL STUDENTS WILL HAVE REHEARSALS AND THE PERFORMANCE ...
SU (SLIDE)
...THE PRESCHOOLERS WILL BE GETTING READY FOR THE FINALE...
JOINT CHRISTMAS EVENT
合同クリスマスイベ
本番までのスケジュ
SCHEDULE WORKING UP TO PERFORMANCE
...AND WE'RE GOING TO BE MAKING THE SNACKS TO SERVE THE GUESTS.
I PUT TOGETHER EVERYTHING SCHEDULE-RELATED YESTERDAY. TAKE A LOOK OVER IT.
AFTER ALL THAT YESTERDAY ...?
WHOA. YOU DID A LOT.
パラ…
PARA (FLIP)
CHIRA (GLANCE)
I...
...CAN'T APPROACH PEOPLE THE WAY YOU AND YUIGAHAMA-SAN DO, SO...
The Little Match Girl

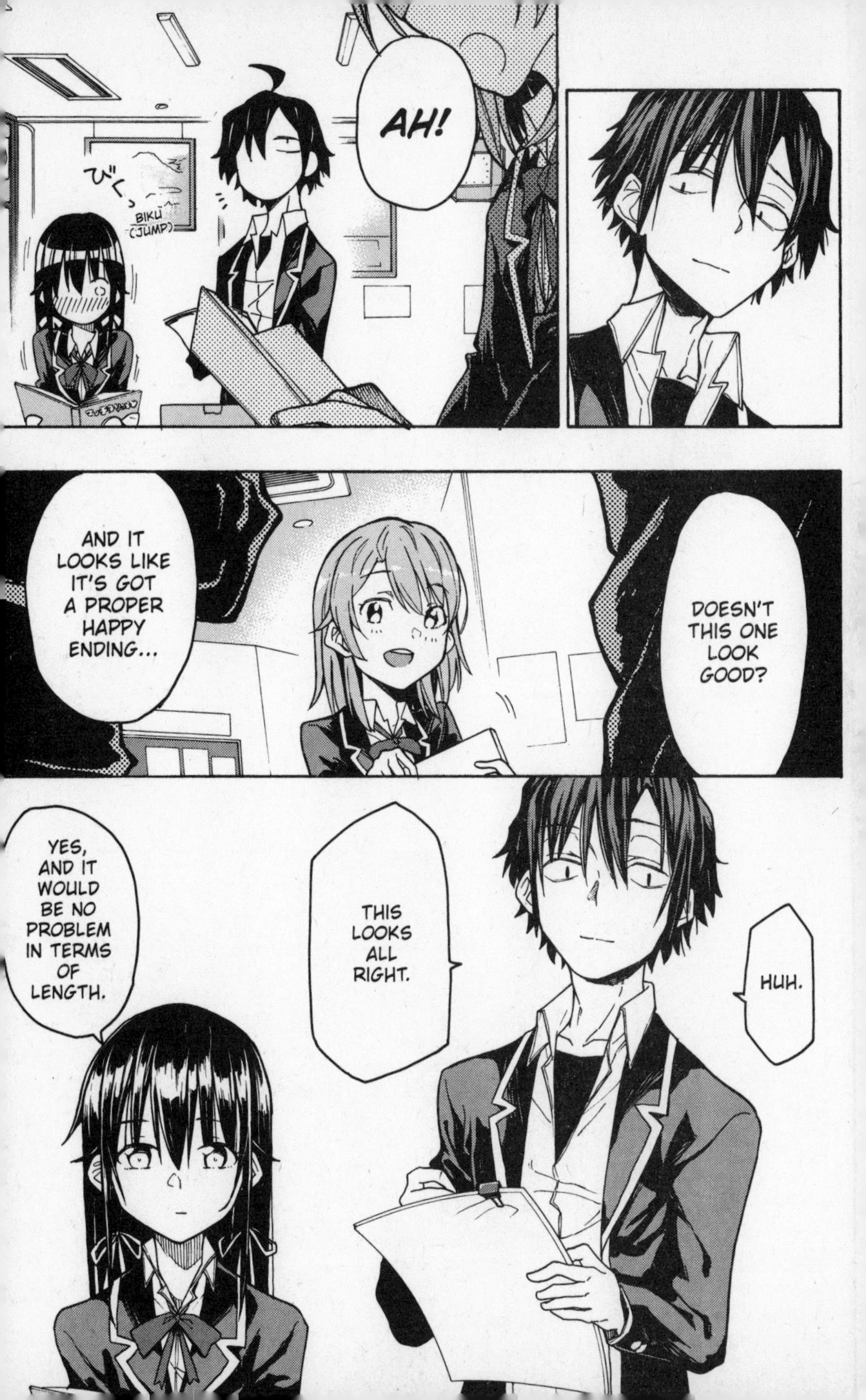
AH!
びくっ
BIKU (JUMP)
DOESN'T THIS ONE LOOK GOOD?
AND IT LOOKS LIKE IT'S GOT A PROPER HAPPY ENDING...
HUH.
THIS LOOKS ALL RIGHT.
YES, AND IT WOULD BE NO PROBLEM IN TERMS OF LENGTH.

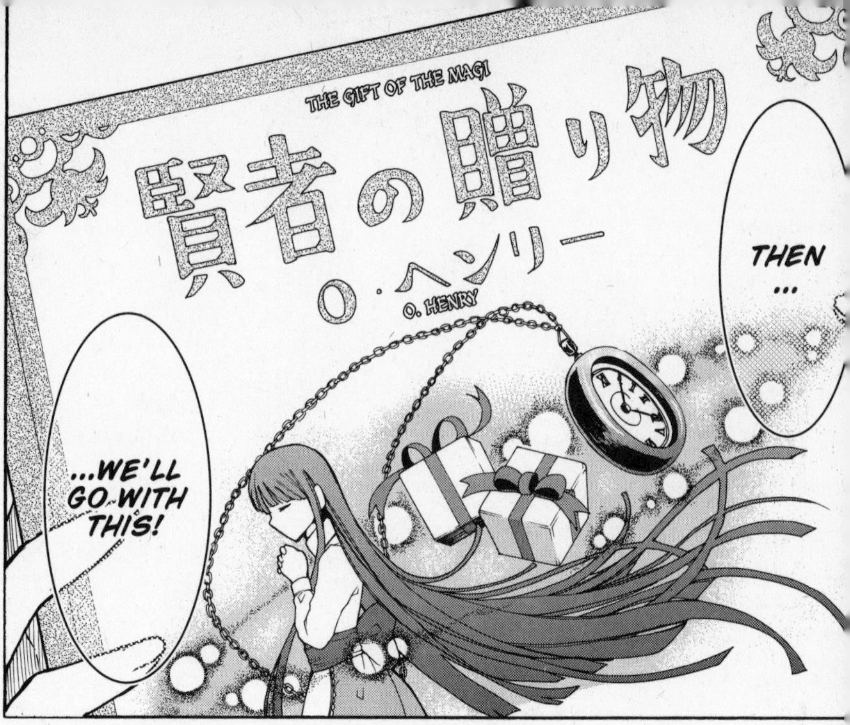
THEN ...
THE GIFT OF THE MAGI
賢者の贈り物
O.ヘンリー
O. HENRY
...WE'LL GO WITH THIS!
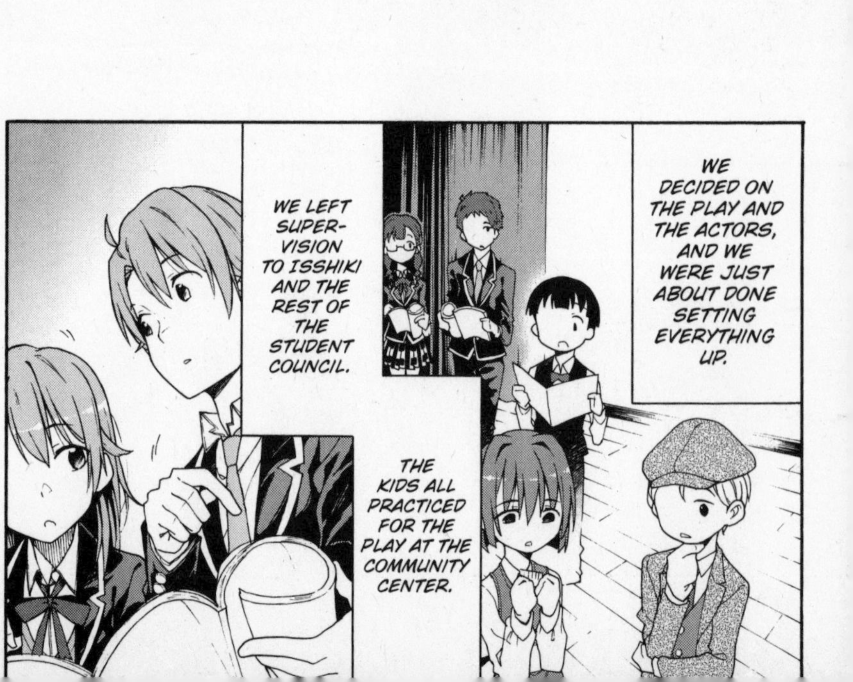
WE DECIDED ON THE PLAY AND THE ACTORS, AND WE WERE JUST ABOUT DONE SETTING EVERYTHING UP.
WE LEFT SUPER-VISION TO ISSHIKI AND THE REST OF THE STUDENT COUNCIL.
THE KIDS ALL PRACTICED FOR THE PLAY AT THE COMMUNITY CENTER.

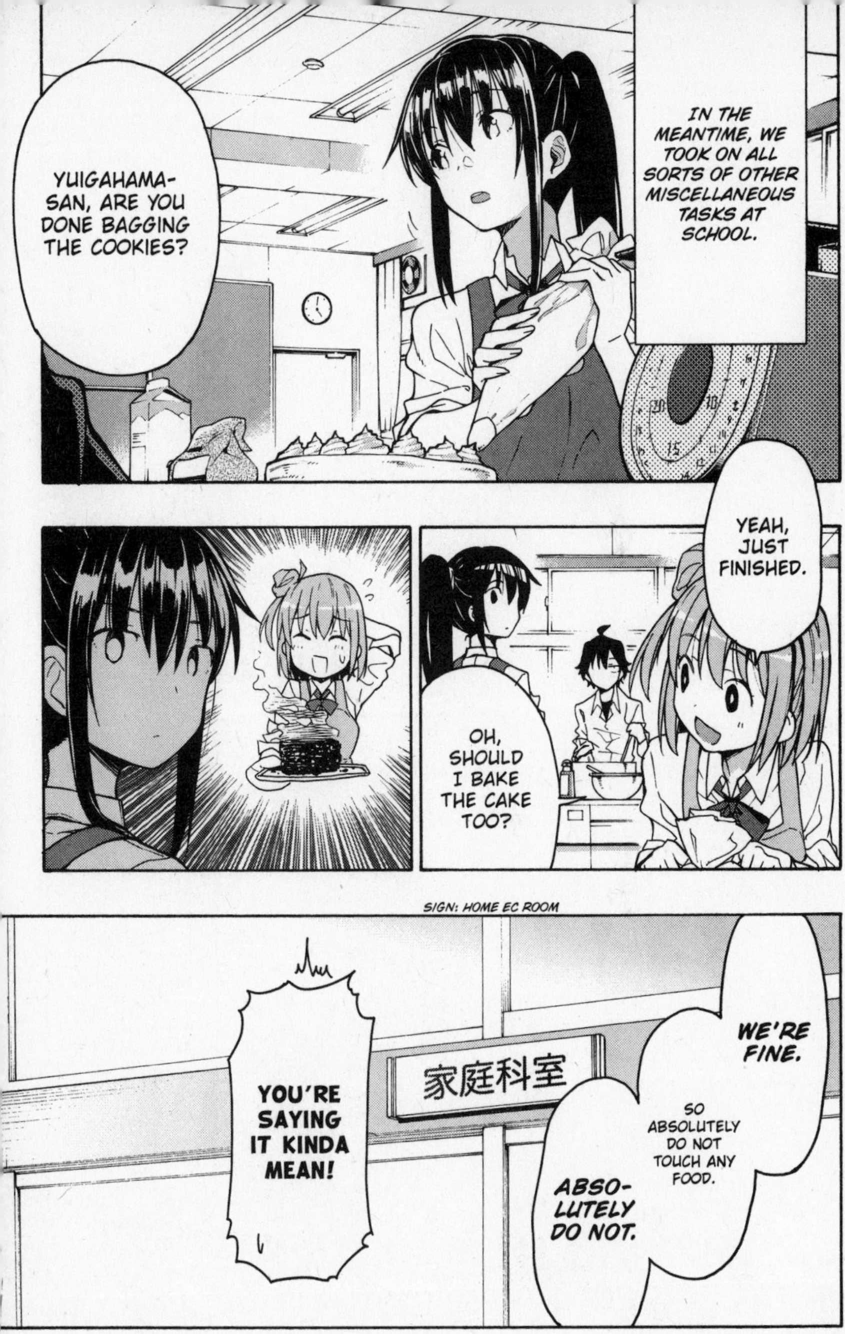
IN THE MEANTIME, WE TOOK ON ALL SORTS OF OTHER MISCELLANEOUS TASKS AT SCHOOL.
YUIGAHAMA-SAN, ARE YOU DONE BAGGING THE COOKIES?
YEAH, JUST FINISHED.
OH, SHOULD I BAKE THE CAKE TOO?
SIGN: HOME EC ROOM
WE'RE FINE.
SO ABSOLUTELY DO NOT TOUCH ANY FOOD.
ABSO-LUTELY DO NOT.
家庭科室
YOU'RE SAYING IT KINDA MEAN!

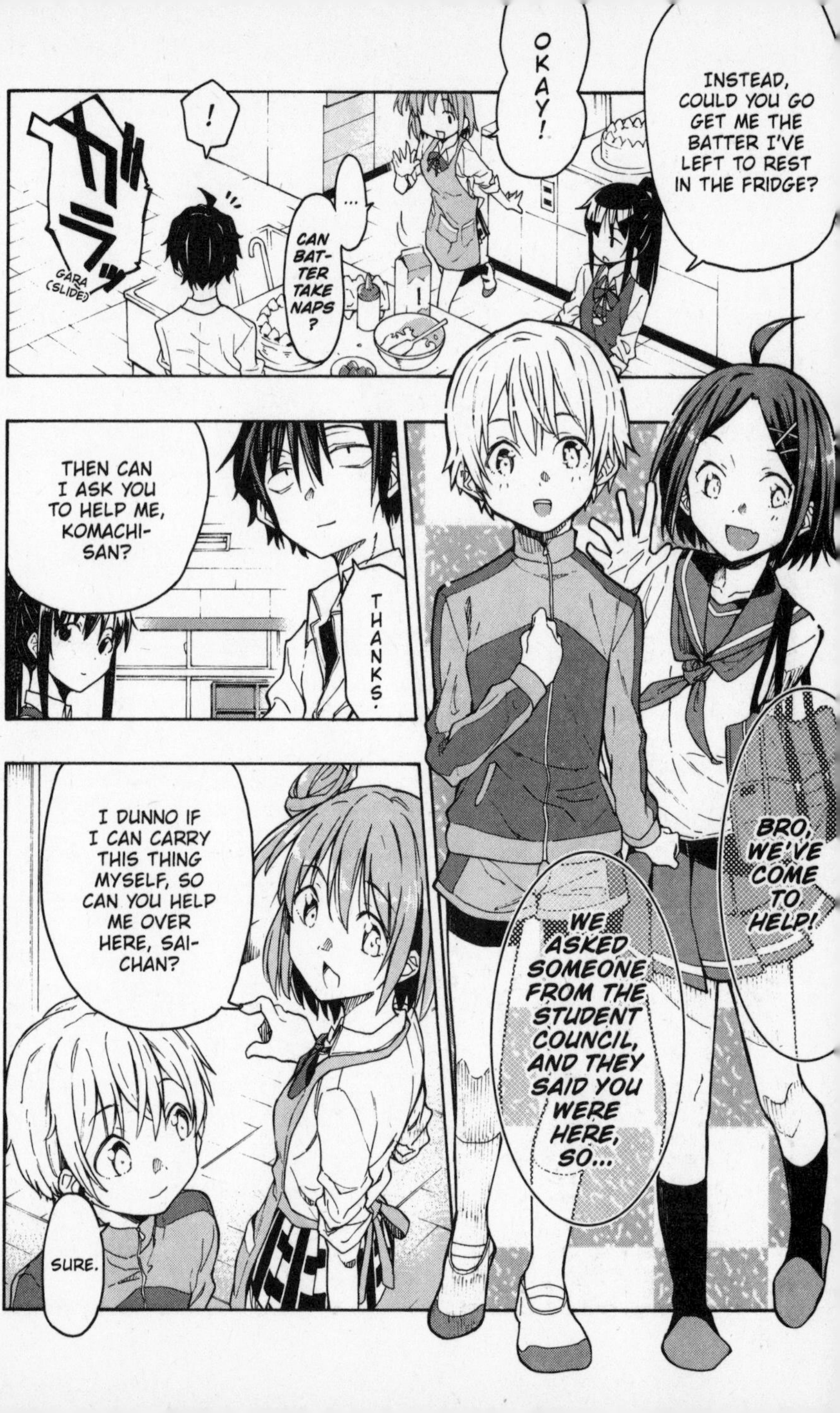
INSTEAD, COULD YOU GO GET ME THE BATTER I'VE LEFT TO REST IN THE FRIDGE?
OKAY!
!
...
CAN BATTER TAKE NAPS?
!
GARA (SLIDE)
BRO, WE'VE COME TO HELP!
WE ASKED SOMEONE FROM THE STUDENT COUNCIL, AND THEY SAID YOU WERE HERE, SO...
THEN CAN I ASK YOU TO HELP ME, KOMACHI-SAN?
THANKS.
I DUNNO IF I CAN CARRY THIS THING MYSELF, SO CAN YOU HELP ME OVER HERE, SAI-CHAN?
SURE.

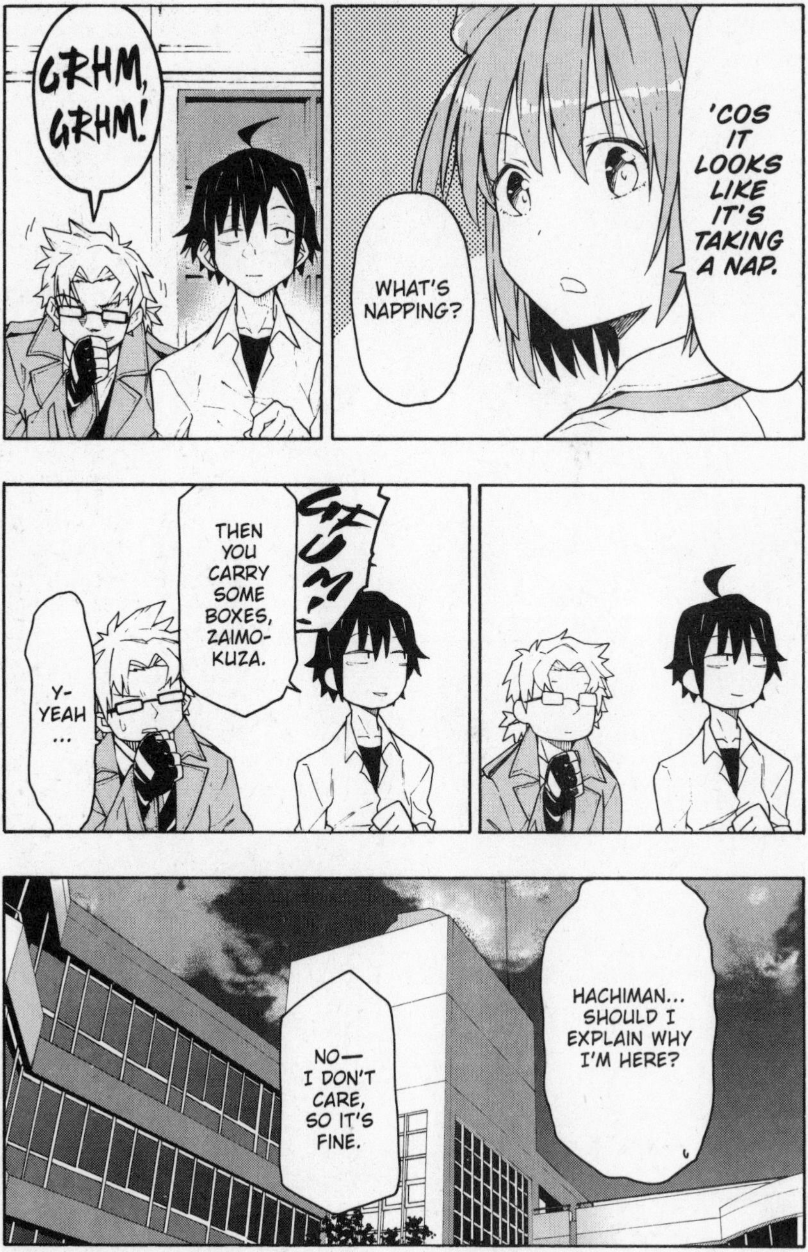
'COS IT LOOKS LIKE IT'S TAKING A NAP.
WHAT'S NAPPING?
GRHM, GRHM!
THEN YOU CARRY SOME BOXES, ZAIMOKUZA.
Y-YEAH ...
HACHIMAN... SHOULD I EXPLAIN WHY I'M HERE?
NO— I DON'T CARE, SO IT'S FINE.

SIGN: PUSH BUTTON

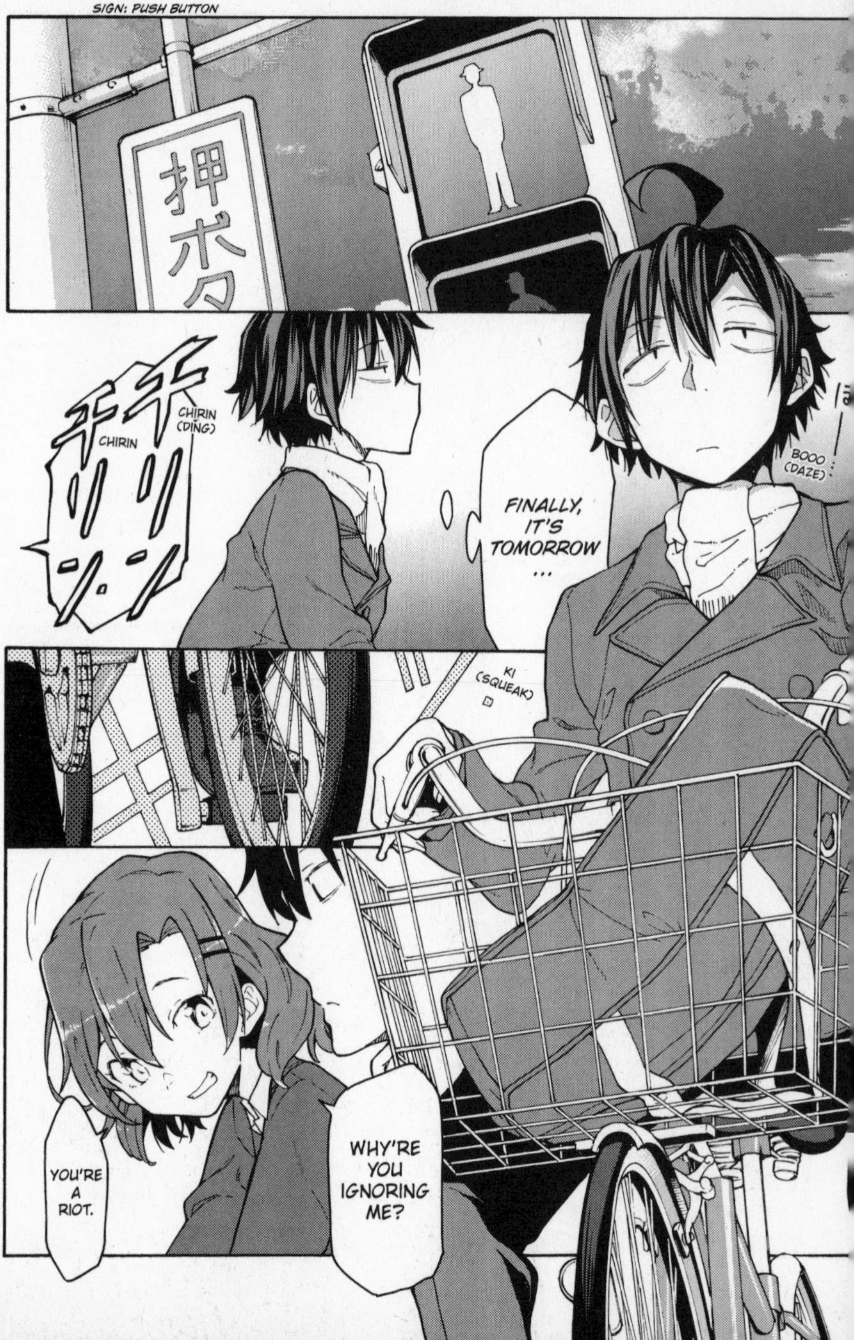

押ボタ
BOOO (DAZE)
FINALLY, IT'S TOMORROW ...
CHIRIN (DING)
CHIRIN
KI (SQUEAK)
WHY'RE YOU IGNORING ME?
YOU'RE A RIOT.

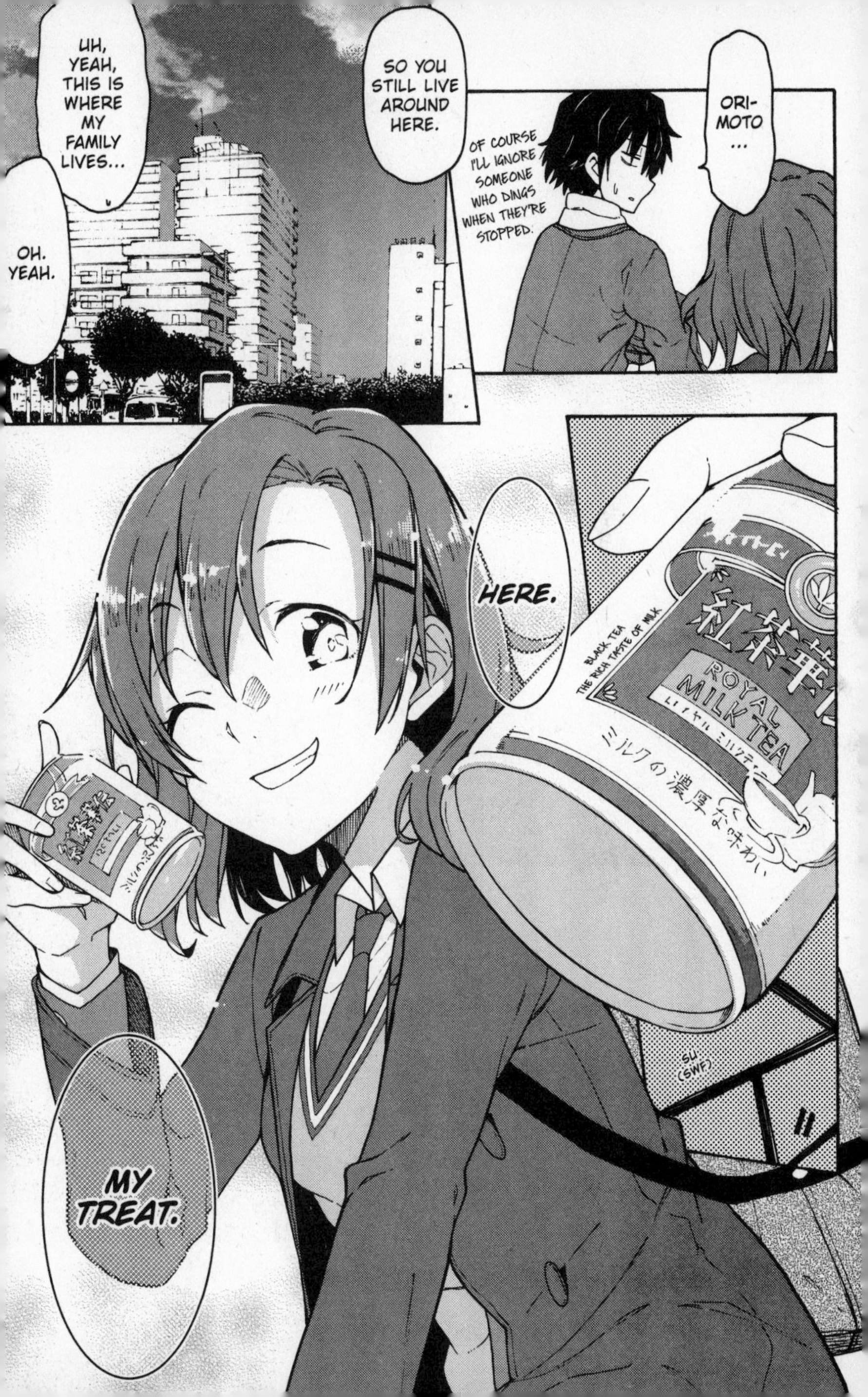
ORI-MOTO...
OF COURSE I'LL IGNORE SOMEONE WHO DINGS WHEN THEY'RE STOPPED.
SO YOU STILL LIVE AROUND HERE.
UH, YEAH, THIS IS WHERE MY FAMILY LIVES...
OH. YEAH.
HERE.
BLACK TEA
THE RICH TASTE OF MILK
ROYAL MILK TEA
ミルクの濃厚な味わい
SLI (SWF)
MY TREAT.

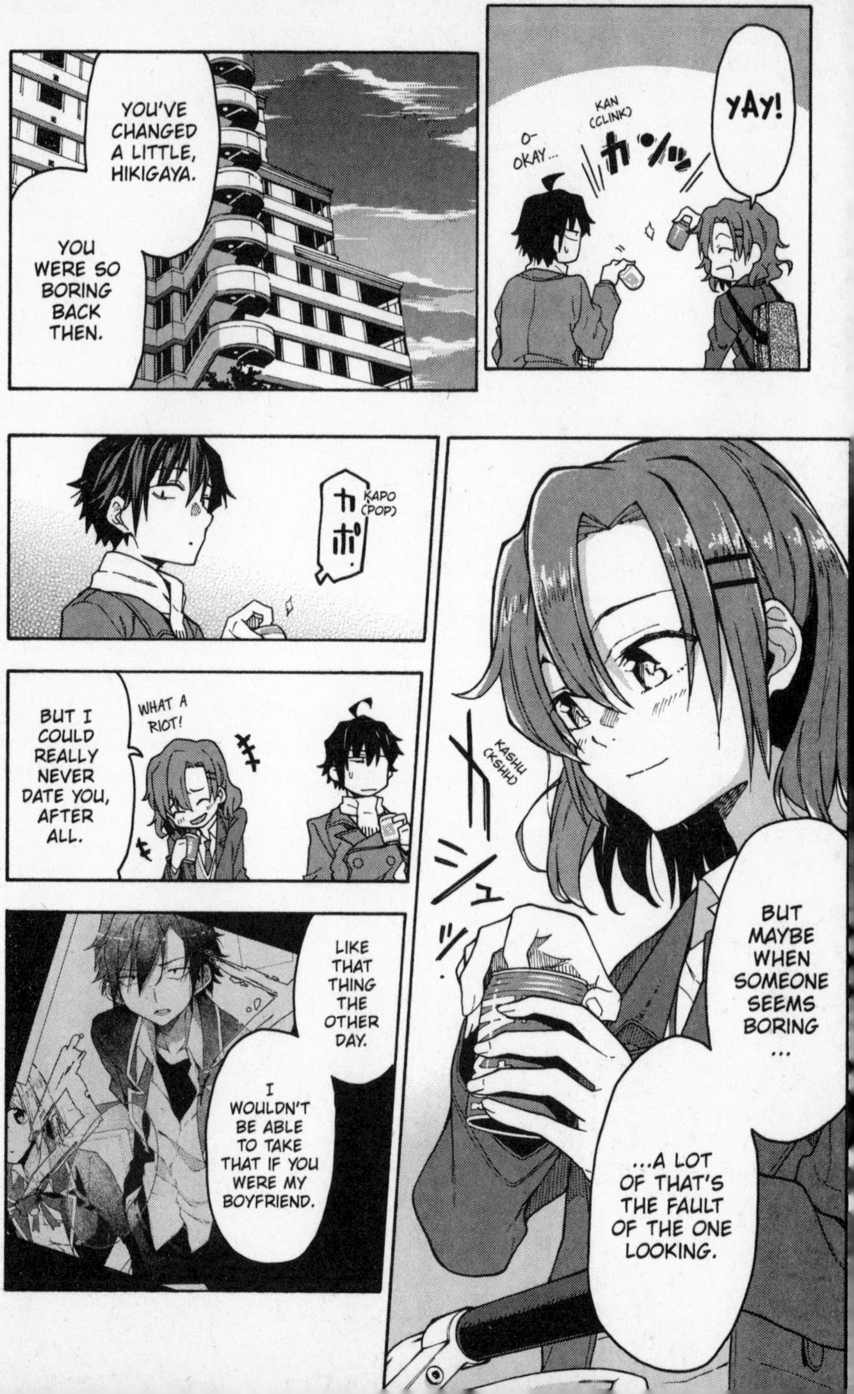
YAY!
KAN (CLINK)
カンッ
O-OKAY...
YOU'VE CHANGED A LITTLE, HIKIGAYA.
YOU WERE SO BORING BACK THEN.
KASHU (KSHH)
シュッ
BUT MAYBE WHEN SOMEONE SEEMS BORING...
...A LOT OF THAT'S THE FAULT OF THE ONE LOOKING.
KAPO (POP)
カポ
BUT I COULD REALLY NEVER DATE YOU, AFTER ALL.
WHAT A RIOT!
LIKE THAT THING THE OTHER DAY.
I WOULDN'T BE ABLE TO TAKE THAT IF YOU WERE MY BOYFRIEND.

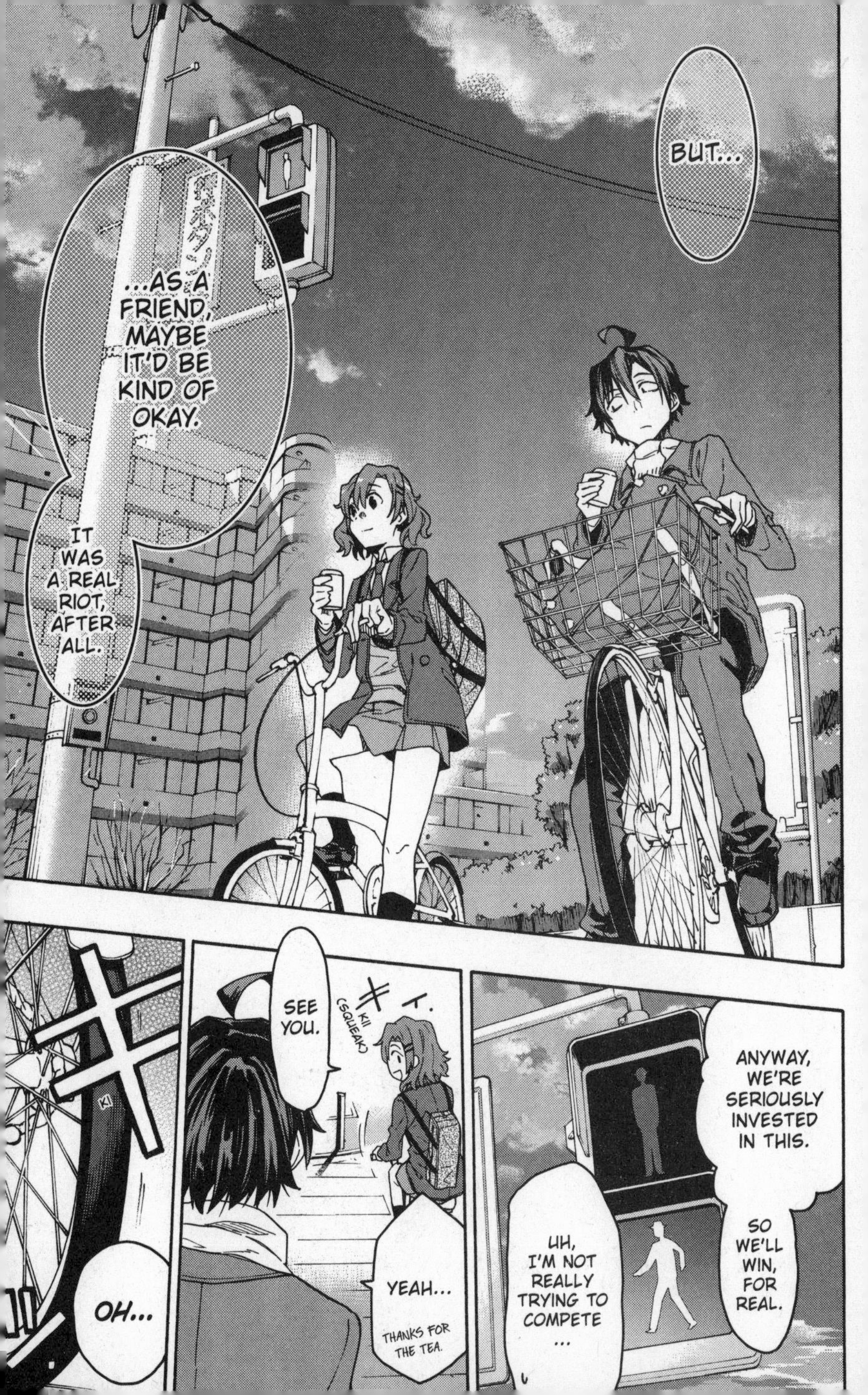
BUT...
...AS A FRIEND, MAYBE IT'D BE KIND OF OKAY.
IT WAS A REAL RIOT, AFTER ALL.
ANYWAY, WE'RE SERIOUSLY INVESTED IN THIS.
SO WE'LL WIN, FOR REAL.
UH, I'M NOT REALLY TRYING TO COMPETE...
SEE YOU.
キィ.
KI (SQUEAK)
YEAH...
THANKS FOR THE TEA.
KI
OH...

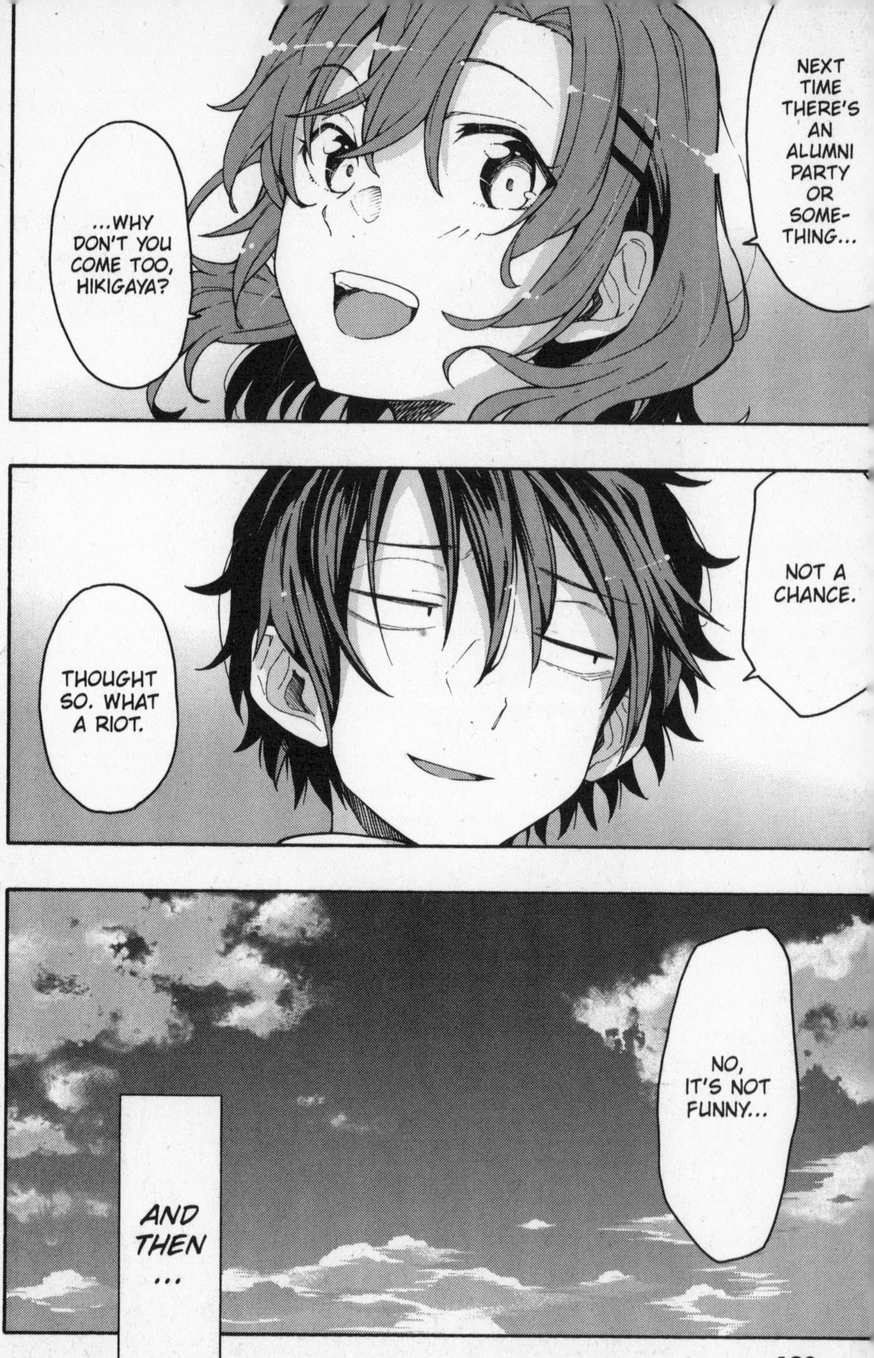
NEXT TIME THERE'S AN ALUMNI PARTY OR SOME-THING...
...WHY DON'T YOU COME TOO, HIKIGAYA?
NOT A CHANCE.
THOUGHT SO. WHAT A RIOT.
NO, IT'S NOT FUNNY...
AND THEN ...

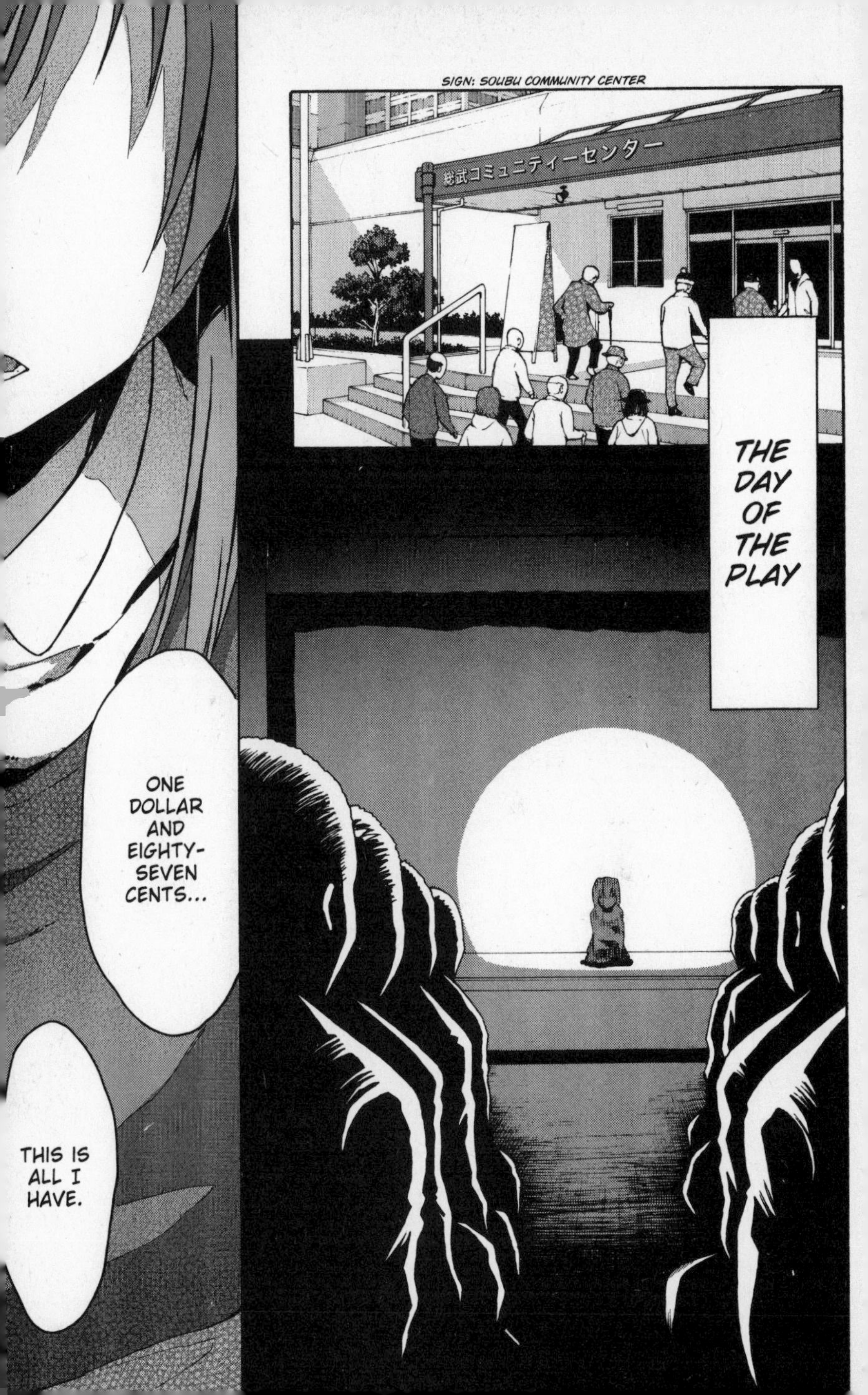
SIGN: SOUBU COMMUNITY CENTER
総武コミュニティーセンター
THE DAY OF THE PLAY
ONE DOLLAR AND EIGHTY-SEVEN CENTS...
THIS IS ALL I HAVE.

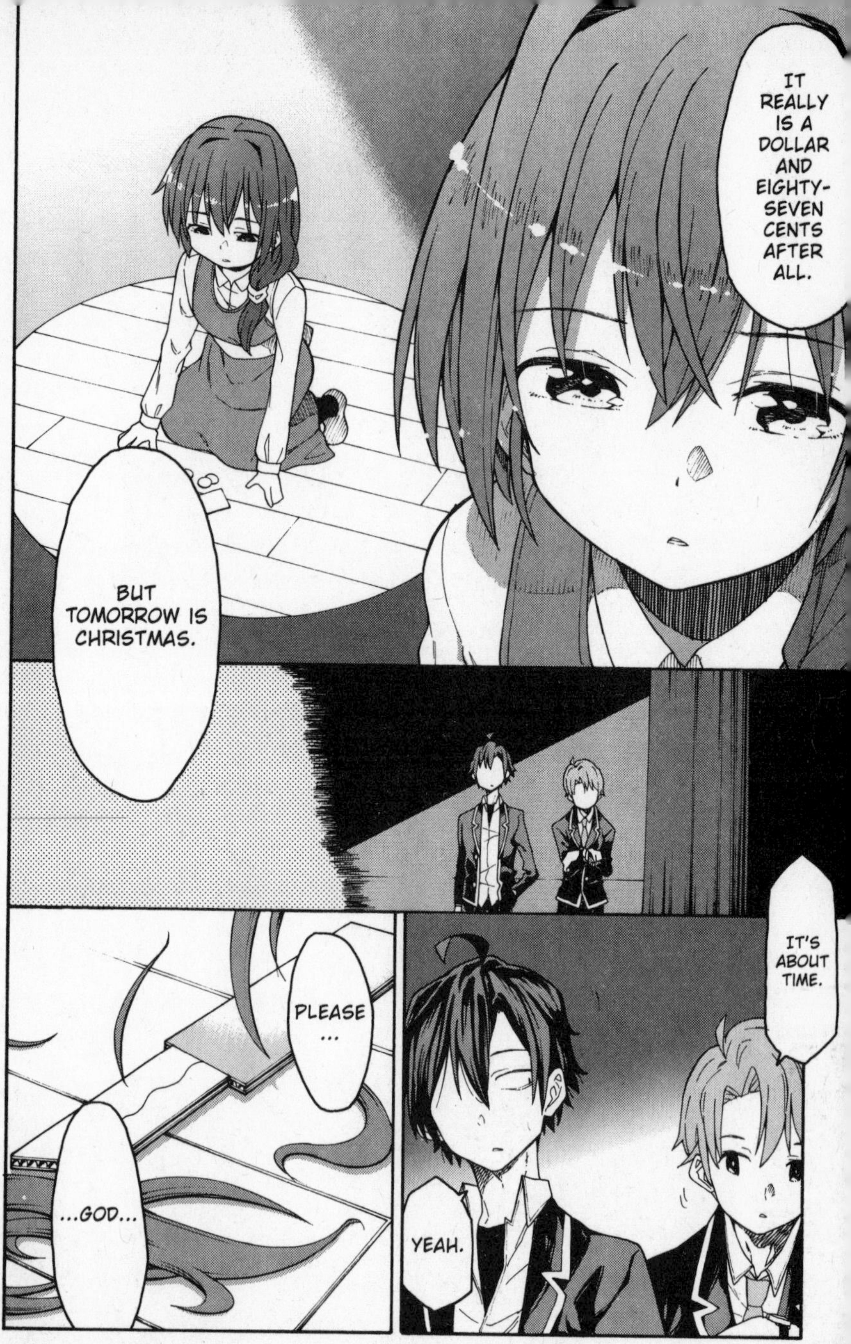
IT REALLY IS A DOLLAR AND EIGHTY-SEVEN CENTS AFTER ALL.
BUT TOMORROW IS CHRISTMAS.
IT'S ABOUT TIME.
YEAH.
PLEASE...
...GOD...

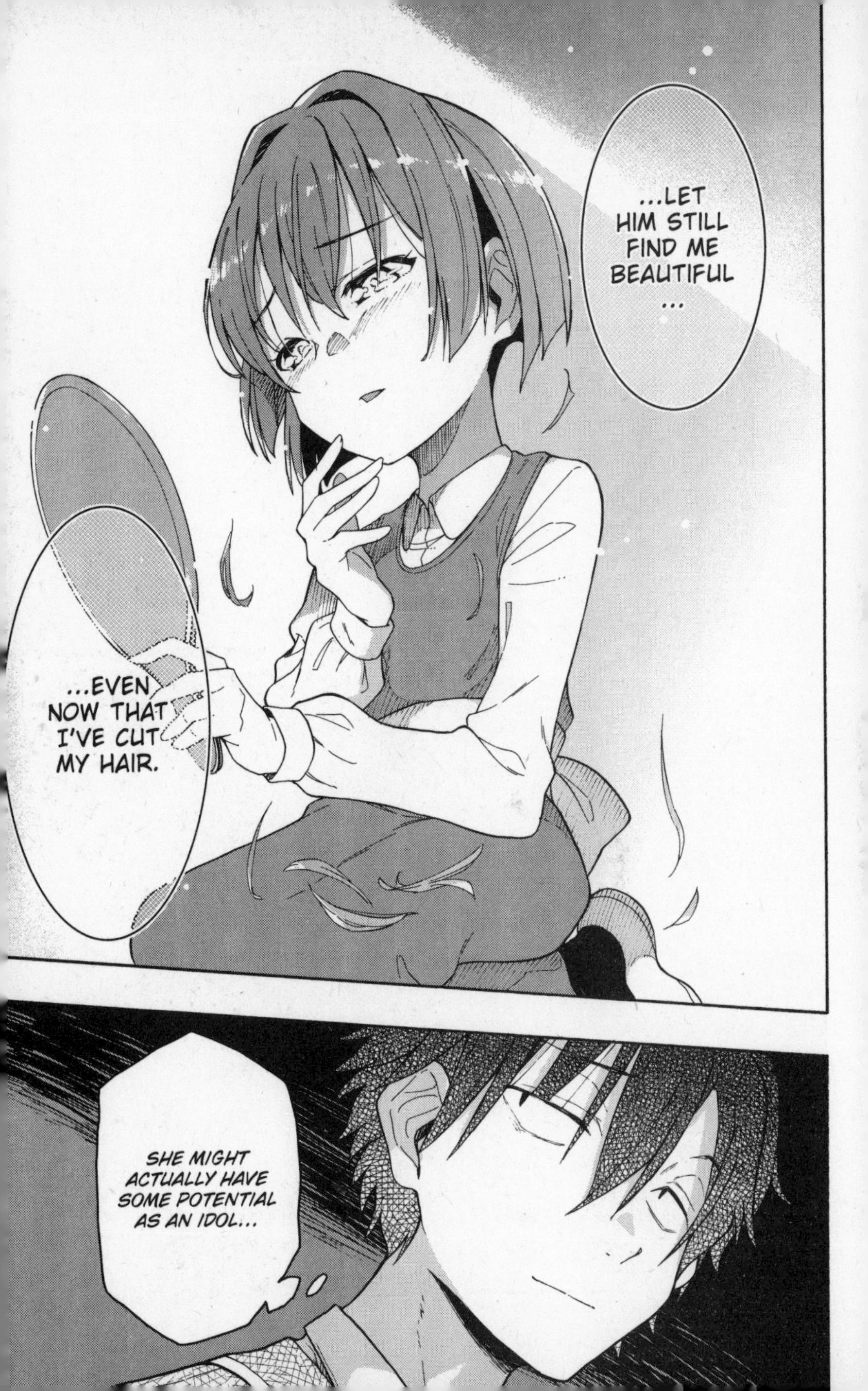
...LET HIM STILL FIND ME BEAUTIFUL ...
...EVEN NOW THAT I'VE CUT MY HAIR.
SHE MIGHT ACTUALLY HAVE SOME POTENTIAL AS AN IDOL...

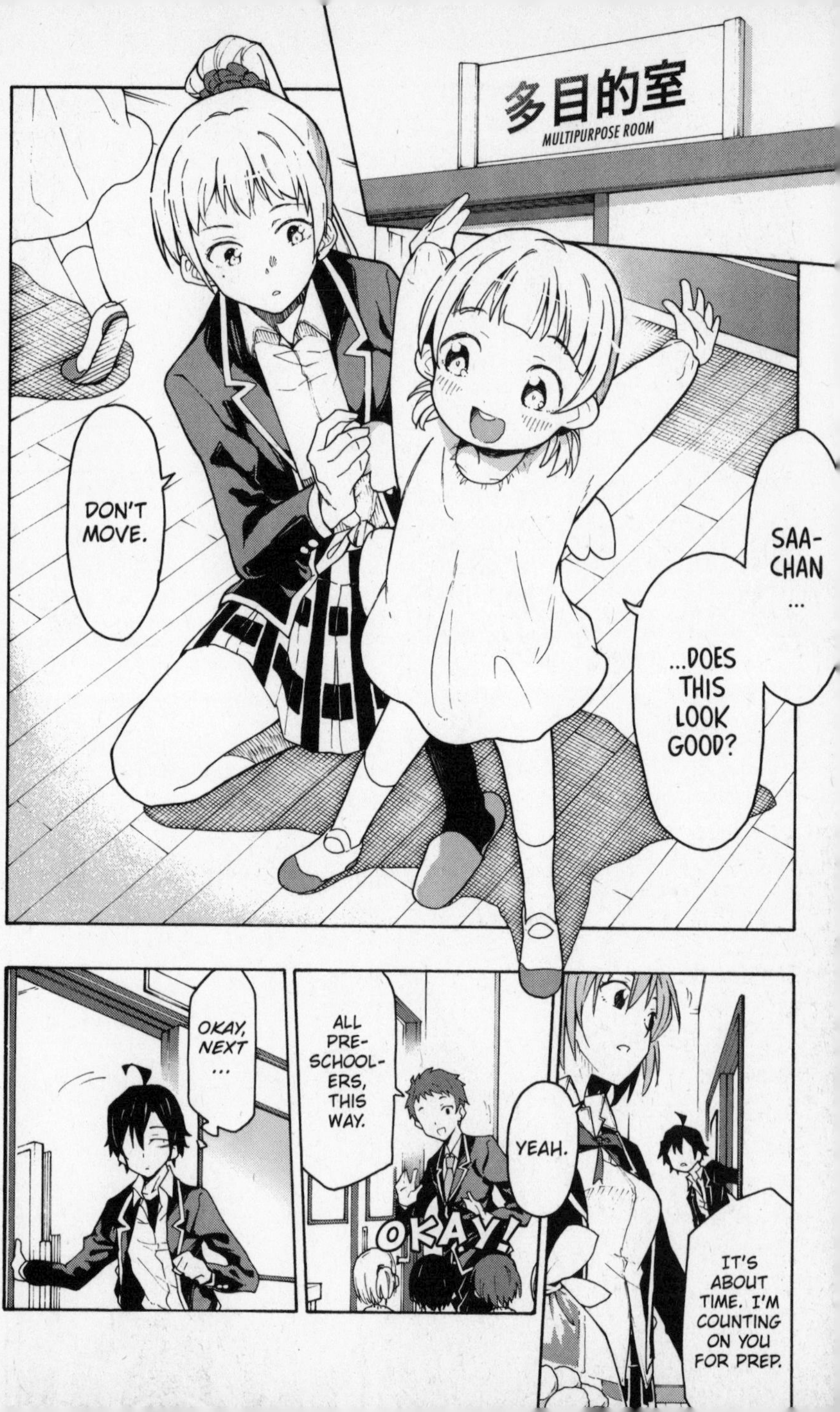

多目的室
MULTIPURPOSE ROOM
SAA-CHAN...
...DOES THIS LOOK GOOD?
DON'T MOVE.
YEAH.
IT'S ABOUT TIME. I'M COUNTING ON YOU FOR PREP.
ALL PRE-SCHOOLERS, THIS WAY.
OKAY!
OKAY, NEXT...

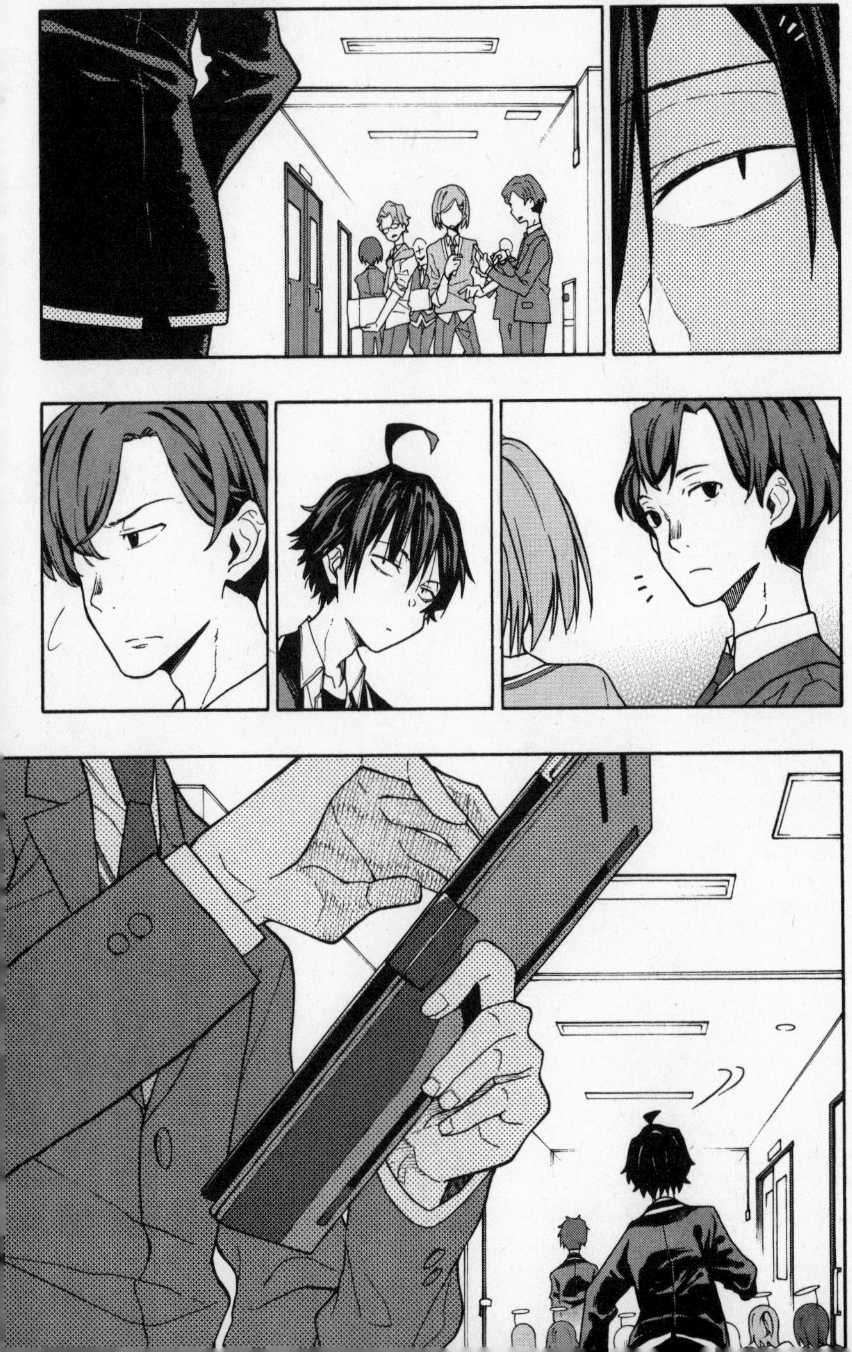

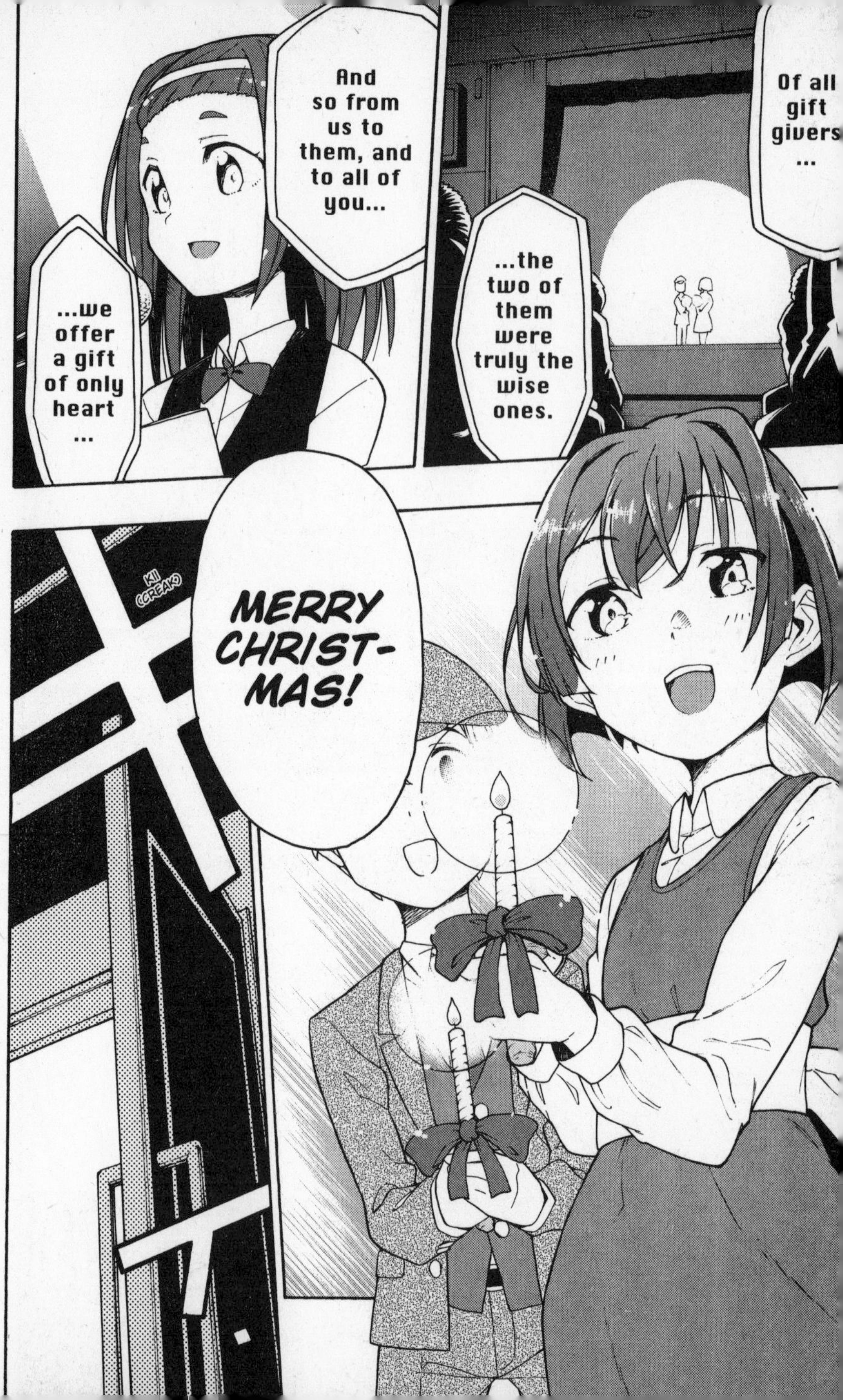
Of all gift givers...
...the two of them were truly the wise ones.
And so from us to them, and to all of you...
...we offer a gift of only heart...
MERRY CHRISTMAS!
KII (CREAK)

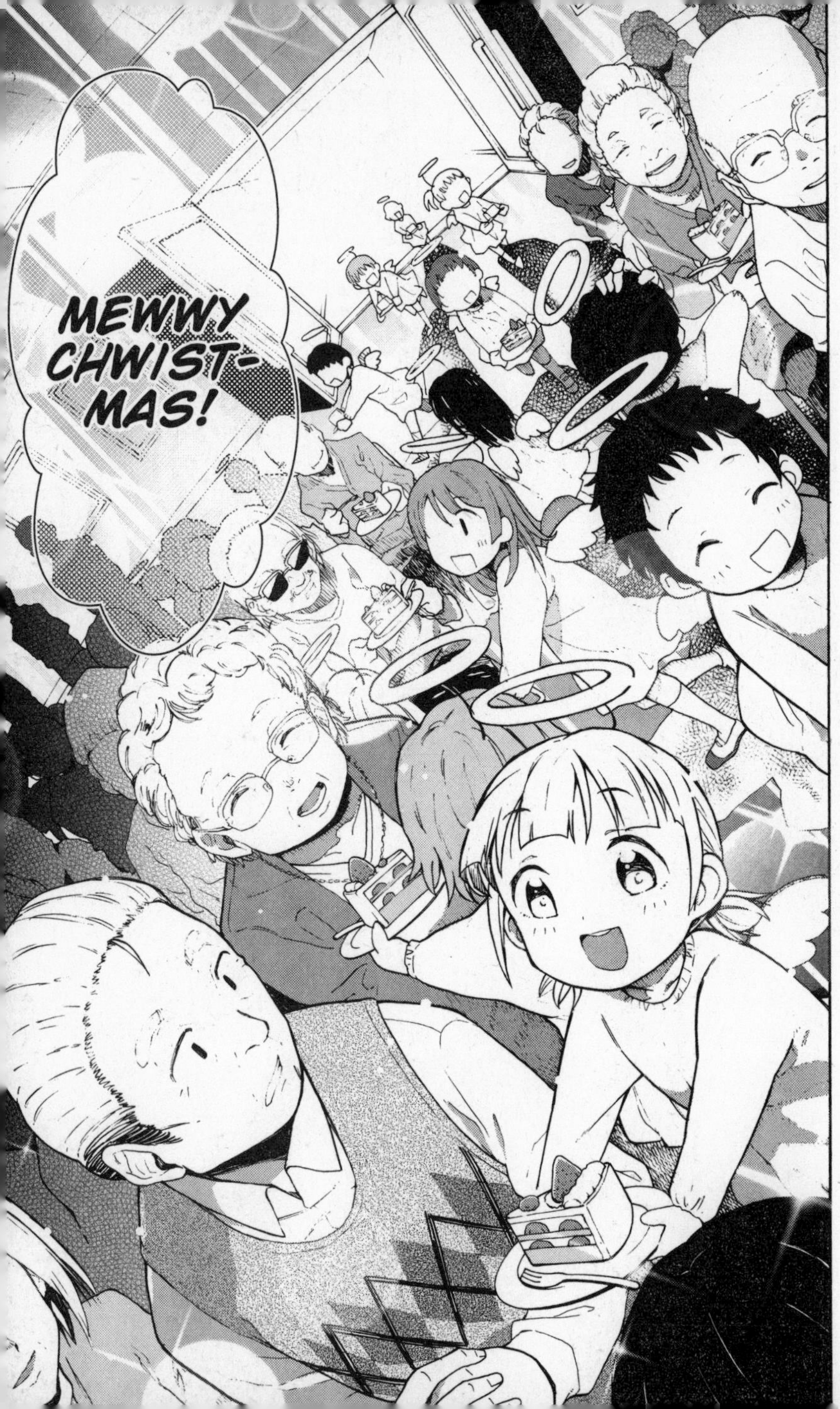
MEWWY CHWIST-MAS!

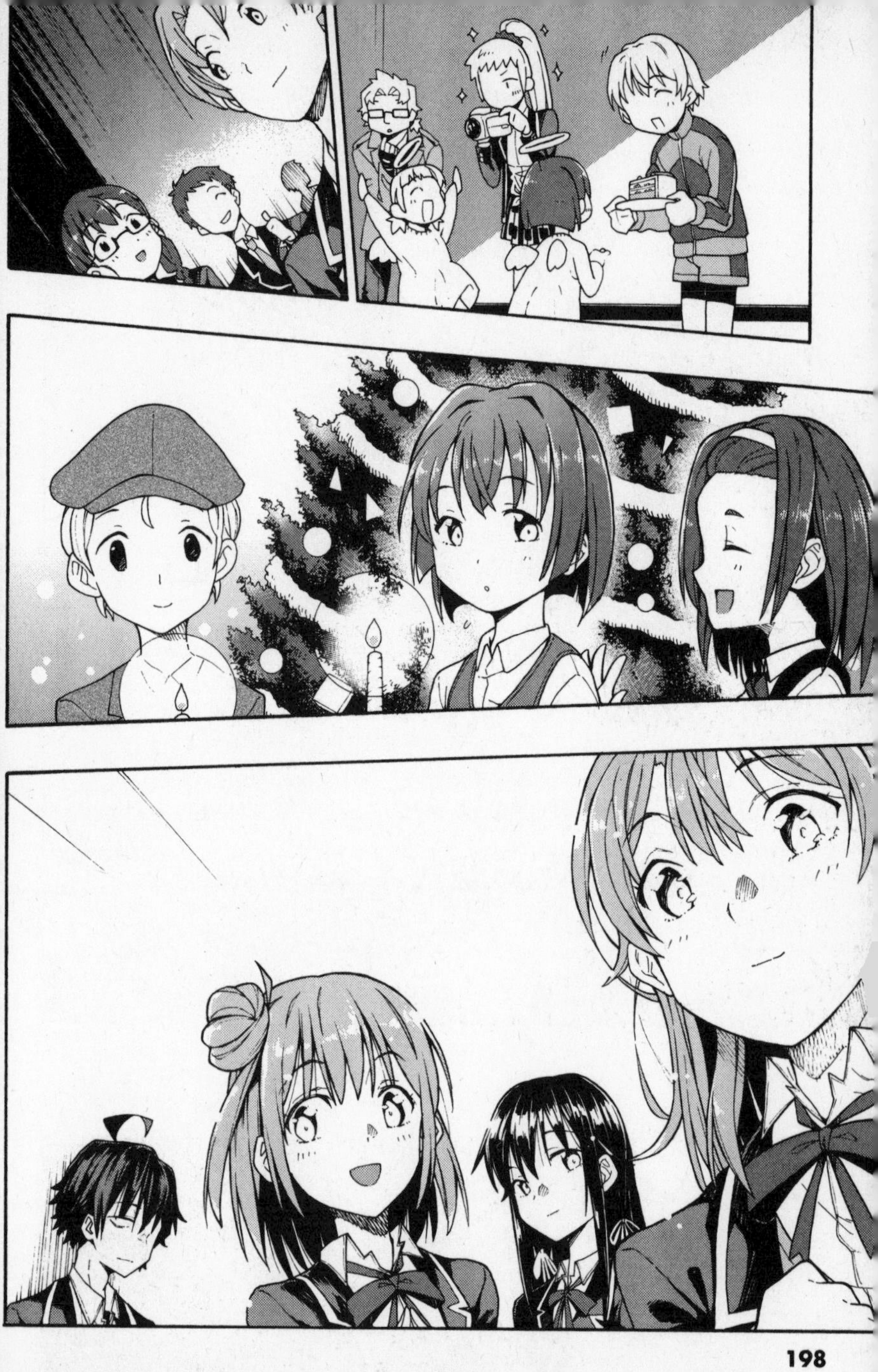

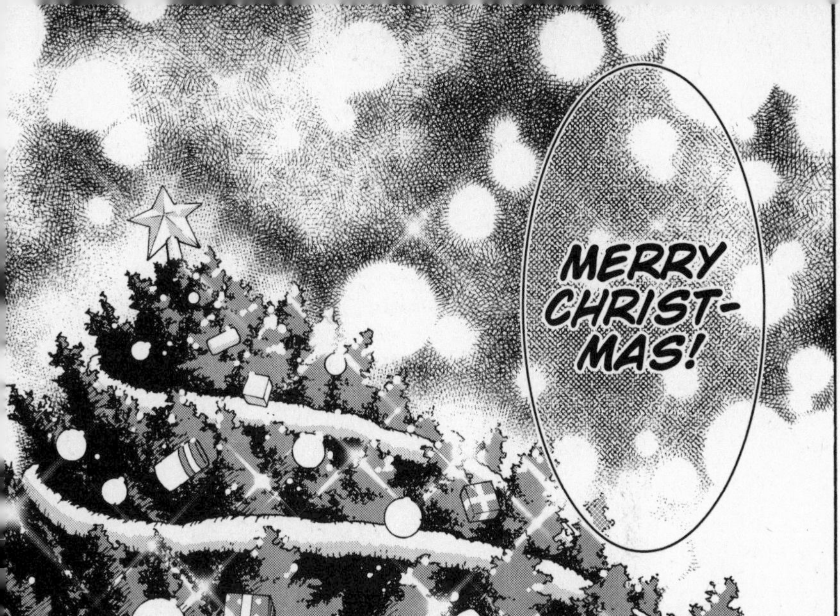
MERRY CHRIST-MAS!

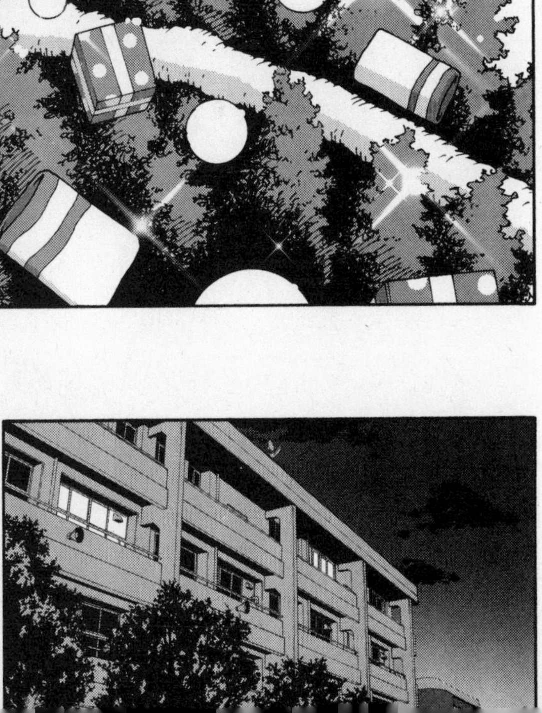

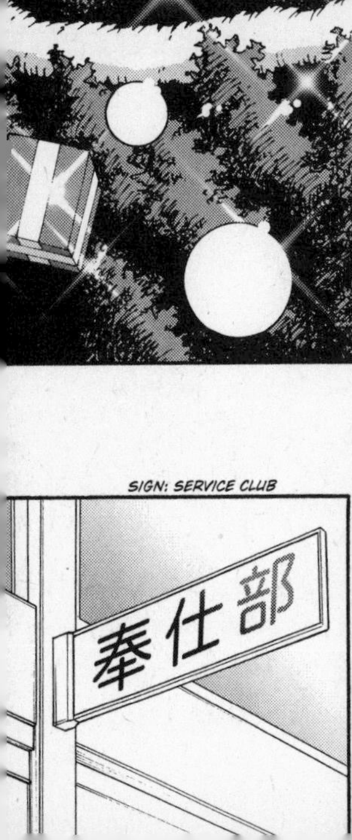
SIGN: SERVICE CLUB
奉仕部

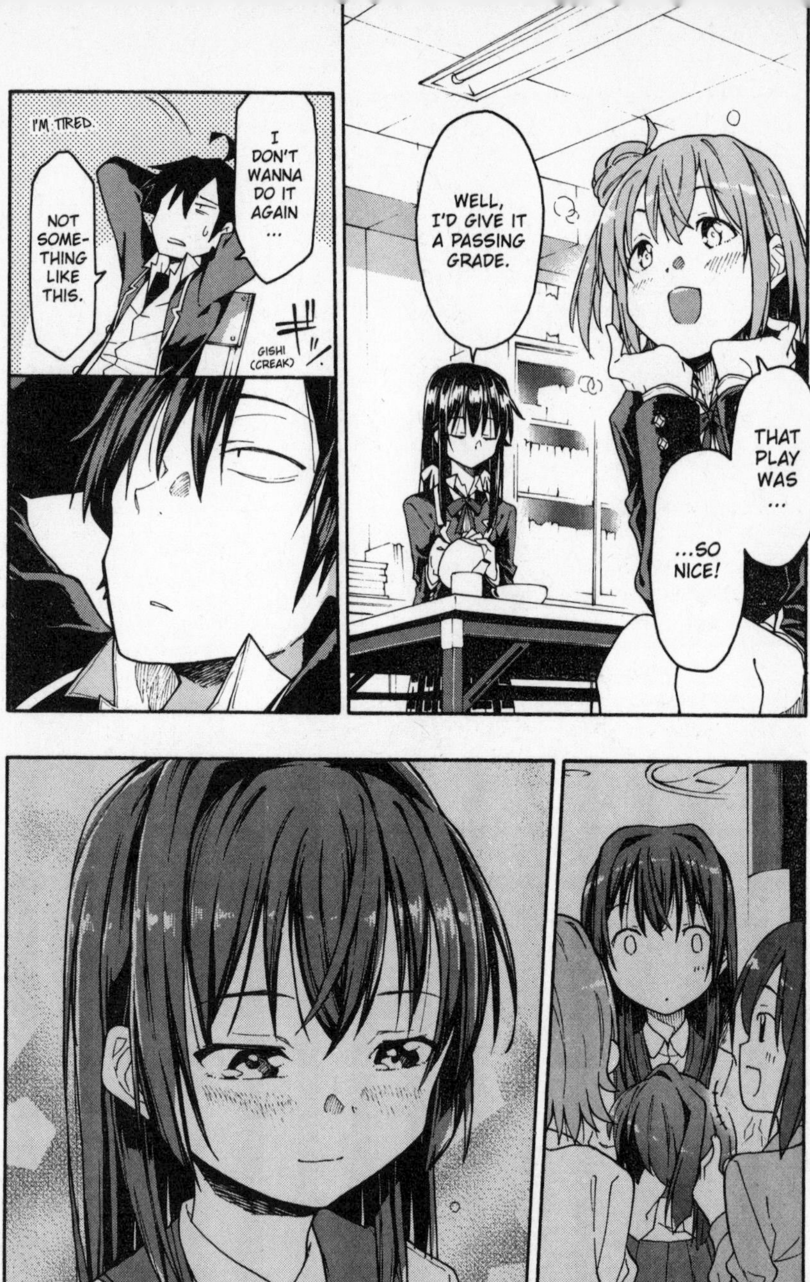
THAT PLAY WAS ...
...SO NICE!
WELL, I'D GIVE IT A PASSING GRADE.
I DON'T WANNA DO IT AGAIN ...
NOT SOME-THING LIKE THIS.
I'M TIRED.
GISHI (CREAK)

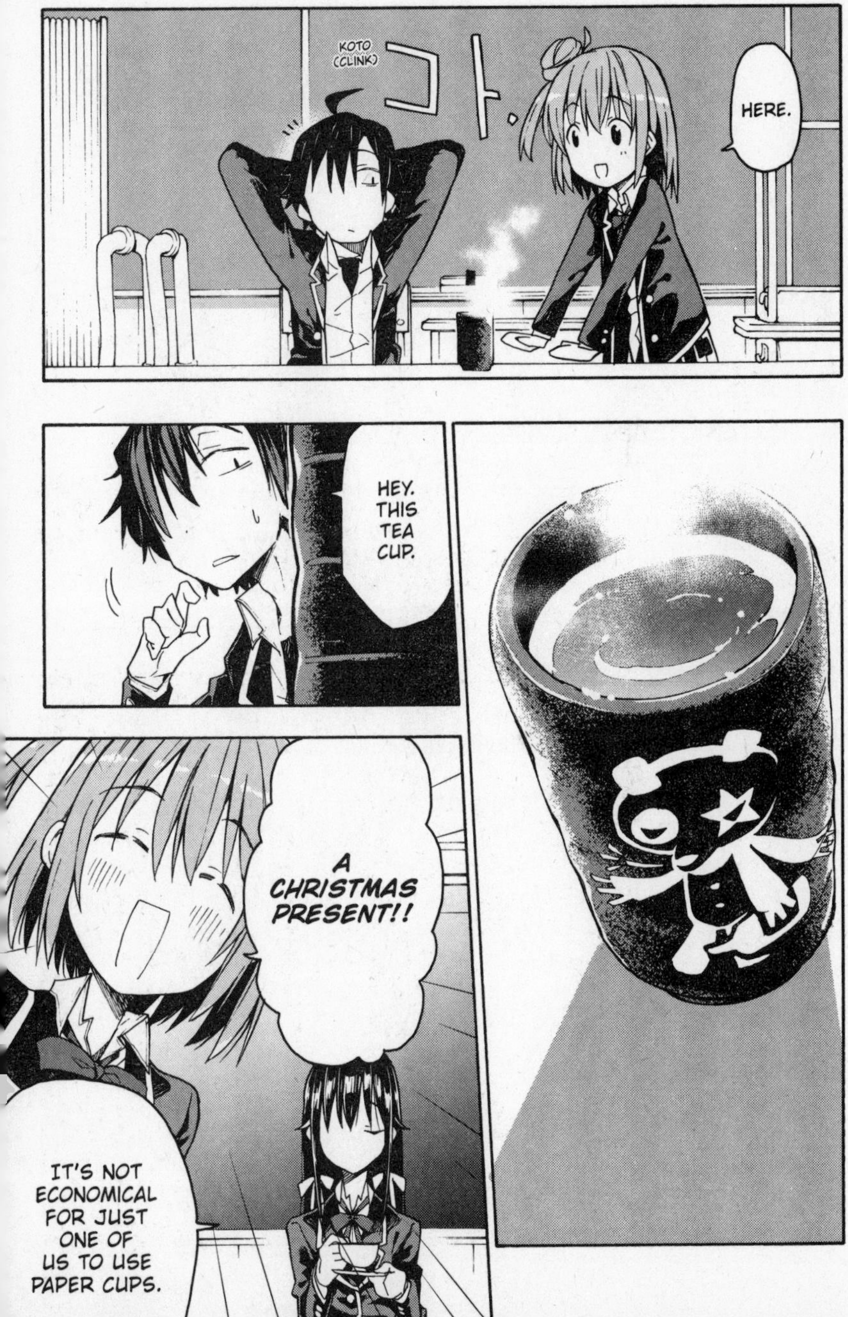
HERE.
KOTO (CLINK)
HEY. THIS TEA CUP.
A CHRISTMAS PRESENT!!
IT'S NOT ECONOMICAL FOR JUST ONE OF US TO USE PAPER CUPS.

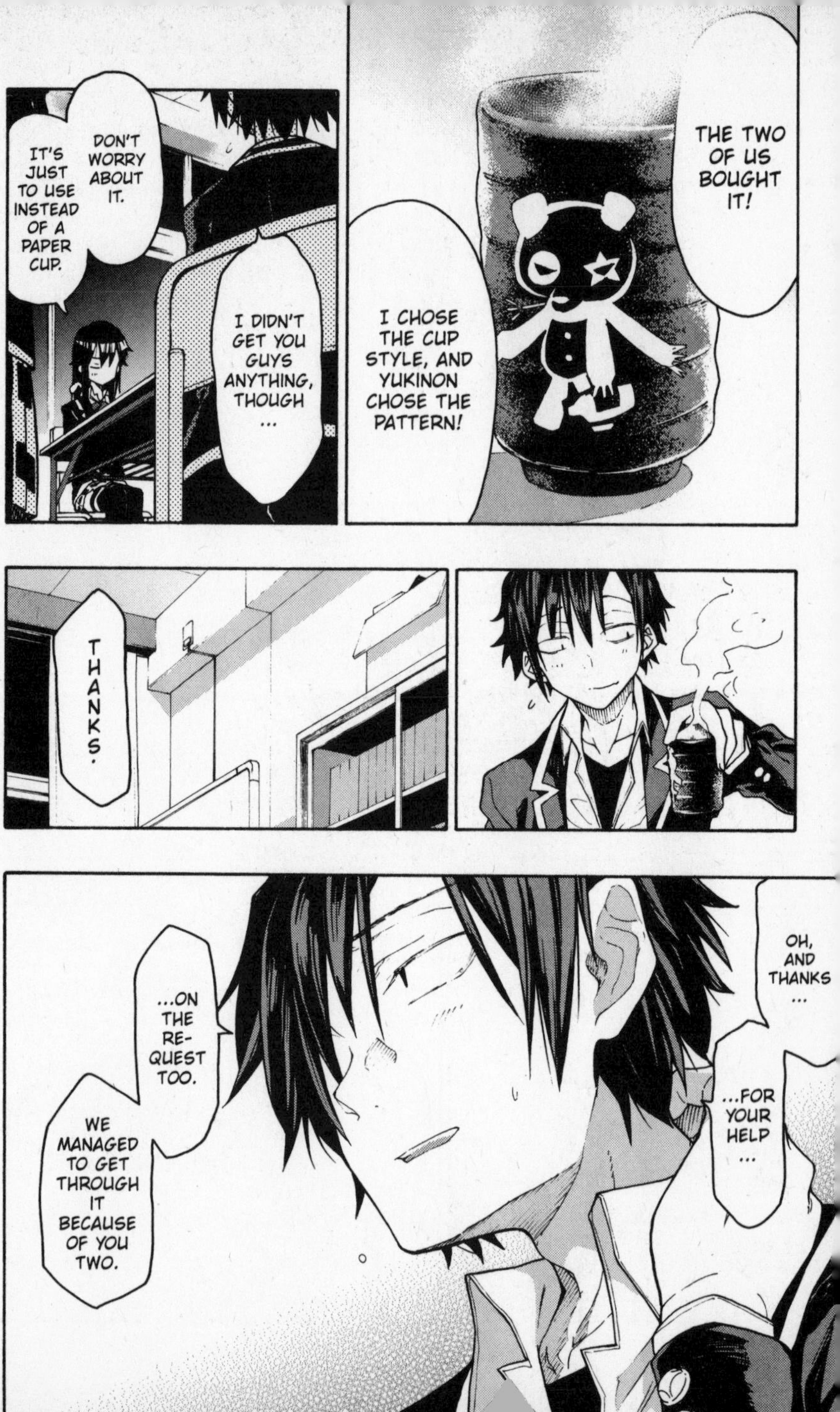
THE TWO OF US BOUGHT IT!
I CHOSE THE CUP STYLE, AND YUKINON CHOSE THE PATTERN!
I DIDN'T GET YOU GUYS ANYTHING, THOUGH ...
DON'T WORRY ABOUT IT.
IT'S JUST TO USE INSTEAD OF A PAPER CUP.
THANKS.
OH, AND THANKS ...
...FOR YOUR HELP ...
...ON THE REQUEST TOO.
WE MANAGED TO GET THROUGH IT BECAUSE OF YOU TWO.

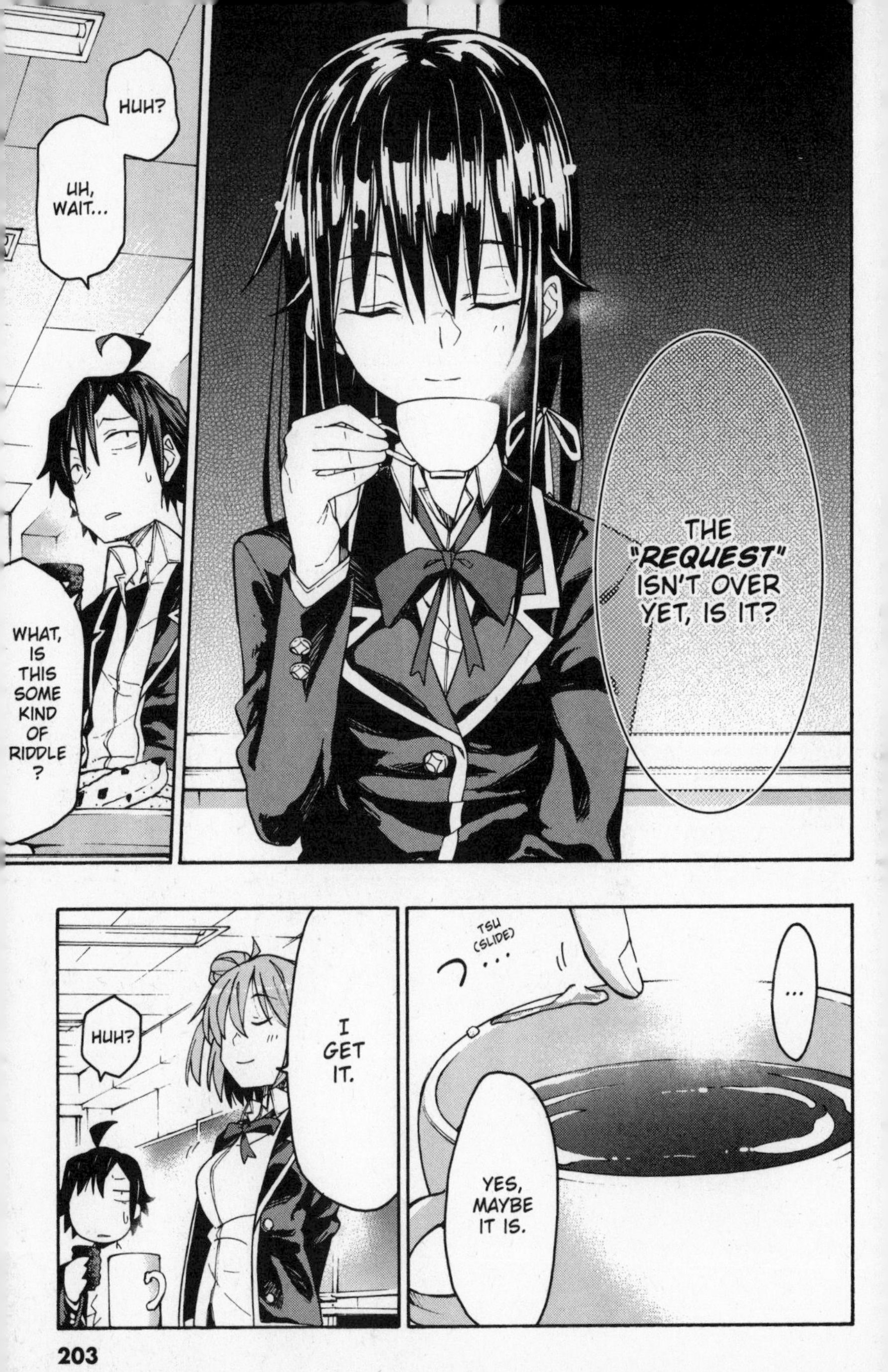
THE "REQUEST" ISN'T OVER YET, IS IT?
HUH?
UH, WAIT...
WHAT, IS THIS SOME KIND OF RIDDLE?
...
TSU (SLIDE)
...
YES, MAYBE IT IS.
I GET IT.
HUH?

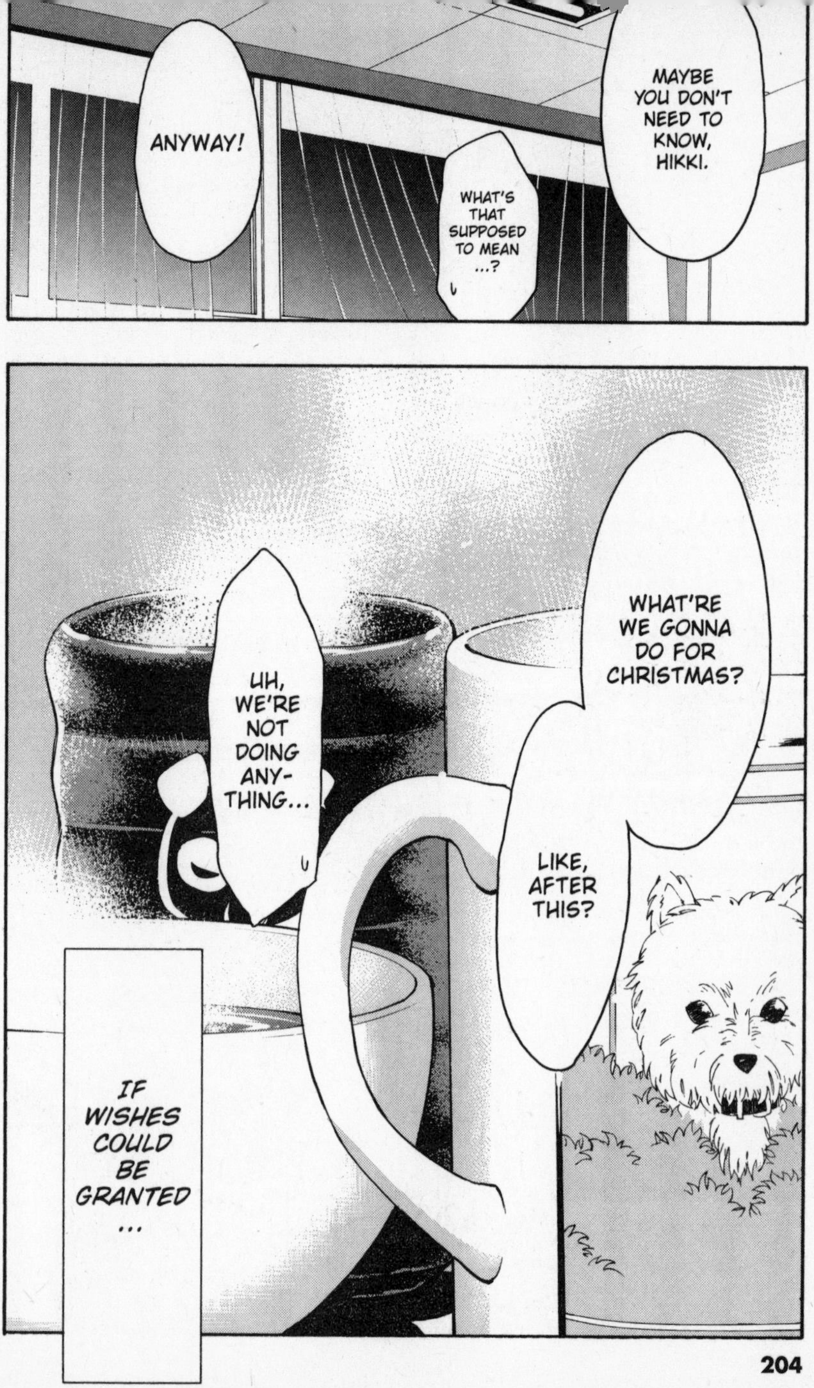
MAYBE YOU DON'T NEED TO KNOW, HIKKI.
WHAT'S THAT SUPPOSED TO MEAN ...?
ANYWAY!
WHAT'RE WE GONNA DO FOR CHRISTMAS?
LIKE, AFTER THIS?
UH, WE'RE NOT DOING ANY-THING...
IF WISHES COULD BE GRANTED ...

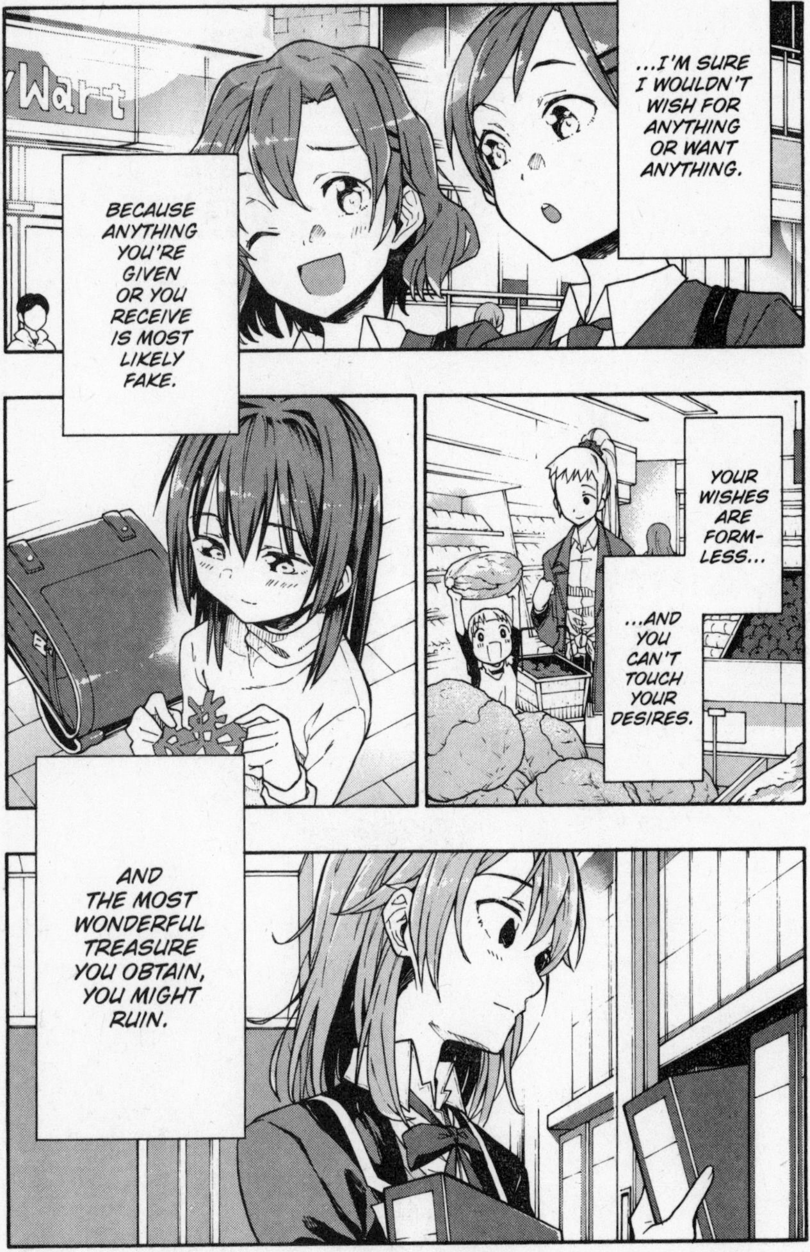
...I'M SURE I WOULDN'T WISH FOR ANYTHING OR WANT ANYTHING.
BECAUSE ANYTHING YOU'RE GIVEN OR YOU RECEIVE IS MOST LIKELY FAKE.
YOUR WISHES ARE FORM-LESS...
...AND YOU CAN'T TOUCH YOUR DESIRES.
AND THE MOST WONDERFUL TREASURE YOU OBTAIN, YOU MIGHT RUIN.

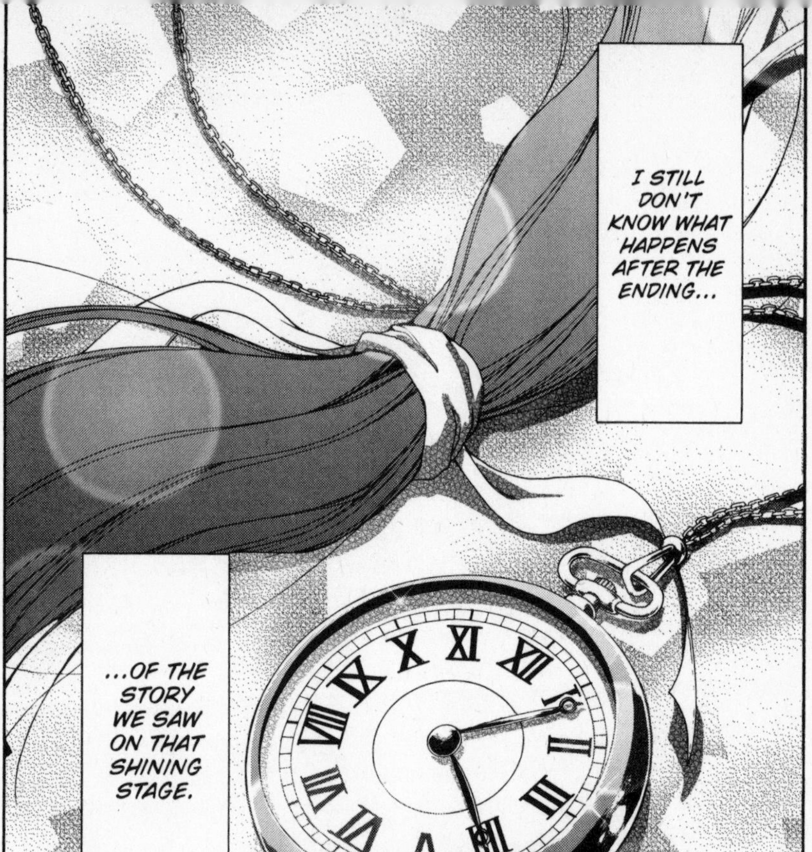
I STILL DON'T KNOW WHAT HAPPENS AFTER THE ENDING...
...OF THE STORY WE SAW ON THAT SHINING STAGE.
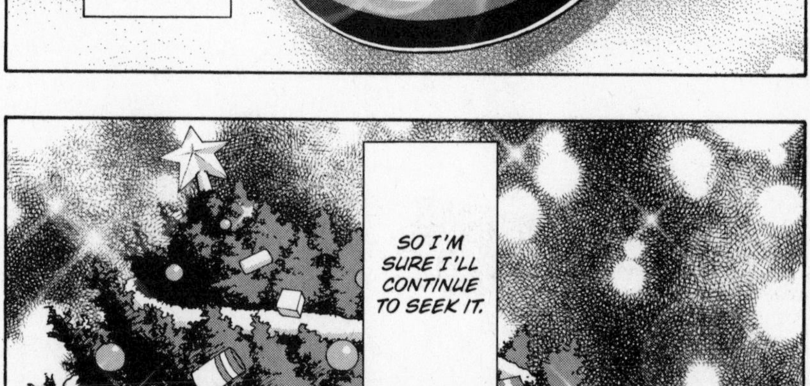
SO I'M SURE I'LL CONTINUE TO SEEK IT.

MY YOUTH ROMANTIC COMEDY
IS WRONG, AS I EXPECTED

...To Be Continued.

CHAPTER 69.5 ··· MEANWHILE, IN THE STUDENT COUNCIL ROOM, A PROPER ROM-COM IS GOING ON.

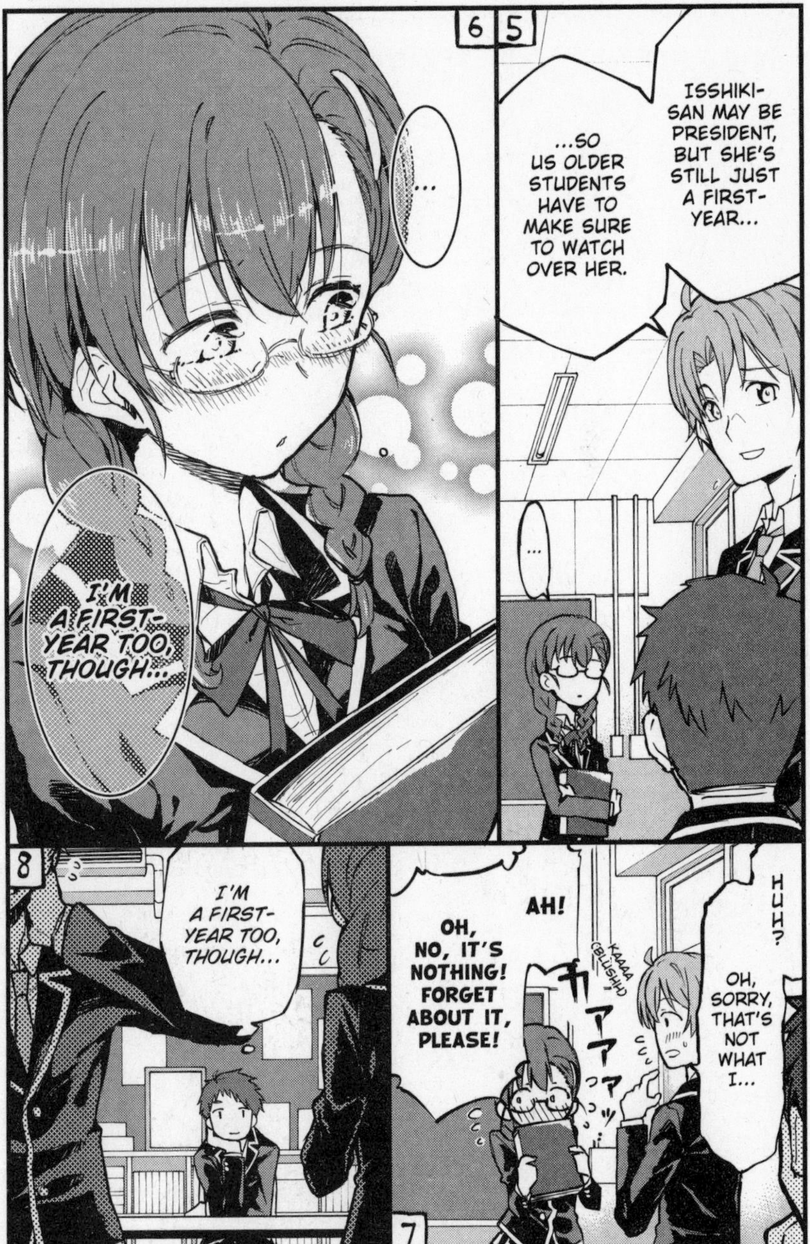
ISSHIKI-SAN MAY BE PRESIDENT, BUT SHE'S STILL JUST A FIRST-YEAR...
...SO US OLDER STUDENTS HAVE TO MAKE SURE TO WATCH OVER HER.
...
...
I'M A FIRST-YEAR TOO, THOUGH...
HUH?
OH, SORRY, THAT'S NOT WHAT I...
KAAAA (BLUSH)
AH!
OH, NO, IT'S NOTHING! FORGET ABOUT IT, PLEASE!
I'M A FIRST-YEAR TOO, THOUGH...

TRANSLATION NOTES

Page 14
Tokyo Destiny Land is a parody of Tokyo Disneyland. There are a number of superstitions related to romance, such as "If you go on a date to Tokyo Disneyland, you're destined to break up" and "If you kiss at Tokyo Disneyland, you'll be together longer."

Page 48
A **Tosho Card** is a kind of prepaid gift card used exclusively for books and magazines. Rather than being limited to any one specific store or chain, it can be used in multiple bookstores.

Page 59
Destiny Sea is a parody of Tokyo DisneySea—a sea-and-nautical-themed amusement park in Japan.

Page 96
In Japanese, a **max-value hand** in mahjong is known as a *yakuman*, and is worth either 32,000 points or 48,000 points. *Yakuman* are exceedingly rare and difficult to obtain, so Hachiman is basically saying everything should be lined up perfectly for Iroha.

Page 112
Iroha's mentions of **strategic prep** and getting **pieces into a favorable position** are references to the strategy board game Go. Revolving around placing pieces called "stones," it's famously known as a game that's simple to learn but exceedingly difficult to master.

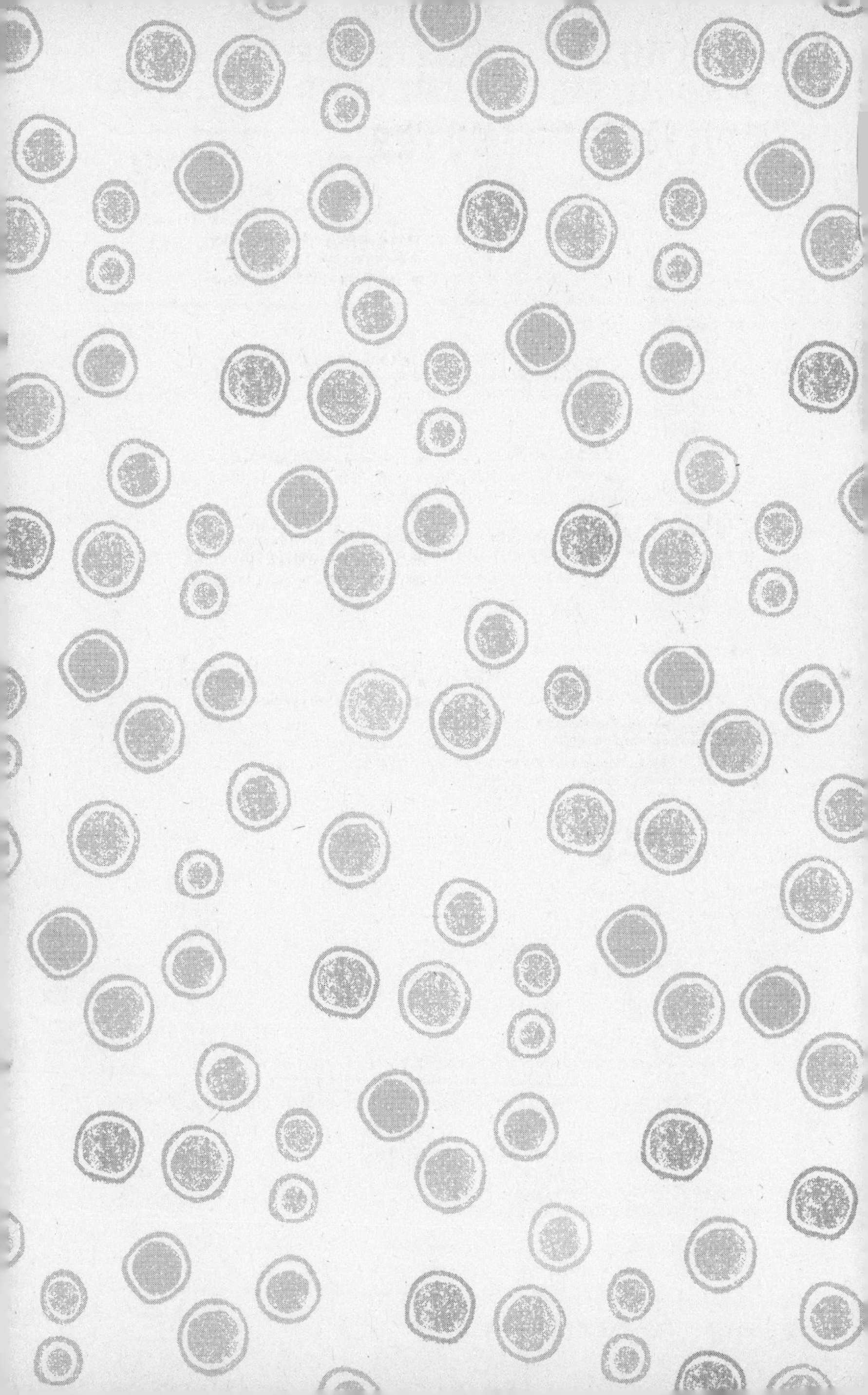

MY YOUTH ROMANTIC COMEDY IS WRONG, AS I EXPECTED @COMIC ⑫

Original Story: Wataru Watari
Art: Naomichi Io
Character Design: Ponkan⑧
ORIGINAL COVER DESIGN/Hiroyuki KAWASOME (Graphio)

Translation: Jennifer Ward

Lettering: Bianca Pistillo

YAHARI ORE NO SEISHUN LOVE COME WA MACHIGATTEIRU.
@COMIC Vol. 12 by Wataru WATARI, Naomichi IO, PONKAN⑧
© 2013 Wataru WATARI, Naomichi IO, PONKAN⑧
All rights reserved.
Original Japanese edition published by SHOGAKUKAN.
English translation rights arranged with SHOGAKUKAN through Tuttle-Mori Agency, Inc., Tokyo.

English translation © 2019 by Yen Press, LLC

Yen Press
150 West 30th St, 19th Floor
New York, NY 10001

Visit us at yenpress.com
facebook.com/yenpress
twitter.com/yenpress
yenpress.tumblr.com
instagram.com/yenpress

First Yen Press Edition: November 2019

Yen Press is an imprint of Yen Press, LLC.
The Yen Press name and logo are trademarks of Yen Press, LLC.

The publisher is not responsible for websites (or their content) that are not owned by the publisher.

Library of Congress Control Number: 2016931004

ISBNs: 978-1-9753-5937-9 (paperback)
       978-1-9753-5937-9 (ebook)

10 9 8 7 6 5 4 3 2 1

WOR

Printed in the United States of America